Coleridge's *Biographia Literaria*

Coleridge's
Biographia Literaria
Text and Meaning

Edited by
Frederick Burwick

OHIO STATE UNIVERSITY PRESS
Columbus

Copyright © 1989 by the Ohio State University Press.
All rights reserved.

Library of Congress Cataloging-in-Publication Data

Coleridge's Biographia literaria: text and meaning / edited by
    Frederick Burwick.
        p.   cm.
    Essays.
    Bibliography: p.
    Includes index.
    ISBN 0-8142-0479-1 (alk. paper)
        1. Coleridge, Samuel Taylor, 1772–1834. Biographia literaria.
2. Wordsworth, William, 1770–1850—Criticism and interpretation—
History.   3. Poets, English—19th century—Biography—History and
criticism.   4. Criticism—Great Britain—History—19th century.
5. Autobiography.   6. Imagination.   I. Burwick, Frederick.
PR4476.C26   1989
821'.7—dc19
[B]   89-31306
                                                            CIP

*The paper in this book meets the guidelines for permanence
and durability of the Committee on Production Guidelines
for Book Longevity of the Council on Library Resources.*

Printed in the U.S.A.

9 8 7 6 5 4 3 2 1

Contents

Introduction

Despite its place among the foremost works of criticism in English, the *Biographia Literaria* has been a difficult book to defend, even more difficult to understand. The structure is imbalanced from padding, the content is riddled with plagiarized passages, the reasoning sometimes lapses into whimsy or prejudice. What Samuel Taylor Coleridge originally conceived as a preface to his *Sybilline Leaves*, grew into two companion volumes which would provide, as he described the changes to John Gutch (Sept. 17, 1815), "Biographical Sketches of my LITERARY LIFE, Principles, and Opinions, chiefly on the subjects of Poetry and Philosophy." Coleridge had apparently decided to write his own version of the "Growth of a Poet's Mind" and to make that biography at the same time a cogent critical theory. However, in editing from his own notebooks, he let himself be distracted from reconciling these two tasks into a single text; other tasks, and other texts, intervene. As a result, Coleridge left us with such a collage that his text, or texts, get in the way of his meaning. The dominant purpose of this volume is to address the conflicts, and explain problematic relationships, between text and meaning; the particular difficulties in understanding the *Biographia* are set forth, chapter by chapter, in terms of differing strategies and methods. The chapters survey several major concerns: the writing, editing, and reading of the text; the critical topoi and privileged discourse of Coleridge's language; the ideological pretensions which shape and direct his meaning.

In the opening chapter, "Editing and Annotating the *Biographia Literaria*," Norman Fruman calls particular attention to the differences between the 1817 and the 1847 editions, arguing that in preparing the latter Sara Coleridge and Henry Nelson Coleridge relied on Coleridge's own revisions and amendments. John Shawcross in his edition (1909) gave preference to the 1847, but the recent edition of James Engell and Walter Bate (1983) returns to the 1817. With due appreciation of their colossal scholarly effort, Fruman shows how their edition adds many new problems and resolves but few of the old ones. Every investigation into Coleridge's use of sources erodes more of what we might want to praise as original in his critical thinking. Nevertheless, the Engell-Bate edition presents the illusion that the German sources are now fully catalogued and the overdue debt is paid. If the original edition, Fruman objects, had provided (as does the Engell-Bate edition) the running heads in the ninth chapter acknowledging "Obligations to Schelling," the plagiarism dispute might well have been forestalled. Although he praises Shawcross for following, at least in part, the 1847 edition, Fruman objects to his abbreviating and deleting the notes in which Sara identified the unacknowledged sources. Suppressing the evidence, Shawcross claims that Coleridge was independent of German thought. Fruman, however, is bothered not just by undocumented sources. Basing his case on the first chapter of the *Biographia*, Fruman addresses another challenge in the editorial task of annotation. Fruman takes a careful look at the autobiographical self which Coleridge introduces here, and he finds it filled with distortions and misrepresentations that all previous editors have ignored.

Thomas Vogler, in "Coleridge's Book of Moonlight," is also concerned with the concept of "editing," both as a textual practice performed by conventional editors on texts, and as a part of the creative process itself as a form of "self-editing." As examples of the latter, Vogler calls attention to Blake in the Urizenic role of editing the *Book of Urizen*, Carlyle editing *Sartor Resartus*, Kierkegaard editing *The Point of View for my Work as an Author: A Report to History*. In editing his own Notebooks into the text of the *Biographia*, Coleridge catches himself in the rational traps of discourse. Vogler emphasizes the importance of textual space: the randomness of the Notebooks versus the ordered structure of an edited book. Citing Foucault's account of the "author function" of the book, Vogler explores Coleridge's reluctance to implicate himself, his struggle against the inevitability of identifying himself with the text. The physical shape of the Engell-Bate edition Vogler describes as an "editorial sandwich," which contains a "philosophical sandwich," which contains, in turn, the "meat." But it is not just the extensive editorial annotation of chapters 5 through 13 that makes the "sandwich" an apt metaphor. Coleridge himself builds up layers of textual space: the philosophical history of chapters 5 through 9, followed by "a chapter of digressions and anecdotes," followed in chapter 11 by an "affectionate exhortation to youthful literati."

In chapter 12, Coleridge presents his "requests and premonitions concerning the perusal of the chapter that follows." The "premonitions," as the annotations make clear, are translations, paraphrases, and summaries pieced together from Schelling. Finally, in chapter 13, Coleridge arrives at the "meat," his promised exposition "On the imagination, or esemplastic power," only to interrupt himself with a "letter from a friend." In a close reading of this interruption, Vogler shows that Coleridge is—in Carlyle's terms—playing the role of "English Editor" to his own alter-ego of the "Germanic Metaphysical Visionary." Coleridge escapes his "metaphysical *cul-de-sac*" by resorting to the aposiopesis of Cervantes or Swift. Rather than be disappointed with Coleridge's evasions, his delays and digressions, Vogler suggests that we should delight in them with full appreciation of the satirical manipulation. Coleridge may have failed to define the imagination, but he demonstrated it. Vogler concludes with an analysis of Coleridge's authorial voice, his revelation of subjective presence and "inward power." Demonstrating Coleridge's art of self-presentation in "The Blossoming of the Solitary Date-Tree," Vogler argues similar authorial presence in other poems ("Kubla Khan," "Hymn Before Sunrise") as well as in the *Biographia*.

Catherine Miles Wallace agrees that the "philosophical chapters" fail to provide a lucid account of the imagination. Where Vogler turns to Coleridge's promotion of a "willing suspension of disbelief" and subjective cooperation, Wallace directs attention to the "rich and lively polemic." Instead of lamenting his digressions, she advises, we should recognize their initiatory function, as part of the author's desire to engage his readers in thinking about ideas. In "The Besetting Sins of Coleridge's Prose," she investigates the metaphoricality of Coleridge's definitions, the disjuncture of his argumentation, and his supra-historical appeal to, and participation in, a presiding intellectual community of minds. Coleridge's thought is *eidetic;* his logic requires visual models. Wallace shows how his definitions rely on manipulating mental pictures. For De Quincey, the secret of great prose was in the art of connection and transition. There is little such art to be found in the *Biographia*. But Wallace suggests that we be patient with the seeming discontinuity of Coleridge's mental leaps: "at such times he is probably doing one of a finite number of reasonable things which he (quite unreasonably) does not signal to us in advance." With a few apt examples, she provides some general exercises in building the logical bridges that Coleridge fails to construct in his prose. She then reveals a visual continuity that Coleridge saw in the great philosophical tradition, a peculiarly ahistorical space into which the mind peers, possessing what it perceives. This is the exalted perception into "the hidden order of intellectual things" (Synesius) praised by Coleridge as an act of the philosophical imagination.

When Coleridge agonizes over text and meaning, it is not because their relationship is disparate, rather because it is arbitrary. Through promiscuous use and equivocation, the finer distinctions and discriminations of language erode. If we surrender to what has been "naturalized" in "general currency," then "language itself does as it were *think* for us." Thus he calls for the desynonimization of words (*Biographia*, ch. 4; *Philosophical Lectures*, ch. 5). But if communication depends upon a general acceptance of arbitrary signs, how can language be creative? In "Coleridge and the Language of Adam," Robert N. Essick paraphrases a Coleridgean text: "Adamic language is one with human perception, an echo of God's creative Word, differing from the Logos only in degree, and in the mode of its operation." Commentaries on Adam's naming of the beasts in Genesis resolved, Essick tells us, into two linguistic ideals: a universal language, known to all mankind; and a language in which there is a real (or, in modern terminology, a "motivated") relationship between the word and the thing it signifies. Essick briefly recounts the rationalist and taxonomic linguistic studies of the seventeenth and eighteenth centuries, noting that the rising interest in primitive poetry carried with it a belief in the presence of a natural, Adamic language. Discontent with the taxonomic view of language, one that limits "the conceivable" to "the picturable" through associationist matching, Coleridge distinguishes this "language of words," or arbitrary signs, from "a language of spirits" in a way that parallels his famous desynonymization of "fancy" and "imagination." Coleridge joins the German romantics in gleaning the mystical wisdom of Jacob Boehme, for whom God's language is infinite and spiritual, man's finite and sensual, while the language in and of the world always strives to reconcile the difference between the individual and the divine. The reconciliation is promised by a semiotics that struggles "to idealize and unify" the binary opposites generated by a fallen, taxonomic linguistics. Like the language of Adam, this ideal mode repeats in the realm of finite discourse the structure of the Logos. Its essential constituent is not the word but the symbol (as defined in *The Statesman's Manual*) in counterdistinction to the "picture-language" of allegory. By partaking "of the reality which it renders intelligible," the Coleridgean symbol becomes the chief romantic form of Adamic utterance. By considering Coleridge's "imagination" and "symbol" from this linguistic perspective, we can perceive something of their historical background—but also the extent to which they are transcendental, even nostalgic, ideals rather than the tools of a practical poetic.

Are any of the tools of Coleridge's philosophical poetic serviceable as tools of a practical poetic? Is the *Biographia* the keystone in the great arch that joins philosophy and poetry, or simply a stumbling block in the way? The questions have been asked before, and variously answered. The answers J. H. Haeger gives us in "Anti-Materialism, Autobiography, and the Abyss of Unmeaning in the *Biographia Literaria*" are positive, but laden with provisos. He reads the "philosophical chapters" as a desperate metaphysical self-defense. Yes, they have practical applicability in analyzing poetry—Coleridge's poetry, especially the "mystery poems" and all those Coleridgean broodings over the dark side of human consciousness. Promising to "investigate the seminal principle" of the fancy and the imagination, and proceeding to explore the epistemological bases of his "poetic creed," these chapters are charged with a personal exposition of a psychological as well as philosophical struggle out of the abyss of dejection. Just as he wavers in his reaction to Schelling's pantheism, so too his account of self-perception shifts uncertainly from confessional to metaphysical discourse. While his philosophical formulations present one perspective, his style suggests another. In appropriating from Schelling the elements of a dynamic or constructive philosophy, Coleridge is more preoccupied with his own response to the metaphorical tensions than he is with the metaphysical implications. Haeger summons telling evidence of the autobiographical/philosophical struggle. Coleridge describes himself as a wanderer in the labyrinth (whose "best good fortune was finally to have found his way out again"), storm tossed on a sea of doubts ("and it was long ere my ark touched upon Ararat, and rested"); other metaphors describe darkness and danger without rescue or salvation. Coleridge's discursive statements point toward increasing mental abstraction and autonomy in relation to the external world, but his figurative language consistently dwells upon the chiaroscuro of an uncertain earthly terrain.

Coleridge considers the tension between meaning and text inherent in language, not just a problem peculiar to the *Biographia*. Because language is shaped by mind, our words are ordered by the same habitual connections we use in organizing sights and sounds, thoughts and feelings. The perceptions may be fallible, but optical illusions and other distortions of the senses are discovered through experience and corrected by reason. This habitual correcting and censoring are all too efficient; through habit the perceptions are numbed, and language loses its sensual vitality. Coleridge recounts in the *Biographia* the origin of the *Lyrical Ballads*, tracing his and Wordsworth's intentions in the poems to a desire to shatter entirely the habits of their readers, and most particularly their visual habits. Although Coleridge and Wordsworth found themselves opposing much in Enlightenment thought, they shared that age's assumption that ways of seeing largely determine what we think and know. Richard Fadem begins his chapter, "Coleridge, Habit, and the Politics of Vision," by recounting the Molyneux question on the relation between perception and experience, and the pondering of that question by Locke, Berkeley, and Hume. When Coleridge journeys through this philosophical territory in the *Biographia*, he tells how he came to recognize habit as an impediment to vision and see the dangers in Hartley and Associationism. He regards habit as drastically skewing and limiting our relation to reality. Fadem shows that the concern with habit in the philosophical chapters leads directly to the chapters on Wordsworth. The poets had agreed, Coleridge writes, that the two "cardinal points of poetry" consisted in "truth to nature" and in "novelty." Novelty would emerge from the play of "the modifying colors of the imagination" upon the natural world (Wordsworth's venue) or from the imagination's lighting up the supernatural world (Coleridge's territory). Despite their very different assignments one element remained common to both poets: "The awakening of the mind's attention from the lethargy of custom." Fadem then calls attention to Coleridge's repetition of the same objective in the motto to "The Rime of the Ancient Mariner." Fadem points out the visual/verbal construct of the poem, its theme of vision numbed and renewed, its visual imagery of deception and discovery, its language of puns and look-alikes. From his study of Coleridge's use of habit, as outlined in the *Biographia* and as evident in "The Ancient Mariner," Fadem concludes by noting that the stick Coleridge employs to beat the Enlightenment turns out oddly to be the same one that such late descendants of the Romantics as Pater and Wilde use to repudiate elements of Romantic vision.

As Fadem sets forth the entangled case of Coleridge's opposition to Locke and the philosophy of the Enlightenment, Stuart Peterfreund studies the opposition to Newton and the science of the Enlightenment. Although literary historians have generally associated the shift from Classicism to Romanticism with the philosophical shift from Materialism to Idealism, both the literary and philosophical movements may be circumscribed by the shift in scientific thinking from a matter-based physics to an energy-based physics. Peterfreund begins his chapter, "Coleridge and Energy," with a selective sampling of Coleridge's references to energy as an efficacious ability to do the work of shaping the world, whether it be the world of Joan of Arc in *The Destiny of Nations* (1796) or the literary world shaped by the secondary, "esemplastic" imagination in the *Biographia*. When Coleridge praises Richard Saumarez's *The Principles of Physiological and Physical Science* (1812) for overthrowing "Sir Iky's System of Gravitation, Color, & the whole 39 Articles of the Hydrostatic, chemic, & Physiologic Churches" (letter to John Rickman, July 17, 1812), his objections to Newton are aptly couched in the metaphor of religion, for matter-based physics ignores the energy of God that Coleridge holds to be manifest in both mind and nature. He looked to science, to Young, Davy, and Saumarez, for something more than a metaphor. Coleridge insists on the relevance of energy in contexts of theology and literature as well as of physics. The theological origin of the term and concept are especially important to Coleridge, since the word *energy* (from its use in the Epistles of the New Testament to its use by Priestley and Wesley) is a word that refers to the workings responsible for the Judeo-Christian theodicy, as it affects and informs the world and the individual. Coleridge begins his career confident that the theodicy of the private life and the larger theodicy of the world are informed by one energy, emanating from the same divine source and responsible for the same positive outcome. But personal setbacks fostered doubts. He grew uncertain as to whether the same energy informed the individual and the world alike; and if it were the same energy, he was no longer certain whether it emanated from a source above, or one below. Divine energy operating in the individual, the world, or both could bring about spiritual renovation of apocalyptic proportions; but satanic energy could bring about untold sorrow and, by displacing the indwelling token of a positive theodicy, could deepen that sorrow by removing the last vestige of hope and consigning world and individual alike to irremediable fragmentation and ruin. The issue—whether energy is on the side of the angels or on the other side—is a central one for Coleridge's poetry and prose alike.

No other topic in the *Biographia* has been more discussed and debated than the plagiarism from Schelling in chapter 12. In spite of all the attention to identifying the passages from Schelling, none of the commentators has explained why Coleridge found it necessary to construct his borrowed argument from three separate sources, representing three different versions of Schelling's attempts to posit self-perception. In "Perception and 'the heaven-descended KNOW-THYSELF,'" Frederick Burwick traces the philosophical problem from Hume's declaration that there is only perception, no self-perception. Burwick then explains how Kant and Fichte accounted for the self as an object in the subjective act of perceiving and how Schelling successively altered his analysis of self-perception in the three works used by Coleridge. What Coleridge wanted from Schelling was the confirmation that "a principle of unity is contributed by the mind itself." But he could find in Schelling no appreciation of the imagistic act in perception, no discrimination of perceptual modes (looking at trees, reading a book, solving a geometric problem), and no God in the absolute. Coleridge therefore freely added and adapted when he pieced his ten theses together from various parts of each of the three different versions he found in Schelling's works. The matter is even more complex, for Coleridge himself changed and altered the organization of the theses in transforming the text from his notebooks into the *Biographia*, and he reshaped it once again in his chapter "On the Logical Acts" in the *Logic*.

Although Schelling's *Von der Weltseele* (1798) led his contemporaries to anticipate an account of God, his *System des transzendentalen Idealismus* (1800) made it clear that Schelling was opposed to the kind of religiosity forwarded by Schleiermacher's *Reden über die Religion* and Novalis' *Die Christenheit oder Europa*. When Coleridge appropriates his theses from Schelling, he needs to demonstrate how self-consciousness enables us to participate in absolute consciousness. Quoting the theses in "Annotating the Annotations: a Philosophical Reading of the Primary and Secondary Imagination," J. Fisher Solomon explains that Coleridge could not possibly wring a revelation of God out of the "philosophic imagination" because the ontological argument of the theses allowed for no reproductive or representative function. The passage on the "primary" and "secondary" imagination has baffled interpreters for so long because it has always been considered in the context of a representational epistemology, according to which the primary imagination would somehow have to re-present or "repeat" the "eternal act of creation" itself, which can finally only be understood as some kind of divine presence. The solution to the puzzle of the primary and the secondary imagination is not in the proper balancing of "reason" and "understanding" by an esemplastic power, but neither is it to be found in a deconstruction of the "mind" whose faculties are so difficult to unify. Arguing that Coleridge's psychology cannot really stand so long as "the eternal act of creation" remains metaphysically unexplained, Solomon turns from psychology to ontology; he interprets Coleridge's distinction between the primary and the secondary *imagination* in the light of Aristotle's ontological distinction between primary and secondary *being* (*ousia*, substance) in the *Categories*. From Aristotle's argument that actuality (*energeia*), potentiality (*dunamis*), and the composition (*synthesis*) of form and matter are all *ousia*, Solomon shows that power-and-difference subsist in the ontic "this." Coleridge utilizes the same dialectical structure: the primary imagination constitutes the ontic "this" and the secondary imagination constitutes the "this" as aesthetic symbol—not as repetition or representation of being, but as being itself.

In the editors' introduction to the *Biographia*, Engell and Bate claim that "we do not face the need, as we so often do in the difficult earlier chapters, to turn to Coleridge's other writings for supplementary help" in reading the critique on Wordsworth. This is misleading advice. As Raimonda Modiano shows us, Coleridge is indeed relying on a hidden agenda drawn from previous writings. Reacting to the rift and rivalry with Wordsworth, Coleridge sought other models of poetic excellence in which he could reaffirm aspects of his own abilities and strengths. In his notebooks and his lectures on literature, the two principle models are Shakespeare and Milton. When he builds his case against Wordsworth in the *Biographia*, Coleridge deliberately sets Wordsworth up as "nearest" to Shakespeare and Milton in diction (ch. 20) and in imaginative power (ch. 22). This is not faint praise, but it is nevertheless damning. In contrast to mechanical constraints of mere "copy," Shakespeare is praised for the dramatic power of "imitation"; "the language of real life" is found in Milton, not among rustic cottagers (ch. 22). Raimonda Modiano turns our attention back to chapter 2 to show how the integrity of Milton, especially his morality and simplicity, are made to work against Wordsworth in chapters 17 through 22.

Because Coleridge's theological and political views direct his philosophy of criticism, the reader of the *Biographia* is well-advised to be alert to the implicit motives of Coleridge's rhetoric. In examining the politics of Coleridge's criticism, Jerome Christensen shows not only the applicability of the deconstructive method, but the propriety of deconstruction in Coleridge. Christensen opens this chapter, "Like a Guilty Thing Surprised: Coleridge, Deconstruction, and the Apostasy of Criticism," by repeating Frank Lentricchia's charges against Paul de Man and the deconstructionists. Lentricchia asserts that "the deconstruction of deconstruction will reveal, against apparent intention, a tacit political agenda after all, one that can only embarrass deconstruction, particularly its younger proponents whose activist experiences, within the socially wrenching upheavals of the 1960s and early 1970s will surely not permit them easily to relax, without guilt and self-hatred, into resignation and ivory tower despair." Christensen answers that deconstructing deconstruction is the task assumed by Jacques Derrida, who taught that embarrassing hidden intentions is constitutive of the deconstructionist method. The problem is not that deconstruction has "a tacit political agenda," rather that deconstruction leads to apostasy. Is apostasy, Christensen inquires, a necessary or contingent consequence? Then he turns the inquiry around. Coleridge, he repeats Hazlitt's phrase, was "always an apostate," or in the Heideggerian formula, "always already an apostate." And his apostasy leads to deconstruction. Coleridge is ever reacting against stasis, detaching himself from all forms. The apostasy that is the inevitable fall from divinity is reenacted in the continuing polemic of his philosophical criticism. His apostate polemics are not only addressed in rebuttal, refutation, correction, and amendment of this or that philosopher, poet, or politician, but Coleridge is his own "man from Porlock." He interrupts and repudiates his own texts.

In discussing Coleridge's abiding commitment to the organic reciprocity of church and state, Thomas McFarland would have us avoid the solipsistic implications of Jerome Christiansen's account of Coleridge's apostasy. If Coleridge was, personally, repeatedly falling away from his divine ideal, he was ever returning to it, reconfirming its social and cultural manifestations. When the *Biographia* was first published, Thelwall objected to its anti-Jacobin statements and rebuked Coleridge as a turncoat. Hazlitt, too, scoffed at Coleridge's "recollection" of his politics. In chapter 10, Coleridge claimed that his principles had always been "opposite . . . to those of jacobinism or even of democracy." Granting that such an assertion "admits of a convenient latitude of interpretation," Hazlitt replied that Coleridge's politics were certainly "still more opposite to those of the Anti-Jacobins, a party to which he admits he has gone over" (*Edinburgh Review*, August 28, 1817). More recently, E. P. Thompson has renewed the charge of Coleridge's apostasy. McFarland's purpose in "Coleridge and the Charge of Political Apostasy" is to explain why Coleridge could endorse neither Jacobin nor anti-Jacobin politics. By documenting the response to the French Revolution and the highly charged reaction to the "Bloody Reign of Terror," McFarland is able to show the complexity and ambiguity of the political issues. He also shows how Coleridge's habit of "mirroring" an auditor's ideals resulted in contradictory interpretations of his political convictions. Not a desire simply to please, to say what his listener wanted to hear, but a dialectical habit of thinking—to reconcile extremes, to restate and synthesize a contrary position—is persistently evident in Coleridge's writings. Because Coleridge interpreted political movements in terms of his organic theory, he responded to the Revolution in terms far more so-phisticated and probing than either Wordsworth or Southey. Long after they had changed their minds, and their politics, Coleridge continued the same mode of analysis. Prone to vacillation in personal matters, Coleridge was nevertheless, McFarland stresses, constant in his intellectual views.

Jerome J. McGann, in "The *Biographia Literaria* and the Contentions of English Romanticism," also examines Coleridge's polemics and his studied attack on "Opinions in fashion." It is for his literary criticism, not for his critique of empiricism nor for his political views and religious convictions that we read the *Biographia*.

But Coleridge engages the questions of literature in contexts that are emphatically political, social, and moral. We need not endorse his re-actionary views, says McGann, to appreciate Coleridge's commitment to a holistic humanism; we must, however, ascertain the polemical set of ideas at work in his theoretical and practical criticism. Modiano studies Coleridge's critique of Wordsworth in terms of his appeal to a Miltonic authority that she traces back through the notebooks and Coleridge's lec-tures and that she sees covertly anticipated in the opening chapters of the *Biographia*. McGann emphasizes, instead, the ideological ground of Coleridge's polemic against Wordsworth's materialism and associationism. Although both believed in the mind-nature dialectic, Coleridge empha-sized a subjective and intellectual aesthetic, while Wordsworth, in Cole-ridge's opinion, was far too attentive to the details of the material world and far too sympathetic to the rustic's language and experience. Coleridge writes poetry of "revelation via mediations," while Wordsworth's purpose is to free his subjects from the very mediations which convey them. Cole-ridge engages the subject-object dialectic to reveal the ordering process of mind, Wordsworth to "see into the life of things." In the concluding section of this chapter, McGann traces the influence of the *Biographia* on Byron's theory and practice. Giving close attention to Coleridge's critique of Maturin's *Bertram* in chapter 23, McGann shows that Byron conceived his *Don Juan* in direct response to the *Biographia*.

Although it had already appeared in the *Courier*, the critique of *Bertram* (along with Satyrane's Letters which had appeared in *The Friend*) provided necessary bulk to round out the second volume of the *Biographia*. What had started out as counter-Wordsworthian Preface to *Sybilline Leaves* had become a separate entity, a book. Even before it spilled over into a second volume, Coleridge felt misgivings about his book as public merchandise. In the final chapter, "Poetry and Barrel-Organs: The Text in the Book of the *Biographia Literaria*," Robert Maniquis examines Coleridge's response to the metamorphosis of his "literary life" into a commodity in the marketplace. Maniquis finds the chary attitudes about commercial contamination, the scornful derision of the "Reading Public," important to an ideological analysis of Coleridge's Christian politics. From the first volume of the *Biographia* Maniquis excerpts a number of Coleridge's references to the commodification of a text as book. In one such passage from chapter 2, Coleridge declares that language is taken away from the "*constructors*," who "alone could elicit strains of music," and given over to the "press-room," where "language, mechanized as it were into a barrel-organ, supplies at once both instrument and tune." Coleridge distinguishes between the "property" of the poet, and the mass-produced commodities of the marketplace. Coleridge does not address the "Reading Public," but a "literary republic," whose members share his republican and Christian ideals. To these readers Coleridge raises his warning against a commodification of art which dictates the opinions of the vast "Reading Public" and threatens to undermine the constitutional republic. Maniquis has said that his study of Coleridge's "Text in the Book" was intended to engage recent ideological criticism, such as McGann's *The Romantic Ideology*. He does not merely engage, he extends.

Every student of literary criticism knows that the *Biographia* is a seminal text: both for its epistemological analysis of the imagination and for its exposition of organic form. Every student also knows that it is a tainted text. For the non-Coleridgean scholar, it should be pointed out that the work has a surprisingly limited editorial history. After the first edition of 1817, a revised version was edited by Henry Nelson Coleridge and Sara Coleridge in 1847. Subsequent editions have largely relied on the 1817 edition:

John Shawcross used a conflation of the two texts in his edition for Oxford University Press in 1907; George Sampson for Cambridge, 1920; and George Watson for Dent/Dutton, 1956 and 1965, tended to follow Shawcross. With extensive annotation, James Engell and Walter Jackson Bate recently completed an edition for the Bollingen *Collected Coleridge*, 1983, but relied wholly on the 1817 version. The Shawcross edition, long privileged as the standard "critical edition," had at last been replaced. Having seen that their edition would be superceded by the Engell-Bate edition, Oxford did not have to deliberate long on how to answer the competition. For their new edition, Fruman bases his text not on the original edition of 1817 but on the edition of 1847, which, as he argues, incorporates Coleridge's own corrections and also has the benefit of Sara Coleridge's meticulous scholarship. Because Fruman in his *Coleridge, The Damaged Archangel* (1971) radically altered the way in which Romantic scholars deal with the problems of Coleridge's sources, the Oxford University Press no doubt felt that Fruman was just the editor needed to counter the Engell-Bate authority.

In confronting the problems of editing the *Biographia*, Fruman raises more than the question of "reliable" text. Whose text is this? In lengthy footnotes, the Engell-Bate edition provides a subtext of Coleridge's sources and verbatim borrowings that offer scholarly reliability while they cover up authorial unreliability. The topics addressed in the ensuing essays concern Coleridge's strategies of editing his own text and manipulating his language and the ideological traps which he created for himself and his readers. In order to provide a thorough examination of the issues in the contemporary critical debate over Coleridge's complex and devious text, the essays address the following in logical succession: editing the text and the self-edited text; language and metaphorical strategies; criticism and philosophy; criticism and ideology. These concerns reflect, of course, the issues being raised virtually everywhere in recent literary studies. Because it contains antecedents to so much of modern criticism, Coleridge's *Biographia* provides a central battlefield for defining and redefining the grounds of interpretation.

1

Editing and Annotating the
Biographia Literaria

Norman Fruman

"Sir Walter Scott made a just observation on the fate of the *Biographia Literaria*," wrote Coleridge's brilliant daughter Sara, "when he said that it had made no impression upon the public."[1] Thirty years passed before the most influential book of literary criticism and theory in English came to a second edition, begun by the poet's nephew and son-in-law, Henry Nelson Coleridge, and completed after his death by Sara.

Since then we have had six more major reprints, and though almost all editors have claimed to reproduce faithfully the first edition of 1817, all but the recently published volumes edited by James Engell and Walter Jackson Bate (1983) in the *Collected Coleridge* set have departed from the original text in extensive ways. The manuscript, it will be remembered,

Some six months after this paper was delivered I wrote a long review-article on the Engell-Bate edition of the *Biographia* for *Studies in Romanticism*, 24 (Spring 1985): 141–73, wherein some of the illustrations and language that are used here in the necessarily brief discussions of textual and annotation problems will be found in greatly elaborated form. To avoid ventriloquism here I might have drawn upon an abundance of fresh examples that the editorial history of the *Biographia* readily supplies, as readers of my *SIR* essay will have no difficulty in accepting. However, I found that my several attempts to do so only weakened the concentration and energy of my original paper, a circumstance which has almost converted me to a belief in the doctrine of organic form.

This essay focuses primarily on chapter 1 and examines not only problems of text and annotation, but also seeks to provide a model for a more realistic and productive reading of the *Biographia* than we have had hitherto. It has therefore seemed inadvisable to unravel and reweave the fabric of a tightly knit argument so as to avoid any overlap with a review-article pursuing related but fundamentally different objectives. Given the history of Coleridge studies—especially the tendency of unwelcome evidence to disappear like vinegar in a sieve—the iteration of certain facts may not be entirely superfluous.

disappeared long ago—one of several related misfortunes which plague Coleridge studies.

Sara Coleridge stated that her edition contained "corrections of the text" (1:ii). Unfortunately, she did not say on what authority she and her husband had done so, and thus it is easy to suppose, as almost everybody does, that the many changes to be found in the text of 1847, when they do not correct "obvious misprints"—a treacherous phrase, as we shall see— lack authority. The 1847 text has two unauthorized deletions, both attacking Francis Jeffrey in personal terms. Sara carefully identified the passages and gave her reasons for dropping them (1:clviii–ix). But for these omissions, and the silent alteration of a false date, the text of 1847 probably reflects the author's intentions more faithfully than any other, including the most recent. John Shawcross runs a very close second.

It is much to be regretted that Shawcross said very little about what principles governed his choice of text for the Oxford edition. "The original edition," he wrote, "(besides numerous misprints, more or less obvious) contains many peculiarities of spelling, which can hardly be laid at the printer's door. Neither this orthography, nor the frequent use of italics and capitals, has been strictly respected by later editors. But they are all characteristic of Coleridge, and as such deserve to be retained. At times, however, it has been difficult to discriminate between the printer's errors and Coleridge's idiosyncracies" (1:xcvii,[1907]). An understatement, surely. One could easily suppose from his brief note on the text that all Shawcross did was correct misprints and decide in a few cases where Coleridge was being idiosyncratic. The fact is that far, far more thought and confrontation with difficult problems went into his textual editing than one would suppose or has ever been commented upon.

Shawcross had before him at all times the texts of both 1817 and 1847, and where they differed, as they do in hundreds of places, he decided sometimes in favor of the one, sometimes the other. In general he retains 1817's thicket of italics and capitals and many inconsistencies of spelling and usage. But where a *verbal* change is concerned—a far more substantive matter—Shawcross is usually guided by 1847. What becomes very clear is that he made a systematic comparison, and that he came to a conclusion which no other editor seems to have given any thought to, namely, that Henry Nelson and Sara Coleridge almost certainly did not make *verbal* changes on their own authority but were adopting Coleridge's own corrections and emendations.

Early in chapter 1 of 1817, for example, there is a reference to "the manly simplicity of the Grecian" (1:7). The 1847 text alters that to "the manly simplicity of the Greek" (1:6). So does Shawcross (1:4). (To forestall the suspicion that I have ransacked the whole work for a few examples, I will be dealing throughout this essay mainly with chapter 1.) Later in the chapter, Coleridge wondered "whether the words should be personifications, or mere abstracts" (1:20). The 1847 text changes "abstracts" to "abstractions" (1:19), which makes more sense. Shawcross silently accepts this change also (1:12). In the same paragraph Coleridge wrote, with uncharacteristic slovenliness, of "the authority of the author" (1:20). In 1847 we find "the authority of the *writer*" (1:20), a simple but felicitous change, which Shawcross again silently accepts (1:13). Here, as everywhere, Engell-Bate rigidly follow 1817 and give no indication that alternate readings, possibly by Coleridge, exist.

One would give much to know why Shawcross was not entirely consistent in accepting verbal changes, since his reasoning cannot always be reconstructed. For example, a memorable passage in chapter 1 begins: "At school I enjoyed the inestimable advantage of a very sensible, though at the same time a very severe master. He early moulded my taste," and so forth (1:7). An asterisk after "He" directs us to a footnote which reads: "The Rev. James Bowyer, many years Head Master of the Grammar-School, Christ [misprint for Christ's] Hospital." The awkwardness of relegating the important name to a footnote becomes apparent when one compares the 1847 text, which reads: "At school, (Christ's Hospital,) I enjoyed the inestimable advantage of a very sensible, though at the same time, a very severe master, the Reverend James Bowyer" (1:6). Strangely, Shawcross does not accept *this* change. One cannot help but wonder why. Would the editors of 1847 have altered Coleridge's language on their own volition? It seems doubtful. If they did so here, why not in multitudes of other places? "Throughout this edition," wrote Sara, "I have abstained from interference with the *text*, as far as the sense was concerned" (1:clviii). This statement is not as clear as one might wish, but I think what Sara means is that she has not altered *words*, but only italics, capitals, punctuation, and the like.

Any discussion of textual authority in the *Biographia* must always keep in mind that the editors of 1847 had in their possession a copy, now lost, of the *Biographia* "corrected" and annotated by the author. In a note to the locus classicus definition of the imagination on the final page of chapter 13, the following appears in 1847, after the phrase "and as a repetition in the finite mind of the eternal act of creation of the infinite I AM": "This last clause . . . I find stroked out in a copy of the *B.L.* containing a few MS. marginal notes of the author, which are printed in this edition. I think it best to preserve the sentence, while I mention the author's judgment upon it, especially as it has been quoted. S.C." (1:297,n.13).

Thus we know, if proof were necessary, that Coleridge had reread at least this particular page with a view toward a second edition. And in the 1847 paragraphs on imagination and fancy there are a few verbal changes from 1817, all for the better. Instead of 1817's "The secondary I consider as an echo," we find "The secondary Imagination I consider as an echo," which makes the reference clearer. And in the description of the fancy, 1847 alters "a mode of Memory emancipated from the order of time and space; *and* blended with" to "*while it is* blended with," and the phrase "But equally with the ordinary memory, *it* must" is amended to "But equally with the ordinary memory *the Fancy* must," thus getting rid of a slightly vague pronoun. Shawcross again accepts these alterations, and they have found their way into practically every anthology of Romantic Poetry and Prose and have been quoted innumerable times by scholars, few of whom have probably been aware that in citing Shawcross they were providing not Coleridge's language of 1817, but that of Sara Coleridge's 1847 edition. Engell-Bate reprint 1817 and do not consider that Sara's altered text may have the author's—excuse me—the writer's authority.

To suppose that the reverentially dutiful Sara—who was acutely, indeed excessively conscious of her limitations as an editor and scholar—would presume to improve upon her father's style seems unreasonable. Since we now know that Coleridge had stroked out a crucial phrase on this very page, why doubt that he took the opportunity to make other changes? Coleridge was *never* loathe to alter a text, his own or anybody else's, including the sonnets of Charles Lamb on the way to the printer. "I charge you, Col. *spare my ewe lambs*,"[2] Charles had pleaded, to no avail. Anyone who has examined any book ever in Coleridge's hands knows that he found it difficult to keep his pen at rest. There are at least six annotated copies of *The Friend*.

The fact is that we just don't know how extensively Coleridge had "corrected" the copy of *Biographia* he gave to Gillman. We do know that he added a number of marginal notes, some of them long, which were incorporated in the 1847 text. It is at least a possibility that wherever 1847 differs from 1817—but for the exceptions I have mentioned, and possibly a few others—Henry Nelson Coleridge and Sara may have been following Coleridge's corrected copy. I don't think that is true with respect to the very many changes in italics and capitals—for reasons I will have to argue in detail elsewhere—but I do believe that most of the verbal changes are the author's.

Astonishingly, neither John Shawcross nor George Watson reprinted any of the additional notes, which Sara said came from her father's own hand. Can there be any question that Coleridge wrote them? Here is a short passage from a long and complex one in chapter 10 (1:207[1847]): "Thus, the attributes of Space and Time applied to Spirit are heterogeneous—and the proof of this is, that by admitting them *explicite* and *implicite* contraries may be demonstrated true . . ." Engell-Bate reprint this, not as a part of the text, but in one of their own notes, with the unnecessarily cautious comment: "presumably an annotation by C on a copy of BL" (1:203,n.2).

The editors of 1983 assert flatly that they follow the text of 1817 because that is "the only authoritative text as it was the only English edition published during Coleridge's lifetime" (1:xix). The conclusion here is not self-validating. This is not the place to argue the nightmare question of what text best represents Coleridge's intentions in a situation as complex as that of *Biographia*, but it can surely be said that unflinching devotion to battalions of inconsistencies and errors, which Coleridge could not possibly have meant to eternalize, does not constitute any authority we need venerate. "Obvious misprints" are silently corrected, the editors tell us (1:xix). Thus "Cowper's task" will be made "Cowper's Task" (1:25[1983]). Is not "the peasant's war in Germany" an obvious misprint (1:197[1983])? The editors dutifully correct "Christ Hospital" to "Christ's Hospital," with a note to inform us of that fact (1:9). Didn't Coleridge know the name of the school he attended for eight years? Why leave "Love's Labour Lost" stand (1:6[1983]), as if Coleridge didn't know the correct title? What purpose is served in reproducing "Jacobinism" in both upper and lower case in the same sentence (1:217[1983])?

Why have "christian" and "protestant" and "bible" all in lower case in the same paragraph (1:229[1983]), when Coleridge spells them in the normal way almost everywhere? This kind of thing appears scores upon scores of times.

And if one is going to reproduce 1817 exactly, then why go about correcting Coleridge's many errors in umlauts, accents, breathings and the like (1:xix[1983]), thus preventing readers with knowledge of such matters from assessing Coleridge's command of foreign languages, a subject in some dispute and importance as regards French and German? The correction of errors in foreign quotations, by the way, the *silent* correction, is an editorial principle of the whole Collected Coleridge enterprise.

Rigid devotion to the 1817 text lands an editor in endless difficulties. In chapter 3 of 1817 there is an incomplete sentence. It occurs in an unusually convoluted construction, immediately following upon a long quotation in Greek. 1847 completes the sentence without comment (1:56). Shawcross accepted this, but noted (1:220), that the final words, thirteen of them, "were added by the editors of the second edition." Watson simply lets the fragmentary sentence stand.

In the final volume of Griggs' edition of Coleridge's correspondence (1971) appears a letter, previously unpublished, to Basil Montagu. By a happy quirk of fortune, the letter contains some thirty lines of chapter 3 of the *Biographia* (1:41[1907]), copied out by Coleridge, in which the defective sentence is completed with exactly the same thirteen words as had appeared in 1847. So there can now be no question as to the authority of 1847 text in this instance. Coleridge wrote Montagu: "I have transcribed the passage from Mr Gillman's Copy corrected by the Author—S.T.C."[3] Between the transcribed thirty lines in the Montagu letter, however, and the text of 1817 or 1847, discrepancies abound. In the first ten lines alone I have counted more than *fifty* changes in language, punctuation, and capitalization; however, 1847 is innocent of any knowledge of them. Why? Because, I believe, the alterations, with the exception of the completed sentence, exist *only* in the letter to Montagu, which the editors of 1847 did not see. Is this really so surprising? Coleridge could not possibly have made the changes shown in the Montagu letter in a printed copy of *Biographia* without filling the entire page, margins and between the lines, with new copy in a small hand. Who can imagine an entire text rewritten that way? I have no doubt Coleridge corrected mistakes—what author would not?—made some verbal changes and added marginal notes, as was his habit elsewhere. But he did not write and repunctuate wholesale. However, any time he actually took the trouble to *transcribe*, he would certainly have taken the opportunity to revise, and revise extensively, as he did in the letter to Montagu.

The *Collected Coleridge* editors ignore all this, though we have it on Coleridge's own authority that he was providing "corrected" copy. If you are going to burden the text with such trivia as that in 1817, an *i* was left out in the word "parish," that Southey was given the initial "W," or that "phantasmal" was printed as "phantasm," (1:42,52,116) and so forth, should not the Montagu variants be recorded? And yet, one may well ask, to what end? The reader interested in these matters can always refer to the original edition and relevant related material. Despite a considerable search, I have not found even one article on textual differences in the various editions that has produced a single material point as to *meaning*. Why entail upon posterity the error-strewn and wildly inconsistent text of 1817, which is now sure to be precisely quoted, warts and all, by the next few generations of scholars, just as some misprints in Shawcross have been faithfully copied?

A final comment about the 1983 text, which I hope to deal with more extensively elsewhere. The 1817 *Biographia* has no running page heads, only page numbers centered at the top. Engell-Bate give the chapter number on the left-hand page, and a running head on the right, based upon Coleridge's language in the summaries at the beginning of each chapter. These running heads, of a kind found nowhere else in the *Collected Coleridge* volumes, provide emphases which are certainly not in the text. The result is especially intrusive in the controversial ninth chapter, where seven pages are headed, "Obligations to—," no less than four of them, "Obligations to Schelling." If Coleridge had actually labelled four pages with the words "Obligations to Schelling," much of the animus in the long and bitter dispute over unacknowledged borrowings would surely have been forestalled. But Coleridge provided no such wholesale advertisement of his massive debts to Schelling. On the contrary. Chapter 9's headnote includes together with several other topics, the words "obligations to the Mystics—to Immanuel Kant . . . Obligations to Schelling; and among English writers to Saumarez." The Engell-Bate headings do not mention debts to Saumarez or any other English writer, but do, to repeat, give over four pages to "Obligations to Schelling." Readers who suppose that the heads were provided by Coleridge—and many will—will be mislead.

It is all too easy for an editor, poring over textual problems, to lose perspective as to the importance of such work. It is perhaps well for an editor to recall now and then Dr. Johnson's remark in his *Preface to Shakespeare*: "it is not very grateful to consider how little the succession of editors has added to this author's power of pleasing. He was read, admired, studied, and imitated, while he was yet deformed with all the improprieties which ignorance and neglect could accumulate upon him."[4] I doubt that Johnson would alter this remark two hundred years later. No matter what text of *Biographia* you read, you are reading Coleridge. The meaning is perfectly clear through whatever typographical blemishes an editor, through ignorance, design, or mistaken judgment chooses to preserve.

This is, however, decisively not true when it comes to the problem of annotation. Coleridge's editors have had, and will continue to have, an enormous influence over how *Biographia* and the prose works in general are perceived. For ninety years (between 1847 and 1956) the only inexpensive reprints of *Biographia* were the old Bohn Library and 1895 Everyman Library editions, both almost devoid of annotation, and the effect of this upon generations of readers has been very great in protecting Coleridge from the hazards to which he had exposed himself.

Since 1817 we have had only three fully annotated editions, those of 1847, 1907—sixty years later—and 1983, seventy-six years later still. George Sampson's richly annotated Coleridge student edition of 1920, still worth consulting, omitted chapters 5 through 13 because, he thought, they were beclouded by "yesterday's philosophy" (vi). George Watson's 1956 Everyman edition omits Satyrane's Letters and the *Bertram* critique, is very lightly annotated, and adds little to what had long been known.

The decision by Coleridge's heirs to republish *Biographia* with an extensive commentary and notes was taken as a direct result of Thomas De Quincey's abrasive disclosures in a series of articles in *Tait's Magazine*, not long after Coleridge's death in 1834. De Quincey asserted that large portions of chapters 12 and 13 of *Biographia* had been taken, without acknowledgment, from a German philosopher then scarcely known in England, Friedrich Schelling. This, together with the charge that the popular "Hymn Before Sunrise" was based on a poem by an obscure Danish-German poet, Friederica Brun, provoked a fierce controversy, all the more exacerbated by the fact that Coleridge had died as a widely respected author of devotional works promulgating the doctrines of Trinitarian Christianity.

The turmoil had scarcely subsided when a ferocious attack appeared in *Blackwood's* (March 1840), written by an incensed Scottish philosopher and academic, James Ferrier. Ferrier's documentation was far more precise and damning than De Quincey's, and extended the range of silent borrowings substantially, including the assault on Hartley's doctrine of association in chapter 5, together with almost all its learned quotations in Greek and Latin, taken, as Ferrier was able to show, from yet another obscure German, J. G. E. Maass.

The form and tone of the edition of 1847 was largely determined by the need to defend Coleridge from his detractors. One can only marvel, in the circumstances, at how brilliantly Sara performed her difficult, psychologically almost impossible task. Her three-volume edition leads off with a passionate, one-hundred-page vindication of her father's character and literary honesty; and I think it fair to say that her explanations of the seeming deliberate plagiarisms and other breaches of literary ethics resisted any serious challenge for the next century and a quarter.

Although one can dispute her conclusions—as I do—she was determined to lay the evidence she had before the reader. Sara has never received anything like the credit she deserves. No doubt there is a bit of sexism in this, and some professional snobbery towards someone who has no formal training as a scholar. "The trouble I have taken with this book is ridiculous to think of," she wrote a friend. "It is a filial phenomenon —nobody will thank me for it, and no one will know or see a twentieth part of it."[5] She consulted hundreds of scarce and difficult books, many of them in Greek, Latin, German, French, and Italian; she followed innumerable tortuous trails, and where parallel passages were involved, she set forth many of them plainly. When a source came from the German, she would often print the German together with a translation. The result was, in my opinion—strictly with respect to the German sources—by far the best edition of *Biographia* until Engell-Bate of 1983.

If Sara Coleridge's work has been sadly underrated, John Shawcross's introduction and textual annotation have been drastically over-valued. His eighty-page introduction was for generations, and perhaps still is, immensely influential. His notes, stuck away at the back of each volume with no indication in the text that a note was to be consulted, add little of value to what could be found in the 1847 edition, on which he leaned very heavily, as everybody knows, and which he forthrightly acknowledged. But where Sara, as I have said, printed many parallel passages with translations, Shawcross was content merely to direct those readers with a command of German to works which could be found only in great libraries. Many key titles had been out of print for generations. How many readers would or could take the trouble to follow up on a note which reads: "With this paragraph, cp. the *Abhandlung zur Erläuterung*, &c. *Werke*, I, i, 403"

(1:269)? Moreover, Shawcross's long introduction trumpets from beginning to end that Coleridge was fundamentally independent of German
thought, the effect of which inevitably was to chill anyone's interest in pursuing the subject. Here are some typical judgments: Coleridge's "conception . . . of the imaginative faculty . . . must have been arrived at entirely independently of German influence" (1:xxiv); "he was a metaphysician long
before he studied the German philosophers" (1:xxvii); "Thus Coleridge,
largely if not entirely by the force of independent thinking, has reached a
mental attitude in sympathy with the critical philosophy and its developments" (1:xxxi); Coleridge's "deepest philosophy was drawn not from the
speculations of other men, but from the teaching of life" (1:xxxii); "to him
[Kant] alone could he be said to assume in any degree the attitude of pupil
to master. Yet even to Kant his debt on the whole seems to have been more
formal than material—to have resided rather in the scientific statement
of convictions previously attained than in the acquisition of new truths"
(i, xli); "While *The Friend* abounds in the fruits of Kant's teachings, there
is nothing in it which we are justified in ascribing to the influence of the
German idealists" (1:xlix). The effect of all this on Coleridge studies has
been incalculable.

Shawcross nowhere confronts the plagiarism controversy directly. He
ignores the specific charges which Sara Coleridge was at such pains to refute, though much had come to light in the intervening sixty years. It goes
without saying that he had no intention of suppressing information. He
simply didn't think the matter worth fussing over: "an investigation of the
exact amount and nature of his debt to German contemporaries would
be a task of but doubtful value or success. Nothing, I believe, is more remarkable with regard to Coleridge than the comparatively early maturity
of his ideas" (1:iv–v).

Shawcross was, of course, entitled to his opinions, which, as everybody
knows, have been shared by generations of Coleridgeans. Nevertheless,
one can object to an editorial approach which deprives readers of information necessary to form independent judgments and at the same time
constantly thrusts forward only one view of an important and highly controversial subject.

Thus it was that between 1847 and 1983, the dominant edition of *Biographia* came from a formidable scholar and ardent champion who did not
think the subject of Coleridge's intellectual debts worth pursuing.

Watson's annotation of the philosophical chapters and the work in general can be quickly disposed of. His one-volume edition provides very light commentary, and his approach to Coleridge in 1956 was traditionally reverential. His views appear to have changed somewhat since then. James Engell's annotation of chapters 5 through 13 deserves to stand, and will, as a monument of scholarship. It is melancholy to reflect upon the fact that so much of the fire and fury that have afflicted Coleridge studies since De Quincey and Ferrier might well have been avoided if only the *facts* had been available. Vigorous controversy will continue as to the *meaning* of the facts, of course, but at least there will be a far more solid basis for discussion. It is easy to suppose therefore, that the major difficulty in editing the *Biographia* has at long last been overcome—the willingness of an editor and publisher to confront what is disagreeable. "Society makes what is disagreeable into what is untrue," wrote Freud in the *Introductory Lectures on Psychoanalysis* of 1916–17. "It disputes the truths of psychoanalysis with logical and factual arguments; but these arise from emotional sources, and it maintains these objections as prejudices, against every attempt to counter them."[6] Something like this was certainly true until very recently with respect to Coleridge's plagiarisms. The very word almost always has cautionary inverted commas around it when used in the vicinity of Coleridge's name. Some fresh air is now blowing through the subject, but there is still plenty of smog to contend with.

There are, and always have been, two fundamental problems in annotating the *Biographia*, which is, among much else, an intellectual autobiography. Its editors, without exception, have not only failed to confront the problems, they have exacerbated them. I refer to Coleridge's extreme inflexibility when writing about himself, and his masterful exploitation of the reader's will not to disbelieve. "Shakespeare," said the fearless Dr. Johnson, "with his excellencies has likewise faults, and faults sufficient to obscure and overwhelm any other merit. I shall shew them in the proportion in which they appear to me, without envious malignity or superstitious veneration. No question can be more innocently discussed than a dead poet's pretensions to renown, and little regard is due to that bigotry which sets candour higher than truth."[7] "Candour," in Johnson's dictionary, is defined as "absence of malice," and "kindliness," thus, "little regard is due to that bigotry which sets kindliness higher than truth."

In annotating the *Biographia* it is simply not possible to lay out the facts in a neutral way and let the reader draw his or her own conclusions. In multitudes of instances, the reader will not know that there is any sort of judgment to be made, unless the editor calls attention to it, and the editor who does that can and probably will be charged with unseemly intrusiveness. It is always much safer to say nothing on a controversial matter, in all human affairs. But to say nothing is also to act. Silence can also be a form of intrusiveness, and a particularly insidious one.

Let me illustrate the difficulties confronting an annotator of the *Biographia* and indicate what I think yet needs to be done. Again, my illustrations are almost all from chapter 1. The *Biographia* begins: "It has been my lot to have had my name introduced both in conversation, and in print, more frequently than I find it easy to explain, whether I consider the fewness, unimportance, and limited circulation of my writings, or the retirement and distance, in which I have lived, both from the literary and political world." No editor has thought it necessary to comment on this astonishing sentence. When Coleridge wrote it, he had for years been a very well-known member of the English literary and political world. In the five years immediately preceding, he had delivered an important series of literary lectures in London and contributed scores of articles to newspapers with large circulations. His periodical *The Friend* had been reissued in 1812, and his play *Remorse* had a considerable success at the Drury Lane Theater in 1813. His three essays "On the Principles of Genial Criticism" were published in 1814. In that year he wrote Daniel Stuart, the owner of several powerful newspapers, that the *Quarterly Review* had "insolently reproved" him "for *not publishing.*" "I could rebut the charge," he continued, "& not merely say but prove—that there is not a man in England, whose Thoughts, Images, Words & Erudition have been published in larger quantities than *mine*—tho', I must admit, not *by* or *for* myself" (*CL* 2:532), one of his many complaints that his own writings and conversations had been widely plundered. In a later chapter of *Biographia*, in quite a different context, Coleridge wrote: "Even if the compositions, which I have made public, and that too in a form the most certain of extensive circulation . . . had been published in *books,* they would have filled a respectable number of volumes, though every passage of merely temporary interest were omitted" (1:148–49[1907]). That is certainly true.

Is an editor to say nothing about any of this for fear of being labelled intrusive, or hostile? Silence almost guarantees that the reader, especially the young student first encountering this towering classic, will begin the *Biographia* with a radically false idea of Coleridge's actual position in English intellectual circles, and ask no questions as to the author's motives in presenting himself in this strange way.

In the first sentence of the second paragraph, Coleridge states that his first volume of poems was published in 1794, "when I had barely passed the verge of manhood," that is to say, when he was 21 years old. 1847 silently corrects this to read "In the spring of 1796." Subsequent editors quietly give the correct date in a note. Should it be pointed out that Coleridge misdated many of his poems, almost always to assign them to an earlier period? The poem "Time, Real and Imaginary," often cited as an example of the precocious flowering of his poetic and philosophical genius, was actually written in his 30's, though he published it in *Sybilline Leaves* as a "schoolboy poem," a "favourite epithet" which, Dykes Campbell bluntly observed, "attached by Coleridge to any poem of his is of no value as evidence."[8] The issue is not irrelevant, for one of the two dominant themes of chapter 1, and a major subtext throughout the *Biographia*, is the author's astonishingly precocious boyhood and youth. "At a very premature age, even before my fifteenth year, I had bewildered myself in metaphysicks, and in theological controversy" (1:9[1907]); this is but one of many similar remarks.

The other crucial theme in chapter 1 is the author's perhaps unique scrupulosity in acknowledging intellectual debts. The many ingenious counterpointings of the theme—worthy of Bach in *The Art of the Fugue*—reach the following crescendo:

> Though I have seen and known enough of mankind to be well aware, that I shall perhaps stand alone in my creed, and that it will be well, if I subject myself to no worse charge than that of singularity; I am not therefore deterred from avowing, that I regard, and ever have regarded the obligations of the intellect among the most sacred of the claims of gratitude. A valuable thought, or a particular train of thoughts, gives me additional pleasure, when I can safely refer and attribute it to the conversation or correspondence of another. (1:9[1907])

Is it neurotically suspicious to suggest a connection between this superbly orchestrated Credo and the long controversy over Coleridge's repeated failure to identify his sources? Is the Divine Ventriloquist fanfare alone to be heard?

Referring to the critical response to his first book of poems, Coleridge emphasized that "even at that early period . . . I saw and admitted the superiority of an austerer and more natural style, with an insight not less clear, than I at present possess" (1:3[1907]). Obviously, it was of the utmost importance to Coleridge to establish that in his early youth he already possessed his mature opinions in almost all important respects, aesthetic and political. In chapter 2, he goes so far as to say: "I had derived peculiar advantages from my school discipline, and . . . my *general* theory of poetry was the same then as now" (1:27[1907]), that is to say, before the age of seventeen Coleridge had arrived at the same *general* theory of poetry as he possessed in middle age. These are matters of great historical interest. If Coleridge's claims are true we can assign him almost everything of enduring value in Wordsworth's Preface to *Lyrical Ballads*, and forget about what he may have learned from German aesthetics, which certain critics have gladly done.

What about those "peculiar advantages" which Coleridge repeatedly claimed to have derived from his "school discipline"? This brings us to the "inestimable" James Bowyer, from whom Coleridge says he learned

> that Poetry, even that of the loftiest and, seemingly, that of the wildest odes, had a logic of its own, as severe as that of science; and more difficult, because more subtle, more complex, and dependent on more, and more fugitive causes. (1:4[1907])

Here is one of the most influential statements in the history of literary criticism, as "exhilarating," according to one scholarly enthusiast, as Sidney's "Defense of Poesy" and Emerson's "American Scholar" (Richard Harter Fogle, *The Idea of Coleridge's Criticism*, ix). One could easily lament that Coleridge neglected to pass on to posterity Bowyer's proof of what even the greatest classical scholars have failed to achieve, despite repeated efforts, namely, a convincing demonstration that Pindar's odes are governed by a clearly discernible logic. Be that as it may, Coleridge did not learn this in boyhood from an amazing schoolmaster. In a letter of 1802, long after he had left Christ's Hospital, he wrote in a letter: "Young somewhere in one of his prose works remarks that there is as profound a Logic in the most daring and dithyrambic parts of Pindar, as in the [Logic] of Aristotle—the remark is a valuable one" (*CL* 11:864). Coleridge's notebooks for 1795[9] show that he was copying and paraphrasing passages from Edward Young's essay "On Lyric Poetry" (1728), which contains the following sentence: "Pindar, who has as much logic at the bottom as Aristotle or Euclid, to some critics has appeared mad." Somewhat surprisingly, the idea was not unusual in the late eighteenth century. Alexander Gerard, in *An Essay on Genius* (1774), wrote: "Pindar is judicious even in his irregularities. The boldness of his fancy, had it been under no control from reason, would have produced, not wild sublimity, but madness and frenzy" (73); and Coleridge's friend George Dyer wrote in the Preface of his *Poems* (1792), which Coleridge certainly saw: "The verse of Pindar is subject to as strict rules, as the most accurate and methodical rhyme" (vii).

Only long after his schooldays, it would appear, did Coleridge perceive the significance of this insight; and when he restated the principle in the *Biographia*, he invested it with resonances and implications which made its origin in a suggestive statement by an eighteenth-century poet scarcely recognizable. And surely one of the unique impulses of Coleridge's genius is his insistent quest for unifying principles governing the creation and criticism of the arts and a philosophical system so embracing as to include all thought and all phenomena. Always he had before him this fiery column as a guide. No man in England had so encompassing a vision of the potential breadth of literary criticism and theory.

The tributes to Bowyer have found their way into many histories of education and are constantly quoted when Coleridge's intellectual development is discussed. Christopher North, in a *Blackwood's* review of 1817, refused to "credit this account" of Bowyer, and noticed that "Mr. Coleridge's own poetical practices render the story incredible."[10] Leigh Hunt, who arrived at Christ's Hospital the year Coleridge left for Cambridge, wrote in his *Autobiography*, rather tartly, that Bowyer's "natural destination lay in carpentry."[11] Hunt was well aware of Coleridge's tribute in the *Biographia*, and he meets it head on: "Coleridge has praised Bowyer for teaching us to laugh at 'muses' and 'Castalian streams'; but he ought rather to have lamented that he did not teach us how to love them wisely, as he might have had he really known anything about poetry . . . Even Coleridge's juvenile poems were not the better for Bowyer's training" (108). According to Charles Lamb, Coleridge's contemporary at Christ's Hospital, Bowyer's "English style was crampt to barbarism. His Easter anthems (for his duties obliged him to those periodical flights) were grating as scrannel pipes."[12]

Bowyer is said to have shown "no mercy to phrase, metaphor, or image, unsupported by sound sense, or where the same sense might have been conveyed with equal force and dignity in plainer words" (1:5[1907]). One might easily deduce that this obscure schoolmaster (and thus Coleridge) had anticipated not only the basic principles of organic unity, but much of Wordsworth's supposedly revolutionary argument about poetic language in the Preface to *Lyrical Ballads*. As Hunt and Christopher North acutely observed, there is nothing in Coleridge's early poetry, and intermittently at all times thereafter, to sustain a belief in the efficacy of Bowyer's instruction. It happens that Bowyer kept a book into which he had his students copy their original verses which met his own presumably severe standards, the so-called *Liber Aureus*. Some time ago I read through that fascinating volume in the British Library, and I found no correlation whatever between Bowyer's supposed principles and the poetry he chose to honor. This is hardly surprising if one credits Hunt's scornful remark that "Coleridge's lauded teacher" had once put into his hands "(for the express purpose of cultivating my love of poetry), the *Irene* and other poems of Dr. Johnson!" [13]

Perhaps the wisest and possibly most comforting conclusion to draw from these conflicting accounts of Bowyer's teaching is that we ought to repose no confidence in student evaluations.

Credulousness is rarely criticized in dealing with the illustrious dead. Skepticism is usually pounced upon as a sign of constitutional antipathy towards one's subject. But the problem of Coleridge's veracity will not go away, though scholars have, down the generations, with a few notable exceptions, left the subject strictly alone, when they have even noticed that a problem exists.

It cannot be repeated too often or emphatically that nothing Coleridge says about his intellectual history is to be accepted, except provisionally, in the absence of outside evidence. In chapter 1 Coleridge says that during his first Cambridge vacation he "assisted a friend in a contribution to a literary society in Devonshire" (1:12[1907]). For a page and a half following, drawing upon his memory of that essay, Coleridge impressively discusses Gray's borrowings from Shakespeare and Milton, the reasons he prefers Collins' odes to Gray's, "drawn from a comparison of passages in the Latin poets with the original Greek," all of which "at that early period [here is that significant phrase yet again] led to a conjecture" which he much later heard independently stated by Wordsworth [priority over Wordsworth again] involving the translation of "prose thoughts into poetic language" (1:12–13[1907]).

The editors of 1847 were unable "to discover any traces of this essay" (1:18,n.22). Shawcross goes further: "This [literary] society was probably the *Society of Gentlemen at Exeter*, a volume of whose essays was published in 1796. . . . As Coleridge was not a regular member his essay was not published in the volume, and it is greatly to be regretted that no other trace of it is to be found" (1:209). Shawcross simply takes it for granted that such an essay was actually written. He does not observe that the literary society's first and only publication, in 1796, was already five years after the date Coleridge says he "assisted" a friend in writing it. And he confidently states as established fact that the society didn't publish it because Coleridge was not a regular member, all this about a society which may have nothing whatever to do with Coleridge! Incidentally, in his Introduction Shawcross has Coleridge *joining* a literary society at Cambridge, for which he "wrote essays [now plural] to vindicate Shakespeare's art" (1:xiv), a remarkable and not entirely uncharacteristic extrapolation. Shawcross might have observed that Coleridge throughout his life referred to unwritten works as actually existing, or even at that very moment in press—but he says nothing because it does not occur to him that there is anything to say.

Engell has a longer note on the subject, gives more information about the literary society, repeats that "C was not a regular member," and concludes that "the essay mentioned by C does not appear [in the 1796 volume], but the preface notes that 'materials for another' volume 'have been preserved'" (1:19–20,n.4). Such comments inevitably tend to establish the existence of a dazzling teenage essay, of which no trace exists. Of course, it is possible that Coleridge wrote it, even though there are no other literary essays from the whole early period. Shouldn't the reader be given some sort of context in which to evaluate its probable existence? More important, much more important, if Coleridge is inventing, what purpose does that serve in the overall design of the *Biographia*?

Such commentary inevitably molds the reader's attitudes and beliefs into shapes consonant with the editor's. I am not suggesting that there is any deliberation in this. What I am saying is that an editor's view of Coleridge determines in multitudes of subtle ways what the reader will think. In view of the exhaustive research into the "lost" essay, it is at least a bit surprising that no editor has thought it worthwhile to comment on Coleridge's claim, in the notoriously unreliable chapter 10, that his political essays had been reprinted "in the federal journals throughout America," and that from his articles on the War of 1812, not only "the sentiments were adopted, but in some instances the very language, in several of the Massachusetts state-papers" (1:148[1907]). Surely when libraries are being ransacked to confirm a trivial date there must have been some curiosity about these widespread state and federal appropriations, a charge which, incidentally, aroused the patriotic indignation of a contemporary American reviewer of the *Biographia*.[14] In his first *Lay Sermon*, Coleridge had declared that his essay on "Vulgar Errors in Taxation," originally published in *The Friend*, had been "reprinted in two of the American Federalist papers."[15] But as Coleridge was just fifteen years old when the American Federalist papers first appeared, we can ignore that particular claim. Shouldn't editors confront facts like these? Of course. The point is that an editor's assumptions will often control what facts impinge upon consciousness.

Chapter 1 closes with an amusing and seemingly irrelevant anecdote about a man who was eager to meet Coleridge, but hesitant because he was "the author of a confounded severe epigram on my *ancient mariner*, which had given me great pain. I assured my friend that, if the epigram was a good one, it would only increase my desire to become acquainted with the author, and begg'd to hear it recited; when, to my no less surprise than amusement, it proved to be one which I had myself some time before written and inserted in the Morning Post." The epigram reads:

To the author of the Ancient Mariner.

> Your poem must eternal be,
> Dear sir! it cannot fail,
> For 'tis incomprehensible,
> And without head or tail.

(1:18[1907])

The "severe epigram," however, was not a *jeux d'esprit* poking good-natured fun at himself, as Coleridge wished the reader to believe, but an attack on the poet-laureate "Mr. Pye, on his *Carmen Seculare* (a title which has by various persons who have heard it, been thus translated, 'A Poem *an age long*')."[16] As George Sampson observed, "There is some point in saying of a *Carmen Seculare* that it 'must eternal be'; none in saying it of The Ancient Mariner,"[17] which I think we will agree is one of the most intense and dramatically concentrated poems in our language. The epigram, moreover, was adapted, without acknowledgment, from Lessing's *Die Ewigkeit gewisser Gedichte* ("The Eternity of Certain Poems.") The 1847 edition does not comment upon this, and Sara discreetly dropped this epigram from her collected edition of 1852. Ernest Hartley Coleridge identified all the poetry in the *Biographia* with the exception of this epigram. Shawcross curtly says, "Coleridge is here inventing." Watson says nothing. And the editors of 1983, unreconciled to the possibility that Coleridge could deliberately say the thing that is not, pirouette on the corpse of credibility in defending Coleridge against the charge of distorting fact (1:29,n.1).

Interesting and even entertaining as these matters may be, they are of little importance in themselves. What matters is that they throw light on a real question: what function does this anecdote serve in the structure of the *Biographia*? Coleridge described the book as a whole as "an immethodical miscellany," but the author of the *Essays on Method* and a bulky treatise on logic will always be found to display method in his miscellanies, and especially in his seeming meanderings. At his best Coleridge was a great writer in prose as well as poetry. It is scandalously disrespectful to Coleridge the artist, who had lived by his pen for twenty years and by his wits and brilliantly concealed shrewdness since adolescence, to suppose that he did not know precisely what he was doing when he scattered inventions through a work purporting to be fact.

If the first chapter of the *Biographia* were the first chapter of a novel, the alert reader would surmise that he was dealing with a formidably unreliable narrator, and would confront the rest of the text in that light. The narrator's genius would not be compromised, and to some readers he might become an even more absorbing figure than the received conception of him. Such readers would, I am convinced, have a far deeper understanding of the text, its subtexts, and the complex motives that have resulted in one of the most difficult, justifiably canonical, and booby-trapped works in world literature.

2

Coleridge's Book of Moonlight

Thomas Vogler

My head-knockings, therefore, have to be real ones, solid and substantial, with nothing sophistical or imaginary about them.

—COLERIDGE

To this End, the Philosopher's Way in all Ages has been by erecting certain *Edifices in the Air* . . .

—SWIFT

I would build that dome in air . . .

—COLERIDGE

What have we MOONITES done?

—STERNE

Like most of my essay, the title presumes to be nothing more than an image thrown out in an attempt to change our conventional way of reading the *Biographia Literaria*. I offer it as an image of the work itself, and introduce the phrase with three quotations. First, from page 46 of Blake's *Notebook*:

Delicate Hands & Heads will never appear
While Titian's &c as in the Book of Moonlight p 5

This statement lies there enigmatically on the page, more teasing even than Nietzsche's umbrella, until we find what I take to be a gloss on it in Wallace Stevens' *Comedian as the Letter C*:

The book of moonlight is not written yet
Nor half begun, but when it is, leave room
For Crispin . . . .
Leave room, therefore, in that unwritten book

> For the legendary moonlight that once burned
> In Crispin's mind above a continent

Keeping with the letter C, and getting closer to Coleridge, we move from Crispin to Carlyle, and his description of Professor Teufelsdröckh as *homo scribens:*

> But the whole particulars of his Route, his Weather-observations, the picturesque Sketches he took, though all regularly jotted down (in indelible sympathetic-ink by an invisible interior Penman), are these nowhere forthcoming? Perhaps quite lost: one other leaf of that mighty Volume (of human Memory) left to fly abroad, unprinted, unpublished, unbound up, as waste paper; and to rot, the sport of rainy winds? (*Sartor Resartus* 77)

Carlyle's description here alludes to the story of Aeneas's visit to the Cumaean Sibyl (*Aeneid*, Bk. 6) whose answers, written on leaves, were blown about on the winds.[1] Coleridge took the title for his "collected" poems from the same source, thereby making an ironic comment on Wordsworth's careful ordering of his work in the 1815 edition, as well as reflecting the scattered and disordered state of his own *oeuvre*. One of the many ways to understand the genesis of his *Biographia* is as a "preface" to these poems, begun in *literal* competition with Wordsworth's preface, but ending up as a work in its own write.[2]

I say its own "write" because it does not presume to exist—insofar as a Book of Moonlight may be said to exist—in its own *right;* it constantly points elsewhere for its provocations, its matter, and its fulfillment, even while presumably seeking to demonstrate and represent "the act of self-consciousness [which] is for *us* the source and principle of all *our* possible knowledge" (1:284). We could argue that the text of the *Biographia* is composed of writing which exists to fill a certain kind of space, a highly charged and problematic "space," the emptiness of which was in part defined by the presence of another preface to another collection of poems, and Coleridge's marginal status in that preface.[3] In it Coleridge, who had once liked to think he was the first Englishman to distinguish between the "fancy" and "imagination" (1:85–86), was relegated by Wordsworth to having coined a phrase for the fancy ("the aggregative and associative Power"), which he introduces only to criticize and correct. Coleridge's "beautiful Poems," which had been "long associated in publication" with Wordsworth's, are missing, because "the time is come when considerations of general propriety dictate the separation." (1815 *Preface* 3:39). But also missing is the "truth" about the imagination—the truth that Wordsworth missed in his attempts to philosophize about his own poetry and poetry in general.

Coleridge's image for this missing space comes in chapter 4, as he turns from his initial encounter with Wordsworth to the "attempt" to "present an intelligible statement of [his] own poetic creed," an attempt which will occupy him for the next nine chapters:

> My friend has drawn a masterly sketch of the branches with their *poetic* fruitage. I wish to add the trunk, and even the roots as far as they lift themselves above ground, and are visible to the common eye of our common consciousness. (1:88)

Kenneth Johnston has aptly observed that for Wordsworth there was "a tendency for *The Recluse* to turn at every critical point into *The Prelude*" (18). Coleridge's description of *The Prelude* in the famous letter to Wordsworth of April 1815 repeats his image of his plans for the *Biographia*: "the Poem on the growth of your own mind was as the ground-plat and the Roots, out of which the Recluse was to have sprung up as the Tree—as far as the same Sap in both, I expected them doubtless to have formed one compleat Whole" (*CL* 4:573). In the same letter he makes an interesting slip, calling it "the Poem on the Growth of your own Support" (576) which he thought would "have laid a solid and immoveable foundation for the Edifice by removing the sandy Sophisms of Locke, and the Mechanic Dogmatists" (574). This is also an apt description of his own project in the following chapters, which set out to present Coleridge's "own statement of the theory" and "the grounds on which I rest it" in the form of "deductions from established premises conveyed in such a form, as is calculated either to effect a *fundamental* conviction, or to receive a *fundamental* confutation" (1:88, italics added). It would seem clear, from preliminary gestures of this sort, that Coleridge was committing himself to producing in the *Biographia* the story of the growth of his own mind (or "support" as in the Wordsworth letter) as a case study or demonstration of the real existence and operation of the imagination.[4]

At the core of the "story" must be the performative or self-constituting utterance of an "I AM." He must write his SUM before he can write his SUMMA, as its existential "ground," for "It is asserted only, that the act of self-consciousness is for *us* the source and principle of all *our* possible knowledge" (1:284). But the SUMMA, the *magnum opus* or *Logosophia* in the form of a philosophical demonstration is also required as "ground" for the SUM.[5] As definitive "epistemology" (*epi* + *histanai* + *logos*, or words "on which to stand"), Coleridge's SUMMA is necessary to provide the ground for his SUM, as a philosophical demonstration of the essential truth that "we can never pass beyond the principle of self-consciousness. Should we attempt it, we must be driven back from ground to ground, each of which would cease to be a Ground the moment we pressed on it. We must be whirl'd down the gulph of an infinite series" (1:285). Without the SUMMA the SUM risks being only the dithyrambic ode of a QUERKOPF VON KLUB-STICK, shouting *ipse Divus*, "myself God":

> Here on this market-cross aloud I cry:
> I, I, I! itself I!
> The form and the substance, the what and the why,
> The when and the where, and the low and the high,
> The inside and outside, the earth and the sky,
> I, you, and he, and he, you and I,
> All souls and all bodies are I itself I!
>
> (1:159)

In this context we can hear a litotes in Coleridge's statement that "Great indeed are the obstacles which an English metaphysician has to encounter" (1:290). To avoid the bathetic dithyramb, he must forge a linked chain of compelling argument; but "a chain without a staple, from which all the links derived their stability" (1:266) is another infinite series, like a string of blind men in a straight line without a guide.

In this attempt to develop a systematic philosophical argument, Coleridge takes up his place in the great enlightenment project to produce an independent, rational justification for a moral human nature, to discover the rational foundations for an objective morality which will inspire the confidence of man as a moral agent, assuring him that his moral practice and utterance are correct. This is the idea of philosophy "as a science" (1:140) which Coleridge takes up in chapter 9, as a consequence of the "*clearness* and *evidence*" of Kant's work and the "adamantine chain of the logic" having taken possession of him "as with a giant's hand" (1:153). To complete the impulse, Spinoza "supplied the *idea* of a system truly metaphysical, and of a *metaphysique* truly systematic" (1:158). Without such *systematic* grounding we run the risk of becoming like Hartley who, though "excellent and pious," assumed "as his foundations, ideas which, if we embrace the doctrines of his first volume, can exist nowhere but in the

vibrations of the ethereal medium common to the nerves and to the atmosphere" (1:121–22). Or still worse, "We might as rationally chant the Brahmin creed of the tortoise that supported the bear, that supported the
elephant, that supported the world, to the tune of 'This is the house that
Jack built'" (1:137–38).

Staples (providing support from above) and grounds (support from below) are figures of "attachment" to something outside in order to avoid
the alternative of an infinite series which simultaneously fills all space and
time and swallows itself into its own gulf. But this figure of attachment
can be turned inside-out in an attempt to avoid the same fate: "We are
to seek therefore for some absolute truth capable of communicating to
other positions a certainty, which it has not itself borrowed; a truth self-
grounded, unconditional and known by its own light. . . . Its existence
too must be such, as to preclude the possibility of requiring a cause or
antecedent without an absurdity" (1:268). Coleridge comes close here to
Blake's insanely "rational" Urizen, another bookish persona caught in the
webs of the book he is and the book he is writing, the book "of" Urizen:

> 5. First I fought with the fire; consum'd
> Inwards, into a deep world within:
> A void immense, wild dark & deep,
> Where nothing was; Natures wide womb
> And self balanc'd stretch'd o'er the void
> I alone, even I! the winds merciless
> Bound; but condensing, in torrents
> They fall & fall; strong I repell'd
> The vast waves, & arose on the waters
> A wide world of solid obstruction
>
> 6. Here alone I in books formd of me—[6]
>
> (*Book of Urizen*, plate 4)

The very figures that seek to image an escape from the devouring trope
of aporia may in fact themselves constitute that trap. Kant, in section 59
of the *Critique of Judgment*, gives as examples of metaphors that are not
reliable from an epistemological point of view a set which begins with
"ground [*Grund*]" and "to depend [*abhängen*])" and includes "to follow
from [*fliessen*]" and "substance" in Locke's sense of "the support of accidents."[7] Kant's warning has been analyzed at length by Paul de Man
(1978), in terms that are pertinent to our consideration of Coleridge at
this point:

> The considerations about the possible danger of uncontrolled meta-
> phors, focused on the cognate figures of support, ground, and so forth,
> reawaken the hidden uncertainty about the rigor of a distinction that
> does not hold if the language in which it is stated reintroduces the ele-
> ments of indetermination it sets out to eliminate. For it is not obvious
> that the iconic representation that can be used to illustrate a rational
> concept is indeed a figure. (27–28)

Coleridge could readily criticize the philosophical approach "which talking of mind but thinking of brick and mortar, or other images equally
abstracted from body, contrives a theory of spirit" (1:235); but a viable
alternative practice was not so easy for him to achieve.

II

> An author is often merely an *x*, even when his name is signed, something quite
> impersonal, which addresses itself abstractly, by the aid of printing, to thousands
> and thousands, while remaining itself unseen and unknown, living a life as hid-
> den, as anonymous, as it is possible for a life to be, in order, presumably, not to
> reveal the too obvious and striking contradiction between the prodigious means
> of communication employed and the fact that the author is only a single indi-
> vidual—perhaps also for fear of the control which in practical life must always be
> exercised over every one who wishes to teach others, to see whether his personal
> existence comports with his communication.
>
> —KIERKEGAARD, *Author* 45

Most of what I have been discussing so far applies specifically to the famous "philosophical chapters" (5–13), which are usually taken to provide
the main intellectual substance of the *Biographia*. I want now to shift my
focus to the physical "packaging" of these chapters, while keeping the
thread of spatial imagery implicit in the dominant image of "ground." The
ground is to provide the basis for erecting a structure, and the structure
in this case is to be a text-edifice. For a variety of reasons it was imperative
for Coleridge to produce a published *book*. His self-consciousness about
this dimension of the project shows at every stage, from his early concern
about duplicating the exact features of Wordsworth's Preface, to the decision that his "book" should be divided into chapters, to the defensiveness
at the end of chapter 10, where he claims that had "the compositions,
which I have made public . . . been published in *books,* they would have
filled a respectable number of volumes, though every passage of merely

temporary interest were omitted" (1:220). "But are books the only chan-
nel through which the stream of intellectual usefulness can flow?" he asks
defensively, for the fact is, as he makes clear at the very beginning of the
Biographia, his publications have not achieved the status and stature of
books. Without the production of a *book* he risks the possibility of having
"lived in vain . . . a painful thought to any man, and especially so to him
who has made literature his profession" (1:219). The same note is struck
in the *Notebooks*, as when he yearns for "time & *ease* to reduce my Pocket-
books and Memorandums to an *Index*" in order to produce at least "one
printed volume" (1:xviii–ix).

For Coleridge the existence of a printed, published book, with his own
name on it, became both the sign for and the demonstration of a personal and intellectual existence. Publications like *The Friend* did not count,
for that work was "printed rather than published, or so published that it
had been well for the unfortunate author, if it had remained in manuscript" (1:175). The physical book could function as material object in that
subject-object relationship in which Coleridge saw "each involving and
supposing the other. In other words, it is a subject which becomes a subject
by the act of constructing itself objectively to itself" (1:273). It is in this
spirit that Coleridge takes the *act* of writing to illustrate the "absurdity" of
the Hartleyan theory:

> Yet according to this hypothesis the disquisition, to which I am at present
> soliciting the reader's attention, may be as truly said to be written by
> Saint Paul's church, as by *me*: for it is the mere motion of my muscles and
> nerves; and these again are set in motion from external causes equally
> passive, which external causes stand themselves in interdependent con-
> nection with every thing that exists or has existed. Thus the whole uni-
> verse co-operates to produce the minutest stroke of every letter, save
> only that I myself and I alone, have nothing to do with it . . . . the poor
> worthless I! (1:118–19)

In writing his book Coleridge must thus perform a self-constituting and
esemplastic *act*, comparable to that he claims to have performed in making
the word: "'*Esemplastic, The word is not in Johnson, nor have I met with it elsewhere*.' Neither have I! I constructed it myself from the Greek words . . . to
shape into one" (1:169). In the act of producing his book, Coleridge was
attempting to put himself together, to shape himself "into one." The degree of success he felt he had accomplished may be accurately expressed
in a letter he wrote to Tulk in August 1817: "In my literary Life you will

find a sketch of the *subjective* Pole of the Dynamic Philosophy; the rudiments of "*Self*-construction, barely enough to let a thinking mind see *what
it is like*" (*CL* 4:767).

Before him most immediately was the example of Wordsworth, who had
just edited himself in the form of the 1815 volumes, where "propriety" and
the sign of his own name had dictated the exclusion of Coleridge's "beautiful Poems." But the extremity of Coleridge's self-consciousness in his
enterprise comes closer to those works which in their *bookishness* as books
exist as parodies of the edited and printed book. *A Tale of a Tub* comes to
mind here as chief example, but *Don Quixote*, the *Dunciad*, *Tristram Shandy*,
Sartor Resartus, and a whole range of Kierkegaard's productions provide
additional examples.

I will discuss some of these works later, but for now would like to point
out the ways in which they exemplify what Foucault has called the "author
function" of a book. Anonymous or pseudonymous publication, or works
which thematize the problems of "authorship," employ strategies which
produce disturbing implications for the concept of the author and its link
with the status of the proper name. The fact that Tristram Shandy or
Lemuel Gulliver or Johannes Climacus exist only by virtue of the printed
texts bearing their names—that they are thereby persons or authors whose
identities are produced only by the printed book—may suggest the way
in which any author can be seen as a "function" generated by publication
and interpretation. In an exaggerated emphasis on the mechanics of the
printed book (with its dedications, introductions, annotations, footnotes,
etc.) the possibility is raised that the author (and even the editor in some
cases) is himself simply another feature of the printed book, a function
of its publication.[8] Thus Kierkegaard, explaining his "pseudonymity or
polynymity," asserts that "it has an *essential* ground in the character of
the *production*." He is "a *souffleur* who has poetically produced the *authors*,
whose preface in turn is their own production, as are even their own
names." He can claim only to be the "foster father of a production . . .
for all poetic production would *eo ipso* be rendered impossible and un-
endurable if the lines must be the very words of the producer, literally
understood" (*Postscript* 551–52). Authors of such works typically publish
their own words under the name of another, simultaneously invoking and
subverting the rule of the proper name. Coleridge, by so frequently publishing the words of others as his own, is differently but equally subversive
of the publication techniques—and their "proprieties"—that he is trying
to use to establish his own authorial identity.

These and other considerations like them seem to me to put the efforts of those engaged in the more conventional aspects of "editing" in a peculiar situation. The *Biographia* has already been "edited" by its author, very self-consciously, and with specific goals in mind. What are new editors to do, and how are they to do it without participating in the strategies of the author, or becoming complicitous with his efforts to produce the book as *book* and himself as its *author*—without entering that magic circle where the text evokes its own "author function" which they take as the literal author of the text? In general, I suggest that we can see much of conventional editing as the staging of the production of a text *and* its author; and the more problematic the nature of the text to be staged, or the author to be imputed, the more effort must go into its production.[9]

With these considerations in mind, let us now look at a recent staging of the *Biographia* by Princeton University Press as an impressive new contribution to that quintessentially Coleridgean goal: the COLLECTED COLERIDGE. In it Engell and Bate, as editors, are continuing a project begun by Coleridge with the *Biographia*, the new edition of which now takes pride of place in the Bollingen series. Both its physical form and the emphasis on size and scale in its presentation demonstrate that this work is too big for one volume, as well as too big for one editor. The hyperbolic dust jacket presents itself as the outermost skin of this "supreme work of literary criticism and one of the classics of English literature."

> Into the *Biographia* Coleridge poured twenty years of speculation. . . . Combining his belief in philosophical principles as the foundation of criticism . . . the *Biographia* is unrivaled except by his Shakespeare lectures as Coleridge's central work of criticism.

Coleridge himself used similar images, describing the *magnum opus,* for example, as "a work, for which I have been collecting the materials for the last 15 years almost incessantly" (*CL* 4:591), or as "the Reservoir of my Reflections & Reading for 25 years past" (*CL* 5:160). The editors of the new *Biographia* echo these tropes in the attempt to establish the effect of an overflowing abundance that resists conventional modes of containment and control. And of course no matter how *much* is here, its abundance will be less than that of the *magnum opus* which McFarland imagines as "continually being raided to produce slighter works that Coleridge did in fact publish" (*Ruin* 354).

The physical form of this two-volume book makes it clear from the beginning that we are approaching a center that is FULL, like a generous deli sandwich bulging at the seams. At the front are cxxxvi pages of "Introduction," demonstrating the work's unity ("actually . . . a series of interlocking unities") and its "unshaken continuity" (cxxxii). At the end hang 161 pages of appended material. For those who like to nibble on footnotes with their textual sandwich, this is the place to eat, for the editors have "poured" in what seems like another twenty years of effort. Even the footnotes that Coleridge provided now have their own footnotes. Textual self-sufficiency is established by the dust jacket announcement of "the first completely annotated edition of this highly allusive work, giving in detail all the sources, ancient and modern, on which Coleridge drew, and illustrating the different ways in which he used them," as if the work can now give birth to itself out of its own sources that it includes within itself.

As we move towards the center of this editorial sandwich, we find that Coleridge's text itself already has the form of a philosophical sandwich, with the meat being the "philosophical chapters" that the editors claim Coleridge dictated to Morgan in August and September of 1815, placing them in the center of the work even though they were the last written.[10] One material index of the density of this "central" material is the increasing frequency and length of Coleridge's notes. Here the form of his text is doubled by the form of the edited text:

> Hence the disparity in bulk of annotation between the latter half of Volume I, containing the "philosophical chapters", and the rest of the edition. Considering how *central* these chapters are to our understanding of Coleridge's thought as a whole, how *crammed* they are with allusions of every kind, and *weighed* by the problem of sources . . . the increase in annotations has been inevitable. (xv–xvi, italics added)

More than a hundred pages later we will be told that "the *Biographia* is a book whose circumference is everywhere and whose center is nowhere" (cxxxvi). This raises several questions, among them whether or not the "truth as a divine ventriloquist" (1:164) has been at work again, since Jerome Christensen has emphasized how Coleridge's texts are "a circle whose center is nowhere and whose circumference is everywhere" (16) and pointed out "how the profusion of the peripheral bears on the absence of the central" (96).

If we tackle these chapters unaided by any editorial guidance except that already so abundantly provided by Coleridge, we see that (starting with the announcement at the end of chapter 4) they present themselves as an arduous and difficult journey for author and reader alike. The first stages are historical, clearing away errors, specifying precise meanings for important words, acknowledging "obligations to Schelling" and others. This occupies us from 5 to 9, which ends with the image of Coleridge as "a writer of the present times" who can only "anticipate a scanty audience for abstrusest themes, and truths that can neither be communicated or received without effort of thought, as well as patience of attention" (1:167). As we turn to chapter 10, however, ready to cultivate our patience and exert our efforts, we may be surprised to find it titled "*A chapter of digression and anecdotes, as an interlude preceeding that on the nature and genesis of the imagination or plastic power*" (1:168). This "digression" goes on for forty-five pages, which makes it two pages longer than what has come before.[11] It ends with an extended defense against "this rumour of having dreamt away my life to no purpose" (1:221), which may gain some urgency from Coleridge's awareness of what he has been doing—and *not* doing—for the last forty-five pages. Chapter 11 continues the deferral for another eight pages with an "affectionate exhortation to the youthful literati" that they should not undertake the course he is pursuing: "NEVER PURSUE LITERA-TURE AS A TRADE" (1:223). This goes on in a light-hearted vein until it becomes an "unpleasant subject" (1:230) and Coleridge realizes that he is on the brink of returning to material already covered in chapter 2.

Chapter 12 seems to get us back on the track, announcing itself as "*A Chapter of requests and premonitions concerning the perusal or omission of the chapter that follows.*" The anticipatory motif is kept steadily in view as the chapter moves through thirty-four pages, much of which is either "direct translation" or "close paraphrase" or "loose paraphrase" or "material summarised (but reworded)" (Appendix A 2:254). At the end of this chapter, having spent forty-three pages giving background for his subject, fifty-three pages digressing from it, and thirty-four pages of premonitions, he announces that "I shall now proceed to the nature and genesis of the imagination" (1:293), and chapter 13 identifies itself as the long-awaited chapter "*On the imagination, or esemplastic power.*"

That chapter starts with one page of quotations, followed by three pages of introductory prose. At that point we reach the end of the journey and the "center" of the book, only to find a row of asterisks, followed by three pages of the "letter from a friend," which prompts the decision by the author to defer publication, leaving only "the main result" of the chapter, in the form of a one-page conclusion that contains twelve lines on the imagination, two of which were apparently later "stroked out" by

Coleridge. The work up to this point has been so carefully and so self-consciously structured and staged that the *absence* of the crucial demonstration of the imagination produces a special kind of structural effect. The center is empty; the foundation, cornerstone, keystone, not there in the place where it was repeatedly announced and long expected—an absence made so emphatic as to be almost the *presence* of nothingness. It is this provocative vacuity that the editors and commentators rush to wrestle with and attempt to fill.[12] In doing so, they contribute splendidly to the effect, which is perhaps best described by the Author of *A Tale of a Tub*:

> It was judged of absolute necessity, that some present Expedient be thought on, till the main Design can be brought to Maturity. To this End . . . this important Discovery was made by a curious and refined Observer; That Sea-men have a Custom when they meet a *Whale,* to fling him out an empty *Tub,* by way of Amusement, to divert him from laying violent Hands upon the Ship. . . . And my Genius being conceived to lye not unhappily that way, I had the Honor done me to be engaged in the Performance.
>
> This is the sole Design in publishing the following Treatise, which I hope will serve for an *Interim* of some Months . . . till the perfecting of that great Work. (325–26)

Dare I suggest that Coleridge's *Tub of a text* is breached in chapter 13 and revealed to be the *text of a Tub*? If we look inside Swift's empty Tub of a tale, we find an even more specific model for the *effect* that Coleridge has staged in chapter 13. In section 9 we encounter the highest reach of the aspiring intellect in the *Tale*:

> The present Argument is the most abstracted that ever I engaged in, it strains my Faculties to their highest Stretch; and I desire the Reader to attend with utmost Perpensity; For, I now proceed to unravel this knotty Point.
>
> There is in Mankind a certain   *   *   *   *   *
> * * * * * * * * * * * * * * *
> (*Hic multa desiderantur*)   * * * * * * * *
> * * * * * * * * * * * * * * *
> * * * *   And this I take to be a clear Solution
> of the Matter. (413)

The Author adds a note to this graphic aposiopesis, suggesting that it *"were well if all Metaphysical Cobweb Problems were not otherwise answered."* An earlier note to a similar *"Hiatus in MS."* is also pertinent:

> *Here is pretended a Defect in the Manuscript, and this is very frequent with our*
> *Author, either when he thinks he cannot say any thing worth Reading, or when*
> *he has no mind to enter on the Subject, or when it is a Matter of little Moment, or*
> *perhaps to amuse his Reader (whereof he is frequently very fond) or lastly, with*
> *some Satyrical Intention.* (340)

Sterne—himself in the line of descent from Swift—also provides examples of the hiatus maneuver, along with the generous provision of in-
structions for reading the book and the grandiose and always-thwarted
plans for writing it that mark both authors. Sterne was so fond of Pliny's
defense of the digression (*"Non enim excursus hic eius, sed opus ipsum est"*)
that he used it as a title-page motto for vols. 7 and 8 of *Tristram Shandy*.[13]
In one of Sterne's most notable gaps (the missing "whole chapter" 24 in
vol. 5) the "demonstration" that "the book is more perfect and complete
by wanting the chapter, than having it" (1:372) is close to the arguments
of Coleridge's "Friend." Joyce will continue this descent after Coleridge,
producing in *Finnegans Wake* a book that contains a remarkable "letter":

> What was it?
> A . . . . !
> ? . . . . O!
>
>   (94)

Joyce's "letter" evokes the "space" between alpha and omega which—being
everything—must "contain" the book which contains them as the letters
of the "letter," transforming the hiatus into a textual ouroboros. A more
direct hint at Coleridge's textual effect comes earlier: "There was once
upon a wall and a hooghoogwall a was and such a wall hole did exist"
(69). Here the textual totality, the "whole of the wall" (69) exhibits the
inevitable "hole" in the "whole" of the book.

A familiar touch from another of Coleridge's favorite authors can be
discerned in chapter 13 if we look closely at the precise point where the
asterisks produce the *scriptor interruptus* effect. Coleridge has prepared
the stage for an encounter between "two equal forces acting in opposite
directions . . . both alike infinite, both alike indestructible" (1:299). It is
precisely at the point where we are poised for the encounter, assured a
second time that "something must be the result of these two forces, both
alike infinite, and both alike indestructible" (1:300) that the interruption
comes. The verbal formulation here suggests an echo of Sterne ("No body,
but he who has felt it, can conceive what a plaguing thing it is to have
a man's mind torn asunder by two projects of equal strength, both obsti-

nately pulling in a contrary direction at the same time" [1:399]). But the situation of a textual crisis that is being contrived here is more like that found at the end of chapter 8 of *Don Quixote*, when

> Don Quixote was approaching the wary Biscayan, his sword raised on high and with the firm resolve of cleaving his enemy in two; and the Biscayan was awaiting the knight in the same posture, cushion in front of him and with uplifted sword. All the bystanders were trembling with suspense at what would happen as a result of the terrible blows that were threatened. . . .
>
> But the unfortunate part of the matter is that at this very point the author of the history breaks off and leaves the battle pending, excusing himself upon the ground that he has been unable to find anything else in writing concerning the exploits of Don Quixote beyond those already set forth. (69)[14]

In his role as "an English metaphysician" (1:290) Coleridge's reading of the German transcendental philosophers may well remind us of the equally vast and specialized reading of Quixote ("The poor fellow used to lie awake nights in an effort to disentangle the meaning. . . ." [26]). But instead of a Dulcinea del Toboso, Coleridge has a different lady, Dame Philosophy, the shimmering elusive beauty of the *Logosophia* which "some evil enchanter" keeps hiding or transforming into the chaotic text of the *Biographia*. The "friend" who writes him the letter is not Brisman's man from Porlock or Christensen's "man of the letter," but himself as Sancho Panza, the letter-carrier or intermediary between the Don and his Dame.[15] In being both Quixote and Sancho Panza, Coleridge becomes Cervantes, the witty master of a text that can't fully be mastered by its readers.

If we turn now to the observation of Engell and Bate, that "no form of writing came more easily and habitually to Coleridge than the *Apologia*" (1:liii), we can see that numerous features of the *Biographia* make it inevitable that the *apologia* (or "away-pushing words") comes easily to his critics and editors as well:

> This is not to excuse the plagiarisms. But a distinction can be kept in mind between "excuse" and a mere explanation of circumstances that could seduce or frighten Coleridge into acts against which the cushions of leisure, financial security, calmer (or firmer) temperaments, or even sheer moralism would preserve others. In connection with the "plagiarisms" the reader should bear in mind the chronology of the work, the

> circumstances, the pressures to get it done rapidly, the self-doubts, the
> exhaustion. (lviii)

The reason for the continuation of this mode of the *apologia* is that the
charges continue to exist in the minds and words of some readers, no less
perhaps in his staunchest defenders than in his more hostile critics. These
charges were already amply invented and documented by Coleridge himself, and the parties to the game seem bent on endlessly repeating the same
moves already inscribed in the book. The task of the Coleridge editor thus
appears like that of Richardson, struggling through successive editions of
Clarissa, appending editorial comments, footnotes, summaries of letters
and the like to the work, in a futile effort to control and predetermine its
reception by the readers. Like his efforts, theirs too can sometimes have
a subversive effect. Rather than assuring us of the authenticity of the text
they so strenuously assert, they remind us of the uncontrollability of a text
that requires such efforts.

What I am urging here is a different way of reading the *Biographia*, and
a different basis of respect for Coleridge's skill as a writer. The choice by
Engell and Bate of the elegant Latin form *apologia* rather than the more
pedestrian English "apology" provides a nice Coleridgean touch, while
safely avoiding the latter's meaning as a "failed effort," with which we
might call the *Biographia* a "sorry excuse" or an "apology" for the *LOGO-
SOPHIA*. But another conventional and time-honored use of the term
apologia may be still more apt for the *Biographia* in its manifestation as a
satura or satirist's overflowing grab bag. Satirists from classical writers to
Pope and beyond have made the *apologia* one of their stock subjects, its
goal to assure the reader that the censor is a *vir bonus,* a man of good will
who has been forced into action against his will.

Thus Pope begins his entry into the satirical ring with the publication of
the *Epistle to Dr. Arbuthnot* and a classical disclaimer: "This paper is a sort
of bill of complaint. . . . I had no thoughts of publishing it, till it pleased
some Persons of Rank and Fortune . . . to attack, in a very extraordinary
manner, not only my Writings (of which, being public, the Public is judge)
but my *Person, morals,* and *Family,* whereof, to those who know me not, a
truer information may be requisite" (215). Compare Pope's opening here
with the first lines of the *Biographia*:

> It has been my lot to have had my name introduced both in conversation,
> and in print, more frequently than I find it easy to explain, whether I

consider the fewness, unimportance, and limited circulation of my writings, or the retirement and distance, in which I have lived, both from the literary and political world. Most often it has been connected with some charge, which I could not acknowledge, or some principle which I had never entertained. (1:5)

The same note continues throughout the work, maintaining the posture of one who had been "for at least 17 years [Pope's "saving counsel" had enabled him to keep the peace for only nine years] consecutively dragged forth by them into the foremost ranks of the *proscribed,* and forced to abide the brunt of abuse, for faults directly opposite, and which I certainly had not" (1:50). Maynard Mack has suggested that no one ever misinterpreted a satire for failure to see that the adversaries were fictional, and it is clear that most of the hordes of Coleridge's detractors that fill the *Biographia* are equally fictional—perhaps the most amusing being the "amateur performer in verse" whom Coleridge invents as the thief of his own epigram, originally addressed *"To Mr. Pye"* (1:28). Coleridge's strategy here, with its self-contained economy in which he plays *both* parts, provides him the double pleasure of reclaiming the lines as his own wit, prompted by his own work, the "Ancient Mariner."

Engell and Bate point out that of the ninety-six extant articles from 1798–1814 that mention Coleridge sixty-three are favorable, often even eulogistic, ten to twelve strike "a middle note," and the remainder "less abusive than Coleridge implies" (1:50). These facts suggest that the much maligned "author" of the *Biographia* is merely an assumed identity or *persona,* the production of the text rather than its producer. Is the "real Coleridge" the one on Napoleon's hit list, or the one who masqueraded as an American when he left his papers in Rome (1:216)? The one who "had translated the eight Hymns of Synesius from the Greek into English Anacreontics before [his] 15th year" (1:247)? Who frequently emphasizes the need for scrupulosity in acknowledging literary debts? Whose fugitive writings published in the *Morning Post* made him the rival of Burke, and prompted Fox to make the charge "that the *late* war . . . *was a war produced by the* MORNING POST" (1:215)? Who drafted more than 100 pages of chapter 13 and cut it down to ten lines, and then complained to Gutch about the need for "writing a *hundred and fifty pages* additional—on *what, I* am left to discover" (lxii)? The one who thought up all of German transcendental philosophy on his own? Or the one who enlisted in the Light Dragoons as Silus Tomkyns Comberbacke? Or is he NEHEMIAH HIGGENBOTTOM? Or Satyrane? Or Spy Nozy?

The thoroughly conventional satiric plot of the *Biographia* claims that a fictitious and degraded "Coleridge" has been textually produced by the press and is circulating in public conversation. This spurious impostor will be refuted by the production of the "real" Coleridge in book form. But the real Coleridge keeps going elsewhere. His letters, his printed words, his lectures, even his conversations appear under the names of other authors. Meanwhile his real work is always provisional, always somewhere else, like the *Logosophia*, which is a commentary on the Gospel of John, which is a commentary on the Logos of God. While he claims the thoughts as his own, the words of others keep speaking themselves through him as he dictates to Morgan. A substantial portion of the work appears under the name of Satyrane, who was and was not a different Coleridge at an earlier time. Another generous portion is a once "anonymous" group of letters criticizing *Bertram* (a play Coleridge thought had taken the rightful place of his *Zapolya*, rejected by Covent Garden and Drury Lane), claimed now as his own but purged of the sarcasm that marked their original appearance.

At least one part of the *Biographia* seems to have been actually written at the appropriate time for inclusion in the work—written with apparent pleasure by a Coleridge who had come to prefer the ease of speech to the effort of writing ("written without taking my pen off the paper except to dip it in the inkstand" [*CL* 4:728]) It appears under the alias of a "friend," a fictional persona who had actually entered and experienced one of the antechambers of that vast textual edifice, the *magnum opus*. What was the experience like? It was *"too much, and yet not enough"* (1:302). Not enough, because *"you have been obliged to omit so many links, from the necessity of compression, that what remains, looks . . . like the fragments of the winding steps of an old ruined tower"* (1:302–03). Too much, because it will *"amount to"* over one hundred printed pages when published, so that it is also like *"one of our largest Gothic cathedrals in a gusty moonlight"* (1:301), both too large and too serious for the present work: *"If you do publish this Chapter . . . you will be reminded of Bishop Berkeley's Siris, announced as an Essay on Tar-Water, which beginning with Tar ends with the Trinity"* (1:303). The chain-conscious friend is suggesting that this missing link in the *Biographia*, which is itself missing *"so many links,"* would be a link too many for the work ("Siris" from the Greek *seira,* "chain"). The result is that we are left with a book of Moonlight, a book in which the disquisition on the imagination would be too much (and too little), but the letter from a friend is *just right*.

III

It would be highly interesting to point out the causes of the pleasure given by this extravagant and absurd language . . . it depends upon a great variety of causes, but upon none perhaps more than its influence in impressing a notion of the peculiarity and exaltation of the Poet's character, and in flattering the Reader's self-love by bringing him nearer to a sympathy with that character; an effect which is accomplished by unsettling ordinary habits of thinking, and thus assisting the Reader to approach that perturbed and dizzy state of mind in which if he does not find himself, he imagines that he is *balked* of a peculiar enjoyment which poetry can, and ought to bestow.

—WORDSWORTH

Weave a circle round him thrice . . .

—COLERIDGE

Thus far I may seem to be in agreement with the view that "Coleridge's attempt to produce a theory of subjectivity in the *Biographia Literaria* spectacularly fails. . . . the definition of subjectivity falls into nonmeaning in the moment of its utterance. Unspeakable and unspoken, the analysis is to be found in the unwritten 100 pages, in the *Logosophia* to be announced at the end of the *Biographia* (it was not announced) and in the essay prefixed to 'The Ancient Mariner' (which was never written)" (Belsey 77). My goal is different, however, for I believe that it is a failure only on one level which, if properly understood, can help us to see the true nature of its "success." One index of that success is the note of ironic humor with which Coleridge was able to extricate himself from his metaphysical *cul-de-sac*— a note he shares with Kierkegaard as one of "these authors who proposed to make the comical a determination in earnestness, and to find in the jest a release from the sorriest of all tyrannies: the tyranny of moroseness, stupidity, and inflexibility of spirit" (*Postscript* 251). But there is also a serious side to the Coleridgean accomplishment, if we take a lack of completion and unity as a special mark of the *literary,* a mode of discourse which both provokes and resists the techniques and satisfactions of a "philosophical" interpretation. I am convinced that Coleridge's philosophic argument can be seen as at all times dependent on and governed by literary and linguis-

tic devices, in which even the *appearance* of a philosophical argument may
be seen as a literary effect.

As poets and theoreticians, both Coleridge and Wordsworth provide
the arguments and examples for that conventional literary criticism which
assumes that poetry is to be read as an expression of the full inwardness of
an author's individual human experience. For Wordsworth poems should
have a "source within my own mind, from which they have proceeded"
(*Essay* 3:80). In this view poetry is a matter of subjectivity, and the Wordsworthian question ("What is a Poet?") is synonomous with the question:
What is poetry? For Coleridge the authentic index of poetry can be seen
as a subjectivity *within* a subjectivity: the imagination, which is the source
and cause of those works which are true poetry. A radically different view
suggests that the subjectivity which authenticates certain works as poems
is the product of a discourse rather than its source, an effect produced
by rhetorical strategies in the poem, and by equally important strategies
of the interpretive discourse, both of which combine to produce the effect of the imagination. This explains in part the persistent emphasis on
the importance of Coleridge's "applied" criticism of Wordsworth in the
Biographia, since by performing a successful reading of Wordsworth, Coleridge was both identifying the traces of the imagination in the poetry and
demonstrating a theory in practice which he had failed to articulate as
philosophy. In Engell-Bate's words

> An impartial and solid "philosophic reason, independent of all foreseen
> application to particular works and authors" [2:110–11], was making his
> *actual* applications of the greatest possible worth when finally they came,
> as they do come profusely in the second volume. (1:lxix)

The originary unity of the subject is the result of a circular process, in
which the poem reveals its true self to a certain practice of reading. Since
all productions of a poet will not have the authenticating marks, a special
canon *within* a canon emerges, consisting of those writings which can be
endowed with a special status, indicative of the author's presence. Thus
Wordsworth can be criticized by Coleridge in the *Biographia* for exhibiting

> an undue predilection for the *dramatic* form in certain poems, from
> which one or other of two evils result. Either the thoughts and diction
> are different from that of the poet, and then there arises an incongruity
> of style; or they are the same and indistinguishable, and then it presents

a species of ventriloquism, where two are represented as talking, while in truth one man only speaks. (2:135)

The subjectivity within a subjectivity, which is the imagination, can only be known by certain signs. One of the most important of these is the presentation of the written poem as the trace of a *speaking voice,* guarantee of the available presence of the poet, and of the spontaneous nature of his "utterance," which simply appears without effort. Lacking any a priori authority to command belief or attention, it is only by strategies of language that the poet can convince an audience of the authority of his voice. The merely material and mechanical aspects of writing do not reflect the essence of the poetry, and poems which exhibit the "mechanical adoption" of "figures of speech" are not true poetry but a "motley masquerade of tricks, quaintnesses, hieroglyphics, and enigmas" (Wordsworth 1802 *Appendix*, 1:160, 162) By contrast, "All good poetry is the spontaneous overflow of powerful feelings" (1800 *Preface* 1:126). "Produce" and "effect" are key words in Wordsworth as he discusses the strategies of those "desirous of producing the same effect" (1802 *Appendix* 1:160) that "genuine" poets produce—those who lack the originary source and rely instead on figurative language and meter to produce its illusion. But when he turns to "genuine poetry" and the question of "how this pleasure is produced" (1800 *Preface* 1:156), he has reached his "limits" and has no space to explain how the genuine poet can "throw over" his subjects "a certain colouring of imagination" (40). "Colour" is of course an ancient synonym for figurative language (cf. 1800 *Preface* 1:144), and it has a strange sound in the theory of a poetry that claims for its language the status of an unmediated transparency. Coleridge writes in the *Biographia* of the distinction between a "counterfeit and artificial persuasion" and "the person's own feelings [of] a real sense of inward power" (1:38), criticizing those whose self-presentations are governed "by their desire to *appear* men of genius" (1:42). The basic distinction is between those who "write orthographically, make smooth periods, and had the fashions of authorship almost literally *at their fingers ends*" and those who "in simplicity of soul, made their words immediate echoes of their feelings" (1:150).

But the absence of conspicuous mechanical signs of writing is itself an effect of a special kind of writing, equally material and equally "rhetorical" in its practice. Coleridge's own writing, from the "conversational poems" to the *Notebooks*, exhibits an impressive range of those techniques and signs which, by a negative logic, we take as the authenticating traces of the presence of a subject, and of the workings of his imagination. A useful example, though seldom commented on, is his "The Blossoming of the Solitary Date-Tree," which can be read as an allegorical example of the practice at its clearest. In his introductory note to the poem, Coleridge first evokes the "guileful false serpent" responsible for the fall, who lacks a soul but knows how to produce the *effect* of soul, pretending "to have the heart of a Man, and to feel the yearning of a human soul for its counterpart" (*Poetical Works* [EHC] 1:395). Coleridge's poem aspires to the status of a genuine "lament" in which the poet, like the date tree mentioned by Linnaeus, "year after year had put forth a full show of blossoms, but never produced fruit, till a branch from another date-tree had been conveyed from a distance of some hundred leagues". The poem itself is presented allegorically as one of those "blossoms" which the reader must approach from a similar distance, to join with the poet and complete his efforts to produce the effects of an authentic lament in isolation:

> The first leaf of the MS. from which the poem has been transcribed, and which contained the two or three introductory stanzas, is wanting: and the author has in vain taxed his memory to repair the loss. But a rude draught of the poem contains the substance of the stanzas, and the reader is requested to receive it as the substitute. It is not impossible, that some congenial spirit, whose years do not exceed those of the Author at the time the poem was written, may find a pleasure in restoring the Lament to its original integrity . . . . (*PW* [EHC] 1:395)

The introductory note is doubled by the poem, whose theme is that " 'What no one with us shares, seems scarce our own.' " The poem's most striking figure is that of a hot air balloon, which needs the cooperating medium of the air for its ascent. But this external, buoyant force will be destructive if it is not matched by "the supporting air from within" the would-be balloon poet: "Deprive it of this, and all without, that would have buoyed it aloft even to the seat of the gods, becomes a burthen and crushes it into flatness."

The first word of the part of the poem that is not "wanting" (stanza 3) gives us the term for the necessary afflatus from within: "imagination." But the part that is "missing" from the manuscript, the part that must be completed by the reader, is also the *inside* part of the system, the imagination, and we must be both inside and outside this air-balloon-poem to assure its ascent. The allegorical "fruit" of this date tree, its authentic status as poem rather than infertile "blossom," is our *hearing* it as the "lament" of a real subject. If we do hear it this way, becoming absorbed in its self-representation, we will be reading the poem as the trace of a subject, and a trace of the imagination of the poet. It will be a genuine poem only if we complete it; but if we complete it according to directions, we will experience our reading as the effect of the poet's imagination, which is the *source* both of the poem and of our affect. The poem does indeed make a powerful plea for our complicity in this enterprise, but that plea is nothing but unfruitful flowers of rhetoric without our cooperation; and the most important and effective of its strategies is the bold and Coleridgean tactic of presenting the poem as a trace or fragment. The inadequacy of the trace, the loss of the "original," prompts the adequation of our reading; its failure as conventional poetry is part of its certificate of authenticity, being too spontaneous, too authentic, too intimate, too "rude" to be captured by the written word. Genuine poetry is what gets lost in translation, and the exhibition of that loss, or fragmentary status, prompts us to fill the void with our own imagination of what is missing. Seen in this way, what might seem to be the special features of this fragment of writing, are an analogue of all written poetry that asks to be read as a trace (or "supplement" in Derrida's terms) of the speaking voice of a genuine subject.

In the late twentieth century we have become accustomed to a variety of abdications of conscious authorial responsibility and intentional rhetoric in the production of a text which appeals to the reader's sympathy and understanding. Freud has taught us to read the surface of discourse as a mode of secondary revision, with the powerfully conflicting (i.e., "authentic") currents of the unconscious only partly or obliquely available through a special reading, or in special cases where the surface is ruptured. Read provides a typical example of the trope:

> We can imagine in certain rare cases a phenomenon comparable to a "fault" in geology, as a result of which in one part of the mind the layers become discontinuous, and exposed to each other at unusual levels. . . . Some such hypothesis is necessary to explain that access, that lyrical intuition, which is known as inspiration and which in all ages has been the rare possession of those few individuals we recognize as artists of genius. (88)

Even those strategies of reading (and increasingly, of writing) which maintain that the writer does not write his language but is himself written by it as a passive agent, can be seen as strategies of authentication, providing access to depth and meaning by reducing the functional presence of the writer's conscious will.

What I have briefly suggested as a way of reading the "Date-Tree" poem is equally applicable to "Kubla Khan" where the presented "fragment" of a poem doubles—or is doubled by—its prose introduction. In that introduction we have the description of an effect produced on the author by his reading *Purchas his Pilgrimage* after taking an anodyne. That effect was the composition of a poem, "if that indeed can be called composition in which all the images rose up before him as *things,* with a parallel production of the correspondent expressions, without any sensation or consciousness of effort" (*PW* 1:296). On waking, before being called out on business, he wrote down "the lines that are here preserved," of "what had been originally, as it were, given to him." And it is those lines which are "as it were, given to" us, not for their poetic merits" but as a "psychological curiosity."

If we take the introduction at face value, we have a remarkable effect produced on the author by a specified set of influences. The effect is the double-production of dream images as *things,* and the correspondent expression of those things in words. In the written fragment we also have an emphasis on a double production of the pleasure dome. First is that of the Khan, whose (presumably verbal) decree effortlessly produces a pleasure dome. An act of conscious will, using language, produces a spectacular material result—but one whose material embodiment is also its vulnerability, so that all that now remains is the remote trace of Purchas's writing. The other production of the pleasure dome imaged in the poem does not throw a "shadow," for it is both immaterial and conditional ("Could I revive within me"). If the author *could,* he would enter the magic circle of the imagination, so that those who "heard" the music would "see" the dome, and would know him as a poet. But as Keats pointed out, if "Heard melodies are sweet . . . those unheard / Are sweeter," and can better express a "wild ecstasy" than our rhyme.

> Words—what are they but a subtle *matter?* and the meaness of Matter must they have, & the Soul must pine in them, even as the Lover who can press kisses only [on] the garment of one indeed beloved . . . . O what then are Words, but articulated Sighs of a Prisoner heard from his Dungeon! powerful only as they express their utter impotence! Life may be *inferred,* even as intelligence is from black marks on white paper—but the black marks themselves *are truly "the dead letter"* (*CN* 2:§2998)

As "garment" the words of the poem remind us of our distance from the signified of the poetic subject, and within that subject of the imagination. But the material garment is necessary to create the effect of the existence of a privileged signification or idea (God, truth, imagination, or even the text) which is beyond logical demonstration or poetic representation, inaccessible to sensory perception. If the external garment is distorted, stretched or torn, the effect is all the more powerful, suggesting "that within which passes show" (*Hamlet* 1:2.83).

In Coleridge it is the result or goal of the poetic practice to hide the original and the source from view, thereby creating even more strongly the effect of their authentic originary existence elsewhere. While this effect is being produced, what is actually present to our perception is effectively being hidden—the *production* of that "miracle of rare device," which is as much dependent on its own tropes and strategies as the rejected mode of merely figurative language. There is no essential difference between "Kubla Khan" and a poem like the "Hymn Before Sun-Rise, In the Vale of Chamouni," which is often considered an embarrassment or scandal in the Coleridge *oeuvre*. Both use rhetorical means in order to produce the effect of our belief in an originary subjective affect ("the mood and Habit of mind out of which the Hymn rose" [*CL* 4:974]). But we have been trained by Coleridge and the Romantic tradition to suspend our disbelief willingly in one case, and to exercise it vigorously in the other. Coleridge had never been in the Vale of Chamouni (as he seemed to claim in the introductory note [*PW* 1:377]), so the poem cannot be the result of an experience of "objects that immediately excite in him sympathies which, from the necessities of his nature, are accompanied by an overbalance of enjoyment" (Wordsworth, *Preface* 51). The poem is not a trace of Coleridge's encounter with the "sovran BLANC," but a trace of his reading. As Fruman observes,

> The *gentiana major*, which Coleridge had found such "an affecting emblem of the boldness of human hope," was plucked from the notes of Brun, while the valley "which must needs impress every mind not utterly callous" with the shallowness of atheism, had never impinged upon the retina of the devout moralist. (*Archangel* 27)

In "Chamouni" Coleridge has apparently tried to hide the traces of his reading, and our discovery of the Brun poem with its notes unmasks the pose of the poem as a deliberate deceit. Yet in "Kubla Khan" the author

reveals a possible "source" of his psychological curiosity in his reading, and we are not so much disturbed by this as we are impressed by what the imagination can do with a few words of ancient prose.

Wordsworth, who emphasized the need for sensuous perception of objects, whose poetry is so often assumed to begin with the fact of witness, can nevertheless assert that the poet is characterized by "a disposition to be affected more than other men by absent things as if they were present; an ability of conjuring up in himself passions, which are indeed far from being the same as those produced by real events" (*Preface* 49). And even if Coleridge had been present in the Vale, to experience what Derrida calls "the natural wealth and original virtue of the sensory image" (*Margins* 210), it would have been only to experience the silent blankness of the mountain as yet another trace of the absent source, the God who resists all representations except those which signify His absence. The link between the signifiers and the transcendental signified that is missing in "Chamouni" is not that of participation or resemblance between the imagery of the poem and the physical location of its ostensible referents. It is the link between the trope of apostrophe (which governs the rhetoric of the poem) and the functional effect of that trope in producing an image of invested passion. As a distortion of ordinary speech, apostrophe can claim to be "a figure spontaneously adopted by passion, and it signifies metonymically, the passion that caused it."[16] According to Wordsworth, this link is broken when a figure "which at first had been dictated by real passion" comes to be used by poets who, "perceiving the influence of such language, and desirous of producing the same effect, without having the same animating passion, set themselves to a mechanical adoption of those figures of speech" (Wordsworth, *Appendix* 63–64). Thus Coleridge reports that "Mr. Wordsworth . . . condemned the Hymn in toto . . . as a specimen of the Mock Sublime" (*CL* 4:974). As a regression to the mainstream of eighteenth-century poetics, it exhibits its rhetorical techniques rather than hiding them.

The labor of composition must be hidden for the effect of the imagination to be produced, since the genuine poem must appear to have been spontaneously produced in the heat of *original* conception, contradicting the mundane belief that a very laborious process lies behind the production of most good poems.

> Imagination!—lifting up itself
> Before the eye and progress of my song

Like an unfathered vapour, here that power,
In all the might of its endowments, came
Athwart me. I was lost as in a cloud,
Halted without a struggle to break through

                    (1805 *Prelude* 6, lines 593–98)

But if the imagination and the poetic traces that it is supposed to produce are themselves poetically produced, and if we read the traces as the
poetic structures which they in fact are, we can see that they provoke us
to experience the effect of the imagination by exerting our own efforts in
cooperation with the poem, internalizing through our reading the same
devices utilized by the poetic text. The poem simulates as its cause that
which it cannot possess, and evokes in us that faith which is "the substance
of things hoped for, the evidence of things not seen" (Hebrews 11:1).[17]
The theory of the imagination demands this faith, as shown by Quixote's
challenge to the merchants from Toledo who asked to see a picture of Dulcinea del Toboso before they would acknowledge her peerless beauty: "If
I were to show her to you . . . what merit would there be in your confess-
ing a truth so self-evident? The important thing is for you, without seeing
her, to believe, confess, affirm, swear, and defend that truth" (45). If we
cooperate with the demand, we find ourselves in the position so vividly
described by Coleridge as his own:

> I have too clearly before me the idea of a poet's genius to deem myself
> other than a very humble poet; *but in the very possession of the idea, I know
> myself so far a poet as to feel assured; that I can understand and interpret a poem
> in the spirit of poetry* . . . . Like the ostrich, I cannot fly, yet I have wings
> that give me the feeling of flight. . . . (*CM* [*CC*] 1:482, italics added)

Hazlitt's early review of the *Biographia* gives us a vision of Coleridge's
efforts to fly that might have been written by the poet himself:

> Mr. Coleridge has ever since [his early poetic efforts], from the com-
> bined forces of poetic levity and metaphysical bathos, been trying to fly
> . . . . going up in an air-balloon and coming down in a parachute made
> of the soiled and fashionable leaves of the Morning Post,—promising us
> an account of the Intellectual System of the Universe, and putting us off
> with a reference to a promised dissertation on the Logos, introductory
> to an intended commentary on the entire Gospel of St. John. (*BL* 1:lxvi)

But if Hazlitt was unable to experience the "feeling of flight" from the
air-balloon of the *Biographia*, or the soiled leaves of the *Post*, he could still

recall the effect of the Sibylline leaves of Coleridge's early poetry, and their author as "the only person I ever knew who answered to the idea of a man of genius . . . . His mind was clothed with wings; and raised on them, he lifted philosophy to heaven," leaving behind the "recollection" that rings in our ears "with never-dying sound" (*Works* 5:167). And that, too, is part of the special effect, not of individual works, but of the career and the canon of works seen as traces of the organic whole or trajectory of an individual subject, providing "the interest which arises from watching the progress, maturity, and even the decay of genius" (*Table Talk* January 1, 1834). Both Coleridge and Wordsworth have become poets whose image of greatness is intimately tied to the relative paucity of their "genuine" work in the vast sea of their "failures". The nonevents of Coleridge's *Magnum Opus* and Wordsworth's *Recluse* are nevertheless emphatically *there* as nonevents, certifying a different kind of genius for their authors.[18] Our continued appreciation of that genius, in the spirit of its self-representation by Coleridge, bears out the maxim made "long since" by his "philosophical Friend" which Wordsworth repeats in the 1815 *Essay*:

> —that every Author, as far as he is great and at the same time *original,* has had the task of *creating* the taste by which he is to be enjoyed; so has it been, so will it continue to be. (3:80)

3

The Besetting Sins of Coleridge's Prose

Catherine Miles Wallace

Coleridge's prose is notoriously hard going. Yet we accommodate to it; we develop some of the conscious and unconscious skills Coleridge demands of his readers. In *The Design of 'Biographia Literaria,'* I argued that it helps to categorize the kinds of difficulties we have in reading Coleridge's prose.[1] The most substantial problems are those created by the complexity of his ideas. Other problems arise from the ideal of discourse toward which he worked, the ideal of engaging us as whole moral beings. And finally, major problems arise from the habitual ways in which Coleridge managed—and mismanaged—the basic tasks of a writer. Yet reading Coleridge becomes much easier going if we know how he handles transition, emphasis, unity, definitions, and the like. I propose to examine three elements of Coleridge's writerly habits: his definitions, the way he structures or develops arguments, and the way he situates himself historically.

Coleridge's definitions always ground themselves in extensive metaphor patterns. The famous definition of imagination in chapter 13 has been examined and cross-examined for generations, but the metaphors anchoring this definition have had far less attention. Most of these metaphors arise when the *Biographia* contrasts imaginative people and imaginative works with the character and the work of fanatics. A crucial early point is the definition of fanaticism in chapter 2. The German word for "fanaticism," Coleridge explains, "is derived from the swarming of bees . . . The passion being in an inverse proportion to the insight, *that* the more vivid, as *this* the less distinct; anger is the inevitable consequence" (1:19).[2] This link between violence and blindness repeatedly comes into play as Coleridge describes the controversy over Wordsworth: "the acrimonious passions, with which the controversy has been conducted by the assailants" provide one good estimate of the intelligence and insight of these critics (2:7).

Anonymous criticism perfectly satisfies the early definition of fanaticism: "These facts, and the intellectual energy of the author [Wordsworth], where it was outwardly and even boisterously denied, meeting with sentiments of aversion to his opinions, and of alarm at their consequences, produced an eddy of criticism, which would of itself have borne up the poems by the violence, with which it whirled them round and round" (2:7). Note how the image of swirling upward, tornado-like, repeats the movement of swarming bees: the philosophic critic's activity is later compared to a windmill's (2:88). Anonymous criticism is blasphemous, personal and "popular" (1:41–42; 2:211); philosophical criticism is principled, systematic, and noble (1:44; 2:87–89). True poets and philosophic critics are genial in both senses of that word: geniuses, to the extent that their imagination supplies genuine insight; and genial because their personalities are literally *above* the petty, personal, and political squabbles of lesser minds.

Anonymous critics admire an equally decadent modern poetry that offers only "the glare and glitter of a perpetual, yet broken and heterogeneous imagery" (1:15). Such glare and glitter differ sharply from the illumination Wordsworth provides: "the original gift of spreading the tone, the *atmosphere,* and with it the depth and height of the ideal world around forms, incidents, and situations, of which, for the common view, custom had bedimmed all the lustre, had dried up the sparkle and the dew drops" (1:59). Wordsworth's *Descriptive Sketches*, Coleridge explains, announced "the emergence of an original poetic genius above the literary horizon" (1:56). Citing Wordsworth approvingly, Coleridge asserts that he knows how to

> add the gleam,
> The light that never was, on sea or land,
> The consecration and the poet's dream.
>
> [cited at 2:124]

Changed light and cleansing water repeatedly characterize the renewed vision genius provides.

Coleridge characterizes modern literature with images of hollow and false *things;* genial works are described with images for the imaginative *acts* they both require and elicit. Moderns are fraudulent:

> In the days of Chaucer and Gower, our language might (with allowance for the imperfections of a simile) be compared to a wilderness of vocal reeds, from which the favorites only of Pan or Apollo could construct

even the rude Syrinx; and from this the *constructors* alone could elicit strains of music. But now, partly by the labours of successive poets, and in part by the more artificial state of society and social intercourse, language, mechanized as it were into a barrel-organ, supplies at once both instrument and tune. Thus even the deaf may play, so as to delight the many. . . . Hence of all trades, literature at present demands the least talent or information; and of all modes of literature, the manufacturing of poems. The difference indeed between these and the works of genius is not less than between an egg and an egg-shell; yet at a distance they both look alike. (1:25–26)

What once demanded divine favor now can be manufactured—apparently —without the least exercise of skill. Such productions lack the truth and permanence of great literature. Coleridge emphasizes this permanence in his first "critical aphorism" in chapter 1: "not the poem which we have *read,* but that to which we *return* with greatest pleasure, possesses the genuine power, and claims the name of *essential poetry*" (1:14). His image for this permanence and value is an act:

[In "a just poem,"] The reader should be carried forward, not merely or chiefly by the mechanical impulse of curiosity, or by a restless desire to arrive at the final solution; but by the pleasureable activity of mind excited by the attractions of the journey itself. Like the motion of a serpent, which the Egyptians made the emblem of intellectual power; or like the path of sound through the air; at every step he pauses and half recedes, and from the retrogressive movement collects the force which again carries him onward. (2:11)

This "pleasureable activity" is the working of secondary imagination, earlier imaged by the water-insect:

Most of my readers will have observed a small water-insect on the surface of rivulets . . . and will have noticed, how the little animal *wins* its way up against the stream, by alternate pulses of active and passive motion, now resisting the current, and now yielding to it in order to gather strength and a momentary *fulcrum* for a further propulsion. This is no unapt emblem of the mind's self-experience in the act of thinking. . . . (In philosophical language, we must denominate this . . . the *Imagination.* But in common language, and especially on the subject of poetry, we appropriate the name to a superior degree of the faculty, joined to a superior voluntary controul over it.) (1:85–86)

This alternately progressive and retrogressive movement images the imagination for us just as the mechanism of the barrel-organ or the hollowness of an eggshell images literary fraud. On the one hand we have an image for a producing faculty; on the other, for a useless product. Lacking the productive faculty, moderns provide only a false and mechanical version of the real thing. Their readers are "carried forward" passively, as perhaps on a whirlwind; readers of genuine works travel under their own power, enjoying that activity as such.

Coleridge subsumes all these metaphors, and the realities they name, in two accounts of the poet as a landscape. The false poet is an irritable character because "men, whose dearest wishes are fixed on objects wholly out of their own power, become in all cases more or less impatient and prone to anger. . . . Even as the flowery sod, which covers a hollow, may be often detected by its shaking and trembling" (1:25). Recall that the *Biographia* is to define the trunk and roots of the distinction between fancy and imagination (1:64). The roots of such "shaking and trembling" poetic flowers are not solidly anchored. The careless observer might not recognize the problem at first; but one need not be much of a gardener to realize how poorly such "flowers" will survive the vicissitudes of an entire season—or the tribulations of the years.

All that is false and perverse and ephemeral about such works is captured by Coleridge's most daring description of anonymous critics as ones "whose intellectual claims to the guardianship of the muses seem, for the greater part, analogous to the physical qualifications which adapt their oriental brethren for the superintendence of the Harem" (1:42). Decadent modern literature and its advocates are but a perversion of mankind's most valuable productive powers: "poetry is the blossom and fragrancy of all human knowledge, human thoughts, human passions, emotions, language" (2:19). Contrast the description of Wordsworth:

> "The soil is a deep, rich, dark mould, on a deep stratum of tenacious clay; and that on a foundation of rocks, which often break through both strata, lifting their backs above the surface. The trees which chiefly grow here are the gigantic black oak; magnolia magni-flora; fraxinus excelsior; platane; and a few stately tulip trees." What Mr. Wordsworth *will* produce, it is not for me to prophecy; but I could pronounce with the liveliest convictions what he is capable of producing. It is the *First Genuine Philosophic Poem*. (2:128–29)

This is not to be read as an allegory, wherein specific poetic abilities correspond to various geological layers; it is to contrast with the metaphors describing all that is hollow and ephemeral in modern literature. Even the flower image reappears, in the magnolias and tulip trees. The lines from Milton in chapter 13 also stand in context:

> O Adam, One Almighty is, from whom
> All things proceed, and up to him return,
> If not deprived from good: created all,
> Indued with various forms, various degrees
> Of substance, and, in things that live, of life;
> But more refin'd, more spirituous and pure,
> As nearer to him plac'd, or nearer tending,
> Each in their several active spheres assign'd,
> Till body up to spirit work, in bounds
> Proportion'd to each kind. So from the root
> Springs lighter the green stalk, from thence the leaves
> More airy; last the bright consummate flower
> Spirits odorous breathes. Flowers and their fruit,
> Man's nourishment, by gradual scale sublim'd,
> To *vital* spirits aspire: to *animal:*
> To *intellectual*!—give both life and sense,
> Fancy and understanding; whence the soul
> *Reason* receives, and reason is her *being,*
> Discursive or intuitive.   *Par. Lost.* b.V.
>
>   (1:195)

The movement from rocks and clay to magnolia magni-flora claims that Wordsworth's genius mirrors God's creation. He is the mirror *and* the lamp, the one whose genius illuminates reality for the rest of us precisely because he exists in such perfect harmony with it.

Throughout the *Biographia* one finds an ongoing tension between the vivid particular world—"the table itself, which the man of common sense believes himself to see"—and the transforming power of imagination— "'The light that never was, on land or sea'" (1:179, 2:124). The fanatic's inability to sustain both poles of creativity reveals—perversely—how genius functions. These complementary accounts are integrated by metaphors that we ignore or slight at our peril because Coleridge's idea of imagination is most lucidly explained not in the abstraction of the "philosophical chapters" but here, in this rich and lively polemic. Chapters 12 and 13 do little more than summarize abstractly what is elsewhere more clearly stated.[3]

Reading Coleridge's prose comfortably also demands sensitivity to the sometimes eccentric ways in which he structures his arguments. At his best, as Bishop C. Hunt, Jr., so aptly explains, "what we might call the 'dramatic' element in philosophy, the process of search and its written re-enactment, assumes a larger significance. Much of Coleridge's best writing can be read as a kind of dramatic monologue in prose, a mimetic representation, like Wordsworth's philosophic poetry, of the mind in the act of thinking something through."[4] This drama may in part arise from the dictating of the *Biographia*. Most transcribed tape-recordings of conversations are astoundingly incoherent because the transitions and connections are lost. Such connections in Coleridge's prose are feeble beyond reason, given the rigor of his thinking. Consider as well DeQuincey's account of how radically fragmented Coleridge's conversation could be even for those present. And yet DeQuincey also says, "I can assert, upon my long and intimate knowledge of Coleridge's mind, that logic the most severe was as inalienable from his modes of thinking as grammar from his language."[5]

Even when Coleridge seems to turn most distractedly—like the White Rabbit to zip past and disappear—at such times he is probably doing one of a finite number of reasonable things which he (quite unreasonably) does not signal to us in advance. Let me sketch three of these: exploring grounds and presuppositions; defining a new perspective on an old issue; or turning back to an issue now that its grounds are clear and various perspectives have been considered. These strategies supply the "dramatic element" that Hunt described. This is far from a complete list, but for present circumstances it is enough.

Chapter 2 analyzes the supposed irritability of men of genius, a subject Shawcross dismisses as "quite irrelevant" (1:212). Yet this chapter first and most richly contrasts the genius and the fanatic. Shawcross is misled by Coleridge's failure to specify the connection between chapters 1 and 2, but the connections are nonetheless there. In chapter 1 Coleridge describes his study of Bowles, and his attempt to understand the basis of genuine literary value—the difference between "the Greek Poets from Homer to Theocritus inclusive; and still more . . . our elder English poets from Chaucer to Milton" and such moderns as Erasmus Darwin (1:14). He also contrasts his own education with that which produces the kinds of minds that become anonymous critics. The chapter ends with a funny little anecdote concerning literary parodies.

There are two sorts of connection between chapters 1 and 2. Locally, or superficially, Coleridge goes from wondering why anyone would think him angered by a parody to wondering why people always think poets are irritable. This sort of connection might be no more than Coleridge's capacity for being "solicited" away from the virtuous path of his argument by a handsome new notion.[6] But he is not wandering off track: he is delving beneath the state of affairs just described. He explores the basis of the difference between great poetry and modern trash, and correlatively between great criticism and anonymous criticism. The transition functions as if an imagined interlocutor interrupted Coleridge to ask, "Why is this so? Why did that fellow think you would be so angry?" In answering Coleridge *refuses* to be "solicited:" he takes his interlocutor to the grounds of what he has been describing throughout chapter 1.

Knowing Coleridge's abiding interests helps us follow such transitions because we know where Coleridge is apt to turn to answer such a question. But why are the transitions so poor? Coleridge's use of his notebooks demonstrates how much he relied on set pieces, and yet any set piece would need minute revision to allow Coleridge to explore the grounds he wants while maintaining reasonable unity in his "local" topic. Such revisions are tedious. Rather than submit to such "professional" drudgery, Coleridge unduly relies on metaphor patterns to hold things together. His habit of dictating and the conversational quality of his prose are again relevant: in conversation it is easy to observe how people relate their abiding interests to the topic at hand, and it is easy to follow such integrations. It is for whatever reason far more difficult in prose, and more difficult yet when the abiding interests are as complex as Coleridge's.

Coleridge also loses readers at the beginning of chapter 5. Chapter 4 ends with the proposal that he investigate the seminal grounds of the distinction between fancy and imagination so as to resolve the controversy over Wordsworth and poetic diction. Chapter 5 ties immediately to that by delving under it, to the more comprehensive issue of mental activity and levels of will. The chapter begins, "There have been men in all ages, who have been impelled as by an instinct to propose their own nature as a problem, and who devote their attempts to its solution. The first step was to construct a table of distinctions, which they seem to have formed on the principle of the absence or presence of the *Will*" (1:65–66). If you were not lost at chapter 2, as of course many are, then the "problem" of our own "nature" might seem a reasonable enough reference to the fanatic/genius contrast. But even those who follow to this point are following tentatively, because what ought to be a crucial connection deserves greater emphasis than Coleridge provides. Because the emphasis is missing, we intuitively downgrade the connection, thereby revising our nascent sense of what the *Biographia* is "about." Almost any reader, then, is likely to throw up hands in despair as chapter 5 gets underway. What has Mackintosh to do with anything? Is the "men of all ages" business just a historical flourish to introduce him?

Coleridge might have made a coherent transition in several ways. Since he attended Mackintosh's lectures in 1800, he might have represented them as one of the series of "influences" which he describes in the first four chapters. Hartley certainly was a major influence who would fit very nicely in that catalogue. He could also improve the transition with a simple bit of emphasis: specify that he will resolve the controversy and explore the roots of imagination and fancy by considering the levels of will, which men of all ages . . . etc. But Coleridge's prose is remarkably without any such aids to orientation. We are to see where we are going by looking about us as we progress. We lose our way here because Coleridge assumes the continuity of his discourse and supplies only the facts. To the extent that we are influenced by the powerful tradition that assumes the discontinuity of Coleridge's discourse, we are blind to relationships which are tolerably obvious but not specified.

(And let me note in passing that this chapter opening is a crucial point for discovering or destroying the unity of the *Biographia* generally, because it is profoundly important to keep in mind the short table of will here provided. Coleridge refers to it, adds to it, argues with other philosophers about details of it, all as if it were written on a blackboard behind him.)

But what *is* going on with Mackintosh, after all? We who were comfortable with critics and poets are now rightly annoyed. And, of course, Coleridge does this to us all the time. At such points of apparently massive dislocation, Coleridge is introducing a new perspective, or a new *set* of perspectives on the issue at hand. The new perspective here is philosophy: Coleridge cannot explore the roots of imagination without talking about the nature of the mind itself. Fair enough. This reaching to first questions and fundamental issues is part of why we value Coleridge so much as a thinker.

But he does more than this. He adds to the contrast between true poets and false poets, or that between anonymous critics and philosophic critics. He adds a parallel distinction between false philosophers and true philosophers and a parallel problem to the evil politics of poetry in a pernicious politics of philosophy, which must in modern times be addressed to the multitudes rather than to an intellectual and moral elite. Later he does this again, drawing the same contrast between fanatic political writers and genial ones (i.e., Burke, and also Coleridge himself in the *Morning Post*). And the politics of philosophy all comes to bear when Coleridge's imaginary friend dissuades him from publishing chapter 13. In short, he is both providing a new perspective—philosophy—and continuing to elaborate the preceding set of issues. His ultimate point is to argue for the cultural importance of secondary imagination, wherever it is manifest. But he does not, as more linear minds might, separate explaining what imagination is from explaining why it is so important. Byron's wicked lines are marvelously apt.

Coleridge's transitions also disorient us when he attempts to close one of his "huge circuits," as he does for instance at the opening of chapter 14. Transitions like these demand a close review of the beginning of that circuit to locate the issues and metaphors that will reappear. Such a comparison of chapters 1 through 4 with 14 to 16 uncovers both new emphases and entirely new issues. Central among these new issues is an argument about the nature of language and the relation between language and consciousness. These are evident in the opening chapters as well, with their concern for purity and precision of diction; but at this point they come richly to the fore.

When Coleridge reaches back like this, we are less seriously disoriented than at other eccentric transitions, because repetition is so rare in his prose that it collects its own emphasis. There is another reason as well. Working as I have with Coleridge's organizing habits has made me scrupulously aware of my own modes of organizing. And at one point I realized—perhaps you will too—that I used such huge circuits in the classroom all the time. A bright student asks a complex question, or reveals a historical or philosophical lacuna that has to be filled. One stops to provide the necessary information or analysis, then takes a deep breath and returns to the original topic at hand, a topic that has now been to some extent transfigured. It is as if the energy of that inhalation is to lift the class with me to see all the transfigurings the new ideas provide.

Coleridge supplies this energy too, or this guidance, in the extraordinary *density* of his prose at such closings-of-circuits. The connections to the origin of the circuit are so many and so potent that they easily force an entire rereading of the chapters to which they refer, which in turn triggers other rereadings and reconsiderations, in what strikes me as a quintessentially Coleridgean way. Although no doubt a master of the fragment, perhaps even of the aphorism, Coleridge is simultaneously a most sustained and systematic thinker. He expends little energy on the niceties of composing, and especially on the small mechanical tricks of transition and structure; but the essential continuities are so obsessively, overwhelmingly present that either we lose our way in the tangle of connections, or we let the text engage us in a closely directed *reflection* upon the topic at hand. We, too, then become "minds in the act of thinking something through."

Finally, allow me to sketch an issue which deserves major new study: how Coleridge situates himself historically. We know that Coleridge saw himself not as an original and innovative thinker, but as one of a substantial and ancient community of thinkers working on closely related issues from roughly the same presuppositions. This idea of an intellectual community underlies not only the famous plagiarisms, but also the seldom-examined problem of how Coleridge changes the texts he incorporates. It also underlies both the anachronism and the teleologism of his version of Western intellectual history. Coleridge's idea of history, in short, is elaborate and complex to an extent seldom properly understood and never adequately defined.[7]

Coleridge's idea of history shapes his texts in innumerable ways, three of which are simple enough to be briefly summarized. First, references to the ancient community of thinkers commonly define major suppositions and starting points. For instance, chapter 5's reference to "men in all ages":

> There have been men in all ages, who have been impelled as by an instinct to propose their own nature as a problem, and who devote their attempts to its solution. The first step was to construct a table of distinctions, which they seem to have formed on the principle of the absence or presence of the *will*. Our various sensations, perceptions, and movements were classed as active or passive, or as media partaking of both. . . . Our inward experiences were thus arranged in three separate classes, the passive sense, or what the school-men call the merely receptive quality of the mind; the voluntary; and the spontaneous, which holds the middle place between both. But it is not in human nature to meditate on any mode of action, without enquiring after the law that governs it; and in the explanation of the spontaneous movements of

our being, the metaphysician took the lead of the anatomist and natural philosopher. (1:65–66)

Coleridge then argues that perception is not passive (as the tradition seems to suggest). Perception, he argues, is a form or mode of the spontaneous, because "the will and reason are perhaps never wholly suspended" (1:77). This eventually leads to his definition of primary imagination as "the living Power and prime Agent of all human Perception" (1:202). The voluntary quality of the mind Coleridge calls "fancy" (1:87, 202). The faculty of the spontaneous is the imagination, although "in common language, and especially on the subject of poetry, we appropriate the name to a superior degree of the faculty, joined to a superior voluntary controul over it" (1:86).

These distinctions and definitions are not quite the commonplaces Coleridge suggests, and not quite original either.[8] He is on the one hand referring to a rich tradition not widely known by his English contemporaries, and on the other asserting that a rich and ancient tradition leads directly to the argument he wishes to make. The truth of the matter is not wholly in either hand. To discover and define that truth, to understand the argument about perception and imagination that Coleridge makes in *Biographia*, we must watch carefully what happens when Coleridge invokes "tradition" (see also 1:89–90, 94, 133–36).

Coleridge also situates himself historically by citing from his "ancient community"—often by plagiarizing. Even when these passages are verbatim transcriptions, Coleridge usually changes what he takes by placing it in a new context that inevitably changes how we read it. Given the extent to which he demands a scrupulous attention to his own contexts, he may have written with great awareness of how he was forcing a rereading of what he incorporated. That might be part of why he did not rewrite sufficiently to preclude the charge of plagiarism: perhaps he is quite in control of the tensions thereby created.

But often he does not simply incorporate. Often there are major interpolations, or major redefinitions of key terms preceding the plagiarized passage. These changes are sometimes just ignored, or worse yet condescendingly brushed aside as the "mere" Christianizing of ideas or systems otherwise too bold or too free for what is then characterized as a rigidly orthodox personality. All such settings-aside are monumentally mistaken: these changes commonly reflect or share in the central issues of the argument Coleridge is making. If we are to understand that argument in all its complexity, these changes need to be mapped in just as much detail as the plagiarisms themselves.

I am not a comparative literature scholar; I cannot offer this mapping with the necessary detail and precision. But let me offer a couple of interesting examples. In chapter 12, in the famous "range of hills" passage, Coleridge compares consciousness to a stream. At the conclusion of this passage, he underscores the metaphor: "That the common consciousness itself will furnish proofs by its own direction, that it is connected with master-currents below the surface, I shall merely assume as a postulate pro tempore" (1:167). Later, then, Coleridge incorporates a considerable passage from Schelling that talks about the "direction" of a point in motion. Coleridge is using the passage to say something different from what it says in Schelling, because what for Schelling is mathematics, for Coleridge is metaphor.[9]

Or again, Coleridge appends to thesis vi a connection between the Schellingian "I am" and the traditional, Biblical, divine "*sum quia sum*" (1:183). It is a mistake, a profound and serious mistake, to blur the difference between Schelling's "I am" and Coleridge's "great eternal *I am*." Let me explain why. The real gap in the *Biographia* is not in chapter 13; it is between thesis vi and its Scholium. The essential connection that Coleridge cannot define to his or our satisfaction is the relation between human cognition and the knowledge and power of God. In the *Biographia*, Coleridge asserts that through faith we have immediate knowledge of both a personal God and a real world of physical objects immediately known (see 1:133–36). The *Logosophia* will explain *how* this can be so (it is necessarily indemonstrable, given its origin in faith and free will). He draws this thorny issue into the *Biographia* in order to ground the moral value of the highest exercise of secondary imagination, "'the vision and the faculty divine.'" Coleridge forthrightly acknowledges that his position can never be proven without losing its moral force (see 1:135–36: "It could not become intellectually more evident without becoming morally less effective."). Schelling, on the other hand, is performing a sophisticated maneuver in a highly technical kind of epistemology. The central issue for Coleridge is not epistemology but theology. To deny the difference is to become blind to the foundation of Coleridge's argument about the cultural centrality of literature and literary criticism.

Coleridge's idea of history also shapes his texts through his proper use

of quotations. Whether separated from his text as headnotes and epi-
grams, or whether embedded as citations that are properly identified as
such, these passages usually summarize and thereby emphasize central
aspects of the issue at hand. Because Coleridge's prose provides so few
structuring elements, these citations deserve and reward thoughtful attention. Chapter 13 begins with three citations, one from Milton, one from
Leibniz, and one from Synesius. Chapters 12 and 13 have been written
about more than any other two chapters in the *Biographia*, yet I have never
seen a discussion of these three headnotes.

Milton's lines trace the relation from God, or pure knowing, to creation.
This is the subjective pole of philosophy, as defined in chapter 12 (1:176).
I quoted these earlier, but they are worth rereading.

> O Adam, One Almighty is, from whom
> All things proceed, and up to him return,
> If not depraved from good: created all
> Such to perfection, one first nature all,
> Indued with various forms, various degrees
> Of substance, and, in things that live, of life;
> But more refined, more spirituous and pure,
> As nearer to him plac'd, or nearer tending,
> Each in their several active spheres assign'd,
> Till body up to spirit work, in bounds
> Proportioned to each kind. So from the root
> Springs lighter the green stalk, from thence the leaves
> More airy: last the bright consummate flower
> Spirits odorous breathes. Flowers and their fruit,
> Man's nourishment, by gradual scale sublim'd,
> To *vital* spirits aspire: to *animal*
> To *intellectual*!—give both life and sense,
> Fancy and understanding; whence the soul
> *Reason* receives, and reason is her *being*,
> Discursive or intuitive.   *Par. Lost.* b.V.
>
>   (1:195)

These lines summarize chapter 12 in far more accessible and familiar
terms, especially for an English audience. God creates and orders the universe, maintaining both our being and the being of the world around us,
and thereby guaranteeing or grounding the possibility of our knowing
that world.[10] Human knowing is the most nearly divine of human powers.

There follows a passage from Leibniz that travels in the opposite direction, from matter to mind. This is the objective pole of philosophy, as defined in chapter 12 (1:175).

> If indeed corporeal things contained nothing but matter they might truly be said to consist in flux and to have no substance, as the Platonists once rightly recognized. . . . And so, apart from the purely mathematical and what is subject to the fancy, I have come to the conclusion that certain metaphysical elements perceptible by the mind alone should be admitted, and that some higher and, so to speak, *formal principle* should be added to the material mass, since all the truths about corporeal things cannot be collected from logistic and geometrical axioms alone, i.e. those concerning great and small, whole and part, shape and position, but others must enter into it, i.e. cause and effect, *action* and *passion,* by which the reasons for the order of things are maintained. It does not matter whether we call this principle of things an entelechy or a power so long as we remember that it is intelligibly to be explained only the idea of *powers.*[11]

The lines from Leibniz recapitulate the major conclusion of chapters 5 through 9: we cannot explain the real world and our knowledge of it by assuming that the mind is passive in perception. The lines say more than this, of course, more that also involves the significance of Kant for the *Biographia*'s argument and for Coleridge's position generally. But the essential thrust here is the inadequacy of materialism as a philosophy, a central and recurrent concern throughout the first volume: "all the truths about corporeal things cannot be collected from logistic and geometric axioms alone."

The lines from Synesius which follow have been variously translated; I follow George Watson.[12]

> I worship the hidden order of intellectual things.
> The Mean dances and is not still.

And this is the imagination, a spontaneous act, a dancing, which at its basic level is perception, but at its highest level is art. Great poetry grounds itself on close and shrewd perception, on a renewed vision of the beauties around us; but it can do so only because it sees within this material world the translucence of the divine. Coleridge argues so bitterly with Wordsworth's emphasis on observation because it seems that Wordsworth undervalues or fails to recognize the necessary priority of the mind who is observing.

Why does Coleridge do this? Why does he supply citations where we surely expect a firm, lucid summary, emphases duly allotted? No doubt there are layers and categories of reasons why; let me select just one. Coleridge's entire argument about the value of Wordsworth's poetry, about the value of great poetry generally, and therefore about the character of imagination and fancy depends at last on Coleridge's assertion that it is contranatural to doubt the existence of a real world correspondent to sense, and to doubt the existence of some divinity (1:133–36). Grant this, you grant him everything; deny this, and the *Biographia* offers only a muddled Shellingeanism and some interesting comments on poetry and a good deal of inconsequential rambling. Faith is at once the strongest and the most fragile of bases. Given that it is impossible to solve the metaphysical problem of mind and matter, faith is as good an answer as we are apt to find. And yet a systematic structure built on faith is fragile indeed: the best answer we are likely to find is nonetheless far less certain than anyone would like. The best guide, then, is tradition. I may err, you may err, but if the One Almighty exists, then surely over time the truth will emerge from the ancient community of those who think about such issues with open minds and hearts. Coleridge cites rather than summarizes to bolster his argument, to persuade us that the "unscientific" argument he is making has its own power, its own prestige, its own history.

And maybe he was lazy, or maybe he was crazy, or maybe he hated revising. Maybe he synthesized with such ease that he thought he was being quite clear. It's an unanswerable question. The best we can do, I propose, is to discover Coleridge's eccentricities and understand them. If we understand his habits as a composer of arguments, we will follow those arguments more easily. We will see his place in history more accurately, and we will learn from his genius more fruitfully. He is a difficult writer, but he is not impossible; and above all, his prose works are worth the effort they demand.

4

Coleridge and the Language of Adam

Robert N. Essick

> And out of the ground the Lord God formed every beast of the field, and every
> fowl of the air; and brought them unto Adam to see what he would call them:
> and whatsoever Adam called every living creature, that was the name thereof.

The exegesis of Genesis 2:19 has played a minor, half-submerged, but
nonetheless initiatory and intriguing role in the history of speculative linguistics. Several idealist dreams of a perfected language and schemes for
returning to paradise, at least in our words if not our bodies, have clustered around this brief verse, so conveniently open to interpretation and
embellishment. Nothing in the passage excludes the possibility that Adam
merely chose sounds at random, matched these with the beasts presented
to him, and thus founded a system of conventions that lasted until its fragmentation at the Tower of Babel (Genesis 11:7–9). However primal the
scene in Genesis, God is little more than a spectator, curious about "whatsoever Adam called every living creature." Language is a human invention, perfect in its referentiality to God's inventions when there was one
tongue, but arbitrary in its sound/thing correspondences. Such a reading is consistent with the opinions of Hermogenes in Plato's *Cratylus*, with
Ferdinand de Saussure's model of the structure of the sign, and generally
with positivist and associationist theories of thought and language.

An alternative reading also takes its cue from what is not stated, but
sees the absence of details as an opportunity for the transcendental. If the
entire scene is viewed *sub specie aeternitatis*, then the names Adam gives to
the beasts can be interpreted as partaking in the Divinity whose creations
they render intelligible. Adam provides each beast with "the name," not
merely *a* name, and thereby recreates in the secondary realm of finite consciousness what the infinite consciousness of God created in the primary

realm of being. Adamic language is one with human perception, an echo of God's creative Word, differing from the Logos only in degree, and in the mode of its operation. The story of Babel dramatizes not only a division between speakers but also a disruption of the unity of word and world from which all subsequent tongues suffer.[1]

My plagiarisms adumbrate my thesis: the reemergence of the transcendental tradition of Adamic language in some of Coleridge's most important statements on mind and its tropological capabilities. Before explicitly confronting that issue, I think it would be helpful to provide an historical context by briefly delineating those facets of linguistic speculation in the seventeenth and eighteenth centuries that speak most directly to Coleridgean themes.

Theories of a universal language which seek a restoration of Adamic unity can be divided roughly into two types, each characterized by a different attitude toward the relationship among the order of things, the order of words, and the processes of mind.[2] In seventeenth century England, several projectors with strong allegiances to Baconian rationalism and the values of the Royal Society published schemes for written languages in which signs would stand for things rather than spoken words. Francis Lodowick's *A Common Writing* (1647) and *Ground-Work* (1652), John Webster's *Academiarum Examen* (1654), George Dalgarno's *Ars Signorum* (1661), and John Wilkins's *Essay towards a Real Character, and a Philosophical Language* (1668) typify the genre. Their goal is most clearly set forth by Wilkins:

> . . . now if these *Marks* or *Notes* could be so contrived, as to have such a *dependance* upon, and relation to, one another, as might be suitable to the nature of the things and notions which they represented; and so likewise, if the *Names* of things could be so ordered, as to contain such a kind of *affinity* or *opposition* in their letters and sounds, as might be some way answerable to the nature of the things which they signified. . . . by learning the *Character* and the *Names* of things, [we would] be instructed likewise in their *Natures*, the knowledge of both which ought to be conjoyned. (21)

The passage embodies a problematic at the heart of the rationalist school of language reform. Wilkins would seem to be searching for a motivated hieroglyph, hence the "real" of his title.[3] The affinity of such pursuits with the exegetical tradition of Adamic speech is made explicit by Dalgarno's desire to discover "some *vestigia* of that primitive and Divine, or purely rational Sematology, taught by Almighty God or invented by Adam before the Fall" ("Discourse" in *Works* 164). Yet the bonding of language to nature, founded on the supposedly common ground of logic, subordinates the former to the latter and must finally lead not only away from the divine Word but from a concern with any signs insofar as they participate directly in the nonverbal. While Dalgarno invokes Edenic naming, it is of no consequence to his "rational Sematology" whether the origin of Adamic language is transcendental or human. Wilkins's emphasis is on the two systems of language and nature and on the internal relationships of their terms. His hope is to be a new Adam and construct a language with a grammar homologous to the structure of nature. Not surprisingly, this is to be accomplished by freeing writing from speaking, thereby eliminating at one stroke those figurative encrustations inhibiting the logical machinery of all known tongues and phonetic alphabets.[4] Words and things will then move on parallel, isomorphic tracks. The mode of their relationship will presumably be a kind of logical allegory constructed by the human mind capable of perceiving one system through the senses and perfectly expressing what it perceives through the other.

Wilkins's proposal foreshadows the attention devoted to syntax in eighteenth- and nineteenth-century linguistics, but attempts to solve the problem of reference by a radical reduction of both nature and language to mere taxonomies.[5] In a simplistic way this returns us to the scene in Genesis—so many beasts, so many names. John Locke soon disrupted this ideal symmetry by the simple but revolutionary observation that "words, in their primary or immediate signification, stand for nothing but *the ideas in the mind of him that uses them,* how imperfectly soever or carelessly those ideas are collected from the things which they are supposed to represent" (*Essay* 2:9). While Locke's anticipation of Saussure's definition of the signified prepared the foundation for the psychological study of language, his nominalism accepted the arbitrary nature of signs and the schematic approach to their organization.

David Hartley follows in the Lockean tradition. He lays particular stress on the difficulties of determining the nature of Adamic speech in a way that suggests the triviality of such speculations. Hartley does propose, however, "that the language, which *Adam* and *Eve* were possessed of in paradise was very narrow, and confined in great measure to visible things," and "monosyllabic in great measure" (*OM* 176). The growth of language occurs only after the fall when "*Adam* and *Eve* extended their language to new objects and ideas" through a process of association and growth resembling "the increase of money at interest upon interest" (*OM* 177). The characterization of the language of paradise descends almost to Hobbesian terms: mean, brutish, and short. In his own proposal for a "philosophical language" (*OM* 186), Hartley notes the "supposition" that Adam and Eve spoke something "of this kind," however "narrow" (*OM* 187), but this is a feeble gesture of little consequence to his goal of establishing the "general Doctrine of Association" (*OM* 188) as it should manifest itself in language. Clearly, we have nearly reached a dead-end of the Adamic tradition. To a romantic sensibility, Hartley's linguistic Eden, like those conjured up by Wilkins and Dalgarno, looks more like a desert than a garden, a place where difference and absence have been planted between word and world. Mind is left in the void separating the order of things from the order of words, furiously switching back and forth between two paths that never merge.

The significance of the Adamic tradition to rationalist schemes of language reform has been disputed,[6] but there can be no question of its importance to an alternative tradition of speculative, even mystical, linguistics. Jacob Boehme is the grand exemplar of this school and the main route through which it became known to Englishmen such as Blake and Coleridge. Boehme's doctrine of signatures, set forth in greatest detail in his *Signatura Rerum* (4:1–140), provides the foundation for his belief that Adam spoke the language of "all Spirits" (3:196) that was one with the essences God invested in things. Thus, "*Adam* stood in the *divine* Image, and not in the *bestial,* for he knew the Property of all Creatures, *and gave Names to all Creatures* from their Essence, Form, and Property. He understood the Language of Nature, viz. the manifested and formed Word in every one's Essence, for thence the *Name of every Creature* is risen" (*Mysterium Magnum* 3:80). Boehme also implies in his *Mysterium Magnum* a rough parallel between the creation of man in God's image and the nature of Adamic speech as a recapitulation, at a lower level of the spiritual will, of the "*Verbum Fiat*" (3:66–67). Unfortunately, Adam's progeny "understood not that God was *in* the speaking Word of the Understanding" and as a result thought that language was only a "Form" divided from its sensual substance (3:197; see also 3:195). To use the fashionable terminology of our own day, man created *difference* as he came to believe in an ontological distinction between the physical signifier and the tran-

scendental signified. This in turn led to false ideas about God and the
misguided attempt to build a tower to reach that which was still present
in the one language of man before Babel (see 3:199–200). Christ, as the
incarnate "living Word" (3:204) rejoining form and substance, offers the
paradigm for the linguistic recovery that will lead man back to paradise.
Christ passed through what Boehme terms the "Death of the Letters,"
overcoming "the *Whoredom*" of fallen conceptions of language (3:204) and
revealing to man "the Spirits of the Letters" (3:208). Guided by this revelation, Boehme claims his ability to recover the spiritual meanings residual
in lapsarian language. By treating words as things, he finds in them their
divine signatures through a process that amounts to little more than pun-
ning and etymological transformations similar to his alchemical treatment
of substances.

It is not difficult to trace fragments of Boehme's linguistics through
Coleridge's scattered comments on language. Some dozen years before he
began to annotate a copy of the so-called Law's edition of *The Works of
Jacob Behmen*, Coleridge hinted in "The Destiny of Nations" at his predisposition for a doctrine of signatures:

> For all that meets the bodily sense I deem
> Symbolical, one mightly alphabet
> For infant minds; . . .

(PW [EHC] 1:132)

In a letter to William Godwin of September 22, 1800, Coleridge ques-
tioned "how far . . . the word 'arbitrary'" is a "misnomer" in reference
to "signs" and expressed the desire, underlying all schemes for the recovery of Adamic language, "to destroy the old antithesis of *Words &
Things*." This he hoped to do by "elevating, as it were, words into Things,
& living Things too" (*CL* 1:625–26) much as Boehme had treated words
as substances subject to alchemical transmutation to recover the linguistic equivalent of gold. Long after he had begun to reject the pantheistic
implications of Boehme's philosophy, Coleridge was not above using the
well-chosen pun as an exegetical instrument, as in his reference to "the
identity of *nomen* [name] with *numen*, that is, invisible power and presence"
in many Biblical passages, including the naming of the beasts in Genesis 2:19.[7] Perhaps we can even sense the incorporation of Boehme's views
in Coleridge's admonition in the *Biographia Literaria* not "to overlook the
important fact, that besides the language of words, there is a language
of spirits." The second half of this sentence—"that the former is only the

vehicle of the latter" (1:290)—leaves intact the hope that one can recover the spirit hidden in that vehicle.

The annotations Coleridge wrote over many years, beginning in 1808, in his copy of Law's edition offer the clearest indication of what he found so compelling in Boehme's theory of language and what he could not accept. "Even in the most startling [paragraphs], those on the correspondency of Letters, and syllables, to the universal sense of words," Coleridge sensed "an important Truth hidden in the seeming Blunder of its exemplification" (*Marginalia* 1:591). To explain this disparity between intuitive principle and the fanciful parsing of German words to find Adam's, Coleridge proposes a "way of saving Behmen's credit" by supposing "that he had seen the truth as to the *Ideal* of Language—and had in his ordinary state confounded the spiritual, perhaps angelic, language with the poor arbitrary & corrupted Languages of men as they actually exist" (629). In short, Boehme had not paid sufficient heed to the fact of man's fall, that "fundamental postulate of the moral"—and linguistic—"history of Man" (*Table Talk* 65).

Boehme's failure to resurrect Adamic speech left as an alternative the rationalist tradition of language reformation. It at least recognized the limitations of contemporary languages. But the substitution of classical logic for the ideal of the motivated sign could not satisfy Coleridge's transcendental instincts, nor perhaps his needs as a poet. His rejection of the taxonomic view of language is implicated in his criticism of its necessary twin, the taxonomic view of nature, in his annotations to Johann Friedrich Blumenbach's *Über die natürlichen Verschiedenheiten.* "The fault common to the Systems & Systematizers of Natural Hystery" is not, in Coleridge's view, "the falsehood nor even the unfitness of the guiding principle," but rather the "forgetting that Nature may pursue a hundred Objects at the same time" (*Marginalia* 1:536). As we have seen, the systematizers of language required the elimination of polysemy. They are blind to the "living powers" of "Words" (*Essays on His Times* 2:249) much as the taxonomists are blind to Coleridge's proto-evolutionary sense of nature's protean dynamics.

Confronted with the narrowness of the rationalist theories of language, Coleridge clung to the essential features of the transcendental position in spite of Boehme's demonstrative blunders. Coleridge's strategy was to preserve the ideal of Adamic language by constructing a motivated sign defined in counterdistinction to the mechanical matching of taxonomic linguistics. The relevant passages in *The Statesman's Manual* are well known, but it is sometimes forgotten that Coleridge's definition of a "symbol" unfolds in the context of a book about the uses of the Bible, not secular literature. The key term is introduced as "a system of symbols, harmonious in themselves, and consubstantial with the truths, of which they are the conductors" (29). This "system" fulfills the requirement, proposed by Wilkins and other rationalists, that the words of an ideal language should be properly related to each other, although Coleridge substitutes an organic sense of the "harmonious" for taxonomic logic. He next moves his system beyond intrinsic harmony among signs to propose a unity of signs and their referents, the former "consubstantial with"—that is, one with the same substantial reality as—the latter. Such a sign, which "always partakes of the Reality which it renders intelligible" (30), is not consubstantial with things but with "truths." Coleridge implicity accepts Locke's insight about all signs, as he explicity does elsewhere,[8] and is able to substitute "truths" for "ideas" because he is considering only ideas in the Bible. This higher mode of signification is contrasted to allegory, a product of "the mechanical understanding" that translates "abstract notions into a picture-language which is itself nothing but an abstraction from objects of the senses" (30). Coleridge's terminology here might seem to refer only to a poetic mode, but it also refers to a method of reading the Bible and, by implication, to those ideal language schemes that propose merely the alignment of the order of words with the order of things, those "objects of the senses" to which the Baconian logician matches his abstract and arbitrary signs.

With his definition of the symbol, Coleridge does nothing less than resurrect the motivated sign of Adamic language. As A. W. Schlegel pointed out, "protolanguage will consist in natural signs, that is, signs found in an essential relation with what is designated."[9] Such a sign arises logically and historically from the exegetical tradition of Genesis 2:19 exemplified by Boehme, although perhaps it would be unfair to say of Coleridge's theory what he said of Schelling's "System": "it is little more than Behmenism, translated from visions into Logic and a sort of commanding eloquence" (to C. A. Tulk, November 24, 1818; *Letters* 4:883). The transcendental nature of Coleridge's symbol is indicated by his use of "consubstantial," a term generally applied to the interrelationship of the Trinity (see *OED*), and by the example he offers from Ezekiel 1:20. Significantly, Coleridge does not take the language of the Biblical passage as *itself* symbolic; that could fall into the same blunders with English or Hebrew that Boehme fell into with German. Rather, Coleridge indicates that Ezekiel's vision of the eyed wheels was the exemplary moment when "the truths and the symbols that represent them move in conjunction and form the living chariot that bears up (for *us*) the throne of the Divine Humanity" (29). Coleridge does not, indeed could not, claim that the languages of man after Babel are the same as the symbolic language of Adam and of divine revelation. Only when we "suppose man perfect" can we claim that his "organic Acts" are "faithful symbols of his spiritual Life and Cognition" (annotations to Boehme; *Marginalia* 1:634). That perfection can be restored through transmundane visions like Ezekiel's, but only then is there a "translucence of the Eternal through and in the Temporal" (*Statesman's Manual* 30). Unlike Boehme, Coleridge does not forget the fall, standing between sign and referent, signifier and signified, as it stands between Eden and England, Ezekiel's wheels and Coleridge's words.

As several critics have pointed out, no one has been very successful in discovering Coleridgean symbols in secular literature.[10] The reason for this becomes clear when we consider the motivated sign from the perspective of prelapsarian or divine language, the only realms in which it can be fully embodied. Any account of the symbolic experience will itself fall short of that ideal. Coleridge's symbol is not an instrument of a practical poetic or hermeneutic. It is, rather, what Coleridge might call the "Hypopœesis" or "subfiction"[11] of a general but transcendental semiotic. The explication of that semiotic always takes the form of an allegory in which the transcendental descends into the rhetorical and the symbolic degenerates into the synecdochic. This linguistic recapitulation of the fall happened even when Coleridge attempted to offer a mundane example of a symbol. In a lecture on *Don Quixote* delivered in 1818, he stated that "The Symbolical cannot, perhaps, be better defined in distinction from the Allegorical, than that it is always itself a part of that, of the whole of which it is the representative.—'Here comes a sail,'—(that is, a ship) is a symbolical expression" (*Miscellaneous Criticism* 99). A sail, as a physical object, is consubstantial with the ship of which it is a constitutive part, but the word "sail" no more "partakes of the Reality it renders intelligible" through synecdoche than does any other sign.[12] The problem is not one of alternative tropes, rhetoric, or grammar, but the crucial difference between a motivated and an arbitrary mode of signification. As Hodgson has stated, this is "the true and inescapable issue for any rhetoric that would strive to be transcendental" (292).

We are left with a disturbing gap between the conceivable and the possible, one that thwarts both the desire for return and reunion and makes problematic the alterity of the transcendental. If the symbol is so far beyond us all, how can Coleridge define it? Man, even fallen man, must have some mental faculty by which he can approach, however asymptotically, the union of symbolic discourse without divine intercession. In some fragmentary notes on Shakespeare, written circa 1812, Coleridge tentatively located that possibility in the poetic faculty, with the implication that figurative language is motivated in a way that literal reference is not.[13] He begins with the familiar and necessary distinction between "the language of man and that of nature" (*Shakespearean Criticism* 1:185). The former is composed, for example, of "the sound, *sun*, or the figures, s, u, n," and these "are pure arbitrary modes of recalling the object." In contrast, "the language of nature is a subordinate *Logos*, that was in the beginning, and was with the thing it represented." Thus, Coleridge has defined this Adamic protolanguage, or system of natural signatures, much as he will define "a system of symbols" some four years later, and relates this language to *Logos* much as he will relate the primary imagination to "the infinite I AM" (*BL* 1:304) some five years later. The consanguinity of "symbol" and "imagination" is evident here even before their separate births.

With his paradigm established, Coleridge next situates Shakespeare along its vertical axis: "Now the language of Shakespeare (in his *Lear*, for instance), is a something intermediate, or rather it is the former [language of man] blended with the latter [language of nature], the arbitrary not merely recalling the cold notion of the thing, but expressing the reality of it . . ." (*Shakespearean Criticism* 1:185). The enabling trope haunting this discourse is not synecdoche but oxymoron of the evanescent and mystic sort soon to be explored by Keats in his attempt to grasp the bourne of heaven. While Coleridge admits that arbitrary signs are "an heirloom of the human race," Shakespeare's language becomes "a part of that which it manifests" (i.e., becomes symbolic) through the "valued advantage of the theatre." This final turn in the argument leads us away from the synchronic structure of signs toward the diachronic mode of their (re)production, as though the transcendent is touched through a dramatic "imitation"[14] somehow consubstantial with the dynamics of God's creative Word. This process is given its definitive formulation in chapter 13 of the *Biographia*.

Coleridge's definition of "imagination" has quite rightly been read, and reread, as a general epistemological statement which assumes a transcendental truth and describes how mind produces art. I hope it will not be inappropriate to shift the perspective a little, place the famous four sentences within the traditions of the language of Adam, and view the whole as a statement about the history of motivated signs and the possibility of recovering them. Coleridge, after all, begins like Genesis with an utterance, God's "I AM." In chapter 12, he characterizes "the great eternal I AM" as the ground of both "being" and "idea" (*BL* 1:275), a speech (or at least semiotic) act linking at their common source both "idea" and "law" as defined in the "Essays on Method."[15] Much as in his evocation of the *Logos* in his comments on Shakespeare, Coleridge has again taken one step back from Adam naming the beasts as the origin of language to God naming himself, perhaps with a hidden pun on "Yahweh" and Hebrew for "I am."[16] Similarly, the nontranscendent "I am" takes on special originary importance in Coleridge's *Logic*, where "the verb substantive ('am,' *sum*, . . .) expresses the identity or coinherence of being and act" and is the "point" from which "all other words therefore may be considered as tending" (16–17).[17] The finite "I am" thus repeats, in the realm of language, the same generative function performed by the Logos in the world of things, just as the primary imagination is a "repetition in the finite mind of the eternal act of creation in the infinite I AM" (*BL* 1:304). The relationship of infinite to finite "I am" is much the same as Boehme's sense of the repetition of the *verbum fiat* in Adamic speech. In each case, infinite and finite, the point of origin is an utterance with the oxymoronic structure of Coleridge's "symbol," for each blends into a unity two disparate categories —being and act, or sign and referent.

The imagination is not, finally, a symbol-making faculty in the sense that it assumes the prior existence of that which it is meant to create. In a *Notebook* entry of April 14, 1805, Coleridge senses this circularity when he describes the production of symbols as a projection of something within the subject, not the discovery of a truth about objects of perception.

> In looking at objects of Nature while I am thinking, as at yonder moon dim-glimmering thro' the dewy window-pane, I seem rather to be seeking, as it were *asking*, a symbolical language for something within me that already and forever exists, than observing any thing new. Even when the latter is the case, yet still I have always an obscure feeling as if that new phænomenon were the dim Awaking of a forgotten or hidden Truth of my inner Nature. (*CN* 2:§2546)

In the *Biographia*, the imagination is similarly characterized as an active and "inner" symbol, and thus the faculty cannot explain *how* we can move from the nonsymbolic language of fallen man to Adamic or divine consubstantiality. That question is answered with the psycholinguistic equivalent of the statement that man can know God because there is something godlike in man, an answer which simply denies the absoluteness of the difference assumed by the question. We are perilously close to Boehme's claims, criticized by Coleridge, about the Adamic traces in lapsarian languages. The secondary imagination, as a willed "echo" of the primary, shares its oxymoronic structure—"at once both active and passive" (*BL* 1:124) and combining both dissolution and unification. Coleridge arranges his definitions as though we are descending hierarchically from the infinite to the finite mind, from logos to poetry, but at no point do we leave the transcendental ideal hidden in the tropology of the motivated sign in any of its several simulacra—symbol, mystic oxymoron, or Adamic speech. Coleridge offers the secondary imagination as "the principle and agent of return" (Christensen 31), but it cannot return our language to Eden because it never leaves that paradise. Indeed, the secondary imagination, as much as the infinite I AM, is defined in counterdistinction to fancy, the mechanical world of arbitrary signs where reside all languages after Babel. The division between imagination and fancy reasserts that ancient division between Adamic and lapsarian language, between motivated and arbitrary signs, with which the ideal language projectors, Boehme, and Coleridge himself all began—and struggled in vain to overcome.

The *Biographia* takes note of another, competing theory of transcendental language. One of the common strategies in the eighteenth century for positing the former existence of motivated signs, or at least a speech closer to nature than contemporary tongues, was to shift the ground of the myth from Eden to the primitive past of whichever tribe (Britons, Celts, Germans, and others) seemed most susceptible to such inventions.[18] This secularizing substitution plays a major role in the 1802 "Appendix" to the "Preface" to *Lyrical Ballads*. Wordsworth claims that "the earliest poets of all nations generally wrote from passion excited by real events; they wrote naturally, and as men: feeling powerfully as they did, their language was daring, and figurative" (1:160). Wordsworth here adds a further variation to the myth, for the motivated association is between words and feelings rather than words and things or words and ideas. His theory of the fall from motivated to arbitrary signs is not centered on Babel, but rather on

"Men ambitious of the fame of Poets" who "set themselves to a mechanical adoption" of the "figures of speech" of the earliest poets and "applied them to feelings and thoughts with which they had no natural connection whatsoever."[19] But just as Wordsworth repeats the familiar story of original union and a fall into division, he also holds out the promise of return. By substituting space for time, he can locate motivated language not just in the primitive past but also in the present countryside. As Wordsworth indicates in the 1800 "Preface," men of "low and rustic life" speak "a more permanent and a far more philosophical language than that which is frequently substituted for it by Poets" who "indulge in arbitrary and capricious habits of expression" (1:124).

Wordsworth's theory of poetic diction is a variation on that same general theory of Adamic language so important to Coleridge. Even the words "philosophical language" intimate something about motivated signs, just as they do in Wilkins's title of 1668. But by locating that higher mode of speech in the language of common men here and now, Wordsworth makes his theories liable to the commonsensical objections offered in the second volume of the *Biographia*. We have already seen much the same pattern in Coleridge's criticism of Boehme's attempt to rediscover Adamic speech in his own modern German. And just as he found Boehme's linguistic idealism appealing, in spite of blunders in application, Coleridge proclaimed Wordsworth capable of writing "the FIRST GENUINE PHILOSOPHIC POEM" (*BL* 2:156) even though he had demolished Wordsworth's own theory of regaining a philosophical (i.e., motivated) system of signs. At the same time, Coleridge has eliminated one of the options for developing his concept of the imagination, at least as it might apply to secular literature. One consequence of this rejection is the lameness of Coleridge's attempt, in chapter 22 of the *Biographia*, to distinguish imagination from fancy in Wordsworth's verse and to claim that Wordsworth is a master of the higher mode while denying his stated method for rising above the lower. The gap remains between transcendental and mundane language, that gap Wordsworth attempted to bridge with the speech of rural Englishmen.

Coleridge's turn toward theology is in part predicated upon his theory of language. His success in defining the essential elements of an ideal language, his failure to find a convincing means for transporting the arbitrary language of fallen man back to that ideal, and his rejection of the facile routes to recovery, such as those offered by Boehme's linguistic alchemy or Wordsworth's poetic rustication, all led inevitably away from

words to the Word as the locus of transcendence. Only by that means can
Coleridge keep from becoming *"merely* a man of letters" (*BL* 1:229) whose
self-possession is based on the arbitrary marks rejected even by Wilkins
and whose spirit is subject to the "Death of the Letters" condemned by
Boehme.[20] Only the Father, whose words become things, and his Son, the
new Adam and Word incarnate, make consubstantial word and world, idea
and law, signifier and signified. While incapable of accepting the presence
of Adamic speech in secular texts, Coleridge could believe in the immanence of God's Word in the Bible even if its literal expression was necessarily in human words. While Coleridge had difficulty finding symbols in
contemporary language, he could claim the fulfillment of their definition
in Christ and in those Christian rituals "of the same kind, though not of
the same order, with the religion itself—not arbitrary or conventional, as
types and hieroglyphics are in relation to the things expressed by them;
but inseparable, consubstantiated (as it were), and partaking therefore of
the same life, permanence, and intrinsic worth with its spirit and principle" (*Aids to Reflection* 15). Even Coleridge's conception of the Trinity as
"Iseity," "Alterity," and "Community" (*Table Talk* 51) replicates the trinitarianism of an ideal grammar he divided into the "being" of the subject,
its "action" on an object, and the community of the two in the "verb substantive" (*Logic* 16–17).

If Coleridge's theology is indeed inscribed with traces of his linguistics,
it is because his linguistics was always a theology. If we now have difficulty
following him along those merging paths, it is because of a difference in
faith, not knowledge. He was too honest and too insightful to claim that
he had recovered the language of Adam this side of divinity, but to do
so never ceased to be an object of desire and a component of Coleridge's
transcendental speculations.

5

Anti-Materialism, Autobiography, and the Abyss of Unmeaning in the *Biographia Literaria*

J. H. Haeger

In an important study some years ago, Thomas McFarland offered a striking point regarding Coleridge's complex response to the issue of romantic nature *versus* philosophy and formal learning:

> . . . [T]he problem cannot be resolved by an easy preference for green and golden life over grey and bookish theory; it is compounded into a gravely perplexing choice. The green and golden meadow beetles dreadfully over the abyss of moral nullity; opposed to it is a chill moral freedom which, though grey, may be seen as the light of a hopeful dawn. And to choose one is to reject the other.
>
> Such a choice Coleridge refused to make. He would accept neither alternative as finally satisfactory, or even as finally bearable, and yet, like Hamlet, he could not bridge the irreconcilability of his interests. (*Tradition* 109–10)

McFarland's thesis that Coleridge remained determinedly both poetic and philosophic—attracted to the phenomenal world of "it is" yet denying it priority, and giving priority to the noumenal intellective "I AM" yet refusing to reduce all phenomena to abstraction—continues to supply an excellent perspective upon his later thought, both in its broad outlines and in its more circumscribed manifestations, such as the series of "philosophic" chapters in the *Biographia Literaria*.

In those famous, or infamous, chapters, Coleridge attempts to affirm ontological and epistemological premises ordering the relations of "it is" and "I am." There, material nature and mental theory, the green meadow and the gray book, take on grim identities. The former, having been reduced to a congeries of masses and motions by the mechanical assumptions of empiricist materialism, is to be reconstituted by the latter, which is an array of metaphysical speculations and systems stretching back over the history of human thought that is ironically being pressed into that service (as Norman Fruman and others have shown) by such intellectual acts of violence as misattribution, distortion, and plagiarism. Overarching all is the paradoxical but undeniable fact of the *Biographia*'s great influence and the equally paradoxical fact that the philosophic chapters, difficult and derivative as their contents may be, have continued to lend force and interest to the work. It is possible that the reasons for this have more to do with the subjective features of Coleridge's discourse in those chapters than with his ideas as such, and that their figural elements of structure and style cause us to react as readers rather like Charles Lamb did to the *Rime of the Ancient Mariner*: "I dislike all the miraculous part of it, but the feelings of the man under the operation of such scenery dragged me along like Tom Piper's magic whistle" (1:266). The convolutions of metaphysics hardly make mesmerizing scenery, but Coleridge's style does convey a sense of the feelings of the man under their operation.

For, as much as Coleridge sought a hopeful dawn in grey mental theory, he also knew that it could be less a refuge from, than a symptom of, "dejection." Indeed, the theme of dejection in Coleridge is a metonym for the dark side of romanticism itself—a side of it which (slighting such counterbalances as McFarland's later study of *Romanticism and the Forms of Ruin*) we ignore at the peril of oversimplifying, as Jerome McGann has recently warned (21–30). It is this that I have in mind in focusing upon the structure and style of the philosophic chapters to explore whether and to what effect the abyss yawns beneath the meadow *and* the theorizing mind in them. I am not primarily interested in Coleridge's affinities with modern existentialism; rather, I am interested in that feature of his work which reflects the sort of "sympathy for the abyss" seen in writings of all ages. This sense of the abyss appears in Coleridge's so-called mystery poems, in the darker passages of the *Notebooks*, and in works like "Limbo" and "Ne Plus Ultra"—which latter, as Frederick Burwick has argued convincingly, were written shortly before, not after, composition of the *Biographia*.

The circumstances of Coleridge's life during this period are well known: his consciousness of the wreck of his past, his heroic efforts to resist the tyranny of his addiction, his resolve to pull himself up by republishing earlier works and setting down his poetic principles—all testify to the magnitude not only of his achievement in writing the *Biographia* but also to the deep need for personal authentication which drove him. Autobiography in the *Biographia*, indeed, is at least as much a matter of *present* exigencies and needs as it is a matter of the past. All autobiography is apologia, to a large extent after the fact, but in Coleridge's case it was also a desperate attempt at reconstruction, at recovery from dejection; thus the biographical elements must not be discounted in the philosophic chapters, even though Coleridge himself referred to some of them as "digressions," for it is the mixture of autobiography and philosophy, or even the *tension* between them, not the philosophy as such, that gives these chapters their peculiar force. This tension, seen in Coleridge's structural motifs, images, and metaphors, supplies a vital subtext to his philosophy and portrays dramatically his struggle to fight his way back from the abyss, in theory.

Because of the elements involved, an overview of the development and subject matter of chapters 5 through 13 may help to set the scene, as it were. We now know that Coleridge wrote the philosophical chapters last—not counting the extra material he was forced to assemble when his publishers insisted on expanding the *Biographia* to two volumes—and that he did so hurriedly, if determinedly, working under a deadline. We know too that this section, as much of the *Biographia* as a whole, reflects Coleridge's relationship with Wordsworth and his desire to articulate his intellectual distinctness *from* Wordsworth by carefully delineating his own ideas respecting language, creativity, poetry, and the function of the poet (*BL* civ–xiv; Whalley *passim*; Christensen 121–37; Wallace 110–43). All of these in turn depend upon the nature of the imagination as an independent force in relation to the external world. This premise was implicit in much that Coleridge had already composed before he turned to the philosophical chapters, but he still felt impelled to explain his metaphysical position explicitly. Accordingly, and with at least half an eye on his future *Logosophia*, he penned a lead-in at the end of chapter 4, then composed a section nearly as long as all that he had already written and inserted it as chapters 5 through 13. In his lead-in, he indicates the importance of the added material by characterizing it as a series of considerations necessary to "an intelligible statement of my poetic creed . . . as deductions from established premises" (88).

Establishing premises begins as decidedly negative work. An elaborate effort of refutation and repudiation makes chapters 5 through 8 one of the most sustained discursive sequences in the book. In chapter 5, Coleridge traces associationism from Aristotle, insisting that whatever merit the concept has is psychological, not epistemological, and shifting credit and authority regarding it from modern to classical thinkers. In chapter 6, he draws heavily upon Johann Maas's critique of Hartley to argue that Hartley's concept of cause and effect in intellection is circular and implies either delirium or a greater mental chaos, wherein all thoughts are present at once (111–12). In chapter 7, he discusses "the necessary consequences of the Hartleian theory" and the "mistake" which led people to accept it. The "consequences" are in effect an obliteration of all sense of individual *agency* in human affairs; the "mistake" was that of confusing "the *conditions* of a thing with its *causes* and *essence;* and the process by which we arrive at the knowledge of a faculty, for the faculty itself" (123). In chapter 8, he widens the attack to dispose of Cartesian dualism and materialism in general as incapable of supplying a theory of perception (129). Translating from Kant and Schelling, and drawing heavily on the ideas of other philosophers, he denies the absolute separation of matter and spirit and the exclusive reign of either in the physical world. With associationism, dualism, and materialism behind him, Coleridge is now ready, it would seem, to move forward to the work of establishing his positive philosophic position.

Chapter 9, however, shifts back to autobiography; there Coleridge recounts the long course of studies which prepared his mind for the ideas of Kant, and he acknowledges his acquaintance with the work of Fichte and Schelling, anticipating charges of plagiarism. In chapter 10, he returns to his purpose by introducing his coinage, "esemplastic," and by reintroducing what he calls the "scholastic" distinction between subject and object; he also sets forth his conception of the distinction between the reason and the understanding—which he insists he had worked out fully before he met with Kant's critiques. But the rest of the chapter shades into an account of his periodical publishing ventures, his early political opinions, the reactionism in England which cast both Coleridge and Wordsworth under suspicion of complicity with France, and finally his retirement in disgust to a cottage in Somersetshire, where he devoted his "thoughts and studies to the foundations of religion and morals" (200). In chapter 11, he gives a short "affectionate exhortation" to young would-be authors not to make the same mistakes he did.

Only after a long interlude, then, does Coleridge return, in chapter 12, to his task of supplying a positive theory of perception and the deduction of the imagination—hedging it with "requests and premonitions," one of which is his plea that the reader either pass over his argument or read it "connectedly," with respect for its place "in the organic Whole" (234). He follows these with a distinction between the transcendent and the transcendental taken from Kant, a discussion of the intuitions of true philosophy and the true philosopher taken from Schelling and Jacobi, and an explanation of "The postulate of philosophy . . . KNOW THYSELF," leading into the ten theses on the nature of knowledge and the imagination—all appropriated from Schelling (252–84). Similarly, chapter 13 opens with a paragraph translated from Schelling and works with materials taken from Fichte and Schelling until it breaks off when Coleridge inserts the celebrated letter from a sage well-wisher advising deferral of further "demonstration."

There is irony in all this, of course: the very sequence which Coleridge insists must be read *connectedly* is the most heavily plagiarized in the book, and the whole argument is undercut and *dis*connected by his one wholly original act of composing in the philosophic chapters, a fictitious letter from an admiring correspondent who is actually himself. Yet, more telling patterns emerge. For one thing, the alternation between autobiography and philosophy suggests a parallel to the approach-avoidance syndrome that McFarland documented in Coleridge's attitude toward pantheism and German idealism. Coleridge is clearly repelled by materialism, but by turning in the other direction he is like Christabel, his hapless heroine who is unable to speak to any good effect. Or, like Geraldine, the other perhaps ego projection in his unfinished gothic tale, he seeks delay. And the delay he finds by recounting the development of his metaphysics and the tribulations in his life he hopes will give him strength. Both with regard to his personal life and the life of his mind he needs to establish that he has "come through." We see this most strikingly in the metaphors that he employs throughout the philosophic chapters.

Most obvious, and indeed almost off handed, is Coleridge's pervasive use of the language of structure—one is tempted to say, of construction and deconstruction. In his assault on associationist and materialist positions, for instance, he systematically charges them with insubstantiality. He faults Hobbes on his idea of contemporaneity as "the *basis* of all true psychology" because "Hobbes *builds* nothing on the principle . . ." (91–93; emphasis added). Likewise, in arguing that absence of conscious agency in the materialist psychology means that morality and intelligence are "reduced" to physical laws (119), he can conclude that "the process, by which Hume degraded the notion of cause and effect into a blind product of delusion and habit . . . must be repeated to the equal degradation of every *fundamental* idea in ethics or theology" (121). But this is all groundless, he concludes in chapter 8 regarding associationist imitation: "We might as rationally chant the Brahmin creed of the tortoise that supported the bear, that supported the elephant, that supported the world, to the tune of 'This is the house that Jack built'" (137–38). Throughout, Coleridge's efforts at refutation employ metaphors which undermine the materialist position as a construct, reinforcing his fundamentally ironic argument that the world of matter, and therefore any metaphysic deduced from matter, is without foundation.

Such "structural" language, it is true, is a familiar feature of all argument; it has long since reached the status of, virtually, "dead metaphor." However, when one employs a metaphoric commonplace so frequently as to call it back to conscious attention, one resurrects the metaphor, albeit grotesquely. Such becomes the case particularly when Coleridge turns to his alternative to associationist materialism. He begins chapter 9 with the question, "Is philosophy possible as a science, and what are its conditions?" (140). Recognizing that the premises of Lockean epistemology, if granted fully, would annihilate all of Kant's categorical forms and their correspondent logical functions "with crushing force," Coleridge offers an engagingly frank special pleading: "How can we make bricks without straw? Or build without cement?" (142). This confession of intellectual and psychological need suggests a more persuasive explanation for Coleridge's recourse to philosophic idealism than his (unacknowledged) use of Maas's assertion, at this point, that Locke's system was based on the logical fallacy of confusing origin with development. Avoidance of that logical fallacy did not necessitate idealism; that idealism *seemed* the only alternative may owe much to the characteristic figuration of structure in the style of the German idealists. Indeed, the language of construction may be as important a factor in Coleridge's attraction to German metaphysics as the concepts themselves. Certainly his English figuration suggests this. After acknowledging his need for straw and cement for his metaphysical bricks and philosophic structuring, he ventures a premise:

> The term, Philosophy, defines itself as an affectionate seeking after the truth; but Truth is the correlative of Being. This again is no way con-

ceivable, but by assuming as a postulate, that both are ab initio, identical and co-inherent; that intelligence and being are reciprocally each other's Substrate. (142–43)

As his editors inform us (143n), the *OED* cites Coleridge as the first to use "substrate" as a noun for "substratum." However, he may have been merely anglicizing the word from Kant and Schelling. So too with even his habit of referring to his transcendental metaphysics as "the *Constructive* philosophy": both Kant, and especially Schelling, exploit the idea of mental *Konstruktion* in their philosophies, drawing upon the analogy of mathematical construction.

Coleridge may have been attracted to philosophic idealism because of its metaphoric exploitation of "structure," then, and he adopted that strategy himself. It is perhaps quite significant, however, that his own prose consistently renders the language of structure more graphic and dramatic than that language appears in his comparatively dispassionate and rationalistic German sources. We see this particularly in the autobiographical dimension of his writing, for instance, when he recounts his philosophic studies with a veritable roll call of ancient, medieval, and renaissance forebears just after he has called for bricks and cement, and has suggested a metaphysical foundation in the reciprocal substrates of intelligence and being. His studies, he says, prepared him for the thought of Kant, whose writing, in "the solidity and importance of [its] distinctions," and "the adamantine chain of [its] logic" so impressed him that Kant's works "took possession of me as with a giant's hand" (153). Eager to extend Kant's philosophy to encompass religion, he was delighted to encounter Fichte, whose theory "completed" Kant's system: "Fichte's Wissenschafts-lehre, or *Lore* of Ultimate Science, was to add *the key-stone of the arch*" (157–58; emphasis added). Or, alternatively, in a letter to J. H. Green, "Fichte . . . has the merit of having prepared the ground for, and *laid the first stone* of, the *Dynamic* Philosophy by the substitution of Act for Thing" (*Letters* 4:792; quoted *Biographia* 1:158n; emphasis added). He burlesques Fichte because "this fundamental idea he *overbuilt* with *a heavy mass* of mere *notions*. . . . Thus his theory degenerated into a crude egoismus . . ." (158; emphasis added), but Coleridge is clearly enthusiastic regarding the "structural" function of Fichte's concept of an act by the self-conscious "I AM." In similarly dramatic fashion during his autobiographical account of the development of his opinions in religion, he explains, "I became convinced that religion, as both *the corner-stone* and *the key-stone* of morality [emphasis added], must have a *moral* origin," for he had come to realize the necessity of assuming God "as the *ground* of the universe" (202–03).

All of this intellectual autobiography, including its figuration, constructs a kind of mask which presents an image of Coleridge as a seeker who has shaped his own philosophy independently through assimilation of the ideas of many others, whose peer he is. Moreover, it prepares his readers to accept the appropriated ideas which will appear in chapters 12 and 13 as his own rightful property no matter who originated them. And the metaphoric emphasis on foundations and structures is also a subtle preparation for the mathematico-metaphysical "constructions"—including Archimedes' lever and all the rest—which he takes straight from Schelling in chapters 12 and 13. In this latter respect the autobiographical account of his philosophic development suggests conscious calculation, but there remains a sense of urgency and even anxiety in Coleridge's metaphors of structure that probably is *not* deliberate, and cannot be explained as mere stylistic reinforcement of thesis.

This point gains confirmation from a striking structural image in the fictitious letter Coleridge wrote as an excuse to break off his reasonings in chapter 13. In the guise of a well-intentioned friend accustomed to modern philosophy, he describes his own system as an eerie Gothic cathedral wherein modern philosophers are represented in statuary "perched in little fret-work niches, as grotesque dwarfs; while the grotesques [i.e., ancient esoteric philosophers] in my hitherto belief stood guarding the high altar with all the characters of Apotheosis. In short, what I had supposed substances were thinned away into shadows, while everywhere shadows were deepened into substances" (301). This, I suggest, is a telling image of Coleridge's philosophic intentions—as is his final characterization of what he has achieved, still speaking in the guise of the friend: "I see clearly that you have done too much, and yet not enough. You have been obliged to omit so many links, from the necessity of compression, that what remains, looks . . . like the fragments of the winding steps of an old ruined tower" (302–03). His conscious intention, obviously enough, is to effect an ironic critique of misdirected modern sensibility, but eeriness and fragmentation overshadow this intent, and the disorientation we feel associates with Coleridge himself. With this image in mind, I wish now to turn attention to another metaphoric strain in the style of the philosophic chapters, one which works as counterpoint to Coleridge's language of construction by opposing fluid horizontal motion to vertical structure.

Coleridge's "affectionate exhortation" to would-be authors in chapter 11 is one of the most directly personal, and also apparently one of the most digressive, sections in the philosophic chapters. Yet it contains a passage which suggests significant parallels between autobiography and philosophy. Speaking of any young person deferring an honorable calling such as the clergy because of doubts and "objections from conscience," he says,

> Happy will it be for such a man, if among his contemporaries elder than himself he should meet with one who with similar powers, and feelings as acute as his own, had entertained the same scruples; had acted upon them; and who by after-research . . . had discovered himself to have quarrelled with received opinions only to have embraced errors, to have *left the direction tracked out for him on the high road of honorable exertion, only to deviate into a labyrinth, where when he had wandered, till his head was giddy, his best good fortune was finally to have found his way out again,* too late for prudence though not too late for conscience or for truth! (230; emphasis added)

The metaphor of the wanderer and the labyrinth is familiar, of course, and Coleridge's implication that he is himself the "elder" person who has come through to serve as damaged premonitor is obvious enough. Given the context of this passage as part of a "digression" from a daunting metaphysical undertaking in his book, however, a question arises whether Coleridge actually is what he represents himself to be, that is, one who has "come through."

At the end of chapter 5, in which he showed that Hartley had departed from the received opinion of associationism as tracked out in a descriptive tradition reaching back to Aristotle, Coleridge promises to prove that Hartley "differed only to err." That done, he will himself explore a correct understanding of the origin and nature of our mental processes—in which task, he says, "I earnestly solicit the good wishes of my readers, while I thus go 'sounding on my dim and perilous way'" (105). The "sounding" (mis)quotation alludes to Wordsworth's dejected Solitary in *The Excursion*, published a year previously. That allusion may be taken as a casual reference, a complimentary acknowledgment of Wordsworth's achievement and a modest confession of the difficulties lying ahead in Coleridge's own book. But to offer Wordsworth's Solitary as analogue of oneself is hardly a positive sign. In *The Excursion*, the Solitary became a foil to Wordsworth's protagonist; whereas the latter had kept to the high road of honorable exertion, the Solitary had entered the labyrinth of Revolutionary utopianism and had reemerged a blasted exemplar of differing only to err. His "sounding on, a dim and perilous way" (*Excursion* 3:701) is his intellectual examination of his past life, attempting to find some meaning in it. Jerome Christensen comments on the relationship of this to Coleridge's current autobiographical account, suggesting that "the Solitary's reflections on his past illuminate the method of Coleridge's text," which is in effect an attempt to find a self by writing of self, and the result is not positive (118–85). Whether we regard Coleridge's project as one of finding a self or of finding and validating a philosophy, his references to himself as labyrinthine wanderer and as voyager through dim and perilous channels characterize his portrayal of his intellectual development in a metaphoric pattern which presents a striking conjunction with his "structural" language regarding philosophic concepts. Terrestrial or aquatic, his way is consistently uncertain, and the sense of disorientation, even alienation, amid constructs of doubtful substantiality overshadows any prospect of successful termination.

In recounting his early philosophic studies at the beginning of chapter 9, for instance, Coleridge asserts that Locke, Berkeley, Leibniz, and Hartley did not provide "an abiding place for my intellect"; moreover, he says, mere reflection without spiritual faith was unable "to afford my soul either food or shelter." During this period, his readings among the mystics had kept his mind "from being imprisoned within the outline of any dogmatic system," and "If [these readings] were too often a moving cloud of smoke to me by day, yet they were always a pillar of fire throughout the night, during my wanderings through the wilderness of doubt, and enabled me to skirt, without crossing, the sandy deserts of utter unbelief" (140–41; 152). And again, in describing his retirement to Somersetshire to study the foundations of religion and morals, he says, "I found myself all afloat. Doubts rushed in; broke upon me . . . and it was long ere my ark touched on an Ararat, and rested" (200). His ark "rested" in "The *idea* of the Supreme Being . . . as the *ground* of the universe" (200, 203), though at this time he "remained a zealous Unitarian" awaiting "A more thorough revolution in my philosophic principles" (204–05). In these two metaphors, each employing allusions to biblical wanderers—Moses in the wilderness, Noah adrift; one subject to shifting sands, the other to wayward currents—Coleridge expresses figuratively a psychic condition the depth and severity of which he was not prepared to acknowledge literally and publicly (his private record in the Notebooks is of course yet another, corroborative, matter).

Again and again in the *Biographia*, Coleridge portrays his metaphysical inquiry in terms of wandering and drifting, seeking an abiding place and probing for foundations in an uncertain universe. "Sounding," indeed, seems the compelling term. To proceed by means of "sounding" is to journey by water; one "sounds" to find the bottom in uncertain channels, to establish the *ground* relationship when one is floating. It is a tedious and doubtful activity, needless to say, not at all comparable to charting one's course by the stars and running before the wind; its attraction is the promise it offers of stability—not of sailing freely, but of coming ultimately to rest. Clichés and simplifications about poetry and philosophy might rush in here, but the famous lament in "Dejection: an Ode" is far behind. In the *Biographia* philosophy and the philosopher are more noble than mundane, for better or for worse. Both metaphorically and literally, indeed, they are called to momentous duties; they are charged with the task of bringing security and stability into an insecure and insubstantial world.

To explain this special calling and special province of the philosopher in chapter 12, Coleridge presents an elaborately extended metaphor drawn variously from Abraham Tucker, Schelling, and Jean Paul, portraying "the scanty vale of human life." Its nearest range of hills is the only horizon conceivable by the majority of the people, and even that region they understand imperfectly and superstitiously:

> But in all ages there have been a few, who measuring and *sounding* the rivers of the vale at the feet of their furthest inaccessible falls have learnt, that the sources must be higher and far inward; a few, who even in the level streams have detected elements, which neither the vale itself or the surrounding mountains contained or could supply. (239; emphasis added)

The "intuitive knowledge" of these few is ultimately mysterious—"The vision and faculty divine" not to be understood by mere mortals—and thus the portrayal of the philosopher here, and consistently throughout the *Biographia*, makes him or her a kind of heroic exception-figure who can master mysteries not penetrable by others. The description of the wizards of the vale of human life suggests, in fact, that the philosopher is particularly important because of his or her mastery of the external world. Coleridge's complaints about the endless flux of matter and the "streamy" nature of associationism are well known; his transcendental philosopher is one who conquers this lawlessness. As in his comparison of the mind thinking to a "small water-insect on the surface of rivulets [which] *wins* its way up against the stream" (124), Coleridge's philosopher, with his faculty of imagination, overcomes the flux. With intellectually constructive power he prepares a fortress in the desert and an island in the sea. He *wins* his way up, indeed, "for man *must* either rise or sink!" (242).

The opposition between material flux and mental construction remains an uneasy one for Coleridge, however. As he moves forward in chapter 12 armed with his premise of that elite faculty "the philosophic imagination, the sacred power of self-intuition" (241), he places himself under the necessity of demonstrating such power in his own reasonings. Adopting the concept of postulates in philosophy from Kant and Schelling, he undertakes to "deduce the memory with all the other functions of intelligence" (247) and to settle the question of the priority of the objective or of the subjective in favor of the latter. Then, turning to "the deduction of the imagination, and with it the principles of production and of genial criticism in the fine arts" (264), he sets down the notorious "Ten Theses" stolen from Schelling, Kant, and Jacobi. In the course of Thesis X, a significant "break" occurs in Coleridge's otherwise virtually whole-cloth paraphrasing and translating from Schelling—a break which dramatically exposes the art of his necessities. Returning to the question of priority between the objective and subjective despite having already dealt with that matter earlier, he insists that

> even when the Objective is assumed as the first, we yet can never pass beyond the principle of self-consciousness. Should we attempt it, *we must be driven back from ground to ground, each of which would cease to be a Ground the moment we pressed on it. We must be whirl'd down the gulph of an infinite series.* But this would make our reason baffle the end and purpose of all reason, namely, unity and system. Or we must break off the series arbitrarily, and affirm an absolute something that is in and of itself at once cause and effect, (causa sui) subject and object, or rather the absolute identity of both. (285; emphasis added)

The ideas here are from Schelling, with possible interlarding of Jacobi, but there is no metaphoric counterpart in the German original to the phrases I have emphasized (284–85n). The vivid image of the ground opening up beneath his feet, and the horrific whirling down the "gulph" of an endless regress, are apparently Coleridge's own. He has inserted them tellingly just before the logical/necessitated choice in his source: "or we must break off the series arbitrarily."

Coleridge finishes chapter 12 still pursuing his rationale of "self construction" (286) and promising to proceed to "the nature and genesis of the imagination" (293). In chapter 13 he attempts to promote the German transcendental concept of the generation of abstract power as the product of opposed and interpenetrating abstract forces. But two far more real forces persist in *destructive* opposition. Mental "construction" has been acknowledged as resting on nothing more than an arbitrary and willful choice made in the face of a sheer materiality so devoid of "unity and system" that Coleridge can see nothing there save the abyss of unmeaning. In this view, that fictive letter, with its tongue-in-cheek image describing his Constructive Philosophy both as a massive cathedral and as a ruined tower is ironic nostalgia indeed.

6

Coleridge, Habit, and the Politics of Vision

Richard Fadem

When in the *Biographia Literaria* Coleridge recalls his first encounter with Wordsworth's poetry, he cites the latter's power to rejuvenate his readers' vision: "above all [Wordsworth possesses] the original gift of spreading the tone, the atmosphere, and with it the depth and height of the ideal world around forms, incidents, and situations, of which, for the common view, custom had bedimmed all the lustre. . . ."[1] The revival of vision was, as we learn, an enterprise to which Coleridge himself quickly became dedicated, for the *Lyrical Ballads* as a whole were committed to exhibiting two sorts of poetry, each of which assailed habitual ways of seeing. Wordsworth's contributions revealed the "truth of nature" by dwelling on the ordinary; Coleridge's demanded more of "the modifying colours of the imagination" and dwelt on the supernatural. For both poets, custom is a distorting glaze that forms imperceptibly over the eye and subsequently the entire mind. Speaking specifically of Wordsworth's mission but including himself in its objective, Coleridge writes that Wordsworth intended to awaken "the mind's attention from the lethargy of custom" and "to penetrate the film of familiarity and selfish solicitude [owing to which] we have eyes, yet see not, ears that hear not, and hearts that neither feel nor understand" (2:6–7).[2]

Coleridge finds in the supernatural an effective lure for taking the reader back from the "dusty high road of custom" (2:121) to a pre-empirical vision that apprehends once more the full moral dimensions of our world. Liberated from "that despotism of the eye" (1:107)[3] which has anchored the mind to a deadly materialism, thought becomes comprehensive and steeped in noumena. Wordsworth dwells on the infranatural, evoking "the Presences of Nature" from the commonplace.[4] He presumes that we think as we see; Coleridge dwelt on the supernatural, and argued that we see only what we are capable of imagining. The suspension of disbelief tends toward belief.

As "The Rime of the Ancient Mariner" shows, those who see the world as unfamiliar experience a vital connection between themselves and what they perceive. Seeing under such circumstances becomes spiritualized. Speaking of Wordsworth, Coleridge writes in the *Biographia* that an un-habituated vision, moreover, restores one's personal past and finally the racial past; such vision is in the nature of it profoundly conservative. One is enabled to "contemplate the ANCIENT of days and all his works with feelings as fresh, as if all had then sprang forth at the first creative fiat" (1:80). To do so, one must "carry on the feelings of childhood into the powers of manhood . . . [and] combine the child's sense of wonder and novelty with the appearances, which every day for perhaps forty years had rendered familiar . . . this is the character and privilege of genius . . ." (1:80–81). Habit and custom, although they are reflexes whose origins are in the past, in fact extinguish the very past to which they pay such dark homage. They make us forget, whereas genius remembers.

Habit is the enemy of genius, the "prime merit" of which consists in one's being able "to represent familiar objects as to awaken in the minds of others a kindred feeling concerning them and that freshness of sensation which is the constant accompaniment of mental, no less bodily, convalescence." So described, genius is the marriage of childhood vision and feeling with mature intellectual powers: "I define GENIUS, as originality of intellectual construction: the moral accompaniment, and actuating principle of which consists, perhaps, in the carrying on of the freshness and feelings of childhood into manhood" (*Friend* [*CC*]1:419). And in Lecture Eight (1811) he summarizes the inverse relationship of vision and habit: "In the Poet was comprehended the man who carries the feelings of childhood into the powers of manhood: who with a soul unsubdued, unshackled by custom can contemplate all things with the freshness and wonder of a child. . . . and where knowledge no longer permits admiration gladly sinks back again into the childlike feeling of devout wonder." It is in this vein that "Dejection: An Ode" recounts his lost birthright. "My shaping spirit of Imagination" has become intermittent, until finally the temper of mind required for "abstruse research" is, he puns, "almost grown the habit of my soul."

"Habit" here has a pejorative religious connotation, just as unhabituated vision is for Coleridge a source of naked spiritual power. Yet we may also think of habit and custom (I shall use them interchangeably, as Coleridge does) as political, as indicating a politics of the eye and of the epistemology upon which they are grounded. Church and state are in vision as in much else for Coleridge inseparable. From one perspective, we might suppose his attack on habit and custom to be that of a radical, and in some senses it is. But we must also take into account the objects of this attack, empiricism and materialism, to grasp Coleridge's aversion to the latent politics of the mechanical philosophy and its epistemology. As I shall argue, Coleridge is responding in part against the democratizing, levelling, massing drift of Locke's epistemology. I shall go on to suggest that Coleridge's thought on the matter of vision and habit constitutes an equinoxial point between the metaphysics of Locke and the aesthetics of Pater and others. Coleridge's deep aversion to Locke's optics and episte-mology—based in part on their political implications—prompts him, and one might include Wordsworth, to respond with a theory of vision and habit whose conservative political implications become fully apparent only later in the nineteenth century.

The "plan" of the *Lyrical Ballads* promised a moral and political revo-lution which of course had secondary aesthetic ramifications. When Cole-ridge recalls in the *Biographia* that the attack on custom was a chief priority on the *Lyrical Ballads'* agenda, we cannot but associate this intent with the radical political rejuvenation to which Wordsworth and Coleridge were also at that time committed. The shattering of habits of the eye was an op-tical revolution with political force, for to see differently was to think dif-ferently about nature and one's fellow man. Conversely, there was implicit in one's optics a politics. The optical revolution that Coleridge and Words-worth sought to effect had a rather more distant enemy. Coleridge in the 1790s had to be sympathetic to *The Second Treatise on Civil Government*, but he could never accommodate himself to *The Essay on Human Understand-ing*. Locke the empiricist was the unnamed adversary of, say, "The Rime of the Ancient Mariner," and it is Locke who haunts the discussion, spread over many chapters of the *Biographia*, of materialism.

Coleridge's references to vision and habit in chapter 4 of the *Biographia* are strategic, anticipating as they do the crucial discussion of association-ism. There are, he maintains in chapter 4, two ways of seeing, one me-chanical and involuntary, one volitional and creative; there are also two faculties which embody these ways of seeing, the fancy and the imagination, one decidedly mechanical, the other organic and esemplastic. Habit is the extension into the moral realm of the mechanical and involuntary. The discussion in chapter 4 of the optical program of the *Lyrical Ballads* leads inexorably to epistemology, a road particularly well travelled by the eighteenth century. It is in this direction precisely that Coleridge is about to conduct us. Preparing us for the philosophical *tour de force* upon which chapters 5 through 9 are about to conduct us, he remarks archly, "It has already been hinted, that metaphysics and psychology have long been my hobby-horse" (85). The point of origin of this journey is the "mechanic philosophy," embodied in Locke and, so far as Coleridge was once concerned, most alluringly presented in Hartley's associationism. For both Locke and Hartley habit is essential, the mainspring which governs physiology, psychology, and epistemology. Focusing on Hartley as now the best coign of vantage for attacking modern materialism, Coleridge assails Hartley's suggestion that our nerves experience a "disposition" to certain vibrations which would be no less absurd than saying "a weather-cock had acquired a *habit* of turning to the east, from the wind having been so long in that quarter . . ." (1:109). So far as Coleridge is concerned the supreme peril in materialism resides in its elevation of habit at the expense of the will ("the infinite spirit . . . an intelligent and holy will"[1:120]), with the expectation that habit will slowly dominate. Habit, like some gangrene, feeds off and destroys living tissue, subtly extinguishing the will. And since the very processes of habit are anesthetizing, we are not even aware of the amputation.[5]

The danger Coleridge finds in virtually all accounts of association is that they "derive association from the connection and interdependence of the supposed matter, the movements of which constitute our thoughts . . ." (1:96). Our thoughts are degraded, leaving them the result of merely mechanical operations. Among the models he lists are billiard balls, nervous or animal spirits that in turn "etch and re-etch engravings on the brain," an oscillating ether passing through the hollow tubes of the nerves, or "chemical compositions by elective affinity, or "an electric light at once the immediate object and the ultimate organ of inward vision" (1:101). Coleridge is prepared to grant that there is some sort of associative power, from which such limited functions of the mind as memory and fancy derive their operations, but he abjures Hartley when it comes to accounting for *all* the mind's faculties by association. The unmitigated evil of associationism is that "the will, the reason, the judgment, and the understanding, instead of being the determining causes of association, must needs be represented as its *creatures*, and among its mechanical *effects*" (1:110). Will would become merely a matter of chance, the accumulation of sufficient mechanical forces at any given moment to overcome our inertia and passivity.

As Professor McFarland has pointed out, Coleridge reserved a special contempt for Locke, even managing to anathematize the teacher while remaining devoted for some time to the disciple, Hartley.[6] After he abandons Hartley, Coleridge has an even clearer conscience for detesting Locke. Not only was Locke the chief exponent of materialism, but he had elevated habit to a position of supreme importance. He maintained that habits of cognition and of conduct prevent experience from atomizing. Instead, they compel the coagulation of experience into ever larger units and generalities. Habit comprises for him the single most dependable integument of daily life. Indeed, experience and habit are for Locke nearly synonymous, habit being the codification of experience, the now involuntary, unconscious logic whose trammels operate and direct the mind.

Coleridge insists that vision and habit are inversely proportional, and therefore he can present the child as the avatar of genius. To Locke maturity and experience alone remedy the inherent stigmatisms of innocent vision. Locke's whole epistemology, and particularly his insistence that correct vision depends upon habit, is dramatically rendered by the famous conundrum known as Molyneux's Question which Locke introduces into the *Essay*. To Ernst Cassirer, Molyneux's Question distills instantly a tangle of Enlightenment metaphysical issues to a single matrix: "A survey," he writes, "of the special problems of eighteenth century epistemology and psychology shows that in all their variety and inner diversity they are grouped around a common center. The investigation of individual problems in all their abundance and apparent dispersion comes back again and again to a general theoretical problem in which all the threads of the study unite."[7] The "center" to which Cassirer alludes is this: "'Suppose a man *born* blind, and now adult, and taught by his *touch* to distinguish between a cube and a sphere of the same metal, and nighly of the same bigness, so as to tell, when he felt one and the other, which is the cube, which the sphere. Suppose the cube and sphere placed on a table, and the blind be made to see: *quaere*, whether *by his sight, before he touched them*, he could now distinguish and tell which is the globe, which the cube?'"[8] Agreeing with Molyneux's own speculations, Locke claims the blind man could not distinguish them by name. Locke's "no" to Molyneux's question is based first on the idea that there is no ur-idea common to all the senses which would permit us to transfer knowledge gained from one to another, and, second, upon his conviction that only extensive experience enables us to have a correct grasp of reality: "For, though he [the newly sighted person] has obtained the experience of how a globe, how a cube affects his touch, yet he has not yet obtained the experience, that what affects his touch so or so, must affect his sight so or so" (1:187).[9] A number of experiments upon the blind and newly sighted verifies Locke's position, which is that we require "experience" and "custom" to make sense of reality.[10] Locke concludes his analysis of Molyneux's question with a moral: "This [the question and answer] I have set down, and leave with my reader, as an occasion for him to consider how much he may be beholden to experience, improvement, and acquired notions" (1:186). His editor reaffirms the link between optics and habit: "The acquired perceptions of sight afford unique illustrations of the large part which habit and suggestion play in the early stages of our intellectual development" (1:187).

From this point habit enters crucially into Enlightenment metaphysics. Berkeley makes Molyneux's Question an issue in *The New Theory of Vision*, seizing especially upon Locke's reliance upon habit. Although he assents to Locke's answer, Berkeley vigorously disputes Locke's reasoning. To Berkeley, visual ideas are categorically different from tactual ideas. He maintains we have no single, common idea of shape or size but a brace of ideas that so entwine themselves as to give the illusion—really the delusion —of a unified sensation.[11] In reality, the five senses provide five discrete landscapes. Only because we have become habituated to a certain short-hand in language are we able to believe that sight and touch converge. Our delusion is perpetuated by grossly distorting habits of our language.[12]

To Locke habits of sight, thought, and language bond our primary to our secondary ideas. On a most rudimentary level we would not, were we not habituated, be able to recognize immediately a tree or a steam engine, nor would we be able to read and do computations with any facility. In effect habit makes reality immediately intelligible. Locke views our susceptibility to habit as promising the happy triumph of nurture over nature, for "Custom possesses greater power than nature." Montaigne had enunciated a similar point in "Of Experience": "It is for habit to give form to life, just as it pleases; it is all-powerful in that. . . ."[13] And Bacon pursues the same line: "Custom is the principal magistrate of man's life." We need only recall that in the Ode custom, along with consciousness, is the warden of the prison-house. But for Wordsworth's predecessors the hope is that, politically, custom will replace anarchy; and that, intellectually, the predictable will extinguish the vertiginous uncertainty occasioned by the constant presence of jostling particulars.

The habituated eye, Locke argues, commands power because it perceives fewer individuations. It consolidates and synthesizes, eliminating the particular in favor of the whole. Children are in effect newly sighted, baffled refugees from the land of the blind not, as Wordsworth insists, eyes among the blind. Locke maintains that

> when we set before our eyes a round globe of uniform colour . . . it is certain that the idea thereby imprinted on our mind is of a flat circle, variously shadowed. But we having, by use, been accustomed to perceive what kind of appearance convex bodies are wont to make in us . . . the judgement presently, by an habitual custom, alters the appearances into their causes . . . (1:186)

Habits of eye and mind are critical to sophisticated cognitive processes, enabling us to translate instantly the black scratches on the page first as letters, then words, then concepts; moreover, custom enables us to respond unconsciously to laws without having to rehearse their premises and test their justice on each occasion. Habit immunizes us against the particular and local. The very opposite of Coleridge, Locke explains that children can only see; they cannot read the visible world. In short, familiarity breeds comprehension.

Locke's dependence on custom turns out to be problematic and, finally, the vulnerable spot in the armed vision. It is precisely on the matter of custom that Hume and Berkeley assail Locke—the one to demonstrate a radical skepticism, the other to close the door in Locke to just such an outcome. In this context we readily discover in Berkeley's response to Locke much of what drew Coleridge to Berkeley after Hartley. Locke's elevation of habit forebodes an attack upon the will, not to mention upon the Romantic axis of child and genius as apostles of the unfamiliar and the particular. Countering Locke, Berkeley argues that we persistently, unconsciously confuse or "embrangle" objects of sight with objects of touch and hearing, a confusion insidiously facilitated by our use of language, which masses together the discrete particularity of everyday life. Habit encourages us to misread reality; habit levels, reducing the etched particular to a lumpish consolidation. The singular and diverse are subsumed in the mass, the class. Hume proceeds a step further, arguing that habit has so insinuated itself into thought as to become an alias for reason. When Hume completes his autopsy of reason, we learn that what Locke calls reason is nothing but habit gussied up in humanist finery: "all our reasonings concerning causes and effects," Hume declares, "are deriv'd from nothing but custom." [14]

Berkeley finds the force of "an habitual connection" of sounds, sights, and words fused into an apparently seamless whole by language to make us stupid before reality. He intends *The New Theory of Vision* to restore to us the proto-language that is omnipresent but which, owing to habit, we cannot read. His purpose is thus repeated in the experimental task of the *Lyrical Ballads*. Returned to a prehabitual, even preassociative state, the eye can perceive with impeccable precision nature broken down into all its particulars. Vision would *mean* for us; we would understand of the tell-tale scratches of a divine cryptogram, which Berkeley describes as the "universal language of the Author of nature," traces of which are yet to be perceived by the unhabituated eye in the palimpsest before it.

The political bias of Locke's epistemology emerges most clearly in his advocacy of the Scientific Method. Locke submits truth to a democratic consensus, not, certainly, to the dubious aristocracy of visionaries who adduce occult qualities or who focus on particulars to the exclusion of generalities. The conclusions the Method reaches are, writes Sir Isaiah Berlin, "true universally, eternally, and immutably; true for all times, and places, and men." [15] Put to the vote, all rational, educated minds must necessarily agree to the Method's conclusions. Presuming such a vote, there would be, Locke submits, "universal assent," a "universal consensus" for his argument against innate ideas. ("Universal" for Locke means the mature, rational, educated, and cultivated; he would exclude children, idiots, and the senile.) Implicit in *The Essay on Human Understanding* is *The Second Treatise on Civil Government*. The Scientific Method describes not only a process of inquiry but the very epistemology inherent to all rational minds. Truth is the residue of repeated siftings and consists of the largest remaining elements and the lowest common denominator.[16]

By contrast, Hume maintains there can be for our mental eye no abstract, universal cat, only Simkin in his furry particularity. It is another instance in which Hume is closer to Coleridge than to Locke. "When," writes Hume, "we have found a resemblance among several objects . . . , we apply the same name to all of them. . . . After we have acquired a custom of this kind, the hearing of that name revives the idea of one . . . and makes the imagination conceive it with all its particular circumstances. . . ." [17] Custom (he anticipates Coleridge) is a filter or film that screens out substantiality, habit an uneventful white sound obliterating the staccato of particulars that once surrounded us. Yet no more than with Hartley can Coleridge console himself with Hume, however useful Hume might be in demolishing Locke. Hume, while degrading "the notion of cause and effect into a blind product of delusion and habit," leaves delusion and habit to reign freely over the merely spectral "now" of an intelligent will.

It is no coincidence that soon after completing the *Biographia*, which assails habit in any of its metaphysical and psychological forms and seeks at every opportunity to vindicate the will and align the self with it, that Coleridge decides to add a motto to *The Rime of the Ancient Mariner*. His choice reflects his concern, voiced particularly in chapters 4 through 9, that we must oppose our enslavement to habits and above all to habits imposed by a constricting, deadening empiricism. Thomas Burnet, whom Coleridge quotes for the motto, importunes his readers to advance beyond an acclimated vision of nature to one that is supernatural or finally sacramental. Burnet was a contemporary of Newton and Locke and an implacable opponent of materialism and the mechanical philosophy. He is hostile to those who glory in the putative perfection of nature, only to slide complacently into deism. Burnet finds it abhorrent that anyone could find nature, as it is, perfect, for what, then, does that say about the genuine perfection of the prelapsarian world. For one, it says they have failed to imagine perfection; they have taken the limits of their own minds as the totality. Having so successfully acclimated themselves to nature, which in reality is "a great ruin, . . . a World lying in its rubbish," they end by exalting what Burnet himself has a visceral contempt for. He admonishes us not to surrender to the apparent blandishments around us, which, like present time and space, are calculated to shrink the circumference of vision and swiftly accustom us to the lowest common denominator of the visible: ". . . Souls that are made little and incapacious cannot enlarge their thoughts to take in any great compass of Times or Things; so what is beyond their compass, or above their reach, they are apt to look upon as Fantastical. . . . Who would set a purblind man at the top of the Mast to discover Land? or upon an high Tower to draw a Landscip of the Country round about?" [18] Surrendering to such democracy of vision, we dismiss the visionary, and with him the apparitions of the supernatural, as a mere idiosyncracy.

Burnet stands in relation to Newton as the elder Gosse, the author of *Omphalos*, does to Darwin. A counterrevolutionary, Burnet resists a battery of scientific evidence to argue that the universe is geocentric and to offer instead an anti-Newtonian, theological theory of rainbows—that there were none before the Deluge. What Newton and Locke stigmatize as "occult qualities" that infiltrate unguarded minds are for Burnet indispensable elements in our understanding of nature's fallen state and hence its vestigial prelapsarian glory.

The motto of "The Rime" points to custom as the servant of a dreary empiricism: "I do not doubt, however," writes Burnet, "that it is sometimes good to contemplate in the mind, as in a picture, the image of a greater and better world; otherwise, the intellect, habituated to the petty things of daily life, may too much contract itself, and wholly sink down to trivial thoughts."[19] Coleridge enlists Burnet to support his own theological beliefs as well as to prepare the reader to exit the cramped landscape dictated by habitual ways of seeing. Ugliness and horror may be the emblems of the fallen world, but habit and the resultant trivializing of the potentially divine are the symptoms of postlapsarian vision, which, regrettably, tends not to discover those traces of a gorgeous beauty among ruin.

"The Rime" provides us with the most dramatic, vivid instance of Coleridgean vision and its antagonist, habit, as they are outlined in the *Biographia*. The poem stands in relation to major elements of Romanticism as Molyneux's Question does in Cassirer's estimate to Enlightenment metaphysics. The Mariner has escaped habitual vision; he has come finally to see, as it were, the *Ancient* of days, apprehending an image of the world in its near nascent splendor and supernatural power. Like Wordsworth's Leech-gatherer, the Mariner's eyes have an uncanny glow that is exaggerated by his body's ghastliness. Both have in a sense dismissed the body and the substantial world; both are associated now, to their perpetual ennoblement, with the lowest of creatures, watersnakes and leeches, things whose primordial marine existence links them above all with the prelapsarian. The brightness of the Mariner's eyes is a gift of the visionary episode which had transfixed them, the moment in which he saw that "every track / Was a flash of golden fire." The Mariner's eyes have caught this light, the repetitions of "glittering eye" and "bright-eyed Mariner" (ll. 20,40,619, and elsewhere) attesting to the capacity of what one sees to irradiate permanently the seer: "This heart within me burns" (l. 585).

As a "rhyme" the poem tells the story of the Mariner's vision, im-

paired by habit, and the restoration of his sight; but as hoar-frost the rime
of the Mariner is precisely that film, that glaze, which freezes over and
deadens the visible world. Rime and rhyme are polarized, one representing the numbing, indeterminate region (a seascape of frost and mist, of
"dismal sheen" and "fog-smoke white" tepidly illuminated by the moon)
that fosters habit and freezes the will, the other the tale or poem itself,
the supreme instance of "an infinite spirit, an intelligent and holy will."[20]
The oxymoronic Mariner—"whose eye is bright, / Whose beard with age
is hoar" (l. 619)—embodies both uses of rime and is himself the incarnation of polarities that, until he blessed the watersnakes, were perceived by
him as opposites rather than as complementary elements of the whole.[21]
The poem recounts a ballet of the antipodean elements—heat and cold,
the worlds below and above the line, and the sun and moon. But at the
critical moment when he is moved to bless the watersnakes, moon and sun
are juxtaposed in an image of a potentially unified vision:

> Her [the moon's] beams bemocked the sultry main,
> Like April hoar-frost spread;
> But where the ship's huge shadow lay,
> The charmed water burnt away
> A still and awful red.
>
> (267–71)

When the Mariner embarked on his voyage the sun itself "shone bright."
But in the polar regions the visible world is deadened, the cold, eery light,
and rimey glaze acting on the eye as an anesthetic: "through the drifts
the snowy clifts / Did send a dismal sheen . . . The ice was all between"
(ll. 55–8); the dreadful groans of the ice reach the Mariner buffered and
hollowed, "Like noises in a swound" (l. 62). The moon finds a dismal complement in the whitened air, which further attenuates the insubstantial
lunar tint: "Whiles all the night, through fog-smoke white, / Glimmered
the white Moon-shine" (ll. 77–8). He shoots the bird under conditions that
give the appearance of an emptied, ghostly seascape, the act as much one
of aggression against the ambiguities of an indeterminate reality as one
of gratuitous violence. For the moment he seems to have elicited meaning. The "good south wind" blew behind, but the mist lingers in which
the sun is "hid." When, at last, the equatorial sun burns off the mist, the
Mariners experience only a new, more terrible occlusion separate them
from nature: they, now, are disembodied, insubstantial, "a painted ship /

Upon a painted ocean" (ll. 117–18). Becalmed, they suffer from heat, thirst, and *tedium vitae*, their stupefaction an apt emblem of the vapidity which made them indifferent to the visible world and their subsequent morality, a scientific morality based as it was exclusively upon cause and effect. The rime that earlier coated the seascape finds its counterpart in the film that now deadens their vision: "glazed . . . How glazed each weary eye." The punishment fits the crime. Yet it is a crime of which Coleridge believes the readers of the *Lyrical Ballads* to be culpable, for Wordsworth and he intended to dissolve the film of familiarity glazing the readers' eyes, thus restoring vision to the morally and aesthetically dead, "those who have eyes yet see not."

At this critical moment in the Mariner's journey, just about the structural midpoint of the poem, he is afforded a "a sign in the element afar off" (Gloss). The "sign" is initially pedestrian and inauspicious, at first merely a something in the sky, a speck, then a mist. At last a shape emerges, and this in turn then resolves itself into a sail. The sign's real significance resides in the process by which the Mariner sees it, not in its being an actual ship. His seeing it in the way he does initiates and bears formatively upon his ultimate recovery by enabling him now to pass from the blurred and indeterminate generalizing vision to the meticulous apprehension of the particular. The visual course he takes from a "something" to a sail is the converse of Lockean perception, which insists we erode and recompose particulars into some general thing. In seeing the "sign" as he does, the Mariner grasps an elementary truth about all nature, the irreversible quiddity of particulars and yet, despite this, the kinship among categorically different things:

> I beheld
> A something in the sky.
> At first it seemed a little speck,
> And then it seemed a mist;
> It moved and moved, and took at last
> A certain shape, I wist.
> A speck, a mist, a shape, I wist!

(147–53)

The evolution of the ship from scarcely a mote to a shape climaxes with the Mariner's slaking his thirst upon his own blood and crying out, "A sail! A sail!" The effect of the metonymy here and of the gathering force of

his swiftly particularizing perceptions (from speck to mist to shape) leading toward that most particular and particularly meaningful of things—
a sail—describes a way of seeing that concludes with and extols the individuated. The passage from speck to mist, shape, and sail initiates the
rebirth of the Mariner's vision. In making sense of the speck, and in his
capacity to get to "ship" and then back to "sail," he begins the reconstruc-
tive process essential to his moral life, a way of seeing that simultaneously
discerns the irreducibly individuated while being capable of recognizing
the fundamentally analogic nature of things. The Mariner here affirms
"the great law of the imagination . . . that a likeness in part tends to become a likeness in the whole."[21] The metonymical way of seeing is, like all
fundamentally imaginative acts, moral. In addition to being its own sort
of particular, the ship is a cluster of discrete parts forged into another
identity, "A certain shape, I wist." Compelled to step through the stages
by which it reaches a notion of a whole thing, to see a thing de-composed,
the mind receives dramatic proof of the inherent likenesses that complete
themselves through the mind's composition of a final unity. Like those
pictures that, when turned in relation to the angle of light upon them,
reveal an entirely different scene, the ship teeters wonderfully between
whole and part; and indeed the Mariner's assurance of its wholeness is
sufficiently certain to permit him to begin to reverse the process when he
cries out "A sail!" His next utterance—"See! See!"—is as much a command
to his shipmates as a jubilant affirmation of restored vision.

There is a connection between the Mariner's sense of a rudimentary
similitude (that suggested also in the well-known Coleridgean distinction
between an imitation and a copy) among apparently disparate things and
the rhyme's visual and auditory presence to us the readers. Coleridge, I
have suggested, means to compare us with the benighted Mariner and
crew. We, too, must learn to see and read, though for us it is the "Rime."
Certainly we must grasp the "moral" of the tale, though Coleridge was
properly impatient with its obtrusiveness and Mrs. Barbauld's density. The
moral lures us away from perceiving and knowing to knowledge, from
gerund to noun; the moral is like saying "ship" instead of seeing it as the
Mariner does or disembrangling the thing and finally the word as Berkeley urges us to do. Coleridge demands we read in that vein, the act being
not only preliminary but ultimately primary to all cognition, intellection,
and knowledge.

He employs the poetry itself of the "Rime" to reeducate the reader with respect to language itself and its alignment with the goings-on of the poem: the profusion of rhymes—internal rhymes, slant rhymes, and sight rhymes, as well as puns such as that in "rime" itself—require of us as readers a recognition of rudimentary analogues, for rhyme itself reinforces the notion of dissimilarity in unity. The likeness between us and the Mariner, and between what he sees and what we read, is born out in the proliferating analogues and look-alikes throughout the poem. If the Mariner dimly perceives kinship through the evolution from speck to sail, and is moved to bless the water snakes as a result, we experience the essential fraternity of things through the poem's various pairings. In "On Poesy or Art," consisting of notes made in 1818, Coleridge mounts a complex argument for the supremacy of poetry—of language—over painting and music: that art will be supreme which has the power of "humanizing nature," which is what language accomplishes, for it is "a translation of man into nature. . . ."[22] Painting excludes the mind and hence the latent analogies between nature and man, while "Music . . . has the fewest analoga in nature," manifesting a superfluity of mind.[23] Sight is for each of us a rudimentary instance of the wedding of mind and nature, but it is finally poetry (meaning language) that best exemplifies all art's capacity to be "a middle quality between a thought and a thing, . . . the union and reconciliation of that which is nature with that which is exclusively human."[24] The various sorts of doubling in "The Rime" force upon the reader an awareness of the deeper analogues, those which insure the presence of "unity in multeity."

Just how closely related the reader's visual education is to the Mariner's becomes apparent through a remarkable succession of linked metaphors that follow shortly upon the Mariner's crying, "See! See!" The setting sun, we are told, is laced by the spars and ribs of the ghost ship and appears to be a face through a dungeon grate. The associations ramify to a comparison of the Mariner's bony body with the "ribbed sea-sand," the ridges left by the receding water. The metaphors carry into the reader's field of view essentially unlike things. Coleridge's capacity to identify the elemental similarities that make possible such a metamorphosis, and our capacity to recognize this variation of speck, mist, shape, ship, and sail, attest to the imagination's capacity to discern (in a sense to give) unity to a cascade of particulars. The images here resemble that unfolding that Wordsworth in the 1815 Preface singles out with respect to the Leech gatherer, who is first perceived as a stone, then a cloud, and finally as a primordial sea beast. Wordsworth writes that this visual evolution demonstrates a function of the imagination, "the conferring, the abstracting, and the modifying powers of the Imagination. . . ."[25] Now, when the Mariner laments that he feels "Alone, alone, all, all alone, / Alone on a wide sea!" and that "the sea and the sky / Lay like a load on my weary eye" (ll. 232–3; 251), we sense that his aloneness and the dispiriting emptiness of his vision are occasioned not by his own vacuity but his need to perceive and affirm relationship in the visible world. In this case, a stunning series of highly individuated images, associated in a manner that seems anything but mechanical, predictable, and hence habitual, lead us to the almost palpable conviction of that associativeness of things which makes metaphor morally true as well as aesthetically pleasing.

As he stares at the movement of the water snakes, "the elfish light, / Fell off in hoary flakes." It is of course *his* image, that of the light's falling off in hoary flakes. His eyes, linked in their restored state often enough with the bright, hot sun, seem to penetrate the rime-like covering that cloaks the slimy things. He sees now "their rich attire: / Blue, glossy green, and velvet black, / They coiled and swam; and every track / Was like a flash of golden fire." He suddenly loses his own dryness. An arterial "spring of love" is pumped from his heart, disinterested and generous and the very converse of his earlier drinking his own blood. With his blessing of the snakes, the albatross, like the rime peeling off the water snakes, also "fell off." His vision is so altered that upon returning home the Mariner must ask, in what is perhaps the most poignant line of the poem, "Is this mine own countree?" But of course he has no country any longer, only transient auditors, such as the wedding guest who listens like a three-years' child, whom the Mariner stuns into "the child's sense of wonder and novelty."

The notion that "the actuating principle of genius" derives from childhood vision, along with the attack upon habit, will have a great impact on later English writers, particularly Ruskin, Dickens, Arnold, and Pater, and upon the Pre-Raphaelite Brotherhood. In *The Seven Lamps of Architecture* Ruskin, employing the imagery and desultory rhythms of Arnold's "The Buried Life" (which is in turn a self-consciously grim re-vision of "Tintern Abbey") maintains that each of us has a true and a false life. In that polarity so favored by the Romantics, Ruskin (bringing together in an extraordinary way much of what I have been saying about will, individuality, and habit) equates our true life with the organic, our false with the mechanical and habitual, the "hoary":

His true life is like that of lower organic beings, the independent force by which he moulds and governs external things. . . . His false life is, indeed, but one of the conditions of death or stupor, but acts, even when it cannot be said to animate, and is not always easily known from the true. It is that life of custom and accident in which many of us pass our time . . . ; that life in which we do what we have not purposed, and speak what we do not mean, and assent to what we do not understand; that life which is overlaid by the weight of things external to it, and is moulded by them instead of assimilating them; that, which instead of growing and blossoming under any wholesome dew, is crystallised over with it, as with hoar frost, and becomes to the true life what an arborescence is to a tree, a candied agglomeration of thoughts and habits foreign to it.[26]

Living the true life, each of us becomes an "independent force," an aristocratic will that transcends the mechanical, the ordinary, the agglomeration.

Coleridge, Ruskin, Arnold, Pater: it is perhaps no coincidence that the most embittered attacks upon habit spring from an essentially Tory mentality—to be precise, a Tory optics, a Tory epistemology—which in addition to detesting the mechanical philosophy, profoundly resents Locke's levelling of the particular, his democratization of experience, his impetus to garner an ever larger consensus on an ever more agglomerated reality. It is not simply the mechanico-utilitarian outlook the Tory critics find offensive; but seen as a politics of perception, it bleeds out the particular and individual, substituting for it the mass of nature, the mob of sensation. In Coleridgean terms, such unity comes at the expense of multeity, and the divergent is swallowed up in the maw of a hollow consensus. No more than Locke, Coleridge's metaphysics are never far from his politics. But Coleridge's are also inseparable from his theology. He is imbued with Burnet's notion that the levelling of vision by personal habit as well as social custom will extinguish the supernatural and holy.

Nietzsche, who contributes a Continental voice to this chorus, singles out the Lockean tradition's dependence on habit at the expense of the organic, idiosyncratic, and aristocratic: "One finds them [the English psychologists] . . . looking for the effective motive forces of human development in the very last phase we would wish to have them found, e.g. in the inertia of habit, in forgetfulness, in the blind and fortuitous association of ideas: always in something that is purely passive, automatic, reflexive, molecular, and, moreover, profoundly stupid."[27] The passage points to

Locke's *Essay* but looks with equal disdain at the *Second Treatise on Civil Government* to indict the somnambulent will-lessness, the automatic and reflexive submission that has settled upon us as both individuals and citizens, the inexorable fulfillment of the democratizing of vision.

Pater carries the absorption in the particular to an exquisite extreme, declaring himself entirely immune to any contamination from the mass. Each "single sharp impression" must be isolated and savored apart from the mass. Pater encourages us to approximate "the impression of the individual in his isolation, each mind keeping as solitary prisoner its own dream of the world." Wordsworth's prison-house of consciousness has now become the hermitic palace of art. Pater so upends the romantic mind that he finds habit acceptable, if, that is, it is the habit of aristocratic vision. In order to burn always with a hard gemlike flame, Pater recommends we habituate ourselves exclusively to the isolated and particular. He writes with a keen awareness of the paradox: "In a sense it might even be said that our failure in life is to form habits: for, after all, habit is relative to a stereotyped world, and meantime it is only the roughness of the eye that makes any two persons, things, situations, seem alike."[28] Habit now becomes a form of hermiticism, not a prison but a monastic cell. Pater's essay on Coleridge, which is maddeningly unsatisfactory in among other things its depiction of Coleridge as an acolyte to a frigid, ossified "absolutism," asks us to forgive Coleridge, reminding us to judge him by our own more pliant relativist standards. But in describing the sort of vision that we should exercise upon Coleridge so as to illuminate his virtues and excuse his faults, Pater in fact helps us to grasp all the more keenly just what Coleridge bequeathed Pater himself and what Coleridge so passionately and effectively insisted upon in the face of the Lockean tradition:

> the dominant tendency of life is to turn ascertained truth into a dead letter, to make us all the phlegmatic servants of routine. The relative spirit, by its constant dwelling on the more fugitive conditions or circumstances of things, break[s] through a thousand rough and brutal classifications . . . [and] begets an intellectual finesse. . . .[29]

Whether or not we can find Pater's use of "absolutist" and "relativist" at all helpful, the fact remains that it was above all Coleridge, advancing a Tory vision and epistemology, who detected the Locke tradition's impetus to make us the phlegmatic servants of habit.

7

Coleridge and Energy

Stuart Peterfreund

Coleridge had a lifelong fascination with the concept of energy and the implications of that concept. In 1794, the year in which he composed *Religious Musings*, Coleridge celebrated a God who is "Nature's essence, mind, and energy!"[1] The antithesis of Newton's Lord God Pantocrator, who is the source of "action at a distance," Coleridge's God is an indwelling divine presence. Energy (as its etymology from *en-ergeia* suggests) means either the potential to accomplish *work* or the actual work itself, latent or actualized *within* the object, rather than impinging upon the object from without, as does Newtonian "action at a distance." For Coleridge in 1794, energy was an indwelling principle responsible for all levels of outcome, up to and including the theodical. Moreover, the Coleridge of 1794 held that energy resided alike in the mind of God and in the human mind, the principal distinction between the two manifestations of energy being one of degree rather than of kind.[2] The heavenly provenance of energy as it exists in the human mind and the assumption that energy constitutes the human maker in the image of the divine Maker[3] are the two articles of faith behind another statement by the Coleridge of 1794; this one is found in the now justly obscure "Lines on a Friend Who Died of a Frenzy Fever Induced by Calamitous Reports": "To me hath Heaven with bounteous hand assign'd/Energic Reason and a shaping mind" (*PW* 1:77,ll. 39–40).

Statements like those above are testaments to a belief on the part of the young Coleridge in a Unitarianism or Pantheism that he was later to abandon in favor of a more nearly orthodox, Trinitarian Christianity.[4] There is evidence for the shift from the former creed to the latter in an undated MS. note to *The Destiny of Nations*, begun in 1796, first published in *Sibylline Leaves* (1817), and revised and republished by Coleridge again in 1828, 1829, and 1834. Glossing his own lines, in which Joan of Arc is made to exclaim,

> "Glory to Thee, Father of Earth and Heaven!
> All-conscious Presence of the Universe!
> Nature's vast ever-acting Energy!"

Coleridge at the same time repudiates their heterodoxy and yet defends their celebration of energy as a vital principle. "Tho' these Lines may bear a sane sense, yet they are easily, and more naturally interpreted with a very false and dangerous one. But I was at that time one of the *Mongrels*, the Josephidites [Josephides = the Son of Joseph], a proper name of distinction from those who believe *in*, as well as believe Christ the only begotten Son of the Living God before all Time" (*PW* 1:146–47,ll. 459–61; 147n.).

Indeed, to the very end of his life, Coleridge maintained a belief in energy as a vital principle that existed in all living creatures in varying degrees and that gave human beings, in whom energy existed in the greatest degree, the ability to participate in theodical or providential design by understanding (though no longer enacting) it. In the *Table Talk* entry for December 3, 1827, Coleridge states that "Internal or mental energy and external or corporeal modifiability are in inverse proportions. In man, internal energy is greater than in any other animal; and you will see that he is less changed by climate than any animal. For the highest and lowest specimens of man are not one half as much apart from each other as the different kinds even of dogs. . . ."[5] And in the entry for March 1, 1834, Coleridge gives some insight into the purpose of such "internal energy"— the discernment of theodical or providential design in the universe. "My mind is always energic—I don't mean energetic; I require in everything what, for lack of another word, I may call *propriety*,—that is, the reason why the thing *is* at all, and why it is *there* or *then* rather than elsewhere or at another time."[6] The energic-energetic distinction marks Coleridge's abdication of his claim for the mind's creative efficacy, celebrated in the *Biographia Literaria* (1816) as "a repetition in the finite mind of the eternal act of creation in the infinite I AM."[7] Some twenty years before the 1834 *Table Talk* entry Coleridge had, in *The Friend* (1809–10), distinguished between nature as process and nature as object, nature as creative and nature as created. The former is the "energetic (= *forma formans*); the latter, the "material (= *forma formata*)."[8]

The preceding examples merely suggest rather than exhaust the range of Coleridge's use of the word *energy* and its derivative forms. Moreover, these examples hardly touch on those instances in which Coleridge discusses the concept of energy without employing the word itself verbatim. For example, the discussion of imagination, on which chapter 13 of the *Biographia* concludes, advances implicitly the claim that the secondary imagination energizes its object by becoming the indwelling vital principle of that object. The secondary imagination, responsible for artistic outcome if not for the theodical kind, "dissolves, diffuses, dissipates, in order to re-create; or where this process is rendered impossible, yet still, at all events, it struggles to idealize and to unify. It is essentially *vital*, even as all objects (as objects) are essentially fixed and dead."[9]

As important as the concept of energy was to Coleridge, he did not discover it, nor did he even popularize it to any extraordinary degree. Virtually all the English Romantics used the word and the concept it denotes with approbation. Even Coleridge's archcritic Carlyle, notwithstanding his reservations about Coleridge's philosophical cogency, paid tribute along with Coleridge to "the primary, unmodified forces and energies of man, the mysterious springs of Love, and Fear, and Wonder, of Enthusiasm, Poetry, Religion, all of which have a truly vital and *infinite* character. . . ."[10] Speaking of Blake's lifetime, the dates of which are nearly the same as those of Coleridge's, Morton D. Paley has, with some justification, concluded that the term *energy* was, during the last third of the eighteenth century and the first third of the nineteenth, "fashionable," approaching the status of a "cult-word . . . employed with an aura of positiveness and varying degrees of precision."[11]

The two-thirds of a century of which Paley speaks may be regarded as an "age of energy," a period in which Blake, Coleridge, and virtually all others who used the term without satirical intent did so with decidedly anti-Newtonian motives and in the service of a decidedly anti-Newtonian program. It was during this period that Thomas Young, writing in *A Course of Lectures on Natural Philosophy and the Mechanical Arts* (1807), first used the word *energy* in its modern physical acceptation, thus replacing the Newtonian *vis*-body explanation of physical phenomena with an explanation based on an indwelling ability, actual (kinetic) or potential, to do work.[12] It was also during this period that Richard Saumarez, writing in *The Principles of Physiological and Physical Science* (1812), criticized Newtonian corpuscular matter as a concept that failed to take into account the qualitative distinctions to be observed between different types of bodies, especially those distinctions to be observed between dead bodies and living ones. The latter manifest an energy that is responsible for creation, development, and outcome. "It is by the energy of this same living power, resident in the seed of plants, and in the fecundated ova of animals, that the acorn becomes evolved into an oak. . . ."[13] Saumarez, as Coleridge notes in the *Biographia*, demonstrated to his satisfaction that no infinite power could be immanent in a finite substance.

The anti-Newtonianism of Young in mechanics and Saumarez in what was to become genetics may at first seem anomalous, not at all part of the whiggish version of the history of science that denies pride of place to Young in favor of Rankine's "energetics" (1855) or Thomson and Tait's "rediscovery" of *energy* (1879), or denies pride of place to Saumarez in favor of Darwin (1859) or Haeckel's "recapitulation" theory (1866).[15] Such a history postulates the orderly, if revolutionary replacement of the Newtonian "paradigm" by a successor only when the "normal science" of the laboratory fell prey to enough "anomalies" to dictate the need for a new "paradigm."[16] But such an account, although it may be narratively satisfying, loses sight of the facts. The same *caveat* that Thomas S. Kuhn advances for those who would treat the development of electrical theory as illustrative of the whiggish scenario of progress and development applies to those who would treat the development of science at large in that way. Just as electrical theory cannot be separated from a larger context of the physical sciences as a discrete discourse with a progressive etiology, science at large cannot be separated from a similar larger context of the human sciences.[17] Young and Saumarez may write as scientists, but they are fully aware of what Gerald Holton would call the "themata" that constitute their larger agenda, as well as the scientific one.[18]

Although it only gained scientific currency later on, when it had been cleansed of its theodical implications, the term *energy*, as used by scientists like Young and Saumarez, represented the attempt to unify the discourses of the human sciences by showing the essential unity of process and theodicy by postulating an indwelling principle responsible for all observable processes and phenomena and connate with God. Young was somewhat circumspect about this agenda, but his Quaker upbringing (*DNB* 68:393–94) predisposed him to a belief in the efficacy of indwelling divine presence.[19] Saumarez was less circumspect than Young. Writing in *A New System of Physiology* (1798), in a chapter entitled "Of the Energy of the Living Principle of the Human Species in the Process of Evolution," Saumarez specifies "the living principle" as being essentially creative, in a figure richly anticipatory of Coleridge. This "principle which the ovum contains, bears the same relation to matter into which it is received, as the painter does to the canvas on which he draws. . . ." The adumbration by this principle of a Maker who works in a living medium as the painter does in his inert one is entirely intentional: "the living principle" takes its rise from God, and its indwelling presence in all living beings brings the life process into harmony with creation's theodical design. In an argument that anticipates Coleridge's regarding the degrees of "internal energy" in different species, Saumarez has the following to say about "the living principle": "That Providence seems to have this principle especially in view, of accommodating the nature of the recipient to the degree of power in the agent, is not only evident from what we have seen in the various systems in general we have examined, but it is illustrated by the human species in particular."[20]

Young and Saumarez were both scientists known to Coleridge through their work.[21] But even before the publication of that work, Coleridge exhibited the same anti-Newtonian predispositions as the two, and for the same purpose—the defense of an agenda that held the essential unity of process and theodicy. In *The Destiny of Nations*, a poem already noted in this discussion for its celebration of the principle of energy, Coleridge condemns Newtonian mechanists for their attempts to separate the phenomena of physical process from a divinely induced structure of causation.

> Proud in their meanness: and themselves they cheat
> With noisy emptiness of learned phrase,
> Their subtle fluids, impacts, essences,
> Self-working tools, uncaused effects, and all
> Those blind Omniscients, those Almighty Slaves,
> Untenanting creation of its God.
>
> (*PW* 1:132,ll. 30–35)

Five years after this attack, Coleridge explicitly condemns Newtonianism and the epistemology that privileges it, calling Newton "a mere materialist" and elaborating on the charge that "*Mind* in his system is always passive—a lazy Looker-on on an external World. If the mind be not *passive*, if it be indeed made in God's Image, & that too in the sublimest sense —the Image of the *Creator*—there is ground for suspicion, that any system built on the passiveness of the mind must be false, as a system."[22]

Coleridge's comments make it clear that the issue is not with Newtonian physics *qua* physics. As Trevor H. Levere notes, Coleridge did not have sufficient mathematics to understand that aspect of Newtonian physics fully, let alone to criticize it.[23] Rather, the issue is with the assumptions on which Newtonian physics rests—assumptions that grant priority to Body over Soul or Mind, to metaphoric vehicle over metaphoric tenor, to the "it is" of the object-world over the "I am" of the subject-world.[24]

Energy as a concept did not come to assume the meaning it had for the likes of Young, Saumarez, and Coleridge by accident. Although even the *OED* does not give full and accurate attribution of the English word's Greek sources, *energy,* from the time that it came into the language in the early sixteenth century, was a word that signified the attempt to merge process and theodicy. The obvious source of the English word is *energeia,* as that word is used in Aristotle, where it refers to the sort of metaphor that describes process, calling "up a mental picture of something 'acting' or moving" (*OED* 3.2:167). For example, in Aristotle's *Rhetoric* (3.11, sec. 2), Aristotle notes that Isocrates' figure " 'thee, like a sacred animal ranging at will' expresses actuality [*energeia*]."[25] But there is also another Greek source for the English word—the New Testament, and there most especially the Pauline epistles. In Ephesians 1:19, for example, Paul writes, "And what *is* the exceeding greatness of his power to us-ward who believe, according to the working [*energeia*] of his mighty power." Paul's claim here is that the "mighty power" of Jesus manifests, in its working, the *energeia* of God's indwelling presence. By means of that presence, the Judeo-Christian theodicy proceeds from old to new, from fallenness to everlastingness.

Given the range of etymological sources at his disposal, it is no wonder that John Skelton, coining what may have been the first English form based on *energeia,* uses that coinage to describe the act of prophecy in its office of reconciling process and theodicy. *A Replycacion* (1528), Skelton's defense of the craft of poetry—and of his laureateships of Oxford and Cambridge—cites as worthy predecessors David, "With his harpe of prophecy," and Saint Jerome, "Warblyng with his strynges / Of such theological thynges." Skelton then goes on to explain

> How there is a spirituall
> And a mysteriall
> And a mysticall
> Effecte Energiall

As the Grekes do it call
Of suche a pregnacy
Of hevenly inspyracion
In laureate creacyon. . . .[26]

This discussion is not the proper context for summarizing the fortunes of energy as a concept and word from the sixteenth century to the nineteenth.[27] Suffice it to say that events as seemingly disconnected as the death of Charles I (and with him divine-right kingship in England), the replacement of Aristotelian physics by the Galilean-Newtonian variety, and the influence of philosophical skepticism on religious orthodoxy caused the word *energy* to assume the negative connotations that it carried down to the turn of the nincteenth century—connotations most offensive to those who fancied themselves spokespersons for religious and political orthodoxy.[28] Notwithstanding such connotations and social pressure, however, the word began to reemerge, with approbation, in contexts where it was used specifically to refer to an indwelling principle responsible for the harmony of process with theodicy. In a 1775 sermon entitled "Working out Our Own Salvation," John Wesley comes startlingly close, in his title and in the sermon itself, to using the word *energy*, albeit in the original Greek form, in the manner in which Thomas Young later uses it. "*To thelein . . .* we render *to will*, plainly indicating every good desire, whether relating to our tempers, words, or actions; to inward or outward holiness. And *to energein*, which we render *to do*, manifestly implies all that power from on high, all that energy which works in us every right disposition, and then furnishes us for every good word and work."[29] And in a 1778 response to Dr. Price's attack on his *Disquisitions on Matter and Spirit*, published in that same year, Joseph Priestley, unedified by Price's *Dissertation on Providence* (1768), which he had enjoined Priestley to read, states that Price's text "only shews, though in a very clear and masterly manner, that the present laws of nature require an *intelligence*, and an *energy*, of which what we usually call matter is not capable. Now I certainly admit to an intelligent and active cause in nature, and have no objection to supposing that this intelligent cause has even more to do with the execution of the laws of nature than Dr. Price is willing to allow."[30]

Priestley's *Disquisitions* "entered significantly into" Coleridge's *Religious Musings*, according to Levere.[31] And while Priestley's Unitarianism may have made him a kindred spirit to the young Coleridge, his use of *Disquisitions* and the concept of energy that that work sets forth has another purpose that remained with Coleridge long after he had renounced Unitarianism and embraced Trinitarian orthodoxy. If one is able to unify process and theodicy under the aegis of energy, that person is in a position to ascribe to process an indwelling presence responsible for a design in the enactment of process that overwhelms any consideration or imputation of evil. In such a scheme, falls become fortunate, not to say temporary; suffering becomes redemptive, not to say purifying; apparent evil becomes ultimate good. Moreover, the apprehensions necessary for the individual to understand the mere appearance of evil and the triumph over it are accessible to the individual while that person is still alive. Such apprehensions, although they may not be Wordsworth's "simple produce of the common day,"[32] wait only on the apprehension of the energy within and the energy without, followed by the insight that it is the same energy in both cases, and that what M. H. Abrams calls "the theodicy of the private life" and "the theodicy of the landscape"[33] depend on one and the same indwelling principle of energy, linking the created world irrevocably to the design of providence itself. Simply stated, Coleridge's adoption of the concept of energy, which he may have had from Priestley, Wesley, or numerous others, is his attempt to come to grips with the problem of evil and to lay it to rest.

Thus Coleridge, convinced at least momentarily that he is possessed both of energy and of the apprehension of its presence within himself and abroad,[34] assumes the prophetic office and addresses the

> numberless,
> Whom foul Oppression's ruffian gluttony
> Drives from Life's plenteous feast!

a mob that includes the murderous highwayman "made wild by want," the seduced and abandoned woman turned prostitute, the old woman turned parish almsperson, and others, telling them,

> Yet is the day of Retribution nigh:
> The Lamb of God hath opened the fifth seal:
> And upward rush on swiftest wings of fire
> The innumerable multitude of wrongs
> By man on man inflicted! Rest awhile,
> Children of Wretchedness! The hour is nigh . . .
>
> (*PW* 1:120–21,ll. 276–308)

On that day, not only will every valley be exalted and every mountain and hill made low, but all of the energized natural world will be etherealized and all of the ethereal world will be naturalized as a way of demonstrating the common indwellingness of the energy within each. At the time of this demonstration, apparent evil will disappear before energy like day before night.

> Thus from the Elect, regenerate through faith,
> Pass the dark Passions and what thirsty cares
> Drink up the spirit, and the dim regards
> Self-centre. Lo they vanish! or acquire
> New names, new features—by supernal grace
> Enrobed with Light, and naturalised in Heaven.
>
> (*PW* 1:112–13,ll. 88–93)

But in the tell-tale phrase "self-centre" and the epic simile that follows, it is possible to glimpse the problems raised by Coleridge's decision to embrace the concept of energy as a solution to the problem of evil. "Passions and . . . thirsty cares" may absorb the spirit and give rise to the solipsistic self-regard that absorbs the fallen and the elect alike. But if the apprehension of indwelling energy is the evidence of one's election, then the means of attaining "supernal grace" is a species of self-contemplation that is difficult to distinguish from the effect of those "dark Passions" that "Drink up the spirit, and the dim regards / Self-centre." When one is truly numbered among the elect and such self-contemplation goes well, then the apprehension of energy indwelling within and the access of grace that follows is "As when a shepherd on a vernal morn / Through some thick fog creeps timorous with slow foot," keeping his eye trained on the partially obscured road ahead, until

> lo! the bursting Sun!
> Touched by the enchantment of that sudden beam
> Straight the black vapour melteth, and in globes
> Of dewy glitter gems each plant and tree . . .
> . . . .
> And wide around the landscape streams with glory!
>
> (*PW* 1:113,ll. 94–104)

But the process may as well lead to solipsistic estrangement and despair. More than thirty years after he wrote *Religious Musings*, at approximately the same time he renounced the energetic faculty of mind, Coleridge brought back the same simile with a difference. Apparently, that vexing problem of evil, which the concept of energy had been intended to solve through the unification of process and theodicy, was still a problem; and therefore the self-contemplation that had earlier been advanced as the means of apprehending the indwelling presence of energy as evidence of election was more likely to maroon the percipient in solipsism than it was to acquaint that person with grace or glory. "Constancy to an Ideal Object" (1825–26) identifies nature as the locus of lapse and loss, the place of all who "veer or vanish," rather than as the locus of any indwelling presence such as energy which, if it exists, has been relegated to the realm of the ideal. And the contemplation of that realm is at best difficult and at worst the sort of false consciousness that leads to solipsism,

> as when
> The woodman winding westward up the glen
> At wintry dawn, where o'er the sheep-track's maze
> The viewless snow-mist weaves a glist'ning haze,
> Sees full before him, gliding without tread,
> An image with a glory round its head;
> The enamoured rustic worships its fair hues,
> Nor knows he makes the shadow, he pursues!
>
> (PW1:455–56,ll. 2, 25–32)

The effect of Coleridge's peculiar need to proceed in his philosophical and theological investigations by beginning with the problem of consciousness—and there with the positing of his own consciousness as object—is precisely the lethargy and intimations of solipsism glimpsed in "Constancy." Not trusting his apprehension of energy within his own mind or abroad, Coleridge sought to verify the means of apprehension, an operation that entailed the willed apprehension of consciousness, which was thought responsible for the unwilled apprehension of energy on the basis of like apprehending like. In contrast to Keats, who understood that such "Things cannot to the will / Be settled, but they tease us out of thought,"[35] Coleridge wished to settle the problem of consciousness to the will, and thereby, he thought, to settle the problem of evil by verifying that the apprehension of energy as the means to overcoming the latter problem was, in fact, a valid apprehension. Although he wrongly attributes Coleridge's dilemma to opium addiction, Laurence S. Lockridge provides an aptly telling analysis of the effect of will in solving the problems he posed for himself.

. . . volition no longer coordinates impulse and motive, will and consciousness. The paradoxical result is that though Coleridge is driven by ever-increasing impulses of a powerful will, he exists in a paralyzed and energyless state. The will sends out a "galvanic fluid" that results in a simulacrum of real motion: the compulsiveness that is identical with loss of freedom. The "Spirit of Life that makes Soul and Body one" is wanting.[36]

At issue in Coleridge's attempt to solve the problem of consciousness[37] as a necessary prolegomena to the problem of evil are the origins and identity of what he would like to consider energy and attribute to origins *and ends* in God. The question is whether the mind, functioning as the vessel of energy, is God's place and thereby a participant in the theodical triumph of good over evil, or whether the mind harbors a willfulness that is the simulacrum of energy—self-originated and self-contemplated —making the mind not God's place, but rather its own, satanic place. Two corollary questions concern mixed influence and total renunciation: If the mind is the battleground on which divine energy and its satanic simulacrum meet, is it possible for the struggle to be resolved on the part of a *tertium aliquid* that inclines to and thereby demonstrates the triumph of the divine over the satanic? And if the mind is in fact wholly under the influence of satanic energy, is there any chance for it to throw off that influence and grant access to the divine?

Like his use of the word *energy*, Coleridge's adherence to this agenda of concerns spanned his mature lifetime. This adherence precedes his reading in German philosophy, to be sure.[38] It is the commitment that draws Coleridge back again and again to what Jean-Pierre Mileur calls "the Protean problem of immanence: immanence of the author in his work, of identity in consciousness, of God in his creation."[39] It is the commitment that leads Coleridge to solve the problem of immanence in one instance by positing the sort of etherealized interpenetration envisioned in *Religious Musings*, then to draw back with the realization that the problem of immanence is in fact a problem of origins.[40] It is a commitment that leads Coleridge to attempt to deal with the problem of origins by proposing a magnum opus geared not only to the "systematic reconciliation of the 'I am' with the 'it is,'" but also to the demonstration that the apparent opposition of these categories may be resolved through the discovery of a divinely originated indwelling principle found to exist in both. In so doing, Coleridge could not only solve "the methexic problem that lies at

the root of all reticulative philosophy"—the reconciliation of apparent opposites through the discovery of a common universal ground—he could
also pursue an explanation of the "unaccountable fact" of Original Sin.[41]

The result of the direct pursuit of this agenda by Coleridge was the
sort of solipsism and despair glimpsed in the closing lines of "Constancy."
Coleridge learned through painful personal experience one of the salient
lessons that follows from the Cartesian sundering of mind and body. The
"ability to know itself incorrigibly ('privileged access')" does not, according to Richard Rorty, necessarily give the mind or the consciousness that
it houses the "ability to grasp universals . . . ability to sustain relations to
the inexistent ('intentionality') . . . [or] ability to act freely. . . ."[42] With specific respect to the question of energy, construed as the ability to perform
work, no poem of Coleridge's more poignantly illustrates an awareness of
the limits arising from the inability to solve the problem of consciousness
than "Work without Hope" (1825). In that poem, the consciousness of the
speaker—both of his otherness and of the lack of hope that characterizes
and enforces that otherness—isolates the speaker from nature awakening
at the passage of winter into spring. And that isolation, not merely from
nature but from nature's theodical potential, is precisely the difference
between work without hope and work with—between *to thelein,* the willing
of "every good desire, whether relating to our tempers, words or actions;
to inward or outward holiness," and *to energein,* the working of "all that
power from on high, all that energy which works in us every right disposition, and then furnishes us for every good word and work." The absence of
the energy that, according to Wesley, so furnishes the individual is evident
from the speaker's description of himself lacking "every good word and
work": "With lips unbrightened, wreathless brow, I stroll: / And would you
learn the spells that drowse my soul?" (*PW* 1:447,ll. 11–12). That absence
means any work attempted by the speaker is willed work—mechanical and
incapable of transforming. "Work without Hope draws nectar in a sieve"
(l.13) at least in part because it is the sort of willed work that cannot trans-
form nectar to honey, as the bees' work can (see ll. 2,6). Willed work does
not work "in us every right disposition," but rather precludes such disposition, isolates the individual from it, or both. Such work, moreover, ratifies
Coleridge's conviction "that man was and is a fallen creature, not by accidents of bodily constitution or any other cause . . . but as diseased in his
will, in that will which is the true and only strict synonyme of the word I,
or the intelligent Self."[43]

Moments as painfully revealing as the last discussed are found with some regularity in the poetry after "Dejection: An Ode" (1802). Through-out most of the prose, and in the poetry up to 1802, Coleridge elected to treat the apprehension of energy and the several problems such apprehen-sion entailed in what, for him, was a scientific rather than a philosophic or imaginative manner. Although Coleridge did not have the mathemat-ics to do so, his treatment has affinities with the strategy devised by the likes of Descartes and Galileo for the treatment of *res extensa*, the world of matter, except that instead of mathematizing nature, Coleridge scientized (or perhaps dialecticalized) it.[44] The end of this strategy was to determine, as Dorothy Emmet observes, whether the powers that Coleridge "found operative in his own mind," as a representative human mind, were "*con-natural* . . . with powers of life and growth in nature, and finally . . . alike depending on a spiritual ground."[45] The oft-discussed chapter 13 of the *Biographia* begins with the goal of making such a determination—not merely the stipulation that the powers operative in the human mind are "connatural" with those in nature, but the proof that the "tertium aliquid, or finite generation" of such powers, manifested as opposed Cartesian forces, is on the order of a positive outcome.[46] The problem with such an undertaking, as Mileur suggests, is that the third term in question depends for its existence on the reconciliation of dualisms—mind and matter, per-ception and will—that are fundamentally irreconcilable.[47] In a poem such as *The Rime of the Ancient Mariner* (1797), discussed below, the way beyond such dualisms is the Christ-like love that allows the Mariner to bless and become one with the water snakes, anticipated to an extent by a "dona-tion" of another sort in Chapter 13—the anonymous letter from a "friend" that specifies the imaginative conditions under which loving, blessing, and a "connatural" state of affairs is possible.

Coleridge's shifting of the problem of consciousness to the realm of dialecticalized science is nowhere more apparent than in his treatment of light and color, an aspect of physical theory with definite theological overtones, most especially since the time of Newton's *Optics* (1704) and its highly suggestive thirtieth and thirty-first queries. Nearer to Coleridge's own time, the theology latent in Thomas Young's theory of light and color, which sought to supplant Newton's theory and its pantocratic point-source of corpuscular light with a wave theory granting light immanent proper-ties, drew down the wrath of the Scottish common-sense philosophers and their spokesperson, Henry Brougham. Calling Young's theory the prod-uct of "a warm and misguided [enthusiastic?] imagination," Brougham illustrated the self-contradictory secularism of this "common sense" New-

tonian legacy. On the one hand, as Richard Olson notes, the Scottish philosophers "consciously emphasized the heuristic value of models"; but on
the other, they conspired to duck the issue of where such models and the
inspiration for them might come from, dissociating "the models and the
theories arising from them from any ontological content."[48]

As Levere notes, although without fully appreciating his theological implications, Young and his theory of light figure into Coleridge's thought
on the subject, as do other writers more obviously aware of theological
issues, such as Schelling and Steffens. Not only did Coleridge undertake to
show that "light and colors illustrated dynamic logic, and [that] their total
influence comprehended many energies, including calorific and chemical
ones," he also undertook to show, as was the case with his development
of the analogy between light and sound, that any explanation of the phenomena of light and colors must be "founded in dynamic philosophy and
Biblical exegesis . . . ."[49] As a mode of inquiry, biblical exegesis must be
understood not only to include the "higher criticism" and its theological and philosophical predecessors, but also the mystics Coleridge read,
including Behmen, and such literary exegetes as Milton.

How, then, does Coleridge propound his theory of the relationship of
light and color? An 1820 notebook entry proclaims that "Gravity in &
subordinate to Light is color. . . . I fear not to call . . . color the body of
Light." The metaphor of subordination is neither incidental nor idle, ap-
pearing three years earlier in a letter to Tieck, where Coleridge proclaims
"Color = Gravitation under the praepotence of light." As schematized in
what Levere terms "a standard Coleridgean pentad," the "praepotence
of light" evolves out of a prior state labelled "Indistinction/(the Mosaic
Chaos):

Prothesis

Indistinction

(the Mosaic Chaos)

Thesis   Mesothesis   Antithesis

Gravity   Heat   Light

Synthesis

Color[50]

Whatever the heuristic value of Coleridge's theory, it is certainly rich in ontological—and—theological content. Even atheists are familiar with the biblical account in Genesis of how God began to fill and give form to a formless and void earth ("[the Mosaic Chaos]") with the efficacious command, "Let there be light" (1:3). But the position of light in Coleridge's pentad is that of the second term (antithesis) rather than that of the first term (thesis) of this dialectical structure, indicating that gravity, (the thesis) preceded light. There is nothing in Genesis itself to justify the sequence, where a gravity-defying "darkness" seems suspended "upon the face of the deep" (1:2) and no *cause* precedes the command for light. And yet Coleridge is clear that light is an older power than gravity, which is subordinate to light: "Color = Gravity under the praepotence of light."

If there is a contradiction involved, it is a contradiction of two conflicting points of view. The pentad attempts to show things from an absolute point of view, uninformed by the fallen perspective of humanity, while the prose statements attempt to explain the phenomena in question from that fallen perspective. In theological terms, the answer to the question "what is light?" is clear enough. Even Newton's "Rules of Reasoning in Philosophy" argues for a common cause of the light observed in a cooking fire and the light of the sun.[51] But what is gravity? Here Coleridge apparently would disagree with Newton (and agree with Blake): gravity for Coleridge is not the action at a distance by a pantocrator-God bent on harmonizing the motions of the solar system by the application of that force. Gravity is, rather, the tendency to fall; and although the Fall of Adam and Eve comes after the creation of light in the Bible, the fall of Satan precedes that creation in *Paradise Lost*. Milton's epic opens with Satan and his rebellious host "Hurl'd headlong flaming from th'Ethereal Sky," those "happy Realms of Light" in which Satan was "Cloth'd with transcendent brightness." From that place Satan and his host fall "With hideous ruin and combustion down / To bottomless perdition, there to dwell" in a realm containing "No light, but rather darkness visible. . . ."[52] Given this scenario, Coleridge's "Mesothesis" of heat may refer either to the infernal circumstances of Satan after the fall from Heaven, the battle between the angelic legions led by Christ and the satanic legions, or both, since both Hell and the battleground in question are certainly hot places.

Heat is also a characteristic of the "*Libyan* air adust" (12.635) that awaits Adam and Eve beyond the East gate of Eden. How is one to overcome the struggle of the two opposing dialectical terms and reach the synthesis of color? Color is conspicuously absent from the descriptions of Hell in the opening books of *Paradise Lost*, as well as from the description of Christ's triumph over Satan in Book 6. As Michael's comments in Book 11 suggest—and as Genesis 6:5–9:17 would tend to corroborate—the synthesis that is color is a phenomenon observed by human beings and pertaining to them alone as *embodied* creatures ("I fear not to call . . . color the body of Light"). Color marks the contingent triumph, in the world, of good over evil—that moment at which light asserts its "praepotence" over gravity and humanity is bound to light through a covenant from God, in token of which he gives his rainbow—color, in other words.[53] In describing the significance of the rainbow that God sets as his covenant following the Flood, Michael explains, in response to Adam's anthropomorphized question about "those color'd streaks in Heav'n / Distended as the Brow of God appeas'd" (11.879–80), that the rainbow is a synthesis, in the sense that a contract, as agreement between two (opposed) parties is a synthesis. The rainbow God shows to Noah, and all subsequent rainbows, are to be viewed as types of

> . . . a Cov'nant never to destroy
> The Earth again by flood, nor let the Sea
> Surpass his bounds, nor Rain to drown the World
> .   .   .   .
> . . . till fire purge all things new,
> Both Heav'n and Earth, wherein the just shall dwell.
>
> (11.893–901)

The reference to the Last Judgment places the rainbow, the covenant it signifies, and the colors (three of them, suggestively) that are the means of signification within the larger context of the Judeo-Christian theodicy. Interestingly enough, at the end of time, when the Last Judgment occurs, color as the token of a temporary synthesis of dialectically opposed forces will no longer be needed or even present. The final images of the City of God in Revelation are of transparency and pure (unrefracted) light: "and the street of the city *was* pure gold, as it were transparent glass. . . . And the city had no need of the sun, neither of the moon, to shine in it: for the glory of God did lighten it, and the Lamb *is* the light thereof" (21:21,23).[54]

From the perspective of this world—the Adamic perspective of *Paradise Lost*, Books 11–12, then, color is a contingent synthesis, a third term (*tertium aliquid*?), the "body of light" that one puts on as a consequence of the Fall into this world and the bodily limits set by the circumstance of Original Sin and that one takes off at that moment when the Resurrection of the Dead sets gravity at nought and signals the annihilation of Satan and the return of pure light "connatural" with God. Seen in a slightly differing perspective, color is what is produced in a body as a result of the conflict between divine and Satanic energies. In Book 4 of *Paradise Lost*, Satan comes to Eve in her sleep to begin tempting her with dreams of the Forbidden Fruit. He "enters," as it were, "at the ear of *Eve*," in hope of coloring the perceptions arising from

> The Organs of her Fancy, and with them forge
> Illusions as he list, Phantasms and Dreams,
> Or if, inspiring venom, he might taint [cf. *tint*]
> Th'animal Spirits that from pure blood arise
> Like gentle breaths from Rivers pure [i. e., translucent],
>   thence raise
> At least distemper'd, discontented thoughts,
> Vain hopes, vain aims, inordinate desires
> Blown up with high conceits ingend'ring pride.
>
>   (4.800–09)

At the distance it assumes as a dialecticalized scientific theory, Coleridge's theory of light and color exists on a level of generality and impersonality that makes it seem almost as though it makes no affective or fideistic claims on lived experience. That "Color = Gravitation under the praepotence of light" may be proven, and it may not. In at least one context, that of the General Theory of Relativity, Coleridge's ideas constitute an uncanny anticipation of the explanation of "red-shift," the phenomenon that occurs when the light waves of a celestial body in motion relative to the observer is viewed through a strong gravitational field that affects the frequency and distribution of the light waves emitted. But in the context of pure theory subjected to impersonal, disinterested observational testing, Coleridge's ideas lose the aura of lived experience joined to theodical significance that those ideas take on in the context of the Bible or *Paradise Lost*. Calling "color the body of Light" in a scientific setting is a way of ignoring the provenance or significance of the concatenated metaphor of color as light's *body*, as well as of ignoring the passion of Adam, Eve, Noah, and all others who experience color as light's body until the Last Judgment.

It is not the Platonic will to power[55] or the Newtonian will to dissemble[56] that leads Coleridge to move the problem of consciousness and the problem of evil to the realm of dialecticalized scientific theory. Afraid of a serious rupture, perhaps even an irreconcilable conflict between process and theodicy, and possessed of a need to see the energies within one and the energies within the world as being ultimately the same theodically informed energy, Coleridge attempts to preserve the theory from any potentially discrediting circumstances by distancing it as far as possible from the ground of lived experience on which the claims of process and theodicy were originally to have been reconciled. There are earlier attempts at such reconciliation in the poetry, but they are incomplete, in large part because the lived experience to verify such a reconciliation is lacking. Without either the egotistical self-confidence or sense of poetic design possessed by Wordsworth, Coleridge did not feel himself sufficiently the prophet of nature to propound "A lasting inspiration, sanctified / By reason and by truth" that tells of everlasting things, such as

> how the mind of man becomes
> A thousand times more beautiful than the earth
> On which he dwells, above this frame of things
> . . . .
> In beauty exalted, as it is itself
> Of substance and of fabric more divine.[57]

The failed attempts at reconciliation have a good deal to do with that characteristically Coleridgean structure, the interrupted work.[58] But such failures are also found in completed works, such as *The Rime*, which was to have provided the occasion for the "essay on the uses of the supernatural in poetry" announced at the end of chapter 13 of the *Biographia*. Limitations of format prevent a full discussion of how Coleridge's theory of light and color operates through the lived experience of the Mariner; however, it is possible in this context to sketch out some of the manifestations of that theory, as well as the implications to be drawn from them.

The vessel on which the Mariner and his shipmates sail, losing sight of the village church, the landscape, and the lighthouse, in that order, is a microcosm of a world subject to original sin—that human version of Satanic pride that is as "unaccountable" but ubiquitous as the gravity that is its physical manifestation as a reminder of prior falls and of one's predisposition to fall further still. Without any particular concern about falling away from their Edenic homeland, with its landscape-dominating church, (green) hills, and (pure) rays of light from the lighthouse, the Mariner and his mates "Merrily did . . . drop" (*PW* 1:187,ll. 22–24). That falling off occurs as inevitably yet unaccountably as gravity of Original Sin. The events that follow, including the killing of the Albatross, are all in their turn both inevitable and unaccountable, not any more susceptible to explanation than why gravity or Original Sin exists. All attempts at explanation, whether they be the cause-and-effect arguments of the Mariner's shipmates or the epigraph from Burnet or the poem's "Argument" or the glosses added to the 1817 edition, are ironic at best and casuistical at worst —the same species of justification that the serpent uses on Eve, that she in her turn uses on Adam, and that he in his turn uses on himself, in order to justify the eating of the Forbidden Fruit that occasions the Fall.

At the outset, there is absolutely no interaction between gravity and light—certainly no subordination of the former to the latter—and no "*tertium aliquid*," as Coleridge calls it in the *Biographia*. The lack of interaction is signalled by the fact that both the ship's motion and the sun's diurnal motion continue without alteration and by the fact that the sunlight does not interact with gravity to produce any color. All that is known about the sun is that it comes up on the left, sets on the right, and shines brightly (without any color, indicating that its "praepotence" is not observed or acknowledged by the shipmates), and is personified as a "he" ("He?" [*PW* 1:187,ll. 25–28]). At the Equator, where the sun shines directly overhead and should have the greatest influence over the ship and its crew, the sun has none and withdraws, not to reappear until the beginning of the second part of the poem, forty-two lines later. Another "he," a "STORM-BLAST" described as "tyrannous and strong" (*PW* 1:188,ll. 41–42), takes the place of the sun. Actually, the storm is only a different aspect of the God figured forth by the sun—a wrathful God rather than the creator-God who says "let there be light." The storm he visits upon the ship is a Noachic storm; and the Albatross, like the raven and the dove in the story of the Flood, is the instrument for regaining access to God's grace, and face, which assumes the colors of the rainbow in Noah's story to indicate that evil has been subordinated to good, not completely vanquished by it. But while Noah is patient and faithful enough to send out a raven that symbolizes the darkly rapacious side of human nature before realizing that the dove, as white as the raven is black, and accounted as selfless as the raven is rapacious, is the better means of achieving landfall and a glimpse of God's grace, the Mariner lacks all such patience. Moreover, the

Albatross, a long-distance flyer even as the dove is a long-distance flyer
in comparison to the raven, is suggestive of how great a distance there is
between the ship and any rapprochement with God. At the Equator, a sort
of point of no return, the ship is far enough away, but when it reaches the
South Pole, which is where the Mariner kills the Albatross, the ship is as
far away from its Edenic home port and the direct rays of the sun (God)
as it is possible to get.

Even when the ship completes its "fall" (southward motion) and begins
its "redemption" (northward motion), there is still no interaction between
light and gravity. The sun has no color—especially no red, one of the
colors of the rainbow (even Milton's tricolored rainbow) and the color of
the blood that Christ must ultimately shed to ransom a sinful humanity
and supplant the Old Man with the New. "Nor dim nor red, like God's own
head, / The glorious Sun uprist . . ." (*PW* 1:190,ll. 97–98). But the Mariner
and his shipmates soon reach a place of suffering and redemption—and a
place of highly significant color, at that, with its "hot and copper sky" and
"bloody Sun" (*ibid.*, ll.111–12).

Blood sacrifice is an important tenet of Coleridge's credo, but it is the
office of the "bloody Son," Jesus, not of the individual. The note to *The
Destiny of Nations*, declaring "Christ the only begotten Son of the Living
God before all Time," preceded *The Rime*. The point is that something else
is wanted for the Mariner's redemption to proceed. Biting his arm and
sucking the blood from it to announce the approach of what turns out to
be a ghost ship (*PW* 1:192,ll.160–61) is a token of the Mariner's fellow
feeling for his shipmates, but not of his redemption.

What is necessary for such redemption to occur is that the Mariner
recognize intuitively the deployment of the dialectically arrayed forces of
good and evil in the world, and that he somehow demonstrate his alle-
giance to the good (light) to bring about the subordination of evil (gravity)
to it. The occasion for redemption arises with the arrival of the ghost
ship, which "drove suddenly / Betwixt us and the Sun," giving the Mariner
and his mates a radically altered view of the sun, which harks back to
the "barred" appearance of the rainbow at the same time it foretokens an
access of grace.

> And straight the Sun was flecked with bars,
> (Heaven's Mother send us grace!)
> As if through a dungeon-grate he peered
> With broad and burning face.

> (*PW* 1:193,ll. 175–80)

The figure of the dungeon-grate of course begs the question of who is in jail, and the answer is that we are *in*, just as surely as the Mariner becomes the thrall of LIFE-*IN*-DEATH.

But being a fallen and death-bounded individual did not prevent Noah from seeing the colors of the rainbow and blessing it for the blessings that its Creator-God conferred on him and his race. And the Mariner also sees such colors and blesses them. Before understanding intuitively that good triumphs over evil just as surely as light triumphs over gravity to create color, the Mariner had seen the water snakes merely as evil unmodified by good. They were "slimy things [that] did crawl with legs / Upon the slimy sea." Their colors were like "death-fires," and "The water, like a witch's oils / Burnt green, and blue and white" (*PW* 1:191,ll. 125–30). A moment of reflection is wanting, and that occurs with the rising of the moon, which stimulates such reflection in its role as a reflector of the sun. With a consciousness that is a reflection of God's, as the result of the divine gift of grace, "a repetition in the finite mind of the eternal act of creation in the infinite I AM," as Coleridge calls it in the *Biographia*, the Mariner views the water snakes and sees that they are good, just as God sees the Creation as good after each separate creative act. The Mariner loves and blesses the snakes, just as God loves and blesses his Creation. The Mariner sees the colors for what they are—"rich attire"—sees the snakes in their proper place upon the sea and, as he explains, "A spring of love gushed from my heart, / And I blessed them unaware." It is a moment of colors—"Blue, glossy green, and velvet black," along with "a flash of golden fire"—and it is a moment of the subordination of evil to good, a moment of prayerful love in which "The Albatross fell off, and sank / Like lead into the sea" (*PW* 1:198,ll. 278–90). It is also a moment of "praepotence," in the sense of "old power." In loving the snakes and their colors, the Mariner harks back to a Creator-God who, in the originary power of Creation, loved the serpent, before it betrayed him in the Temptation and the Fall.

The problem with "praepotence" is that it is doomed in the reenactment of the fall, just as the paradisal realms that Wordsworth would reattain through the marriage of the mind to nature are doomed to be lost all over when they are reattained.[59] The Mariner's triumph is a triumph of life, but it is a life that is under the sway of LIFE-*IN*-DEATH. The reconciliation of the life-process with theodicy is possible, but only momentarily so, and doomed to reenactment in life without any hope of durability or permanence. The Mariner's fate of passing from land to land and repeating his tale to audiences in whatever language they may speak arises not from a

neurotic (or psychotic) repetition-compulsion, but from the fact that repetition is the only possible strategy for achieving even momentary reconciliation between the life-process and theodicy and thereby valorizing the
former. The Mariner's gift of tongues also evokes the story of the Tower
of Babel (Genesis 11:1–9), which occurs just after that of the Flood. Not
only is Babel the locale of a second fall—this one into separate and mutu-
ally incomprehensible languages—it is also the place at which humanity
learns that it is impossible to build any sort of durable link between the
world of process and the realm of theodicy. God simply will not remain
accessible with anything like permanence, instead choosing to reveal Himself momentarily, and sometimes even obscurely in the moment. Thus it
may be, as McFarland claims, "that Coleridge was the 'living link between
religion and philosophy' for his own age."[60] But that linkage, which is but
another version of the linkage between theodicy and process, is a severely
qualified one, subject to the sort of ephemerality and parallactic distortion that arises from trying to view a fixed and unchanging object from a
moving and otherwise shifting perspective, the very organs of perception
changing from moment to moment.

Ultimately, Coleridge's was an impossible task. Energy as a common
term of linkage could cleave to the part of process or the part of theodicy, but it could not remain between the two as a linkage. Coleridge
backed away from the concept of energy in his poetry early on, and he
constrained and qualified it increasingly throughout his prose. The energy that Thomas Young observed and named, purged of its theodical
trappings by thermodynamics, leads not to a new heaven and new earth
but, ultimately, to entropy, a circumstance in which the sum of all energy
within a system is zero. And the energy of which Saumarez spoke, leads to
an ontogeny that, in the fetal state, recapitulates phylogeny, not to a reconciliation with All-in-All. On the level of phylogeny itself, such energy is
responsible for evolution, not Providence, a circumstance dictated by fit-
ness relative to a given environment, not by election. If God disappeared
from the world of process in the nineteenth century, it is not for lack of
an effort on the part of Coleridge and others to keep him in it. And even
the truths about energy that we have realized in his aftermath may say
more about human beings as the projectors of the metaphors that order
the phenomenal world than about the final cause of that world.

8

Perception and "the heaven-descended KNOW-THYSELF"

Frederick Burwick

How does (if indeed it does) perception lead to apperception? So long as I refrain from pretending to offer an answer, the task of investigating Coleridge's labors with this question will remain fairly simple. Arduous labors they were for Coleridge, arduous and desperate as he tried to construct an answer in the *Biographia Literaria*. After waxing rhetorical in his enthusiasm over "the heaven-descended KNOW-THYSELF," Coleridge proceeded to construct the conditions necessary to apperception, the transcendental apperception, in the Kantian sense, of self-consciousness, self-intuition, self-knowledge.[1] The effort, as has been well documented,[2] led Coleridge to verbatim borrowings from the works of Schelling in the presentation of the ten theses in chapter 12. When he again addressed the relation of perception to apperception in his chapter "On the Logical Acts," also fully documented in J. R. de J. Jackson's edition of the *Logic*, Coleridge once more returned to these same theses in reordering and reshaping the argument.[3] When compared with the presentation of the theses in the *Biographia*, however, the argument in the *Logic* may be seen to differ in structure as well as in conclusion. For that matter, in neither case does Coleridge hold to Schelling's argument. He rearranges it.

None of the commentaries which have pointed out Coleridge's appropriations from Schelling have explained why Coleridge found it necessary to construct the argument from three separate sources, *Vom Ich* (1795), *Abhandlung zur Erläuterung der Idealismus* (1797), and *System der transcendentalen Idealismus* (1800), sources that represent Schelling's early indebtedness to Fichte (until 1797) but leap over the permutations of the *Natur-*

philosophie (from 1797 through 1799) to the emergent *Identitätsphilosophie* (beginning in 1800). Coleridge's selection and manipulation of texts from such differing sources are all the more peculiar, for he could have drawn a cohesive version intact from any one of these works, or from the *Naturphilosophie* which he ignores here although he borrows from it elsewhere. A fundamental question, then, is why Coleridge has taken the trouble to reconstruct an argument drawn from the various stages of Schelling's attempts to resolve perception and apperception.

Before I look at Coleridge's reshaping of Schelling in the *Biographia*, and the reshaping of the reshaping in the *Logic*, it may be useful to review the history of the problem in order to explain why the relation of perception and apperception had become such a philosophical crux for Kant and his followers; and why, too, Coleridge would not accept here, as he often did elsewhere, a facile solution to the problem. Gian Orsini has told part of this story,[4] but a few details should be corrected and a few more added pertinent to Coleridge's peculiar wielding of the passages from Schelling. The story begins with the dissolution of self in Hume's epistemology:

> For my part, when I enter most intimately into what I call *myself*, I always stumble upon some particular perception or other. . . . I never can catch *myself* at any time without a perception, and can never observe anything but the perception.[5]

As Orsini so aptly put it, "the reason why Hume could not find the self in himself was that he looked in the wrong direction." He was so intent upon searching out a lurking "me" or "myself" that he never turned around to confront the "I" who "enters most intimately," who "stumbles" and tries to "catch." Yet this "I," whom Hume has sent on the quest for "myself," is there all the time, asking, deliberating, learning. Hume's position is an extreme yet logical consequence of the empirical definition of the mind as the passive receptor of sense experience; with no activity of its own, the mind is simply the reflex of the continuous and multiple registry of sensations. Thus when Coleridge describes "the necessary consequences of the Hartleian theory" (*BL*, ch. 7), he complains that "the consciousness considered as a *result*" renders "the poor worthless I" as nothing more than a reflection, "the mere quick-silver plating behind a looking-glass."[6]

After Hume had awakened Kant from his dogmatic slumbers, Kant proceeded to sort out the "spontaneous" from the flux of "receptive" data of the external senses. These spontaneous acts provide the form, temporal and spatial, for receiving impressions. Sensory experience is possible only because the mind spontaneously gives form to the continuous stream of sensory data. Not only does this spontaneous inner sense give form to experience, it also organizes. In his "Transcendental Analytic," Kant develops his categories of "quantity," "quality," "relation," and "modality," the a priori frame in which the judgment of experience is possible. But more fundamental in his answer to Hume than the temporal and spatial forms of inner sense and the categories, is the very arena of consciousness that brings awareness to experience. Kant calls it "the supreme principle of all employment of the understanding" (B136).[7] Orsini is disconcerted that Kant virtually buried this crucial principle in the "Transcendental Deduction," not even giving it the structural recognition of a paragraph heading. Orsini suggests that the apparent neglect and subordination of the principle of "self-consciousness" may have come about because it was introduced late in the long period of Kant's composition of the *Kritik der reinen Vernunft.* But Kant himself has another explanation that Orsini has overlooked. Prominently featured in the headings of the second section of the Deduction (§§15–27, esp. §§16–19) is the concern with the synthetic unity of apperception. Orsini does not observe that for Kant the immediacy of self-consciousness is only an illusion, an affect. Kant not only carefully distinguishes apperception from the inner sense, he calls attention to the erroneous tendency "in systems of psychology" to equate the two. In §24 he recalls his first exposition of the inner sense in §6. Everyone will have noticed, he says, the paradox in explaining how the inner sense presents consciousness to the self. The paradox arises not from the condition of the self as it actually is (*an sich*), but only as it appears in introspection. Because we only view our self as we are inwardly affected, we must presume a passive, responsive (*leidend*) comport with our self. This, he says, may seem to be contradictory. Inner sense, after all, has been defined as spontaneous, in contrast to the receptive sensations. Now we find that in order to discover self within the inner sense, the inner sense must become receptive to its own spontaneity as internal affect. This means that self-consciousness, in spite of a compelling illusion, is not immediate; rather, it is mediated, just as the other affects in the receptivity of sensation (§24, B152–53).

Hume lost the self in consciousness, because "I can never catch *myself* at any time without a perception, and can never observe anything but the perception." Kant reaffirms self-consciousness as the transcendental I (*das transzendentale Ich*) by observing the form of time given to perception. In that act of transcendental synthesis he observes also the unity of synthesis from which he deduces apperception, the consciousness of self. The synthesizing and unifying act of apperception is in itself spontaneous. It belongs to the subject as self-activity (*Selbsttätigkeit*), exercized only by the subject (§15, B130). Further, the synthesizing, unifying act of apperception reveals the Kantian *cogito* (*Das: Ich denke*) which determines being (§25, B157n). Because he overlooks Kant's explanation of the apparent paradox here, Orsini finds Kant inconsistent: sometimes, according to Orsini, Kant "speaks practically like Fichte," wading into the idealism of scholastic dogma and "getting into very deep water indeed"; "at other times," Orsini adds, "Kant succumbs to his habitual fears of transcendent speculation, and says that the 'I think' is only 'a representation' and that it merely 'accompanies' all other representations" (B 132).[8] The confusion is Orsini's not Kant's. Kant does not make the mistake in some "systems of psychology" of identifying the unity of apperception with the inner sense as a thing-in-itself (*Ding-an-sich*), the noumenal center of consciousness. Indeed, Kant allows no compromise on this point: self-consciousness is a mediated affect, a phenomena; like all other noumena, the noumenon of our own inner nature remains inaccessible to consciousness (§24, B153–56). The unity of apperception presents the phenomena of self-consciousness that accompanies all the form-giving activities of perception, all the categorical organization of thought, all activity of mind *per se*.

Kant describes a self-consciousness that, to be sure, has an a priori given form and determination, but that can be known only as a reflection. Clearly, such a self-consciousness cannot be Coleridge's "heaven-descended KNOW THYSELF." Coleridge anticipates the problem in chapter 10, when he first acknowledges "obligations to Immanuel Kant," whose doctrine "took possession of me as with a giant's hand." Even after fifteen years of reading Kant "with undiminished delight and increasing admiration," Coleridge confesses that a "few passages . . . remained obscure to me." He points in particular to "the chapter on *original apperception*." Coleridge's difficulty is precisely that which we have just seen repeated by Orsini: the belief that Kant was caught in "contradictions." As Coleridge explains, Kant really wanted to affirm that apperception was noumenal and revealed universal idea, but "he was constrained to commence at the point of *reflection*, or natural consciousness" because "he had been in imminent danger of persecution." Coleridge's alternative, a "heaven-descended

KNOW THYSELF," would not set well with the "priest-ridden superstition." The religious censorship prompted such acts of "confiscation and prohibition," Coleridge argues, "that the venerable old man's caution was not groundless." He thus presumes a "difference between the letter and the spirit of Kant's writings"; specifically, Coleridge refuses to believe that "it was possible for him [Kant] to have meant no more by his *Noumenon*, or THING IN ITSELF, than his mere words express; or that in his own conception he confined the whole *plastic* power to the forms of the intellect, leaving for the external cause, for the *materiale* of our sensations, a matter without a form, which is doubtless inconceivable" (*BL* 1:155). This interpretation of Kant, as Wellek has shown, follows Schelling in close paraphrase. But it is indeed Coleridge's disappointment that Kant allowed for no heaven-descending in his deduction of the unity of apperception.

For such an explicit avowal of idealism, Coleridge turned to the *Wissenschaftslehre* of Fichte which he praised as "the key-stone of the arch." Fichte made precisely the equation which Kant denied. For Fichte, self-consciousness is immediate. The Kantian abyss between the noumenal and the phenomenal is bridged, for Fichte claims access to one noumenal presence: the "I" itself. To be sure, the "I" is no thing-in-itself. Just as Kant presented the *cogito* (*Das: Ich denke*) as verb rather than noun, as act, so too for Fichte the "I" (*das Ich*), as Coleridge emphasizes, is "an *act*, instead of a *thing* or *substance*." Departing from his mentor, Fichte made it an act exercized in and through the dynamism of universal idea. If Coleridge approved Fichte's "key-stone" which linked the phenomenal with the noumenal "I," why then did he add his harsh "burlesque on the Fichtean Egoismus"?

> Here on this market-cross aloud I cry:
> I, I, I! I itself I!

Coleridge explains that Fichte's "fundamental idea" was "overbuilt with a heavy mass of mere *notions*, and psychological acts of arbitrary reflection." The net result, Coleridge charges, was that the *Wissenschaftslehre* "degenerated into a crude egoismus, a boastful and hyperstoic hostility to Nature, as lifeless, godless, and altogether unholy." Having closed the arch to the noumenal, the universal "I," Fichte was unable to cross over. His system became ever more encumbered with subjective apparatus. Instead of access to the divine, Fichte proved only self-centered deductions and grammatical postulates of God. As Coleridge's mock-Fichte proclaims:

> Self-construed, I all other moods decline:
> Imperative, from nothing we derive us;
> Yet as a super-postulate of mine,
> Unconstrued antecedence I assign
> To X, Y, Z, the God infinitivus!

The keystone, nevertheless, was in place; only the way across, the way to postulate all things in the absolute, was missing. "My *Faith* is with Fichte!" Coleridge exclaimed in an 1804 notebook entry. But even here, where he appreciates Fichte's reduction of the trinity—feeling, perception, thought —to the one universal of pure thought, Coleridge balked at the dehumanizing consequence: "never let me lose my reverence for the *three distinctions,* which are human & of our essence, as those of the 5 senses" (*CN* 2:2382).[9]

In his commentary on Coleridge's references to Fichte, Orsini has included a remarkable identification of the Fichtean element in Coleridge's 1801 notebook entry on *Tintern Abbey*. Orsini could neither relate this passage to the Fichtean matter in the *Biographia*, nor describe its relevance to Coleridge's further concern with perception and apperception. His identification, however, provides valuable evidence. Dating the entry "February-March 1801," Coleridge begins with the Wordsworthian lines and proceeds to discuss apperception in the act of perception.

> —and the deep power of Joy
> We see into the *Life* of Things—
>
> i.e.—By deep feeling we make our *Ideas dim*—& this is what we mean by our Life—ourselves. I think of the Wall—it is before me, a distinct Image —here. I necessarily think of the *Idea* and the Thinking as two distinct & opposite Things. Now let me think of *myself*—of the thinking Being —the Idea becomes dim whatever it be—so dim that I know not what it is—but the Feeling is deep & steady—and this I call *I*—identifying the Percepient & the Perceived—.

Why, Orsini asks, should Coleridge think of a wall? Such an obtrusive image must have a pertinent source, he reasons. After a round-about search, he traces "the wall" through Henrik Steffens back to Fichte. Steffens recollects Fichte's lectures at Jena in 1799. Fichte had devised a mental experiment to demonstrate to his students the self-conscious presence in the act of perception:

> 'Gentlemen', said he, 'collect yourselves—go into yourselves—for we have here nothing to do with things without, but simply with the inner

self'. Thus summoned, the auditors appeared really go into themselves . . . 'Gentlemen', continued Fichte, 'think the wall',—(*Denken Sie die Wand*). This was a task to which the hearers were evidently all equal; they thought the wall. 'Have you thought the wall?' asked Fichte. 'Well, then, gentlemen, think him who thought the wall'. It was curious to see the evident confusion and embarrassment that now arose. Many of his students seemed to be utterly unable to find him who had thought the wall.

Fichte, Orsini finds, had used as early as 1797 this mental experiment to demonstrate in the very act of thinking the unity of the thinker and the thing thought of.[10] Orsini is so preoccupied with the Fichtean "wall" in Coleridge's entry that he pays no attention to the non-Fichtean emphasis on feeling in Coleridge's version of the mental experiment. Nor is Coleridge's emphasis, however peculiar, merely an amalgam of Wordsworth and Fichte, for the commentary is as non-Wordsworthian as it is non-Fichtean. Wordsworth, to be sure, stresses feeling in describing memory's first gift of "beauteous forms" in his isolation "in lonely rooms, and 'mid the din / Of towns and cities." Here the remembered images bring "sensations sweet" which are felt through the body as they pass into "purer mind," a process perhaps accompanied, Wordsworth suggests, by other "feelings . . . / Of unremembered pleasure." The first gift of memory prompts a second,

> Of aspect more sublime; that blessed mood,
> In which the burthen of mystery
> In which the heavy and the weary weight
> Of all this unintelligible world,
> Is lightened.

Just as he described the bodily process of sensations "Felt in the blood, and felt along the heart," he now describes the affections which "lead us on" spiritually yet suspend bodily motion until the very pulsation "Felt in the blood" seems still. At this moment, "we are laid asleep / In body, and become a living soul." It is not the body stirred by feeling that can "see into the life of things," but the soul "made quiet by the power / Of harmony and the deep power of joy." For Wordsworth, material being is suspended in order to attain spiritual intercourse between the "living soul" and the essential "life of things." Feelings are subdued that ideas may be released. Coleridge quotes these lines but describes the opposite process: ideas are subdued by feelings. The very dominance of perceptual sensation renders the idea "so dim that I know not what it is—but the Feeling is deep & steady." For Coleridge, the domination of feeling reveals the "I."

This very same emphasis on feeling, the aesthesis of sensory engagement, produces the peculiar tension with the German texts in Coleridge's efforts to adapt Schelling's construction of apperception out of perception. This moment of identity, Schelling declared, was most fully realized in art. The act, which for Fichte provided the keystone in the arch between phenomenon and noumenon, Schelling recognizes as an aesthetic act. Thus the philosophy of art becomes the keystone for the entire philosophical structure (*SW* 3:349). Although Schelling argues that the most complete unity of subject and object, conscious and unconscious, is attained in aesthetic activity, he does not enter into the activity. He merely posits it, then traces its history. Principles and powers are the concern of Schelling's discourse; he does not indulge the mental experiments of Fichte or verbally reenact the processes of perception. Even in his repeated examples of mental construction, Schelling limits his visual metaphors to bare geometric shapes: the circle, the triangle. Coleridge, of course, elaborates the visual metaphors. But his reshaping of Schelling is no mere cosmetic application of apt images. Coleridge delineates the process of perceptual engagement in order to confirm the *Gestalt* of the aesthetic act. Before examining this crucial modification, I shall briefly review Schelling's presentation of apperception.

It is not enough for Schelling to declare that in apperception, subject and object coincide. He has to explain the coincidence. In opposition to Kant, he argues that this principle is independent, unconditional, immediate. Unlike Fichte, who began with the discovery of the perceiver in the thing perceived, Schelling plotted a two-fold course. The essays in his *Zeitschrift für spekulative Physik* pursued +/− polarities as primal and formative principles in physical nature. The *Jahrbücher der Medizin als Wissenschaft* represented a parallel endeavor addressing human physiology. Schelling sought to establish these same formative principles in the living organism and its capacities of conscious reflection.[11] Acknowledging that Coleridge owned the journals both on physics and medicine, Orsini apparently didn't take them seriously as sources for Coleridge's thought, for the jest with which he dismisses them seems pointless: "one can only hope that he [Coleridge] did not use them to prescribe for himself." But Coleridge did indulge their prescriptions.[12]

In the *Naturphilosophie*, Schelling drew from contemporary physics the argument that the material world was wrought through the dynamism of electricity, magnetism, and galvanic or chemical affinity. But so, too, was mind. The energy of mind, he claimed, was identical to the energy of nature. Consciousness is a temporal affect of the spatial construct of electrical-magnetic-chemical interaction. In tracing that identity from the subjective rather than the objective perspective, Schelling defined his *System der transcendentalen Idealismus* as a necessary counterpart to his *Naturphilosophie* (*SW* 3:332). Through fundamental geometric postulation and construction, Schelling sought to demonstrate the principles of spatial and temporal intuition. The geometry does not merely demonstrate, as Kant would have it, the organizing activity of individual consciousness, it reveals the absolute.[13] The *System* has six parts: 1) He posits self-consciousness as the highest principle of philosophy and deduces this principle from the coincidence of knowing and being in perception (here is the initial source for the ten theses in the *Biographia*); 2) he defines the productive imagination as a subject-object dialectic and demonstrates that its activity is potentially limitless, therefore absolute; 3) he recapitulates the activity of self-consciousness in the deduction of the absolute and recounts the three major "epochs" in the rise of self-consciousness: from sensation to productive imagination; from productive imagination to reflection; from reflection to the absolute act of will (the source for Coleridge's four stages of "inner sense");[14] 4) he investigates the practical implications (freedom, morality) of the self-consciousness as willing and acting; 5) he reviews the problem of freedom versus determinism in the teleological argument of nature; 6) he presents the philosophy of art based on the identity of mind and nature, freedom and necessity.

By affirming that the world known through perception is the real world, Schelling intended to deflate the counterargument of the Empiricists and Realists, whom he accused of leaving the perceiver isolated from reality and trapped in a world of illusions. But in avoiding the causality of sense impressions, Schelling simply assumed the truth of perception without delineating how sensations and feelings are transformed into images, or how the rapid and multiple barrage is unified into the whole of conscious experience. Even in his first effort to extrapolate the pertinent theses from Schelling's *System*, in his notebook entry of September, 1815 (*CN* 3:4265), Coleridge resisted the argument by principle and attempted to reinvoke the perceptual process. From Schelling's discussion of the relation of content to form, presented as a vicious circle[15] in which every pretension to form becomes a content yet to be ordered, Coleridge assembles thesis 2 (thesis 4, Scholium, in the *Biographia*). Schelling asked how to close this apparently open circle. Coleridge answers by taking the paradoxical circle as a literal, or rather, as a visual illusion, thus transforming the thesis into an account of the "endless cycle, a perpetual Interfusion . . . in a common Chaos" as opposed to the ordered circle or sphere.

But Coleridge does not stop here: when he elaborates the point in the *Biographia*, Schelling's endless train of philosophers searching for a systematic form, which always becomes subset within a yet unordered science, becomes "a string of blind men, each holding the skirt of the man before him." Not content to allegorize the fallacy of "a chain without a staple," a logical sorites without a valid first principle, Coleridge goes on to explain how perception, as well as reason, can be duped into overlooking the absurdity, "owing to a surreptitious act of the imagination, which instinctively and without our noticing the same, not only fills out the intervening spaces, and contemplates the *cycle* . . . as a continuous *circle* giving to all collectively the unity of their common orbit; but likewise supplies by a sort of *subintelligitur* the one central power, which renders the movement harmonious and cyclical" (*BL* 1:267).

The account in the *Logic* carries the problem of perceptual order even further. Here, before he introduces the Schellingian theses, he ponders the "mental forms or primary moulds" through which the mind has its "power of conferring unity." Indebted to Schelling's use of geometric construction as "primary intuition," Coleridge talks of "predetermining the figure" in the mind as an act of conception that precedes and informs perception. He presents apperception as catching the mind in this very act of imposing conception upon perception. He might have followed the arguments in *Ideen zu einer philosophie der Natur* (1797), *Von der Weltseele* (1798), or *Erster Entwurf eines Systems der Naturphilosophie* (1799). But these emphasize construction as physical energy rather than as cognitive process. Instead of adopting Schelling's terms of construction, *scheme, image, symbol,* Coleridge introduces the eidetic imagination.[16] In order to reveal the informing activity, the *energeia theoretike*, he chooses to rely on some mental experiments of his own: "there is but one way—that of placing yourself in such situations, or as it were positions, of mind as would be likely to call up that act in our intellectual being and then to attend to it as its necessary transient and subtle nature will permit" (*Logic* 73–74). His first situation is commonplace: the eye "connecting two bright stars" and seeming, at the outset, "to have something between a sense and a sensation of length" and then, "to find myself acting as it were in the construction of that length undisturbed by any accompanying perception of breadth or inequality which must needs accompany all pictures of a line." From this simple situation, he turns to one more complex, cited from a report of Reaumur and confirmed, twice Coleridge says, by his own experience: the triangles and circles or spirals seen in the night-flight of ephemerae by torchlight or moonlight.[17] The purpose of "this apparent digression," he declares, is to call attention to "acts of imagination that are one with the products of those acts" and to reveal the mind "as a subject that is its own object, an eye, as it were, that is its own mirror, beholding and self-beheld" (*Logic* 75–76).

In the notebook Coleridge relies on the *System des transcendentalen Idealismus* (1800) without the recourse to the earlier Fichtean position. In revising the argument for the *Biographia*, he returns in the first six theses to Schelling's early response to Fichte's presentation of sensory engagement; he alters 5 and 6, and expands 7 and 10. Then, in revisiting the argument in his *Logic*, he builds a more careful introduction on perceptual processes and rearranges the theses: 7, 5, 6, 2, 4. This sequence, from individual to universal, reiterates the act of perception in each extension of apperception as the ultimate principle of unity.

There is no departure from Schelling in Coleridge's confirmation that "a principle of unity is contributed by the mind itself." However, it is only Coleridge, not Schelling, who discriminates the perceptual modes, even when he declares that "it is altogether indifferent whether it be the matter of a waking perception, as a perception of a rainbow, or the matter of a waking intuition, as in the imaginative formation of a diagram in the geometrical contemplations, or lastly the matter of a phantasm, 'the stuff that dreams are made of'" (*Logic* 77). It is only Coleridge, not Schelling, who describes how the "percipient energies" give form and shape and how the mind discovers this activity in reflection. Schelling merely posits; Coleridge reenacts the performance.

9

Annotating the Annotations:
A Philosophical Reading of the
Primary and Secondary Imagination

J. Fisher Solomon

> The IMAGINATION then I consider either as primary, or secondary. The primary IMAGINATION I hold to be the living Power and prime Agent of all human Perception, and as a repetition in the finite mind of the eternal act of creation in the infinite I AM. The secondary I consider as an echo of the former, co-existing with the conscious will, yet still as identical with the primary in the *kind* of its agency, and differing only in *degree*, and in the *mode* of its operation. It dissolves, diffuses, dissipates, in order to re-create; or where this process is rendered impossible, yet still at all events it struggles to idealize and to unify. It is essentially *vital*, even as all objects (*as* objects) are essentially fixed and dead.
>
> —*BL* 1:304

Playfully gnomic and self-consciously evasive, Coleridge's famous definition of the primary and secondary imagination challenges its annotator to provide not only a genealogy for the passage in question, but a meaning as well. Each project equally relies upon the other, and each is equally ambiguous. For if Coleridge's meaning is unclear, the synthetic nature of his work obscures his intellectual line of descent as well. Thus, one of his most recent annotators can remark that "if Coleridge had a main source he also had many other sources—and his own thoughts as well" (*BL* 1:lxxxviii). Influence and inspiration blend here in a baffling amalgam whose precise nature is difficult to judge. Without some determination of the influences behind the theorem, we can hardly begin to interpret it; but without some sense of these sentences' meaning, we cannot be certain just who is behind them.

But Coleridge presents us a third challenge as well. That is, once we

have determined the genealogy and the meaning of Coleridge's speculations, we have still to consider just what they accomplish. The decline of
the "imagination" as a vital philosophical topic has ushered Coleridge out
of philosophy into history and literature; but while we need not restore
the imagination as such to its former speculative prominence, we may still
reconsider it as a response to some fundamental epistemological and ontological problems that have hardly gone away. In other words, Coleridge's
remarks on the imagination lay a philosophical as well as a historical claim
upon us, and we can respond to that claim profitably.

Before pursuing this philosophical line of analysis, however, we still
must begin where the annotators begin—with a historical survey of what
the concept of the *imagination in general* once meant and what philosophical problems it meant to resolve. We cannot begin to distinguish degrees
of the imagination, in other words, without first determining what the
imagination in general is. But I will focus here not on the many functions
that the imagination came to serve for philosophy, but rather on the basic
philosophical questions that the theory of the imagination seeks to answer.
And at first, of course, the scope of such questions was rather limited.

As James Engell and W. J. Bate report, the role of the imagination
was traditionally restricted to the "old task of the perception and retention of sense images for re-presentation" (*BL* 1:lxxxvi). Thus conceived,
the imagination answered a strictly empirical question: How do we perceive our world? Constituted in so narrow a sensory context, the imagination is a rather empty, passive human faculty, but later developments in
eighteenth-century philosophy would eventually lead to its promotion to
at once a more active and a more "metaphysical" status. Entire volumes,
of course, have been written to trace this evolution of the imagination
from a passively perceptual to an actively productive concept; but rather
than attempting to reproduce the course of that evolution here, we might
more efficiently limit our discussion to the changing questions that the
imagination-as-a-faculty concept came to address. Our focus, then, is not
so much on the imagination *as such* as it is an inquiry into the problems
that the imagination came to be involved in. And it is by so staging the
imagination in general that we may determine its relevance to contemporary
philosophy.

Our inaugurating question now is not "how do we *perceive* our world?"
but "how do we *know* our world?" Cartesian rationalism answered this second question in such a way as to exclude the first. Knowledge for this

tradition is constituted in accordance with the innate ideas supplied by the intuitive reason. Perception cannot be trusted. Such a perspective, as Engell remarks, has little room for a positive imagination (Engell 1981, 20); but as the British empiricists came to ask the same question, their restriction of the empirically unaided reason to "deduction, logic, and effort" (Engell 1981,19) necessarily expanded the epistemological role of the imagination. Accordingly, the old perceptual faculty found a new conceptual field in which to flourish.

Still, if John Locke had simply restricted our knowledge to the purely objective perception and retention of direct experience, had held, that is, to the most simplistically positivistic interpretation of the "*tabula rasa,*" then no pressure for an expanded *imagination in general* would have been exerted upon English (and continental) philosophy. All that would have been needed would have been a theory of sense perception (of the eyes, ears, and touch). But, of course, Locke conceived the mind in a productive as well as a reproductive sense (see Engell 1981, 18–19). The mind has to organize its simplest experiences in order to constitute its knowledge. It is active as well as passive. A voluntary association of ideas, in other words, presumes some organizational, constitutive power. And here the imagination found its opportunity, eventually becoming a name for this new faculty (see Engell 1981, 19–20).

But what I wish to suggest is that in the Romantic development of the "imagination," the failure to rid it of its lingering reproductive and representational nature would eventually lead to its own ontological contradiction. That is to say, as the imagination came to occupy a greater and greater place in Romantic epistemology, the fact that it continued to carry with it a representational as well as a constitutive connotation finally led to the sort of metaphysical contortions that we find in our own passage from chapter 13 of the *Biographia Literaria.* But rather than announce that the "imagination" therefore constitutes its own contradiction, I will argue that the ontological difficulties that a representational imagination may raise can be resolved once we see that the power that the Romantics called the imagination (and which might be called something else) has no simply reproductive or representative side at all. The mind is *not* both passive and active: it is wholly active. And the implications of this require of us not only a rethinking of the imagination, but (in a more contemporary context) a rethinking of ontology itself.

To demonstrate the wholly nonrepresentational nature of the imagination, we might begin with the same Kantian epistemological challenge that Coleridge faced. When Kant divided reality into its phenomenal and noumenal realms—arguing that outward "objects are quite unknown to us in themselves, and what we call outward objects, are nothing else but mere representations [*Vorstellungen*] of our sensibility" (Kant 1884, 28)—he effectively inscribed a gap between *knowing* and *being,* a representational spacing that would quickly raise a new question for philosophy. That is, we now have to ask just how phenomenal subjects can ever achieve ontological unity with the noumenal objects that ground their experience. How does "mind" match "reality"? Taking his lead from Schelling, Coleridge himself first decided that if such questions were to receive any answers at all Kant's own remarks concerning the *Ding an sich* would have to be reexamined and qualified. And so, in chapter 9 of the *Biographia,* Coleridge observes how:

> In spite of [Kant's] declarations, I could never believe, it was possible for him to have meant no more by his *Noumenon,* or THING IN ITSELF, than his mere words express; or that in his own conception he confined the whole *plastic* power to the forms of the intellect, leaving for the external cause, for the *materiale* of our sensations, a matter without form, which is doubtless inconceivable. (*BL* 1:155)

For Coleridge, in other words, nature in itself could not be conceived as mere shapeless matter. It too had to embody a formal principle, had to be creative just as the mind is creative. As *natura naturans* (as well as *natura naturata*) nature thus had something in common with phenomenal subjectivity, and what it had in common, of course, was the imagination (see Engell 1981, 333).

To demonstrate this imaginative essence of outward nature, the transcendental philosopher had first to demonstrate that the material phenomena of our categorical experience are finally ephemeral. Matter has to be sublimated to uncover the formal principle within. In this, too, Coleridge closely follows Schelling, remarking in chapter 12 of the *Biographia* that:

> The phaenomena (*the material*) must wholly disappear, and the laws alone (*the formal*) must remain. Thence it comes, that in nature itself the more the principle of law breaks forth, the more does the *husk* drop off, the phaenomena themselves become more spiritual and at length cease in our consciousness. . . . The theory of natural philosophy would

> be then completed, when all nature was demonstrated to be identical
> in essence with that, which in its highest known power exists in man as
> intelligence and self-consciousness. (*BL* 1:256)

Thus in the grand Romantic dialectic, human intelligence discovers
through its own imaginative acts of self-consciousness that nature too, as
it is governed by laws, is also an intelligence. The spirit of man and the
spirit of nature finally meet: the gap between mind and matter is crossed.

But there's a hitch. For if, as Coleridge notes in chapter 12 of the *Biographia*, subjective intelligence must be "conceived of as exclusively representative" (*Vorstellende* in Schelling) and objective nature must be conceived
"as exclusively represented" (*Vorstellbare* in Schelling), then we *still* have
a representational gap inscribed between being and knowing, a difference between the representation and the represented (see *BL* 1:255 and
253,n.3). Coleridge tries to resolve this contradiction in his own definition
of the imagination, but we have yet a stubborn representational space to
cross, and in attempting to cross that space Coleridge finally obscures his
own solution.

At this point we may turn back to our passage from chapter 13 of
the *Biographia*. Epistemologically, Coleridge's definition seems quite clear.
The primary imagination, which we might see to be a kind of synthesis
of Schelling's *erste Potenz* (or sensory perception) and *zweite Potenz* (or productive perception: see Engell 1981, 306–07), is that faculty responsible
for our essential perception of the world. It both receives and organizes
sensory stimuli, passively responding to and actively reproducing its perception of outer reality. The secondary imagination, or the esthetic power,
reorganizes what the primary imagination has received and constituted
in order to create supranatural configurations still tied *to* nature through
their connection to the primary imagination but not to be found, as such,
in nature. But even Coleridge saw that his epistemological explanation
did not wholly achieve what it had set out to do. That is, the concept of
the *imagination in general* was conceived to answer not only the question
"how do we know our world?" but also "how can we be reunified *with* our
world; how can being and knowing be reconciled?" So Coleridge adds
to his epistemological definition of the imagination an ontological dimension, insisting that the primary imagination functions "as a repetition in
the finite mind of the eternal act of creation in the infinite I AM." But now
we are faced with yet another spacing, for if the finite primary imagination *repeats* the acts of an infinite imagination, how can the two ever be

brought into unity? What mediation can there be between finitude and infinitude?

That such questions are no mere anachronism (questions we impose upon the past) can be seen through Coleridge's own attempts to ontologically ground his conception of the *imagination in general.* He too sought for a convincing point of mediation between an infinite and a finite imagination. Thus, in chapter 12 of the *Biographia,* Coleridge tries to demonstrate how self-consciousness must lead necessarily to absolute consciousness: how finite knowledge leads us irresistibly to infinite Being. Coleridge's proof runs as follows:

THESIS I.

Truth is correlative to being. Knowledge without a corresponding reality is no knowledge . . . To know is in its very essence a verb active.

THESIS II.

All truth is either mediate, that is, derived from some other truth or truths; or immediate and original. The latter is absolute . . . the former is of dependent or conditional certainty . . .

Thus:

THESIS III.

We are to seek therefore for some absolute truth . . . a truth self-grounded, unconditional and known by its own light. In short, we have to find a somewhat which *is* simply because it *is.* In order to be such, it must be one with its own predicate . . . to preclude the possibility of requiring a cause or antecedent without an absurdity.

But:

THESIS V.

Such a principle cannot be any THING or OBJECT. Each thing is what it is in consequence of some other thing. . . .

But neither can the principle be found in a subject as a subject, contradistinguished from an object . . . It is to be found therefore neither in object or subject taken separately, and consequently, as no other third is conceivable, it must be found in that which is neither subject nor object exclusively, but which is the identity of both.

And so:

THESIS VI.

This principle, and so characterized manifests itself in the SUM or I AM; which I shall hereafter indiscriminately express by the words spirit, self, and self-consciousness. In this, and this alone, object and subject, being and knowing, are identical, each involving and supposing the other. . . . It may be described therefore as a perpetual self-duplication of one and the same power into object and subject, which presuppose each other, and can exist only as antitheses. (*BL* 1:264–73)

In chapter 13 of the *Biographia*, of course, Coleridge will equate this self-duplicating power with the imagination, thus identifying the *imagination in general* (as knowledge) with absolute truth (as being). But the success of Coleridge's dialectical union of knowing and being through the imagination finally relies less upon logic than faith, as Coleridge openly proclaims in his ninth thesis how "We begin with the I KNOW MYSELF, in order to end with the absolute I AM. We proceed from the SELF, in order to lose and find all self in GOD" (*BL* 1:283). In later experimental attempts to synthesize religion and philosophy, Coleridge will continue to identify the dialectical ground of knowing and being with a personal God (as a *Prothesis*), and with each successive readjustment first of the Pythagorean Tetractys (see Engell 1981, 364–65) and then of his various Pentads, Coleridge will increasingly shore up his philosophy with religious appeals that his own sources felt compelled to resist. Indeed, Schelling himself observed "that theoretical philosophy cannot, given its own criteria, successfully assert that God is the ground of our *knowledge*" (*BL* 1:274,n.2).

But I do not raise this sufficiently obvious objection in order to dismiss Coleridge's philosophy of the imagination out of hand as a mere appeal to an undemonstrated presence. Rather, I suggest that if we look less at what Coleridge's words seem to *say* and more at what they actually *do*, we may discover how his philosophy leads to a new ontological reconciliation between being and knowing on the basis of a power that we need neither ground in God nor strictly identify with a transcendency, but which can be discerned precisely within Coleridge's own definitions.

So let's repeat the problem: as an epistemological faculty, Coleridge's primary and secondary imagination offers us no particular difficulties. As a nonphysiological explanation for the facts of sensory perception and esthetic construction, the imagination simply names a psychological agency (accounts, that is, for our knowledge and creativity). But when this same concept attempts to explain just *how* our knowledge transcends itself to attain union with *what* it knows, our epistemological problem becomes an ontological one. Knowing must become being, and in the imagination, Coleridge thought that he had found the dialectical link. But without an

appeal to a divine imagination able to mediate fully with our finite imagi-
nations, knowing remains cut off, as Kant predicted, from the noumenal
being that grounds our knowledge. All that we really have are representations, and even Coleridge's primary imagination can only come so close
to absolute reality as a *repetition* can afford.

But what if we look at knowledge differently? What if outward objects
are not conceived as mere representations, *Vorstellungen,* of our sensibility?
The whole problem of a "knowing" cut off from "being," I suggest, begins
precisely where we define knowledge as representational at all, as *Vor-*
stellen: something placed before, a substitution. And although the Romantic development of the imagination was constituted exactly to combat the
passive sense of representational knowledge, the imagination, either as
Vorstellungskraft (see *BL* 1:lxxxvi) or even as *Einbildungskraft,* still retains a
duality that it cannot really overcome as so conceived. But this does not
mean that the power that the concept of the imagination seeks to name is
itself so frustrated.

Before turning to the words that might more accurately define the dy-
namically constitutive nature of the power that the term "imagination"
tries to designate, we might first explore the shortcomings of the available terms further. As *Vorstellungskraft,* the imagination only substitutes a
sensory image for what it perceives; it places something before and hence
erects a barrier between knowing and being. It connotes a purely representative, substitutive power. But as *Einbildungskraft,* the imagination still
erects a barrier, albeit an inadvertant one. To refer to Coleridge's own
understanding of this term, we find *Einbildungskraft* meaning "the power
of forming into one, an act on which all creation is founded. It is the power
through which an ideal is also something real, the soul the body . . ." (see
Engell 1981, 304). Or, as Engell glosses Schelling's understanding of the
imagination as *Einbildungskraft*:

> In each object or work of art it creates, the imagination fuses a universal
> form, the infinite or '*Unendliche*,' and a finite, individual manifestation.
> The idea of form, and form's concretion as matter, become indivisibly
> one and exist in and through one another. In the imaginative act two
> unities are formed, each of which is really the other. Form becomes being
> and being becomes form. (Engell 1981, 305)

But so long as we conceive reality in terms of any polar oppositions at
all (infinitude/finitude, ideal/real, form/matter), we have set up polarities
that we need not have set up. Indeed, when we do set them up, even in

the name of a power that will reconcile them, we find ourselves in such ontological difficulties that we must speak of one "unity" that is "really" another. What does it mean, ontologically, to say that one thing *is* only insofar as it is something else? Doesn't this suggest a dialectical ontology that is "always already" divided by a prior difference; that nature itself is hinged, and thus never fully available to knowledge?

Readers of Jacques Derrida will immediately recognize such observations as these, but I raise them here not to suggest that the imagination must thus face up to its own contradictions. To the contrary, I suggest that the power (*Kraft*) that the imagination (either as *Vorstellungskraft* or as *Einbildungskraft*) seeks to define is not well served by terms that either work by representational substitution or by oppositional unification. But if, as I am arguing, "imaginational knowledge" is not representational, then what is it? And if "being," or "reality," is never present *either* in oppositional terms *or* as the unity of its oppositions, then what is *it*? How can we say that "being" is neither dualistically divided nor fundamentally unified?

What I wish to suggest is that when we look closely at the power that the imagination names, we discover an ontology that is neither precisely dualistic nor unified, neither dyad nor monad, and that it is only by this understanding that such statements as Engell's that in "the imaginative act two unities are formed, each of which is really the other" can make any sense. I am not arguing that Schelling and Coleridge are "wrong"; however, their descriptions of the imagination imply an ontology according to which we have neither finite singularity nor infinite universality available at any moment for unification. Instead, the ontology of the power before us appears the moment we cease to oppose any two such "unities" for even an instant. We have neither a simple (or unified) self-present power (the imagination) nor the dialectical difference between dissolved oppositions. What we have, as I shall argue, is a power *with* a difference: what I shall call "power-*and*-difference."

At this point our project becomes enormous, but some outlines for a demonstration of the imagination as an ontological and epistemological structure in power-*and*-difference may be briefly provided by examining a fragmentary commentary of Coleridge's on Aristotle's *Categories* that we find appended to the Bollingen edition of his *Logic* (1981, 287–89). Here Coleridge seeks rather desperately to sort out exactly what Aristotle meant to say about the relation between knowing (or "what is said," *ta legomena*) and being (or "what really is," *ta onta*) in the *Categories,* crossing out one explanation after another only to finally abandon the attempt. But before abandoning his essay, Coleridge precisely indicates the problem at hand and even a possible solution.

The trouble, Coleridge finds, is that Aristotle appears to make a distinction between "what is said" (the *legomenon* or "Dicta") and "what is" (the *onta* or "Entia"), a distinction that Coleridge "confesses" he "cannot at all understand" (289). "But," Coleridge continues, "it by [no] [sic] means appears, that Aristotle meant absolute distinction" (289). Coleridge thus questions the distinction between *legomena* and *onta* because of his discovery that if *legomena* are "general terms" rather than singulars, so too are *onta* (as universal substance, particular accidents, and universal accidents: 288). *Both* the *legomenon* and the *onta* appear to be "general terms," knowledge: "what is said." But if this is the case, what has happened to the "what is"? Have we only knowledge without being?

Coleridge, however, remarks a fourth species of *onta*, Aristotle's "particular substance" ("Thomas," "John," or "Peter"), which appears to resolve our difficulty. Certainly "John," as a *particular* substance or entity, is no mere general term. Certainly "John *is*" whether we say so or not. Aristotle evidently thought so, and took care to categorize the individual entity as the primary ground for knowledge and being, defining it thus as *primary ousia* (C5, 2a, 11–14). And yet, even primary *ousia* has its implicit complications, as well as certain explicit ones. That is to say, as Joseph Owens points out with respect to the *explicit* intentions of Aristotle's later definitions of primary *ousia* in the *Metaphysics*, what is most primary in primary being is not a solid individual but a *form*, a "this," a *tode ti* (Owens 317, 388–89). "What is," then, qua "form," "cannot be a singular," Owens explains, "because it is knowable and definable," and ". . . cannot be universal, because it is Entity, and the primary instance of Entity" (388–89). But if primary being is thus neither singular nor plural, then we must find some name for it. "The term 'a this,'" Owens remarks, "serves the purpose quite conveniently" (389).

Let us look at this "this," this *tode ti*, a moment. As the *Metaphysics* makes clear, it is not the *sole* "entity" (or "substance," or "being"), only the most prior. Matter, and the composition of matter and form, are also "entity" (see Owens 330). But now (to depart from Aristotle) we might ask if it is either necessary or possible to so prioritize being. If matter consists in its potency (*dunamis*) or its power to become formally actual, is it not the *composition* of potency and actuality, matter and form, that determines a being, a "this"? This is not Aristotle, but it might be Coleridge, because in this dialectical complement of matter and form in the non-Aristotelian "this" we may find a model for an imagination that is also a kind of "this": a being that is neither singular nor plural.

If we may regard the "thisness" of being, that is, as a dialectical structure that can be reduced neither to material potency alone nor to formal actuality alone, then what is required is a power to perform the composition of the "two." But do we really need to transcendentalize this power as, for example, an "efficient cause" or an "Infinite Imagination"? Might we not say that the power (*dunamis*) or potency for the composite is immanent in the very relation between matter and form? Could it not be argued that every "this" constitutes the dialectical complement of a material potency and an actualizing form (which, by determining its material complement, simultaneously differentiates or discriminates it from undetermined matter) whose very potential is inscribed within the relation? Do we not have here a certain power with its own differentiating capacity which is never "outside" it, a neither singular nor plural "being" that we might equally call "power-*and*-difference"?

In so questioning, I do not mean to identify such questions with either Aristotle or Coleridge (Aristotelian "difference," for instance, cannot be equated with "form"), but if we look at the "this" in this non-Aristotelian way we find a being that is actually quite close to the Romantic "symbol." For in the symbol's own complementary dialectic of matter and form or expression and meaning we find a similar phenomenon that is neither singular nor plural, but not simply a pure form. And the imagination that is so involved in the symbol is not something that is outside the symbol: it is the *idea* that both particularizes matter and is expressed by matter. It, too, is a structure in power-*and*-difference.

Thus, we might say that the infinite I AM is simply the dialectical being, the "this," of nature: the power-*and*-difference of material potency and formal determination. The primary imagination, in constituting its own "this," and the secondary imagination, in constituting *its* own "this" as esthetic symbol, thus instantiate the structure of being on the order of the *same*, not as a mere repetition or representation. Should we not say that our knowledge and our symbols are not simply substitutions (*Vorstellungen*) for being, but are being itself: that is, a complex, dynamic process of phenomenal constitution that cannot be differentiated simply from any *tode ti*? Is not "what is real," finally, the *structure* of such constitutions, and isn't the imagination one such structure, one such "this"?

Perhaps we might see that the imagination neither *unifies* opposites (*Ein-bildung*) nor *repeats* a "higher" power. It is its own power and potency with its own formational actualization. I have called this integration of undifferentiated potency (*dunamis*) and differentiated actuality "power-*and*-difference" in order to suggest by hyphenation and italic emphasis a term which, like a "this," is neither singular nor plural.[1] This is where Coleridge's mysterious pronouncements on the imagination may possibly lead us: to an understanding that nothing, neither imaginational knowledge nor the world that it knows, ever subsists either simply or with any order of priority. "What is" has no singular component, no *first* principle, but it may still be *principled*.

10

Coleridge and Milton: The Case against Wordsworth in the *Biographia Literaria*

Raimonda Modiano

Coleridge's lavish praise of Wordsworth as a writer equal in imaginative power or even superior to Milton has had the effect of concealing the extent to which Coleridge identified with Milton and used him to expose Wordsworth's numerous defects as poet and critic. U. C. Knoepflmacher, for example, believes that in chapter 15 of *Biographia Literaria*, Coleridge's analysis of the merits of Shakespeare's early writings was meant to draw Wordsworth's attention to the limitations of his dramatic capabilities and reinforce his sense of the Miltonic vocation, which he seemed to have "unwittingly forsaken."[1] In my view, here, as elsewhere in the *Biographia*, despite his statements to the contrary, Coleridge sought to undermine Wordsworth's aspirations to be the Milton of the Romantic age, and to demonstrate the impropriety of placing Wordsworth in the company of Milton, as well as Shakespeare, an association which Wordsworth unabashedly claimed for himself in the preface to his 1815 collection of poems.[2]

Harold Bloom's theory of the "anxiety of influence" has also misrepresented Coleridge's relationship to Milton, for Coleridge's real competitor and feared rival was not Milton, as Bloom indicates, but Wordsworth.[3] Instead of becoming an object of anxiety for Coleridge, Milton in fact mitigated Coleridge's debilitating complex of inferiority toward Wordsworth, enhancing his self-esteem. Bloom oversimplifies the case when he notes that Coleridge transferred his earlier anxieties toward Milton onto Wordsworth and lumped both into a composite father figure.[4] As I will show toward the end of this essay, although Coleridge encouraged the identification of Milton with Wordsworth in an effort to achieve an ideal self-image, he also emphasized the incompatibility between Wordsworth's and Milton's standards of performance. In the period of growing alienation between Coleridge and Wordsworth, as Coleridge became aware of the radical difference in their views on poetry, he found in Milton a set of beliefs that helped him articulate his divergence from Wordsworth with greater confidence. Milton became the intermediary, or *"tertium aliquid,"* in Coleridge's terms, binding the two friends in an ongoing relationship of mutual dependence and barely suppressed antagonism. While Wordsworth used Milton to undo a seemingly flattering representation of his friend,[5] Coleridge devised an extremely idealized portrait of Milton in order to mock Wordsworth's exaggerated sense of his importance as the "Head & founder of a *Sect* in Poetry."[6] As Lucy Newlyn argues, Miltonic allusion becomes "a shared habit, a token of exchange" between Coleridge and Wordsworth, but also "a signal of divergence."[7]

In the following discussion, I examine Coleridge's private writings prior to the composition of the *Biographia* which show that Coleridge's unreserved admiration for Milton was triggered by his disenchantment with the work of a contemporary writer, be it Bowles, Southey, or Wordsworth. Subsequently, I point out Coleridge's covert tactics of using Milton as an ally against Wordsworth in the *Biographia*. Milton enables Coleridge to advance an alternative conception of simplicity, superior to Wordsworth's view as formulated in the poems of the *Lyrical Ballads* and the 1800 preface. Furthermore, Coleridge represents Milton as a writer whose works epitomize the ideal of organic unity to the fullest, an ideal which becomes Coleridge's most viciously successful tool for humiliating Wordsworth. In this matter I differ from critics who have taken Coleridge's statements on organic unity all too seriously either in a positive or negative sense. Although Coleridge was genuinely attracted to this ideal, its extreme formulation in the *Biographia*—which, as critics have often complained, conflicts so glaringly with the actual process of poetic composition or Coleridge's own practice,[8]—was not an article of faith on Coleridge's part but a conscious strategy designed to settle his scores with Wordsworth once and for all. Throughout the *Biographia* Coleridge consistently evaluates Wordsworth's achievements in light of his organic theory, whereas he judges his own works according to an entirely different standard that privileges dynamic change and self-conscious improvement rather than the production of the impeccably organic work of art, as unchanging as the pyramids of Egypt.

II

Coleridge's earliest references to Milton indicate that he was not, from the very start, as keen an admirer of Milton as his later writings might suggest. In 1794, for example, under the powerful impression made by his reading of Schiller's *Robbers*, he wondered why "we ever called Milton sublime," adding that Satan "is scarcely qualified to attend" Moor's "Execution as Gallows Chaplain" (*CL* 1:122). By 1796 Coleridge was willing to grant sublimity to Milton in relation to Homer and Virgil, but compared to the Bible even Milton seemed to him "barely tolerable" (*CL* 1:281). Although some of Coleridge's comments on Milton during this period are apprecia-tive, and occasionally he appealed to Milton to justify his pursuits as poet and political reformer, Coleridge did not as yet perceive Milton as a writer of unique accomplishments. In a letter to John Thelwall of December 17, 1796, Coleridge proudly confessed his capacity to "admire, aye & almost equally, the *head* and fancy of Bowles, the solemn Lordliness of Milton, & the divine Chit chat of Cowper." Here Milton appears to be as good and as bad as Coleridge's contemporaries for, as he puts it, "whatever a man's excellence is, that will be likewise his fault" (*CL* 1:279). Of particular note is Coleridge's claim that Milton merits no more admiration than Bowles, whom he praises in this letter as "the most tender, and, with the excep-tion of Burns, the only *always-natural* poet in our Language" (*CL* 1:278). In later documents Coleridge pointed out the unquestionable superiority of Milton to Bowles, especially as Bowles became a foil for Wordsworth, enabling Coleridge to isolate the faults of a poetry dominated by fancy rather than the imagination.[9]

The first significant assessment of Milton in an unambiguously positive light occurs in a letter to Joseph Cottle of early April 1797. Here Coleridge complained of a dreadful depression that came over him after his return to Nether Stowey, quoting the well-known lines from *Samson Agonistes* that became the source of stanza 2 of "Dejection: An Ode." The "calm hope-lessness" Coleridge described in this letter, which again anticipates the mood of "Dejection," must have been triggered by his sense of inferiority toward Robert Southey, whose overwhelming productivity had the effect of increasing Coleridge's dissatisfaction with his own literary output. Evi-dently Wordsworth, who was visiting Coleridge, criticized Southey for writing verse with too much facility, an opinion which Coleridge readily endorsed in a subsequent attack on the unevenness of Southey's poetry and his preference for "*story* and *event* in his poems, to the neglect of those *lofty imaginings,* that are peculiar to, and definitive of, the poet." Against Southey's rushed and facile poems Coleridge presents the example of Milton, "his severe application, his laborious polish, his deep metaphysical researches, his prayers to God before he began his great poem" and "all that could lift and swell his intellect" which became "his daily food." Coleridge concludes the letter with his well-known plan, extravagantly ambitious in conception, concerning the labors he would undertake to write an epic poem. Unlike Southey who rushed poems into print, Coleridge, prompted by the example of Milton, was willing to spend no less than twenty years to produce an epic poem, ten to become conversant with all branches of science and "the *minds of men,*" and ten to compose and revise the poem (*CL* 1:319–20).

One is struck by the dual role Milton fulfills here, offering Coleridge a language for articulating his hopelessness and sense of dwindling "genial spirits," as well as a language of self-assertion by projecting an ideal that Coleridge hopes to accomplish in some distant future and puts his immediate rivals to shame. Coleridge clearly invests Milton with qualities that represent his own strengths and potential achievements, for, undoubtedly, Coleridge was well versed in metaphysical studies and keenly interested in science, a concern which he maintained throughout his life. Milton emerges as Coleridge's ideal *alter ego* and becomes a figure of fantasy on whom Coleridge pins his wildest projections. More importantly, the letter indicates that Milton surfaces in Coleridge's discourse as an object of adulation at the point when he feels directly threatened by the work of a contemporary with whom he had formed close personal and literary ties. We shall observe the same juncture in documents connected with Coleridge's complicated relationship with Wordsworth. In fact, Coleridge's complaint that Southey produced insignificant poems due to his emphasis on story and event at the expense of "*lofty imaginings*" is almost identical to his critique of Wordsworth after 1800, as is his use of Milton in self-defense.

Coleridge's most outspoken attack on Wordsworth prior to the *Biographia* appears in two letters to Robert Southey (July 29, 1802) and Thomas Poole (October 14, 1803), both of which reveal the link between his deteriorating friendship with Wordsworth and his deepening need to see his beliefs reflected in Milton's achievements. In the letter to Poole, Coleridge criticized Wordsworth's involuted personality, his dangerous

withdrawal within the protective circle of his close admirers, and his abandonment of his great work *The Recluse*, which would have focused his
"attention & Feelings" on "great objects & elevated Conceptions." Wordsworth comes off here no better than Southey in the letter to Cottle. He,
too, appears to be engaged in writing insignificant poems instead of under
taking, like Milton, the laborious task of producing a poem of genuine
philosophic import. "I have seen enough," Coleridge states with unusual
forthrightness, "positively to give me feelings of hostility towards the plan
of several of the Poems in the L. Ballads." Coleridge was particularly of-
fended by Wordsworth's ambition to be "or rather to be called, the Head
& founder of a *Sect* in Poetry: & assuredly he has written—& published . . .
poems written with a *sectarian* spirit, & in a sort of Bravado" (*CL* 2:1013). It
is important to bear in mind this open critique of Wordsworth's "*sectarian*
spirit*," for this underscores Coleridge's attack on Wordsworth in the *Biographia*, where he establishes through writers like Shakespeare and Milton
the ideal of a poet who has no experimental predilections, and whose subjects are "very remote from" his "private interests and circumstances." [10]

A year earlier, in the letter to Robert Southey, Coleridge voiced as
vehement a critique of Wordsworth as in the letter to Poole, noting in
Wordsworth's compositions a "daring Humbleness of Language & Versi-
fication, and a strict adherence to matter of fact." Again Coleridge seems
irritated by the "Bravado" exhibited by Wordsworth in accomplishing the
experimental goals set up in his 1800 preface. Even though the preface
was "half a child of" Coleridge's "own Brain," Wordsworth's recent poems
led him to perceive the "radical Difference" in their "theoretical opinions
respecting Poetry." Hence, Coleridge informs Southey that he plans to
write a treatise on "the Canons of Criticism respecting Poetry," a plan
which, as critics have often noted, is the early nucleus of the *Biographia*.
Less noted, however, is that even in this early formulation, Coleridge is
thinking of Milton as the writer who will provide him with an alternative
to Wordsworth's misguided theory of poetry. [11] "What an admirable Definition Milton gives quite in an obiter way," Coleridge writes, "when he
says of Poetry—that it is '*simple, sensuous, passionate*'!—It truly comprizes
the whole, that can be said on the subject" (*CL* 2:830).

What Coleridge means by this definition becomes clearer from a letter
to William Sotheby of September 10, 1802, and from its later elaboration
in Coleridge's lectures on Milton and Shakespeare. From the former, we
derive an important clue regarding Coleridge's assessment of passion as

a main ingredient in poetry; from the latter, we begin to understand the special meaning Coleridge attributed to the standard of simplicity as a way of differentiating between Wordsworth's and Milton's beliefs.

In the letter to Sotheby, Coleridge connects passion with the intellect and not with sensibility, as one might expect. The letter contains a vituperative attack on Bowles for his transparent "trick of *moralizing* every thing," his inability to unite the head and the heart, and his indulgence in fanciful similes. Bowles, Coleridge complains, "has indeed the *sensibility* of a Poet; but he has not the *Passion* of a great Poet. His latter Writings all want *native* Passion—Milton here & there supplies him with an appearance of it—but he has no native Passion, because he is not a Thinker" (*CL* 2:864). Milton, then, contrary to Bowles, is a poet of genuine passion precisely because of his "severe application" to "all that could lift and swell his intellect," as Coleridge had praised him earlier (*CL* 1:320). Passion, as Coleridge conceives it here, is an intellectual power that unifies what would otherwise remain disparate data of sensibility loosely connected with the mood of a speaker through "formal similes," as in Bowles. Drawing on his poem "To Mathilda Bentham from a Stranger," Coleridge illustrates how the intellect leads to the profoundly unified logic exhibited by the best of poems, providing consistency and endurance to feelings, like a trunk that remains fixed however impetuously its branches "Toss in the strong winds." In this context passion differs minimally from the intellect or the imagination for that matter, which Coleridge defines in this letter as the "*modifying,* and *co-adunating* Faculty" as opposed to fancy or the "aggregating Faculty of the mind."

Just as passion for Coleridge means something other than mere sensibility,[12] springing from the head as much as from the heart, simplicity takes on a different meaning, referring neither to unadorned diction, nor to the representation of the affections of ordinary people, as Wordsworth thought. In fact, in a notebook entry of 1808, in which Coleridge provides one of the few clearer statements on simplicity, we detect a distinct anti-Wordsworthian agenda. In this entry, which, significantly enough, was a draft for a projected lecture on modern poetry, including an examination of Wordsworth's "System & Compositions,"[13] Coleridge draws attention to the extraordinary importance of unravelling the true meaning of Milton's parenthetical definition of poetry as "simple, sensuous, passionate." Had this definition been properly understood, Coleridge reflects, "not only almost a Library of . . . false Poetry would have been either precluded or still-born, but what is of more consequence, works truly excellent, and capable of enlarging the understanding, warming & purifying the heart, and placing in the centre of the whole Being the Germs of noble & manlike Actions, would have been the . . . common Diet of the Intellect instead." After this preamble, Coleridge attempts to elucidate Milton's conception of simplicity, arguing that simplicity is the distinguishing mark that differentiates poetry from science. While science labors "towards an end not yet arrived at," poetry "supposes a smooth and finished Road on which the Reader is to walk onward easily, with streams murmuring by his side, & Trees & Flowers, & human dwellings to make his journey as delightful as the Object of it is desirable, instead of having to toil with the Pioneers, & painfully make the road, on which others are to travel . . ." (*CN* 3:3287).

It is not immediately apparent in what way Coleridge has given here a definition of simplicity. He shows rather that the ultimate aim of poetry is pleasure rather than the attainment of a given end, which is the main business of science. This distinction is familiar to readers of the *Biographia*, as is Coleridge's point that in all good poetry the reader is not "carried forward . . . chiefly by the mechanical impulse of curiosity, or by a restless desire to arrive at the final solution; but by the pleasureable activity of mind excited by the attractions of the journey itself" (*BL* 2:14). But there is something provocative about Coleridge's notebook entry, particularly if we recall that in the letter to Southey of 1802, Coleridge thought of Milton's definition as a direct reply to Wordsworth's mistaken opinions regarding poetry. In what way, then, does this explanation of simplicity challenge Wordsworth's critical program as carried out in the *Lyrical Ballads*?

My sense is that Coleridge sets up a distinction between science and poetry in order to suggest a more important distinction between experimental poetry and a poetry based on universally shared ideals. The former is written by authors who are bent on being "Pioneers" and who take the readers along a toilsome journey on a newly made road; the latter secures for readers a pleasant journey along a "smooth and finished Road" paved by generations of travellers. Readers of experimental poetry will be naturally impelled by curiosity, desiring to know where the new road is leading; whereas readers of poetry that has the sanction of traditional values, like the spectators of a Greek play who already know the plot, will enjoy "the attractions of the journey itself." From this perspective it is possible to see why Coleridge thought that the standard of simplicity conflicted with Wordsworth's goals in the *Lyrical Ballads*. Simplicity for Coleridge is a quality which is least likely to be achieved by writers who, like Wordsworth, aspire to be "the Head & founder of a *Sect* in Poetry." By contrast, simplicity comes naturally to writers who undertake a "submissive study of the best models" of art which have "the consent of ages"[14] and whose works confirm Aristotle's notion that poetry is "essentially *ideal*" (*BL* 2:45). This explains why at the end of chapter 1 of the *Biographia* Coleridge indirectly mocks Wordsworth's affectations of simplicity;[15] but at the close of chapter 22, he attacks openly and with uncontrolled indignation Wordsworth's admirers who congratulate the poet for his "turn for SIMPLICITY" (*BL* 2:158). By such a framing device, Coleridge may have deliberately intended to demonstrate how little Wordsworth earned the praise of simplicity, for the true meaning of this term, as Milton understood it, escaped him altogether. It is no wonder that Coleridge was "not half as much irritated by hearing" Wordsworth's "enemies abuse him for vulgarity of style, subject, and conception," as he felt "disgusted with the gilded side of the same meaning, as displayed by some affected admirers with whom he is, forsooth, a *sweet, simple* poet!" (*BL* 2:158).[16]

Coleridge's notebook entry also clarifies a passage in chapter 14 of the *Biographia* where there is an elision in the text. Here Coleridge defines his conception of a "*legitimate* poem" in light of his organic theory and reiterates the view expressed in the notebook entry that a good poem will spare the reader the "restless" activity of laboring after "an end not yet arrived at," offering instead the "attractions of the journey itself." At this point Coleridge introduces an illustration which bears a tenuous connection with this statement: "Like the motion of a serpent, which the Egyptians made the emblem of intellectual power; or like the path of sound through the air; at every step he pauses and half recedes, and from the retrogressive movement collects the force which again carries him onward" (*BL* 2:14).

It is by no means clear how the movement of the serpent pertains to the pleasurable journey of the reader in the encounter with a "*legitimate* poem." Coleridge complicates matters when he describes the serpent as an emblem of "intellectual power," because we are led to infer that such power belongs to authors themselves and not to readers. In an early notebook entry, Coleridge used the same emblem to represent the "Inventive faculty" in a writer of genius, quoting Milton's description of the serpent in Book 9 of *Paradise Lost*. But in this entry, Coleridge emphasized the serpent's continuous movement forward as a way of exposing a writer's endless digressions. By contrast, a writer of genius, like the serpent in Milton's description, varies his course yet moves onward continuously (*CN* 1:609). It is apparent that in the *Biographia*, as Coleridge takes over the emblem of the serpent, he gives it a different twist. Here Coleridge stresses the importance of the serpent's movement backward, showing that it is precisely through its retractions that the serpent gathers the strength to move forward at all.

My assumption is that Coleridge was using part of his 1808 notebook entry in this section of the *Biographia*, but concealed the reference to Milton's definition of simplicity. The fact that Milton was very much on his mind is evident from his use of the emblem of the serpent drawn from *Paradise Lost*. But the serpent image makes more sense in the context of the notebook entry than by itself in the *Biographia*. In the notebook entry, as I have shown, Coleridge criticized the ambition of the experimental writer who always wanted to charge forwards, opening a new road before him. The serpent image reinforces this critique, by suggesting that a writer of genius will first move backward (take stock of the best models of composition that precede him), before taking a distinct direction of his own. It is in this sense that radical creativity takes place only through a process of imitation. The hidden implication here is that Wordsworth missed the mark when he fell prey to his ambition to originate a new trend in poetry, and, like the naive "Pioneers," only saw the road on which he was travelling himself.

It is by such detective work of suppressed or partially concealed references that one can unravel Coleridge's relentless assault on Wordsworth in the *Biographia*, especially in sections where Wordsworth is marginally present. In the *Biographia* Coleridge drew extensively on notes he kept in his journals in preparation for his lectures on Milton and Shakespeare. Between 1808 and 1815 Coleridge had developed some of the main weapons he was to use against Wordsworth in the *Biographia*, including his organic theory of poetry and the Shakespeare-Milton dichotomy. Although Coleridge failed to deliver his projected lecture on Wordsworth, he was clearly relying on his Shakespearean criticism to work out a theory of poetry contrary to Wordsworth's opinions. Milton, too, was very much on his mind during this period, so much so, that (as Kathleen Coburn remarks in an editorial note to one of Coleridge's journal entries) "when Coleridge thinks of WW and/or of the mental processes behind poetry, he thinks also of Milton, and *vice versa*" (*CN* 3:3257 n.). I should like to turn now to the *Biographia* and show not only that Milton and Wordsworth were inseparable in Coleridge's mind, but also how Coleridge consciously manipulated this association to Wordsworth's disadvantage.

III

In chapter I of the *Biographia*, Coleridge establishes from the very beginning his personal alliance with Milton and Shakespeare, to whom he attributes an important formative influence on his career as a poet. Milton and Shakespeare, Coleridge claims, taught him the severe economy and tight logic essential in all good poetry, a lesson he integrated in his formulation of the organic theory of art. By identifying with Milton and Shakespeare, Coleridge is able to make even his defects look like virtues. For example, Coleridge's scrupulously self-critical admission that he overused double epithets in his early poetry, upon closer examination, turns out to be a confession of his strength rather than weakness; in a strategic footnote Coleridge draws attention to the same fault in Milton's and Shakespeare's juvenilia (*BL* 1:6–7). His point is that a writer of genius does not exhibit a perfect command of his craft from the very start. As Coleridge put it in a lecture of 1811, it "would be a hopeless symptom" if one "found a young man with perfect taste" (*BL* 1:6n.2). The proof of genius will be found in writers who are able to assess their faults and develop as radically as the caterpillar undergoes its metamorphosis into a butterfly in the ancient emblem for the "poetic" soul. It "is remarkable" (Coleridge notes in chapter 4) "how soon genius clears and purifies itself from the faults and errors of its earliest products" (*BL* 1:78), a statement ostensibly directed at Wordsworth, but which applies just as well to Coleridge himself in chapter 1 where he demonstrates how mercilessly he "pruned the double epithets" in his later writings, as did Shakespeare and Milton before him.

In the process of using the authority of Milton and Shakespeare to redeem the sins of his early poetry, Coleridge surreptitiously establishes the ideal of a self-improving artist whose strength lies not in an immediate mastery of organic form, but in his capacity to perceive his weaknesses and correct them accordingly.[17] And yet in subsequent references to Shakespeare and Milton both in the first chapter and later on, these writers are consistently brought up as examples of the power of genius to produce a flawless work of art. Thus Coleridge shows how, thanks to his stern teacher Reverend James Bowyer, he came to appreciate the value of an organically integrated work, as exemplified by Shakespeare and Milton. This informs his self-consciously "bold" claim that "it would be scarcely more difficult to push a stone out from the pyramids with the bare hand, than to alter a word, or the position of a word, in Milton or Shakespeare, (in their most important works at least) without making the author say something else, or something worse, than he does say" (*BL* 1:23).

It is apparent that Coleridge introduced two models of creativity in the opening chapter that require different kinds of competence from a writer. The two models are not antithetical to one another, and may even be shown to conflate partially, but they remain distinct nonetheless. One emphasizes the imperfections that exist in any work of genius, the other the perfections. One encourages dynamic change and gradual progress toward higher forms of art, the other privileges the already perfected and immutable work of organically interlocked parts. In judging his own works, Coleridge refers only to the standard of a developing artist and conspicuously avoids subjecting his poetry to the exacting norms of organicity that he so eloquently defends in the *Biographia*. On the other hand, Wordsworth's poems are severely tested according to the organic model, as well as the standard of progressive change, both of which highlight his various shortcomings.

The organic model is the dominant code in Coleridge's examination of Wordsworth's artistic transgressions in chapter 22 of the *Biographia*. The leitmotif of Coleridge's critique is the disunity present at the core of so many of Wordsworth's compositions. Caught between his compulsion to prove the validity of a poetry based on the language and emotions of ordinary people and the "natural tendency" of his mind to become attached to "great objects and elevated conceptions," Wordsworth was bound to produce poems lacking in organic wholeness and made of incongruous parts, some written in a strikingly original style and others in a language "not only unimpassioned but undistinguished" (*BL* 2:121). Wordsworth's tendency toward mental and verbal "bombast" also resulted in poems marked by discontinuities between expression and thought, or between the intensity of feelings and the objects that occasioned them. A further source of Wordsworth's violation of organic unity was his stubborn "*matter-of-factness*" evident in his "laborious minuteness and fidelity in the representation of objects" that imposed on the reader the unpleasant labor of attending to successive visual details, "not very dissimilar to that, with which he would construct a diagram, line by line, for a long geometrical proposition." Unlike Milton who in his descriptions of natural scenery engages the imagination—allowing the reader to apprehend the "whole picture flash'd at once upon the eye"—Wordsworth in his descriptions appeals to the fancy and produces a "mode of poetic painting" rather than genuine *"creation"* (*BL* 2:126–28).

If in light of the organic model, Wordsworth is defeated not only by his glaring faults but also by his "excellencies,"[18] he seems to fare better by the norm of a developing artist, at least temporarily. In chapter 4 Coleridge concedes that, like Shakespeare and Milton, Wordsworth was able to overcome the weaknesses of his earlier writings. Coleridge cites "Guilt and Sorrow" as a poem in which all traces of "strained thought, or forced diction" had disappeared almost entirely, marking a significant progress over a poem such as "Descriptive Sketches." But in volume 2 of the *Biographia*, Coleridge systematically undermines the illusion of Wordsworth's perfectibility as a poet. For example in chapter 15, Coleridge's enthusiastic eulogy of Shakespeare is clearly aimed at Wordsworth because the very qualities he singles out in Shakespeare's early writings mirror as many faults in Wordsworth's poetry. Although Coleridge's ostensible purpose in chapter 15 is to illustrate not just the merits of Shakespeare's juvenilia but likewise the "obvious proofs of the immaturity, of his genius" (*BL* 2:19), the reader will be hard pressed to find any indication of Shakespeare's weaknesses, being given an impressive list of his incomparable strengths. By contrast in chapter 22 Wordsworth's defects are set in bold relief, while his presumed excellencies seem as negligible as Shakespeare's faults. Coleridge's analysis suggests that as late as *The Excursion*, Wordsworth was still struggling to accomplish goals that Shakespeare had already achieved in his earliest composition. The inescapable conclusion is that although Shakespeare had little to improve on, Wordsworth began his career with such colossal handicaps that his chances of fulfilling the promises of his genius seemed doubtful at best. Coleridge clearly relies on the force of such a conclusion when he remarks toward the close of chapter 22 that although Wordsworth was capable of producing "the FIRST GENUINE PHILOSOPHICAL POEM," it was difficult for him to "prophesy" what Wordsworth *"will* produce" (*BL* 2:155–56). An equally uncharitable prognosis of Wordsworth's artistic career is suggested at the end of chapter 15 where Coleridge divides the spoils of poetic power evenly between Milton and

Shakespeare, conspicuously excluding Wordsworth from the seats on the "glory-smitten summits of the poetic mountain" that are already occupied (*BL* 2:27–28). It is worth noting that in his 1815 preface, Wordsworth used the distinction between Shakespeare's dramatic and Milton's egotistical imagination, as developed by Coleridge during his 1811–1812 course of lectures, without acknowledging his debt to his friend.[19] It is possible that at the end of chapter 15 Coleridge perceived an opportunity to penalize Wordsworth for this offense. Certainly the quotation from one of Wordsworth's sonnets with which Coleridge ends the chapter could not have been intended kindly. Coleridge's allusion to Wordsworth's own praise of Milton and Shakespeare is insidiously ironic, for Coleridge makes it clear that Wordsworth does not belong to the illustrious company he so unwittingly celebrated.

Commentators have sometimes viewed Coleridge's distinction between Milton and Shakespeare as an attempt to isolate two fundamentally incompatible forms of the poetic imagination. This was not, however, Coleridge's intent, as indicated by his statement in chapter 15 that the two writers were not to be regarded as "rivals" but as "compeers" (*BL* 2:27). I agree with Stephen Bygrave that for Coleridge, the protean and egotistical imagination (as represented by Shakespeare and Milton) were "two sides of the same (circulating) coin."[20] In a notebook entry of 1805, which features one of the earliest anticipations of the Milton-Shakespeare dichotomy, Coleridge described his own personality as uniting an attraction toward becoming "great & good by spreading thro' and combining with all things," with the opposite tendency of absorbing all things into his being (*CN* 2:2495), an opinion confirmed by Coleridge's contemporaries, some of whom regarded him as characterless, others as egotistical.[21] This suggests that Milton and Shakespeare can be viewed as opposites only in the special sense that this term acquires in Coleridge's dynamic philosophy: like two poles of a magnet, they share the same essence and presuppose one another.

Throughout the *Biographia* Coleridge carefully documents the affinities between Shakespeare and Milton, the bond between the two writers that secures Wordsworth's exclusion from Parnassus. Both writers are credited with the achievement of impeccably organic works, both are identified with the poetic imagination characteristic of genius, and last but not least, both are praised for their unflinching commitment to the life of the mind. Coleridge's analysis of Shakespeare's abundant gifts in chapter 15 culminates with his eulogy of the writer's "DEPTH, and ENERGY of THOUGHT," proving a point upon which the whole project of the *Biographia* depends, namely, that "no man was ever yet a great poet, without being at the same time a profound philosopher" (*BL* 2:25–26).[22] Milton, too, amply attests to the veracity of this belief, for, as Coleridge had pictured him all along, he was the quintessentially intellectual poet, and for that matter genuinely passionate. It is to Milton that Coleridge attributes his earliest interest in metaphysics[23] and from whom he seeks support for his theory of poetry based on the faculties of the mind. Milton's authority is invoked at key points in the *Biographia* when Coleridge advances some of his leading philosophical ideas, including his definition of intuition (*BL* 2:172), his theory of the imagination,[24] his distinction between reason and understanding (*BL* 1:173–74), between fancy and imagination (*BL* 2:127–28), between illusion and delusion (*BL* 2:134). Like the mythical Atlas, Milton is the omnipresent deity supporting the architectonic of Coleridge's metaphysics, which becomes the foundation of his critique of Wordsworth. Indeed, Coleridge grew so accustomed to relying on Milton as a counterexample to Wordsworth that in the heading to chapter 17 he included as part of the chapter's contents the argument that Milton's language was "as much the language of *real* life, yea, incomparably more so than that of the cottager" (*BL* 2:40); yet Coleridge never took up this subject in the course of discussion, as if by this point in the *Biographia* this conclusion should have been obvious to readers.

Milton ultimately allows Coleridge to show that the same deficiencies found in Wordsworth's work also characterize his personality as a whole. This happens early in the *Biographia* in a chapter which seems to be a detour from the main concerns of the book but which, upon closer scrutiny, contains a scathing critique of Wordsworth. It is not immediately clear why in chapter 2 of the *Biographia* Coleridge bothers to refute the charge that men of genius are irritable. Coleridge compiles an impressive list of writers from the past who remained calm and cheerful under the most testing circumstances, ending with a moving portrait of Milton, who, though "poor, sick, old, blind, slandered, persecuted," maintained his faith in himself and continued to listen to "the music of his own thoughts" (*BL* 1:37). To emphasize Milton's plight in his old age, Coleridge quotes a line from Wordsworth's description of Milton in book 3 of *The Prelude*. We are immediately alerted by this seemingly unimportant allusion that Wordsworth may well be at the center of Coleridge's discussion, because it is by such incidental remarks that Coleridge characteristically plots his campaign against his friend. It is hard to imagine that Coleridge is not thinking of Wordsworth when he states, shortly after quoting from *The Prelude*, that "From others only do we derive our knowledge that Milton, in his latter day, had his scorners and detractors; and even in his day of youth and hope, that he had enemies would have been unknown to us, had they not been likewise the enemies of his country" (*BL* 1:37). Certainly the same could not be said of Wordsworth who in his "Essay, Supplementary to the Preface (1815)" angrily denounced his critics charging them with gross ignorance and an incompetence even more "flagrant" than their malice.[25] In chapter 22 of the *Biographia* Coleridge deliberately draws attention to the vituperative tone of Wordsworth's response to his critics, begging the readers not to judge his friend too harshly for "having expressed himself too indignantly, till the wantonness and the systematic and malignant perseverance of the aggressions have been taken into fair consideration" (*BL* 2:156). But surely if the example of Milton carries any force, readers are not likely to sympathize with Wordsworth, for it is the business of genius to mind "the music of his own thoughts" rather than be concerned with the abuse of critics, however unmerited.

A number of pieces both from the *Biographia* and other writings converge in what appears to be an increasingly clearer picture of Coleridge's hidden agenda in chapter 2. Coleridge's earliest refutation of the opinion concerning the presumed irritability of genius occurs in a letter to Sotheby of September 10, 1802, the same letter in which he praised Milton as the poet of passion and intellect, and damned Bowles as the poet of fancy, implicating Wordsworth in this charge. In this letter, as in chapter 2 of the *Biographia*, Coleridge presents an idealization of himself as a writer least interested in the opinion of the world concerning his works, be it praise or blame, and by implication, least likely to be aroused by anger at an unfair accusation (*CL* 2:863). The view that he is by nature unaffected by anger is also expressed in Coleridge's letter to Poole of October 14, 1803, both directly and by means of a highly loaded portrait of his son Hartley, which succeeds his outspoken critique of Wordsworth's personality and his experiment in the *Lyrical Ballads*. Hartley, Coleridge notes with unconcealed admiration, is "an utter Visionary," moving "in a circle of Light of his own making." "Of all human Beings," he writes, "I never yet saw one so utterly naked of *Self*—he has no Vanity, no Pride, no Resentment / and tho' *very passionate*, I never yet saw him *angry with* any body" (*CL* 2:1014).

Here in full view is the very nucleus of chapter 2 of the *Biographia* in a context where the connection with Wordsworth is unmistakable. Hartley is clearly presented as an antitype to Wordsworth and as Coleridge's *alter ego*. While Wordsworth isolates himself in a small circle of "Devotees" because he is oversensitive to criticism and seeks only praise, Hartley lives securely and happily within the "circle of Light of his own making," his sense of self being completely independent of all external agency. Furthermore, Wordsworth's ambition to establish a new "*Sect* in Poetry" anchors him in the fickle world of public opinion, exposing him to the ravages of self-doubt and aggressive self-assertion, but Hartley's life as an "utter Visionary" makes him immune to vanity or pride, and hence to any manifestation of anger. As Coleridge reflected in a highly personal notebook entry concerned with his wife, Sara, anger "will be found in those most" who become slaves "of the Eyes and Ears of Others," that is, who "most hang upon the opinions of others, & to whom these opinions are of the most importance" (*CN* 1:979).

We can now better understand the source of calm and self-possession that Coleridge attributes to the writer of genius in chapter 2 of the *Biographia*. Like Hartley, all writers of genius are visionaries living in an ideal world of their own making. They are profoundly disinterested in the opinion of the world concerning their works, listening, like Milton, solely to the "music" of their "own thoughts." This explains why Coleridge was so adamant in defending Milton's egotism as an attractive feature of his personality.[26] Clearly all visionaries are egotists in the sense that their identity is generated from within, and their self-assurance is undisturbed by the opinions of others. Paradoxically, visionaries are so entirely all self, as to be, like Hartley, "utterly naked of *Self*"; their very self-absorption protects them from vanity, envy, and resentment which always beset those who construct their self empirically in relation to external objects. This underlies Coleridge's statement in chapter 2 that from Milton himself one would never have known that he had any enemies. Milton evidently was too secure about the worth of his mission as a writer to be affected by or impelled to respond to the merciless attacks waged by his detractors. Hence anger never disturbed his peace of mind, for anger is always a sign of personal insecurity in a writer, stemming from a "debility and dimness of the imaginative power, and a consequent necessity of reliance on the immediate impressions of the senses" (*BL* 1:30). It is easy to see how Coleridge pointed this critique of the irascible writer at Wordsworth. In light of Coleridge's analysis here, Wordsworth's *"matter-of-factness"* discussed in chapter 22 emerges as the obvious source of his angry response to his critics. Wordsworth's excessive concern with objects of sense at the expense of *"lofty imaginings"* ultimately affected his self-confidence and quality of mind, making him prey to expressions of "Indignation at literary wrongs." As Coleridge put it in one of his most cruel remarks addressed to Wordsworth as well as the anonymous critics, "Experience informs us that the first defence of weak minds is to recriminate" (*BL* 1:31).

At long last Coleridge found a way of repaying Wordsworth for describing him in book 4 of *The Prelude* as a hopeless metaphysician, whose mind, "Debarred from Nature's living images," was "Compelled to be a life unto itself" and became "unrelentingly possessed by thirst / Of greatness, love, and beauty" (ll. 305–16). Coleridge invalidates Wordsworth's assumption that those who live in a circle of their own making are liable to "thirst" for greatness, showing that this trait of character is more likely to be found among those who, like Wordsworth, are tied to objects of sense and become slaves of "the Eyes and Ears of Others." Metaphysics, then, is not to be lamented as a sickness for the self, for it attaches the self to "ideal creations," leaving it untainted by vanity or anger. Throughout chapter 2, Coleridge stresses now and again his utter indifference to the fate of his works to the point of "ostrich carelessness and ostrich oblivion" (*BL* 1:45–46), and his disinterest in expressing his "Indignation at literary wrongs," a task which he leaves to others "born under happier stars" (*BL* 1:45). Coleridge thus fully assumes Milton's deportment in the face of unmerited persecution and asserts his superiority to Wordsworth. By showing the link between Wordsworth's preoccupation with objects of sense and his equally damaging preoccupation with the public reception of his works, Coleridge proves that the faults of mind and art are likewise faults of character, the mind containing the full picture of the self. In a roundabout way Coleridge implicitly affirms the superiority of the *Biographia* to *The Prelude*. He shows that his "Literary Life and Opinions" is more purely a story of the "Growth of a Poet's Mind," than *The Prelude*.[27] Although the *Biographia* contains no references to events of Coleridge's personal life or childhood experiences in the midst of nature, it is by no means incomplete. In the end, the story of the growth of one's mind is identical to the story of the writer himself. Coleridge implies that his intellectual biography is a full autobiography and the only kind of autobiography worth writing.

IV

Given Coleridge's attack on Wordsworth in the *Biographia* and his recurrent use of Milton and Shakespeare as counterexamples to Wordsworth, how seriously can we regard his belated statement in chapter 22 that "in imaginative power" Wordsworth "stands nearest of all modern writers to Shakespeare and Milton; and yet in a kind perfectly unborrowed and his own" (*BL* 2:151)? This conclusion has by no means been "variously evident all along," as Catherine Wallace asserts.[28] In the context of the *Biographia* the claim sounds more like a species of Coleridgean "bombast," as it highlights the disproportion between Coleridge's elevated opinion of his friend and Wordsworth's actual accomplishments. And yet it would be a simplification to dismiss this statement as perversely insincere, particularly as we have earlier documents, such as Coleridge's letters to Poole of March 21, 1800 (*CL* 1:582) and to Richard Sharp of January 15, 1804 (*CL* 2:1034), where Coleridge expresses similar views with unmistakable conviction. We are faced, rather, with a profound ambivalence in Coleridge's sentiments toward Wordsworth, which gives rise to his vacillating opinions concerning Wordsworth's proximity to Milton or his radical divergence from his great predecessor. Coleridge actually desired to aggrandize rather than humiliate Wordsworth, for he sought in him a strong partner that would bring to fruition his own genial capacities. Even in the *Biographia*, which represents Coleridge's most aggressive attempt to assert his difference from Wordsworth, he remained dependent on Wordsworth's success as a poet to validate his own literary enterprise. Hence every attack on Wordsworth was bound to feel as a diminishment of Coleridge's own reputation.[29] It is not surprising, therefore, that at the end of chapter 22, after having demystified Wordsworth, Coleridge attempted to reidealize him, as it were, granting him powers equal to those of Shakespeare and Milton. But this extravagant eulogy of Wordsworth comes too late and lacks persuasiveness, as its foundation is completely demolished by Coleridge in his preceding analysis of Wordsworth's "defects." In the end, Coleridge cannot sustain the idealization of Wordsworth, and Milton fulfills better his need to find in another an ideal image of himself.

Temperamentally Coleridge was predisposed to worship men of superior qualities, a proclivity which was reinforced by the ethos of the Romantic age, in which idealization of another was held in high esteem and viewed as the characteristic way of attaining self-knowledge. Jean Paul

Richter, for example (in a passage Coleridge marked in his journals) wrote eloquently about "the eternal thirst" in "every noble heart" for "one more noble, a thirst in every beautiful heart for one more beautiful; such a heart desires to see his Ideal outside himself as a physical presence, an idealized or imagined body, in order that he may reach it the more easily, because a superior man will mature only in contact with a superior man, just as diamonds are polished only by diamonds" (CN 3:4276n.). In relation to Wordsworth, Coleridge undoubtedly wanted to feel ennobled by recognizing in him his likeness embodied in ideal form. His eulogies of Wordsworth, therefore, although not disinterested, are sincere to the extent that they suited his need to seek an ideal outside himself. Furthermore, by celebrating the work of a contemporary poet, Coleridge also gained a pleasing self-image as a writer who was able to promote the work of a rival with exemplary equanimity. It is of interest in this respect that in 1808 when Coleridge was preparing for a projected lecture on Wordsworth, he intended to win his audience by assuming the role of a gifted writer eager to revere the work of a contemporary in whom he recognized the achievement of an ideal. More importantly, Coleridge found in the following passage from Milton the exact language of adulation and selfless prostration before Wordsworth which suited his purposes:

> What besides God has resolved concerning me I know not, but this at least: He has instilled into me, if into any one, a vehement love of the beautiful. . . . Hence it is that, when any one scorns what the vulgar opine in their depraved estimation of things, and dares to feel and speak and be that which the highest wisdom throughout all ages has taught to be the best, to that man I attach myself forthwith by a kind of real necessity, wherever I find him. If, whether by nature or by my fate, I am so circumstanced that by no effort and labour of mine can I myself rise to such an honour and elevation, yet that I should always worship and look up to those who have attained that glory, or happily aspire to it, neither gods nor men, I reckon, have bidden nay. (CN 3:3257n.)

The quotation from Milton identifies a source that tells us why Coleridge could not sustain the high sentiments toward Wordsworth of which he thought himself capable. It shows rather patently that a large ego is required to ensure the success of all projects of idealization. Certainly Milton's worship of another is not articulated from a position of inferiority. Milton seems in no doubt that he, more so than others, was endowed with "a vehement love of the beautiful," for which he has the consent of both men and gods. Richter, likewise, emphasized the equality of the pur-

suer to the ideal he places above him, as is evident in the striking image
of diamonds that "are polished only by diamonds." But Coleridge did not
possess a strong sense of self-esteem and Wordsworth often left him with
a disabling awareness of his own infirmities. In Wordsworth's presence
Coleridge did not feel like a diamond catching the glitter from another,
but more like an undistinguished piece of glass. His eulogies of Wordsworth, however sincerely felt, border so closely on self-contempt that one
cannot easily tell which is the cause and which the effect. This fact was evident to Coleridge's close friend Thomas Poole, who after receiving a letter
from Coleridge in which he praised Wordsworth above Milton, immediately inquired why Coleridge had to prostrate himself before his friend
instead of thinking of his own creative powers. In his reply to Poole's letter, Coleridge strongly reiterated his position that Wordsworth may turn
out to be a greater poet than Milton, but his confession at the end of the
letter that his imaginative powers were "dwindling" and on their way to
be "dried up wholly," confirmed Poole's original suspicion that Coleridge's
masochistic self-denigration was the root of his elevation of Wordsworth
to extravagant heights (*CL* 2:582, 584).

Coleridge's idealization of Wordsworth was not only threatened by his
lack of confidence but also by Wordsworth's failure to reciprocate the love
and admiration that Coleridge felt he had consistently bestowed upon his
friend to the point of "enthusiastic self-oblivion" (*CL* 3:888). As Coleridge
elaborated in another context, the construction of an ideal self cannot be
accomplished through the efforts of a single person but only by "the action
of kindred souls on each other" (*CL* 2:1197).[30] But Wordsworth constantly
frustrated Coleridge's project of idealization, remaining unresponsive to
his need for sympathy and adulation and discouraging Coleridge's effort
to move in a "distinct current" of his own. Under such conditions it is small
wonder that idealization turns into disillusionment and disillusionment
into anger and contempt. As Burke well knew, when an object viewed as
sublime is demystified, the subject will experience a feeling of contempt
proportional to the awe with which he previously regarded the same object.[31]

Idealization is a tricky business, for while it requires a personal stake
to be desired at all, it is doomed when carried out on a personal rather
than purely abstract level.[32] Perhaps intuitively, Coleridge felt this when
he replaced Wordsworth with Milton. As a poet of the past, Milton could
not be made answerable to the requirement of reciprocity that Coleridge
expected so keenly from Wordsworth. This may explain why, paradoxi-

cally, Coleridge, who was by nature so dependent on others, worshipped Milton's egotism as a form of self-reliance closely approximating that of the deity. Clearly in relation to a figure who attracted "all forms and things to himself, into the unity of his own IDEAL" (BL 2:27–28), Coleridge felt unconcerned about lack of reciprocity, learning instead a measure of self-reliance in the pursuit of an ideal which he badly needed to offset his dependence on Wordsworth. Furthermore, Milton freed Coleridge from the conflicting needs of copying and opposing a rival, of wanting to be like him and unlike him at the same time. As Coleridge well knew, one's identity was always constituted by likeness and difference. Consciousness itself, Coleridge wrote, is in essence the "perception of identity and contrariety; the least degree of which constitutes likeness, the greatest absolute difference." Although in relation to Wordsworth, Coleridge experienced the anguish of these extremes, he desired to attain a peaceful state beyond difference that he could barely describe by alluding to a passage from *Lycidas*. In this ideal state, "all things are at once different and the same; there alone, as the principle of all things, does distinction exist unaided by division; there are will and reason, succession of time and unmoving eternity, infinite change and ineffable rest."[33]

Here, then, we have Coleridge's vision of what literary influence and the relationship between two writers should be: a relationship in which difference is not attained at the expense of sameness, nor likeness at the expense of distinctness. This relationship is conspicuously free of oedipal tensions or rivalry and remains a pure abstraction, almost religious in nature. That Coleridge could not sustain this ideal in his complicatedly human interaction with Wordsworth but projected it onto the distant and absent figure of Milton, is not particularly surprising. In fact, the ideal state Milton represents for Coleridge is essentially (and appropriately) theological because the demands Coleridge places upon this form of literary idealization are comparable to those at work in his conception of the Trinity: a unity which does not threaten individuality, and a form of distinction that does not generate division.[34] This ideal is present in *Biographia*. It is a strain that surfaces in Coleridge's theory of the imagination in chapter 13 and completely dominates his concluding chapter. In a work in which Coleridge is so profoundly afflicted by fits of self-loathing and self-aggrandizement, so beset by transgressions large and small, his need for a figure of idealization approaching divinity is supreme. From Milton, so much a God unto himself, to the "I AM" there is, for Coleridge, a rather short leap.

11

"Like a Guilty Thing Surprised": Coleridge, Deconstruction, and the Apostasy of Criticism

Jerome Christensen

Apostasy's so fashionable, too.

—LORD BYRON, *Don Juan*

In *Criticism and Social Change* Frank Lentricchia melodramatically pits his critical hero Kenneth Burke, advocate of the intellect's intervention in social life, against the villainous Paul de Man, "undisputed master in the United States of what is called deconstruction." Lentricchia charges that "the insidious effect of [de Man's] work is not the proliferating replication of his way of reading . . . but the paralysis of praxis itself: an effect that traditionalism, with its liberal view of the division of political power, should only applaud." He goes on to prophesy that

> the deconstruction of deconstruction will reveal, against apparent in-
> tention, a tacit political agenda after all, one that can only embarrass
> deconstruction, particularly its younger proponents whose activist ex-
> periences, within the socially wrenching upheavals of the 1960s and
> early 1970s, will surely not permit them easily to relax, without guilt and
> self-hatred, into resignation and ivory tower despair." [1]

Such is Lentricchia's strenuous conjuration of a historical moment in which he can forcefully intervene—a summons fraught with the pathos excited by any reference to the heady days of political enthusiasm during the war in Viet Nam. Lentricchia ominously figures a scene of rueful soli-tude where de Manian lucidity bleakens into the big chill. And maybe it will, but Lentricchia furnishes no good reason why it should. De Manian deconstruction is "deconstructed" by Lentricchia to reveal "against appar-

ent intention, a tacit political agenda." And this revelation is advertised
as a sure embarrassment to the younger practitioners of deconstruction
—sweepingly characterized as erstwhile political activists who have, wide-
eyed, opted for a critical approach that magically entangles its proponents
in the soul-destroying delights of rhetoric and reaction. Left unexamined
in Lentricchia's story, however, is the basis for the initial rapport between
radicalism and deconstruction. Why should collegiate activists have turned
into deconstructionists? Is not that in Lentricchia's terms the same question as asking why political activists should have turned to literary criticism
(or indeed literature) at all? If we suppose this original turn (to criticism,
to deconstruction) to be intentional, how could the initiates of this critical
approach ever be genuinely *betrayed* into embarrassment by time or by its
herald, Frank Lentricchia? On the face of it, the traducement of a secret
intention would be unlikely to come as a surprise, since deconstructing deconstruction is not only the enterprise of Marxist critics like Lentricchia,
but also of Jacques Derrida, arch deconstructor, who unashamedly identified the embarrassment of intention as constitutive of the deconstructive
method. If deconstruction is at once a natural outlet for activists and the
first step on a slippery slope that ends in apostasy (for surely it is that hard
word which Lentricchia politely suppresses), it suggests a phenomenon
with contours more suggestively intricate, if not less diabolically seductive,
than the program Lentricchia outlines. And it is a phenomenon as wor-
risomely affiliative as it is bafflingly intricate. We need to know whether
the relations between deconstruction and radical politics, between deconstruction and apostasy, between deconstruction and criticism, and between
apostasy and criticism are necessary or contingent, or neither and both at
once.

   I do not intend to address those questions head-on but instead to follow the path of what Edmund, not Kenneth, Burke called "philosophic
analogy."[2] Philosophic analogy is a way of doing history that is probably
more conservative and certainly more literary than the mode Lentricchia
prefers—though not than the one he practices, for the prophecy that he
makes depends on a buried analogy. The analogy exploits the similarity
between the experience of the proponents of activism in the late 1960s
and their English predecessors in the 1790s, who likewise started out in
glad political agitation and ended in sad aesthetic contemplation. The
analogy derives a specific historical gravity from the notable intersection of
the heyday of campus activism in the late sixties with the first enthusiastic

reception of deconstruction in America, the latter signalled by the publication of the Johns Hopkins symposium "The Languages of Criticism and the Sciences of Man" as *The Structuralist Controversy* in 1970, and with the aggressive revival of romanticism by what has since become known as the Yale School, announced by Harold Bloom's landmark collection *Romanticism and Consciousness* in the same year. Both of those books were preceded by Paul de Man's masterly essay "The Rhetoric of Temporality" in 1969.[3] If there is such a thing as coincidence, this connection of political turmoil with deconstruction with Romanticism is not one. The dominant model of our modern understanding of the relation between politics and poetry is derived from Romantic experience and Romantic practice. For the relation between politics and criticism it is possible to be even more precise: the pattern is the career of Samuel Taylor Coleridge. If it is true, as Lentricchia affirms, speaking existentially, that there "is a de Man in us all," it is because, speaking historically, there is a Coleridge in de Man.[4] The deconstructive method makes a neat fit with the Coleridgean text—a fit so neat as to suggest a propriety for deconstruction in Coleridge. Without understanding that fit, it is impossible to understand how apostasy comes so naturally to modern critics, how we can greet our embarrassment and guilt like old friends.

That decorum of deconstruction has historical dimensions: deconstruction takes its appointed place within what M. H. Abrams once described as the "prosecutorial tradition" of Coleridgean criticism, one which supplements the two great themes in Coleridge, originality and fidelity, with their dogged specters, plagiarism and apostasy. This accusatory line of Coleridgean criticism, earliest associated with the names of his contemporaries and friends DeQuincey and Hazlitt, is now most closely identified with the names Norman Fruman, author of *Coleridge, the Damaged Archangel*, and E. P. Thompson. Although I shall follow out the apostasy branch of the family here, I do not mean to imply that it has any precedence or that it is ultimately distinct from the fraternal line. It would be an easy matter to demonstrate that the coalescence of plagiarism and apostasy is Coleridge's very signature: STC.[5]

Thompson, who first addressed the issue of apostasy and its relation to the decline of creative power in the finely textured and acute essay "Disenchantment or Default? A Lay Sermon," later put the case against Coleridge with renewed severity in a review of David Erdman's edition of *Essays on His Times*, the collection of Coleridge's journalism. Coleridge, he proclaims, "is chiefly of interest, in his political writings, as an example of the intellectual complexity of apostasy. He was, of course, a political apostate. . . ."[6] If we trace back the pedigree of Thompson's indictment, it takes us, as he forthrightly admits, to Hazlitt. Indeed, he compares the two, to Coleridge's embarrassment, but we cannot rest there. The very problem of apostasy as Hazlitt conceived it was derived from Coleridge's early, dangerously insightful profile of Edmund Burke. The figure of Burke that Coleridge painted in *The Watchman*, "this *Cameleon* [sic] of *hues*, as *brilliant* as they are *changing*," was the pattern for the figure of Coleridge that Hazlitt later acidly engraved in essays and reviews. The lavish irony with which Coleridge characterized Burke's apostasy—"At the flames which rise from the altar of Freedom, he kindled that torch with which he since endeavoured to set fire to her temple"[7]—is the same trope with which Hazlitt, applying less color and more vitriol, attempted to diminish his former oracle. "*Once a Jacobin and always a Jacobin*," he remarks (ironically quoting Coleridge who was ironically quoting Pitt), "is a maxim which, notwithstanding Mr. Coleridge's see-saw reasoning to the contrary, we hold to be true, even of him to this day. *Once an Apostate and always an Apostate*, we hold to be equally true: and the reason why the last is true, is that the first is so. A person who is what is called a Jacobin. . . . that is, who has shaken off certain well known prejudices with respect to kings or priests, or nobles, cannot so easily resume them again, whenever his pleasure or his convenience may prompt him to attempt it."[8] As for Burke, the irony of Coleridge's reversal from Jacobin to ministerial tool is that there has been no real change at all.

But if Hazlitt shows that Coleridge is constrained by a compulsive rhetoric of reversal, Hazlitt himself is not free of the Coleridgean figure. By equating Jacobin and apostate under the act of "shaking off," he curiously vitiates the moral force of his indictment: he formalizes change into a pattern of mechanical repetition that is more exigent than any ethical posture or political program. Hazlitt captures Coleridge within the restraints of his ironic equation only to open a trapdoor through which Coleridge escapes, leaving behind any responsibility, let alone culpability, for actions that are compulsive rather than wicked, paradigmatic rather than perverse. Hazlitt's assertion, "Once an apostate and always an apostate," is true but only if modified in a way that discharges it of its polemical force: "Once an apostate and *always already* an apostate" is the better, not to mention more fashionable, motto. At every point we examine him, even at the beginning,

Coleridge is already falling away from every principled commitment—commitments which are, indeed, endowed with significance solely by that lapse and the critical reflection it allows.[9]

Partisan grievances aside, the label of "apostate" is accurate. A metaphysics of apostasy is explicitly adumbrated by Coleridge in the notebooks of 1818 and in his marginal notes on the *Works* of Jacob Boehme, worked out at roughly the same time.[10] Coleridge introduced the technical term *apostasis* as part of his endeavor to employ Schelling's model of dynamic polarity defecated of its pantheistic implications. Specifically, he aimed to avoid the Schellingian error of the "establishment of Polarity in the Absolute."[11] At first Coleridge hoped to find an alternative to Schelling in Boehme. His marginalia record his disappointment: "As I read on, I have found that this first Chapter [of the *Mysterium Magnum*] is a deceptive Promise: that Behmen soon deviates into his original error . . . and places the polarities *in* the Deity, [making] them eternal. . . ." In other words, Boehme is guilty of an "anticipation of the Apostasis in the Stasis" (*Marginalia* 1:678.). The terms are important. Coleridge has come to regard *apostasis* as the crucial articulation of a cosmogonic paradigm that would take account of the law of polarity and yet preserve the determinant, singular unity of an absolute which is not nature, not, that is, the mere copula or exponent of polar energies.[12]

Coleridge sketched out this paradigm in a notebook entry. Contrary to both Schelling and Boehme, Coleridge insists that there "must be [and here I rely on Kathleen Coburn's translation of Coleridge's Greek]

> the way downwards and the way upwards—but this is because there are two Spheres. . . . the Plenitude and nature—the way downwards commencing with the Fall from God, Apostasy—the path of transit with the Chaos and the *descent* of the Spirit—the way upwards with the genesis of Light.—Thus in my Logosophia I have four great Divisions. I. That which is neither ascent or descent—for instead of a way, it's that "*from* which" and "to which," not a road at all, but at once the starting-post, and the Goal,—Call it then Stasis. II. Apostasy or the way downwards. III. Metastasis. IV. the way upwards. More neatly thus: I. Stasis II. Apostasy III. Metastasis IV. Anastasis.[13]

Immediately following this arcane deduction, Coleridge asks the question which must be in the mind of every uninitiated reader: "Well but what is the use of all this?" My answer is not the same as his. The use, clear from our neo-Hazlittian perspective, lies in the transformation of "Once an Apostate and Always an Apostate" into a cosmogonic crux. Apostasy is the crucial, or rather, the *critical* stage of Coleridge's paradigm because it is the first break in the stasis that precedes all paradigms, the standing away that precipitates the creation. The first move, apostasy is also the essential move—a move in the service of essence: for only the standing off permits the manifestation of the godhead—either as stasis or as what, in the marginalia on Boehme, Coleridge calls Prothesis: "For in God the Prothesis is not manifested for itself, but only in the Fountain which he is from all eternity because he never can subsist but with the Light in the bosom of the Fountain, whence proceeds the Spirit. But in the Creation as conditioned by the Fall of Apostasis, the Prothesis is manifested as the hardness, the Austerity, the stone indeed of the foundation, but likewise the Stone of offence" (*Marginalia* 1:649). Apostasy is, then, that *once*, the detachment or fall of man from the divine that was originally his base, as it also is in a curious sense, that *always*—for the continual standing forth of man's will is a continual apostasy that reenacts his providential fall—providential because, though a fall, it manifests the divine stasis and promises the anastatic return of the human to that eternal light.

Although proved on the ragged pulse of Coleridge's social and political life, his apostasy is supposedly redeemed when referred to the life of that life, that "I am," which is the finite repetition of "the All-might, which God's Will is, and which he knoweth within himself as the Abyss of his Being—the eternal *Act* of Self-constitution" (*Marginalia* 1:659), and which endows all human action with meaning. Coleridge's metaphysics could be read as a transcendental excuse for the moral weakness of the political journalist—one example, among many, of the Coleridgean aptitude for turning diseases into pearls and a maneuver not less effective for its transparency.[14] From that perspective Coleridge's super-Boehmenist paradigm does not so much rebut the indictments of Thompson and Hazlitt as annul them by referring them to a higher court, the preserve of a purer, more categorical law.

If this sublimation thwarts the attacks of the Hazlittian line, it is, however, also the move that invites the intervention of the deconstructionist. Without mounting a full-scale assault, it is possible to outline the procedures that would be undertaken to problematize the authority of the metaphysical construct on which Coleridge relies. They would consist of a criticism of the enabling distinction between an absolute stasis and a consequent but completely distinct polarity, a disenfranchisement of the priority given to the former over the latter, and a challenge to the unicity of the one as well as to the bivalence of the other. There would follow an exploitation of the dependence of the system on a difference (that between stasis and apostasis) which is not a polarity, a probing of the infelicitous reliance of the absolute on the fall for its very manifestation. The plot would inexorably ravel towards the conclusion that the metaphysical necessity of this movement to the outside is not something that accidentally befalls the absolute stasis but the genetic destiny of a logos that is always only a formation by virtue of that which is about to be extrinsic to it.

The certainty that a deconstruction could be carried out makes the execution unnecessary. Such a supplemental maneuver would only confirm that Coleridge's plot had already provided for its deconstruction, that deconstruction is just another version of the apostasy which Coleridge has already embraced. Supplementarity is Coleridge's device as the margin is his home. To put it another way, metaphysics or philosophical criticism was for Coleridge both apostatic, an ostensible turn away from political activism and poetic ambition, and an apology for apostasy as the prerequisite for critical reflection, indeed, as the preliminary and continual "Act of Self-constitution" which grounds all meaningful action.

The pattern for Coleridge's strategic apostasy was neither Schelling nor Kant but Edmund Burke, in whose "writings indeed the germs of almost all political truths may be found" (*BL* 1:217) and whose *Reflections on the Revolution in France* is the chief eighteenth-century instance of the deployment of the apostatic trope. Here again, my concern is not partisan nagging; I do not care to judge whether Burke actually reversed his earlier political principles. In retrospect, far from the hurly burly pamphlet mongering of reform and reaction, the distinctive achievement of Burke's *Reflections*, that which makes a certain kind of historical reflection —call it Burkean—*possible,* is his promulgation of the idea of an ancient constitution. For Burke, as J. G. A. Pocock has convincingly argued, the ancient, prescriptive constitution "has two characteristics: it is immemorial —and this is what makes it prescriptive and gives it authority as a constitution—and it is customary. . . ."[15] Nowhere detectable by the physical eye, the constitution is, like our revered forefathers, all the more imperiously present by virtue of its empirical absence. The idea of the ancient constitution presupposes an aboriginal law from which Englishmen have necessarily fallen—not morally, as Pocock shows, but historically and hermeneutically, in what Burke calls a "liberal descent" (*Reflections* 121).[16]

Descent produces the metaphor of genealogical connection but also functions as a metonym which inscribes the irreducible distance that *makes* it both possible and necessary that men act "upon the principle of reference to antiquity" (*Reflections* 117). Englishmen can never hope to be those fathers, nor could their forefathers hope to be those fathers who are constitutionally already there before them. The absoluteness of the paternal anteriority, however, is the precondition for a liberal descent. Descent succeeds to a primordial detachment of son from father, reader from writer, which inscribes a contingency in the relation between the present and the past, thereby requiring that any necessity in the connection between past and present be adduced retrospectively, chosen by the son rather than imposed by the father. "We wished," writes Burke, "at the period of the Revolution, and do now wish, to derive all we possess as *an inheritance from our forefathers*" (*Reflections* 117). The emphasis should fall not on "inheritance" but on "wish" and "derive." Wishes may not be horses, but in the absence of any father except the one he imagines, even the most beggarly Englishman (or Irishman) can ride his wishes into an inheritance that is wholly his option, that is, indeed, nothing other than his interpretation of it: in "this *choice* of inheritance we have given to our frame of polity the image of a relation in blood: binding up the constitution of our country with our dearest domestic ties": we "have *chosen* our nature rather than our speculations, our breasts rather than our inventions, for the great conservatories and magazines of our rights and privileges" (*Reflections* 120–21; emphasis added). The aporia between the static and immanent grammar of an absolute law and its performative application to particulars, which de Man has analyzed in Rousseau's *Social Contract*,[17] is exactly the dynamic by which Burke's text and Burke's nation thrives. The distance between the law and its application, as between the father and the son or between the ancient constitution and contemporary cases, is that distance which we have descended consequent upon our turn from grammar, from law, from the past, and which enables us, apostates all, to return in the full force of our wishful derivations, to return in a reading of the history of our descent, a history that is always ancient but which would not be there to be read had we not figured it through our apostasy.

Each manchild is born into this chartered island as a reader of that law which sponsors his historical existence and which by its "penetrating style has engraved in our ordinances, and in our hearts, the words and spirit of that immortal law" (*Reflections* 104). Burke insists that this reading is entailed, but he repeatedly demonstrates that its impression on our hearts is only made possible by our voluntary standing away from a past law or father in order that it can represent itself in us. The text is *constituted* by the head's bloodless detachment of itself from its heart in order to read the history of the mystical body (a history which presupposes such "deviations" [*Reflections* 105–06]), in order to return and metaphorically "frame a polity in blood." For Burke, England exists in time and space as a self-reading text; its history is nothing but the allegory of its reading.[18] England reproduces itself in a male parthenogenesis, fathers endlessly propagating sons who, never coincident with the original law from which they have fallen, have as their historical mission endless reflection on it. *English* history is simultaneously fidelity to and apostasy from the law, a paradox that makes and preserves the constitution by insuring that it is at once ancient and continually reconstituted by reflection.[19] The content of individual reflections is not important to Burke, nor is indefinite interpretability a problem—so long as the indefinite is disciplined and redeemed by the shaping spirit of a continual apostasy, a continual alienation from some undiscovered country of the past.

A crossing from Burke to Coleridge can be made via the following passage, a good example of the kind of attention to principles for which Burke was consistently applauded by his successor:

> On what grounds do we go to restore our constitution to what it has been at one definite period, or to reform and reconstruct it upon principles more conformable to a sound theory of government? A prescriptive government, such as ours, never was the work of any legislator, never was made upon any foregone theory. It seems to me a preposterous way of reasoning, and perfect confusion of ideas, to take the theories which learned and speculative men have made from that government, and then, supposing it made on those theories, which were made from it, to accuse the government as not corresponding with them.[20]

The best Coleridgean gloss on this ridicule of the preposterous is the famous Leibnizian aphorism from the *Biographia*, "There is nothing in the mind that was not before in the senses, except the mind itself,"[21] which, to adapt it to Burke, should be revised thus: "There is nothing in the constitution that was not first the work of a legislator, except the constitution itself."

In the *Biographia*, the equivalent of Burke's ancient constitution, that which grounds and entails all our reflections, is the mind itself: "I began

then to ask myself, what proof I had of the outward *existence* of any thing?
. . . I saw, that in the nature of things such proof is impossible: and that
of all modes of being, that are not objects of the senses, the existence
is *assumed* by a logical necessity arising from the *constitution of the mind*
itself. . . ." (*BL* :1:200). "The constitution of the mind"—the phrase is not
in Johnson but may be met with at the beginning of Burke's "Letter to
a Noble Lord," where Burke summons the idea of a "complete revolution" that has "extended even to the constitution of the mind of man."[22]
Coleridge's usage is thoroughly Burkean; it comprises the way the mind
is constituted and the way the mind constitutes, which ideally come to
the same thing, for "Truth is the correlative of Being" (*BL* 1:142). This
identity is ancient because it must be postulated as subsisting before any
moment in which we can come to know it: "During the act of knowledge
itself, the objective and subjective are so instantly united, that we cannot
determine to which of the two the priority belongs. . . . While I am attempting to explain this intimate condition, I must suppose it dissolved"
(*BL* 1:255). For Coleridge as for Burke, all understanding is reflection on
a past moment that is the condition of our knowledge but that can never
directly be known. The mind is a self-reading text reproducing itself in an
aporetic descent.

As is the *Biographia*, which resolutely rejects all readers except that one
who proves his gentleness by absenting himself in favor of the author: "If
however the reader will permit me to be my own Hierocles," Coleridge
requests at the beginning of chapter 12, referring to the Alexandrian commentator on neo-Pythagorean texts. If the reader does consent, he lets the
Biographia be what it wants to be, at once (or almost at once) Pythagorean
oracle and Hierocletian commentary. The *Biographia* is a continuous falling away from itself that is a reading of itself, falling to know its constitution, falling to know the course of its descent—a narcissism providentially
flawed by the apostasis that motivates a theoretically endless tracking.[23]
Coleridge continues,

> I have now before me a treatise of a religious fanatic, full of dreams
> and supernatural *experiences*. I see clearly the writer's grounds, and their
> hollowness. I have a complete insight into the causes, which through the
> medium of his body had acted on his mind; and by application of re-
> ceived and ascertained laws I can satisfactorily explain to my own reason
> all the strange incidents, which the writer records of himself. And this
> I can do without suspecting him of any intentional falsehood. As when

in broad daylight a man tracks the steps of a traveller, who had lost his
way in a fog or by treacherous moonshine, even so, and with the same
tranquil sense of certainty, can I follow the traces of this bewildered
visionary.

De Man never said it better, though say it he did:

[Insight] exists only for a reader in the privileged position of being able
to observe the blindness as a phenomenon in its own right—the question
of his own blindness being one which he is by definition incompetent to
ask—and so being able to distinguish between statement and meaning.
He has to undo the explicit results of a vision that is able to move toward
the light only because, being already blind, it does not have to fear the
power of this light.[24]

In Coleridge's usage the very insight of the visionary, the coincidence
of the spiritual eye with its ideal object, is identical to his blindness and
known only by his fall into bewilderment. As night passes into day the
visionary's tracks lead to the understanding Coleridge, who stands apart
from his benighted predecessor. The commentator can explain a blinded
insight because he has fallen farther; he can stand back from the experience that enfolded its author and see it as a page, as something already
written; and he can follow the betrayed man's tracks to a source where he
understands the visionary's ignorance but where, in his very lucidity, he
becomes equally blind to his own.

There are numerous places in the *Biographia* where such a procedure
could be illustrated. Some of them, such as the anecdote of the 'possessed'
German maid in chapter 6, the interruption of the letter from a friend
in chapter 13, the criticism of "Fidelity" in chapter 22, and the account
of the epiphany of Wordsworth's genius in chapter 4, I have analyzed
elsewhere with the objective of releasing the uncanny rhetoricity of this astonishing book. My objective here is to persuade that such tropism serves
a purpose. Let us refer to the autobiographical account in chapter 10 of a
strange evening during the young Coleridge's subscription campaign for
his radically evangelical periodical *The Watchman*. Suffering equally from
the "poison" of tobacco and the tonic of the night air, surrounded by a
crowd of well-wishers and potential subscribers, he had "sunk back on the
sofa in a sort of swoon." On awakening from "insensibility" and being
asked, "by way of relieving [his] embarrassment," "*Have you seen a paper to
day, Mr. Coleridge?*", Coleridge, like a guilty thing surprised, confessed to

his doubts regarding the morality of a Christian reading "newspapers or any other works of merely political and temporary interest"—a repudiation of the very course of action to which he had applied all his energies (*BL* 1:182).

Not only is this an instance of Hierocletian commentary, of the insightful, self-reading autobiographer tracking the bewildered visionary of his youth; that bewilderment, an emblematic moment of social blindness, is itself presented as an insight into an apostasy which has *already* occurred and been repressed. Coleridge had earlier adapted Wordsworth to describe his autobiographical progress as "'sounding on my dim and perilous way'" (*BL* 1:105). In this passage resonate soundings both canny and uncanny. Coleridge's daylight, journalistic intention to sound out support for his radical newspaper is thwarted by nocturnal soundings from the land of smoke and mist. The spirit of apostasy, "which the writings of Burke" legitimated for "the higher and [for] the literary classes, may like the ghost in Hamlet, be heard moving and mining in the underground chambers. . . ." (*BL* 1:192). Hearkening to that spirit, the aroused Hierocles awakens from his Jacobinical slumber and, in a moment of spontaneous reflection, sounds out his own "grounds, and [exposes] their hollowness." The return of the Burkean specter, ventriloquizing like truth itself, bewilders the visionary, mocking the "pert loquacity" of the social critic and political activist, and undermining any practical, worldly action whatever. Even in the first flush of his enthusiasm, as a wiser Coleridge tells us, he had already turned away from the faith he was proselytizing.

The objective correlative of his apostasy, Coleridge's dramatic swoon amidst a group of left-wing sympathizers both makes possible his blindly insightful ejaculation and protects it from censure. Because clearly he cannot mean what he says, he is released from the consequences of his utterance by a general laughter. But, of course, one point of the anecdote in the context of chapter 10 is that eventually Coleridge, who devotes much of the *Biographia* (as he had *The Friend*) to attacks on the production and consumption of periodicals and novels, *did* come to mean what he said. When did *coming to mean* occur? Could the turning point be pushed back to the moment (prophetic, as things turned out) of coming out of the swoon? Was Coleridge then confused or canny in his utterance? Did the swoon release an inadvertent prophecy, or did Coleridge swoon in order to tell *a*, if not *the*, truth? Does Coleridge the autobiographer mean to raise the question of meaning or is it an exegetical imposition? We enter the zone of that undecidability that de Man has glossed with reference to Proust: ". . . no one can decide whether Proust invented metaphors because he felt guilty or whether he had to declare himself guilty in order to find a use for his metaphors. Since the only irreducible 'intention' of a text is that of its constitution, the second hypothesis is in fact less unlikely than the first. The problem has to be suspended in its own indecision." [25] De Man works hard to produce these aporias in the texts he reads. Coleridge, as we know from the preface to "Kubla Khan" that tells of another drug-induced swoon, is at work even when he is asleep; and there is work being done here that produces the curious suspension that de Man identifies as quintessentially literary, and work that pits the literary so defined against all forms of ideology. The autobiographer endorses a self-reading that stands apart from any political or social goal whatever: it is, as the amused reaction of the reform-minded audience shows, exempt from the judgment of worldlings, beyond good and evil. The anecdote represents a Coleridge who was an apostate from the beginning and who approves apostasy as at worst an innocent act of some amusement to "the multitudinous public," or, at best as a method for incisively discriminating between the temporary and the permanent, for transforming social and political "realities" into texts able to be read, for suspending action in favor of reflection.

What are opposed to works of "merely political and temporary interest?" Works of permanent interest—and permanent because productive of true and lasting pleasure. Poetry, in other words. But not just any poetry, and not necessarily even that poetry which yields the most immediate pleasure: "not the poem which we have *read,* but that to which we *return,* with the greatest pleasure, possesses the genuine power, and claims the name of *essential poetry*" (*BL* 1:23). Opposed to works of science by its object, poetry is opposed to works of politics by the durability of its pleasure. The merits of poetry are neither substantive nor intrinsic. If poetry is in some sense the hero of the swooning episode as it is in some sense the hero of the *Biographia* as a work of philosophical criticism, the action which proves the merit of the hero—the allegory of its matchless identity—is a commentary. Every hero requires his Hierocles; every poem requires a critic. As the vindication of Wordsworth's genius is not its actual epiphany *in illo tempore* but Coleridge's return to and dramatic repetition of that revelation in chapter 4 of the *Biographia,* so does the merit of every poem depend on such a return—anastasis. And every return requires an initial departure, a standing away or apostasis, which is metastatically hinged to its successor.

That plot comprises the moves identified by de Man in "Literary History and Literary Modernity" as "the three moments of flight, return, and the turning point at which flight changes into return or vice-versa."[26] De Man abstracts those three moments from a plot shared by Nietzsche, Rousseau, and Baudelaire, who, exemplary modernists all, aspire to a clean rupture with literature and the past and who suffer the ironic consequences of that ambition: "The continuous appeal of modernity, the desire to break out of literature toward the reality of the moment, prevails and, in its turn, folding back upon itself, engenders the repetition and the continuation of literature. Thus modernity, which is fundamentally a falling away from literature and a rejection of history, also acts as the principle that gives literature duration and historical existence."[27] De Man is repeating a Coleridgean insight and mystifying it as he goes along, for de Man insists that his story is told from "the point of view of the writer as subject," whereas both his examples (Boileau, Fontenelle, Nietzsche, and Baudelaire) and the Coleridgean precedent argue that the actual point of view from which de Man tells his story is that of the writer as critic. If we are to accept that "the only irreducible 'intention' of a text is its constitution," it should be added that the only constitution of a text is its criticism. Coleridge's aphorism of departure and return is the story of criticism, which is distinguished from common reading insofar as it is motivated, insofar as the standing away is an apostasy (or flight) and insofar as the return is an anastasis (or reflection). It takes a critic to tell the common reader those works which he should reread.

The best critic is the lapsed poet. The high drama of the Wordsworthian epiphany in the *Biographia* is owed to Coleridge's endeavor to depict it as a rapturous stasis from which he can fall away into the seminal imagination-fancy distinction that concludes chapter 4 and that ordains his blossoming as a genuine critic. Coleridge manages a double flight: from Wordsworth and from his own poetic ambitions. This apostasy makes possible and prepares for the reading of Wordsworth that occupies most of volume 2—completing the constitution of Wordsworth's genius and, incidentally, modern poetry. This is not by any means the only story in the *Biographia* or the only apostasy in a text that moves from faith to faith, master to master (Bowyer, Bowles, Hartley, Wordsworth, Kant, Schelling) —all the while subjecting each authority to an allegory of apostasy mastered only by Coleridgean criticism. The critic derives his inheritance; like Burke, he engineers the metalepsis of coming to author the text he reads: hence the curious coincidence between becoming one's own Hierocles and being the commentator on a poetic text. The critic is always the author of the texts he reads, constituting literature as his autobiography, as the history of criticism. By claiming *always* I do not appeal to logic but to history; this state of affairs is not necessarily so, but it has ever been so since Coleridge. We critics would not know what social reality is if Coleridge had not fallen away from it. His falling away makes the "criticism" of social reality possible by rendering it as a *topic* completely interchangeable with any other "god" term that criticism symbolically substitutes for that absolute whose given name is "poetry" or "literature" and which criticism uses retrospectively to motivate and glorify its flight—to turn metonymy or mere contingency into apostasis. Every celebration of the recuperative powers of literature assists in the institution, elaboration, and reproduction of modern, that is, post-Coleridgean criticism.

Apostasy is to metonymy as the Fall is to a lapse. The distinction measures the distance between Coleridge's early nineteenth-century and Paul de Man's late twentieth-century projects. Imagine that distance as two points of view on difference. Coleridge wants to motivate a difference that de Man aims to abstract from all intention.[28] Writing at Highgate and trying to salvage something from a spendthrift career of erratic brilliance, humiliating dependency, and steady marginalization, Coleridge uses "apostasy" to render the possibly contingent as somehow necessary and to figure the ostensibly compulsive as somehow purposeful.[29] Writing after the storm of mid-century European history, centered and chaired within a prestigious department within a powerful university, addressing a profession whose most engrossing critical debates have always taken place on familiar Coleridgean ground, de Man can afford the *askesis* that strips literature to its blind mechanisms, defrauds it of its glory. Surely Lentricchia is right that there is nothing subversive or risky about this maneuver. It is because Coleridge is writing in the wilderness outside an academy yet to come that he needs to motivate the "same" move and give it purpose, so that the plot of criticism he identifies can presuppose its history, establish its tradition, simulate permanence and progression—in short, make the world safe for Paul de Man.

Permanence and progression are key concepts in Coleridge's most explicitly constitutional work, *On the Constitution of the Church and State.* This, the clearest, most controlled, and, by all odds, most influential of Coleridge's critical works, begins, characteristically, with an exculpation. Coleridge introduces his volume as a defense against "the name of APOSTATE," which he fears will be applied to him because of his reversal on the issue of Catholic Emancipation.[30] As a defense *Constitution* proceeds dialectically, both refuting and profiting from the allegation of apostasy. The inaugural move, familiar to any reader of Coleridge, is to apply to the topic of the State the platonic distinction between the Idea or principle and its phenomenal, merely historical, expressions. The Idea functions contextually to impose a vague topography on political discourse and to permit the sublimation of circumstantial differences, mere politics; it functions intertextually as a Coleridgean substitute for the Burkean concept of an enabling legal fiction, the "as if," that makes tradition possible. A critic bent on legitimacy rather than a parliamentary lawyer intent on policy, Coleridge is concerned to defecate the potentially dangerous play and the suggestion of arbitrariness that "fiction" conveys.

According to Coleridge, the idea of the State is its "ultimate aim," which is identical with its underlying and determinant principle, its constitution: "A CONSTITUTION is the attribute of a state, *i.e.* of a body politic, having the principle of its unity within itself. . . . (*CCS* 23). What the constitution ideally unifies, brings into "harmonious balance," are the "two great correspondent, at once supporting and counterpoising, interests of the state, its permanence, and its progression (*CCS* 29)—interests identified with the two "antagonist powers" (*CCS* 24) of the realm: the landed class, whose concern has always been for continuity, and the commercial class, whose interest has always been in change. The agent of that balance is not the state itself, but "the National Church, the third remaining estate of the realm, [whose object] was to secure and improve that civilization, without which the nation could be neither permanent nor progressive" (*CCS* 44). The model could be diagrammed on a blackboard: the State divides into permanence and progression, a reciprocal relation sustained by a single civilizing force, the Church, which contains within it the dual capacities of securing and improving and which, taken as a unit, balances with the State in the harmonious unity of the Nation, the idea that comprises all oppositions.

The sheer schematic clarity of this model would annihilate all dynamism were it not for the crucial past tense with which Coleridge characterizes the National Church, whose object, he says, "*was* to secure and improve." The past tense opens the scheme to history, to rhetoric, and to apostasy. The "was" signifies a specific transformation of the class of persons, who were once responsible for the cultivation of the nation:

> THE CLERISY of the nation, or national church, in its primary acceptation and original intention comprehended the learned of all denominations:—the sages and professors of the law and jurisprudence: of medicine and physiology . . . ; in short, all the so called liberal arts and sciences, the possession and application of which constitute the civilization of a country, as well as the Theological. (*CCS* 46)

But at a certain time,

> the students and possessors of those sciences, and those sorts of learning, the use and necessity of which were indeed constant and perpetual to the *nation*, but only accidental and occasional to *individuals*, gradually *detached* themselves from the nationalty [sic] and the national clergy, and passed to the order [i.e., the mercantile and commercial], with the growth and thriving condition of which their emoluments were found to increase in equal proportion.

Although the detachment of those who would come to be grouped under "the common name of professional, the learned in the departments of law, medicine, &c," significantly altered the balance of the correspondent interests in the nation, Coleridge insists that it

> can in now way affect the principle nor alter the tenure, nor annul the rights of those who remained, and who, as members of the permanent learned class, were planted throughout the realm, each in his appointed place, as the immediate agents and instruments in the great and indispensable work of perpetuating, promoting, and increasing the civilization of the nation. . . . (*CCS* 50)

But if the detachment did not affect the tenure or rights of the clerisy, it did straighten their resources, a curtailment violently institutionalized by the "first and deadliest wound inflicted on the constitution of the kingdom," Henry VIII's immoral refusal to restore the balance after the reappropriation by the state of that wealth, monopolized by Romish hands and dedicated to Romish ends, which had been consecrated to the civil health of the nation. Coleridge describes Henry's fraud as a "sacrilegious alienation"—the exact phrase he had earlier used to denounce Rome's control of the same wealth. Both "detachment" and "alienation" are forms of apostasy, albeit the former mild and accommodating compared to the latter. The three acts of separation are vital to Coleridge because they introduce the destabilizing contingency that is the pretext for his own rhetorical intervention, which justifies its historical existence as necessary to persuade that the wealth that had been detached or alienated, whether by the professions, the Catholics, or Henry VIII, be returned to those for whom it was in principle reserved and that the clerisy be reconstituted according to its original idea. Coleridge retrospectively motivates the contingent in order to give a form to history and to establish his position as critic within that history. No member of the clergy could have written *On the Constitution of the Church and State* for he would not have the necessary detachment to cultivate the ground for a persuasive argument regarding the importance of cultivation. No lawyer would make the argument because as a member of the professions,[31] which have their distinctive status among the estates, he has no interest in returning to the clerical stasis from which he had stood away. Only someone detached from all estates, only someone truly disinterested, only a critic could have written it.

Coleridge is more generous to the apostasy of the learned than to that of king and pope because it is the rubric under which he falls. Historically, the journalism he practices owes whatever claims it has to professionalism to its descent from that fifteenth-century detachment. Biographically, the crucial decisions in his life were his renunciations of a clerical career first in the established church and then in the Unitarian ministry.[32] Coleridge can now redeem those decisions by representing them as not apostasy in the vulgar sense but a detachment which, like all his changes of opinions, was authorized by a prevenient principle—even while he can metaleptically affirm that that apostasy was crucial to his recognition of the causal principle. The deviations of autobiography and history return to truth under the rubric of the idea. The apostate Coleridge returns to the center from which he fell under the rubric of criticism, which normalizes detachment and makes it socially useful. By demonstrating the social and historical function of reflective detachment, Coleridge cultivates the grounds for the institutionalization of the clerisy and constitutes the clerisy as criticism. *On the Constitution of the Church and State* is first and foremost the constitution of criticism and, apart from the *Biographia*, the single most important text for understanding the idea of criticism that harmoniously unifies the writings of Arnold, Eliot, and de Man.

After Coleridge there is no criticism without apostasy. And there are no heroes of criticism who were not first apostates. Kenneth Burke is no exception. Lentricchia begins his "pursuit of the issue of criticism as social force" by recalling an episode, recounted by Kenneth Burke, in which Burke delivered a paper "Revolutionary Symbolism in America" to the first American Writers' Congress at Madison Square Garden in 1935. Burke's paper, in which, according to Lentricchia, he rewrote and elaborated Marx's first thesis on Feuerbach, proposed to

> America's radical left not only that a potentially revolutionary culture should keep in mind that revolution must be culturally as well as economically rooted, but, as well . . . that a revolutionary culture must situate itself firmly on the terrain of its capitalist antagonist, must not attempt a dramatic leap beyond capitalism in one explosive, rupturing moment of release, must work its way through capitalism's language of domination by working cunningly within it, using, appropriating, even speaking though its key mechanisms of repression.[33]

Lentricchia admires Burke's unscared awareness of the force of ideology, his keen sense of the cultural basis of domination and, in stark contrast to the de Man of "Literary History and Literary Modernity," his disavowal of a "romantic" notion of revolutionary rupture, which is a prescription for failure, whether espoused by American Marxists or Yale critics. Lentricchia notes, however, that when Burke recalled the incident, he gleefully attested to the irate reaction of his audience: it "produced hallucinations of 'excrement . . . dripping from my tongue,' of his name being shouted as a 'kind of charge' against him, a 'dirty word'—'Burke!' " Lentricchia applauds the "heresy" and "deviance" of Burke's portentous and prophetic remarks but fails to comment on the circumstantially specific irony that Burke's "challenge to the Marxist intellectual," to forswear self-defeating, paralyzing notions of rupture, is just such a moment of rupture. In that locale, Burke's turn to symbolism and culture, a move that, for Lentricchia, is the paradigmatic action constituting a socially effective criticism, was in fact an apostasy. To what are we to attend, Burke's text or his performance? Which has more social force? Which is more symbolic? Or is there any difference? Who can say? What is to be done? Who can tell the saying from the doing? Lentricchia does not risk his confidence in intervention by taking up those rhetorical questions. But if his avoidance saves him from the more overt symptoms of paralysis, it decisively blinds him to the preternaturally acute insight expressed by Burke's audience, who, with a wit of dreamlike velocity and aptness, instantaneously deployed

"Burke" as a "kind of charge," as "dirty word," catching the pun that twins Kenneth with that Edmund whose surname has been, ever since the explosive publication of *Reflections*, a byword for political apostasy. To follow out that dreamlike association, to inquire into the complicities between revolution and reaction under the rubric of "culture," would be to derive the descent from Burke's Burke to Burke's obsessive identifications with Coleridge to the beginning of de Man's *Allegories of Reading*. Here de Man cites Burke's mention of *"deflection* . . . defined as 'any slight bias or even unintended error,'* as the rhetorical basis of language"—a notion which de Man subsequently employs to deconstruct all intentionalist, not to mention interventionist, notions of rhetoric.[34]

It is not merely the work of Paul de Man, then, that has "the insidious effect . . . of paralyzing praxis itself." The sleep of praxis is the birth of criticism. Or so it is if we take Coleridge as our canonized forefather and regardless of whether we opt for Paul de Man or Kenneth (not Edmund) Burke as godfather. Paralysis or a constitutional "aversion to real action" is the characteristic that this critical Hamlet installed at the center of the literary culture of which he was the chief, if not only, begetter. To freely adapt the critic:

> The critical mind. . . . unseated from its healthy relation, is constantly occupied with the world within, and abstracted from the world without —giving substance to shadows, and throwing a mist over all commonplace actualities. . . . Hence it is that the sense of sublimity arises, not from the sight of an outward object, but from the beholder's reflection upon it:—not from the sensuous impression, but from the imaginative reflex. . . . Hamlet, like Coleridge, like de Man, like Burke, feels this; his senses are in a state of trance, and he looks upon external things as hieroglyphics."[35]

Having abjured the outside world, fallen into the trance of literature, there is no reference except to antiquity, that ghostly father who haunts our latter days. No doubt the tacit political agenda of deconstruction is apostasy, but with no less doubt that apostasy is the imaginative reflex or trope that constitutes modern criticism. And it is because of that inaugural apostasy, which after Coleridge has become the ticket of admission into the clerisy, that if we deconstruct Coleridge we deconstruct a deconstruction; we return to a scene where we, like that bewildered visionary, wake up embarrassed to discover ourselves apostate, having already fallen from the sunlit world of action into the treacherous moonshine of interpretation.

12

Coleridge and the Charge of Political Apostasy

Thomas McFarland

An interesting and unresolved question that occupies the border between literary history and political history is posed by the career of Coleridge. Did Coleridge's political attitudes over the course of his adult life represent a coherent development from primary assumptions, or, on the contrary, did they represent an incoherent line of thought characterized by opportunism and outright apostasy? To address the question is not simply to re-enter the political milieu of the Romantic era, but to shed renewed light on Coleridge's mental attitudes and idiosyncratic modes of thought.

Both of the opposing cases were urged in Coleridge's day and are still being put forward in our own. The historian E. P. Thompson has repeatedly charged that Coleridge lacked political integrity and that he in fact virtually defines one form of discreditable apostasy. In an essay called "Disenchantment or Default? A Lay Sermon," Thompson attempts to distinguish between apostasy and disenchantment:

> There is nothing in disenchantment inimical to art. But when aspiration is actively denied, we are at the edge of apostasy, and apostasy is a moral failure, and an imaginative failure. In men of letters it often goes with a peculiar disposition towards self-bowdlerization, whether in Mr. Southey or in Mr. Auden. It is an imaginative failure because it involves forgetting—or manipulating improperly—the authenticity of experience: a mutilation of the writer's own previous existential being. . . . Hazlitt commented that there need be no objection to a man changing his opinions. But:

> he need not . . . pass an act of attainder on all his thoughts, hopes, wishes, from youth upwards, to offer them at the shrine of matured servility: he need not become one vile antithesis, a living and ignominious satire on himself.[1]

And then Thompson says: "Coleridge fell into this phase soonest." Thompson argues that a creative tension between "Jacobin affirmation and recoil" was good for Romantic poetry, but that apostasy, the abject giving up of former opinion, was bad: that for Wordsworth the moment of creative tension "was far more protracted than it was for Coleridge." He thus sees Coleridge's apostasy as not only an index to moral bankruptcy but as the prime agent in his loss of poetic power, though others have ascribed that loss to other factors.

If Thompson's distinction may seem to raise more questions than it answers, it at least serves as an introduction to his distaste for Coleridge. Ten years later, in a review of David Erdman's edition of Coleridge's *Essays on his Times*, Thompson indulged that distaste with greater vehemence. Coleridge's political essays, he says, are "the spurious rhetoric of a chameleon"; Coleridge himself underwent "interior redecoration"; "Coleridge," says Thompson, "was an apostate, with a voracious appetite for hatreds"; "These articles then are, in the main, both irresponsible and unprincipled." "These books are most damaging to Coleridge's reputation as an exalted political thinker, and, moreover, it is altogether proper that this inflated reputation should be so damaged. The *ingredients* of Coleridge's political thought—historical, philosophical—were exceptionally rich, but the results were always half-baked."

In truth, Thompson simply cannot abide Coleridge. "I find these essays objectionable, not on account of their opinions—although most of these are lamentable—but on account of the unction with which they are delivered." Again: "As one lays the volumes down one is sickened by the surfeit of pharisaism and cliché. Coleridge is always writing 'from my inmost soul,' he offers himself as 'a teacher of moral wisdom.' But the content might be better entitled 'Coleridge's Compendium of Cliché.'" Still again: "The more he tried to work up his impulses into finished thoughts, the more unprincipled he became. He is chiefly of interest, in his political writings, as an example of the intellectual complexity of apostasy. He was, of course, a political apostate, and critics have confused the matter only because they have removed it from a political to an aesthetic court of judgment." In a zenith of irritation Thompson even declares that "Coleridge was wrong on almost everything."[2]

Now not everyone is likable to everyone else, and doubtless there could never be any possibility of rapprochement between the styles and opinions of Edward Thompson and Coleridge. But that Coleridge was a committed Jacobin who then became an apostate Tory seems to me demonstrably not the case. Thompson's own political orientation is very unlike that of Coleridge, and we should heed Coleridge's own statement that

> he who infamizes another man as an Apostate and Renegado, does, *ipso facto,* confess that he himself continues to retain the opinions and principles which the other had *reneged* and *turned against.* Had no other fragments of the works of the heretic Faustus been preserved but those in which he calls St. Augustine, Apostate and Deserter, yet these would have been amply sufficient to make it *certain* that Faustus himself had remained a Manichaean.[3]

Nor does Thompson's quoting Hazlitt against not passing an act of attainder on all one's previous attitudes serve as more than a merely rhetorical point against Coleridge. After all, Coleridge himself said the same thing, more subtly:

> Why do we so very very often see men pass from one extreme to another. . . . Alas they sought not the Truth but praise, self-importance, & above all to see something *doing.*—Disappointed they hate and persecute their former opinion, which no man will do who by meditation had adopted it, & in the course of unfeigned meditation gradually enlarged the circle & so got out of it—for in the perception of its falsehood he will form a perception of certain Truths which had made the falsehood plausible, & never can he cease to venerate his own sincerity of Intention. . . .[4]

The setting up of Hazlitt against Coleridge, indeed, is a more complex matter than would appear on the surface. First of all, Hazlitt had not really been mature enough to experience the before-and-after shock of the Revolution, which as we shall presently see, is so necessary to an understanding of the changes in political sentiment endemic to the time. Second, Hazlitt took a special, indeed a unique pride in not changing his opinions once they had formed, and this temperamental feature cannot be separated from the validity of his position as such:

> In matters of taste and feeling, one proof that my conclusions have not been quite shallow or hasty, is the circumstance of their having been lasting. I have the same favourite books, pictures, passages that I ever had: I may therefore presume that they will last my life—nay, I may indulge a hope that my thoughts will survive me. This continuity of impression is the only thing on which I pride myself.[5]

That statement occurs in an essay called "A Farewell to Essay-Writing." In an essay called "On Consistency of Opinion" he proudly says:

I am not to be brow-beat or wheedled out of my settled convictions. Opinion to opinion, I will face any man. Prejudice, fashion, the cant of the moment, go for nothing. . . . If 'to be wise were to be obstinate,' I might set up for as great a philosopher as the best of them; for some of my conclusions are as fixed and incorrigible to proof as need be. I am attached to them in consequence of the pains, the anxiety, and the waste of time they have cost me.[6]

Hazlitt was particularly "fixed and incorrigible" with regard to the French Revolution, which he calls "the great cause, to which I had vowed myself." As he said in a haunting statement that affirmed his pride in the constancy of his beliefs, "my earliest hopes will be my last regrets":

What sometimes surprises me in looking back to the past, is . . . to find myself so little changed in time. The same images and trains of thought stick by me: I have the same tastes, liking, sentiments, and wishes that I had then. One great ground of confidence and support has, indeed, been struck from under my feet; but I have made it up to myself by proportionable pertinacity of opinion. The success of the great cause, to which I had vowed myself, was to me more than all the world: I had a strength in its strength, a resource which I knew not of, tille it failed me for the second time [i.e., Napoleon's defeat at Waterloo]. . . . It was not till I saw the axe laid to the root, that I found the full conviction of the right was only established by the triumph of the wrong; and my earliest hopes will be my last regrets. One source of this unbendingness, (which some may call obstinacy,) is that, though living much alone, I have never worshipped the Echo. I see plainly enough that black is not white, that the grass is green, that kings are not their subjects; and, in such self-evident cases, do not think it necessary to collate my opinions with the received prejudices.[7]

Coleridge was quite different. He was not, however, different in the tenacity with which he held to his positions; for as I have elsewhere emphasized, he maintained the same principles throughout his adult career.[8] He was different rather in the complex structure of his tenacity; for unlike Hazlitt, who prided himself on seeing that black was not white, Coleridge was always trying to encompass both black and white. He was temperamentally on all sides of a question at once,[9] and he was forever attempting to reconcile and include, rather than to discriminate and reject:

My system, if I may venture to give it so fine a name, is the only attempt I know, ever made to reduce all knowledges into harmony. It opposes no other system, but shows what was true in each; and how that which was true in the particular, in each of them became an error, *because* it was only half the truth, and therewith to frame a perfect mirror. I show to each system that I fully understand and rightfully appreciate what that system means; but then I lift up that system to a higher point of view, from which I enable it to see its former position, where it was, indeed, but under another light and with different relations; so that the fragment of truth is not only acknowledged, but explained.[10]

Coleridge, in brief, agreed both with what the Jacobins were attempting to do, and with what their opponents urged against them. In attempting to incorporate all positions into his own, Coleridge might well seem to one who encountered him only on special issues not to honor the difference between black and white; but I myself have described this being on both sides of a given issue as the idiosyncrasy and defining merit of his mental activity. As I affirmed at the conclusion of a work that surveyed the entire course of his thought:

... through all the transformations of his 'it is'/pantheist interests on the one hand, and of his 'I am'/moral interests on the other, he remained true to the ineradicable fact of their tragic opposition—longing for their reconciliation, but foundering, as do we all, before the mysteries of existence.

In this equipoise Coleridge's philosophical achievement is both of its time and out of its time. His thought shares with that of his German contemporaries an emphasis upon the central importance of Spinozistic pantheism. But it differs in its idiosyncratic refusal to decide, either by pantheism or by solipsistic scepticism, that which cannot be decided.[11]

So, too, as this essay shall argue, Coleridge's voyage down the political stream, steering a course between the opposed banks of radicalism and reaction, seeming now to adhere to one side and now to the other, is entirely consistent with his mental procedure on all topics of thought. Hazlitt sardonically recalled of a walk with him, that

I observed that he continually crossed me on the way by shifting from one side of the foot-path to the other. This struck me as an odd movement; but I did not at that time connect it with any instability of purpose or involuntary change of principle, as I have done since. He seemed unable to keep on in a strait line.[12]

But Hazlitt, despite his disgust at what he thought of as Coleridge's defection from the libertarian position, really did understand that Coleridge's political progress was precisely an intellectual version of the idiosyncratic fact that "he continually crossed me on the way by shifting from one side of the foot-path to the other." Coleridge did keep moving on the path; the shifting, however peculiar to his mode of progression, was not an opportunistic abandonment of one faith and adhesion to another:

> I can hardly consider Mr. Coleridge as a deserter from the cause he first espoused, unless one could tell me what cause he ever heartily espoused, or what party he ever belonged to, in downright earnest. He has not been inconsistent with himself at different times, but at all times. He is a sophist, a casuist, a rhetorician, what you please; and might have argued or declaimed to the end of his breath on one side of a question or another, but he never was a pragmatical fellow. He lived in a round of contradictions, and never came to a settled point.[13]

Despite Hazlitt's scorn, his characterization of Coleridge here is compatible in its structure with what I praise, in the passage quoted above, as the special "equipoise" of Coleridge's intellectual achievement. Moreover, to cleave, as did Hazlitt, to an unvarying course through all the subsequent vicissitudes of the French Revolution, was, as he himself conceded, "unbendingness" and "obstinacy"; for such a course could only be maintained by radically downplaying—conniving at, really—the institutionalized murder that for Coleridge and for others changed the entire moral ambience of that Revolution. As Hazlitt says, ready to change reality rather than change his opinions,

> The Cant about the horrors of the French Revolution is mere cant— every body knows it to be so: each party would have retaliated upon the other: it was a civil war, like that for a disputed succession: the general principle of the right or wrong of the change remain untouched. Neither would these horrors have taken place, except from Prussian manifestos, and treachery within: there were none in the American, and have been none in the Spanish Revolution.[14]

But the American Revolution, Hazlitt should have known, was not a true revolution at all; and Hazlitt could not know that the next true revolution, the Russian Revolution, would precisely repeat the horrors of the French Revolution. In sum, if Coleridge's seeming vacillation between progressive and conservative modes entailed a cost, so too did Hazlitt's steadfastness. And Coleridge, it must emphatically be repeated, was in his own way steadfast too.

To be sure, Coleridge was more conservative in the second decade of the nineteenth century than he had been in the last decade of the eighteenth. As Lewis Patton summarizes Coleridge's language of reform in *The Watchman* of 1796, we hear the tropes likely to be used at that time by any young man of mind and heart. Thus Coleridge in 1796

> charged the Church of England with teaching hatred in the name of the God of love (11) and ridiculed the miracles of the New Testament (52); he called the Two Acts breaches of the Constitution (13); he declared that the possessions of the rich rightfully belonged to the poor (64); he predicted that by providential means kings and potentates would shortly be overthrown, and a good thing, too (65–66); he quoted with approval a declaration in favour of the rights of man (372) and that nations other than France and the United States, which had been "too long the dupes of perfidious kings, nobles, and priests," will eventually recover their rights (373); he urged the enlargement of the right of suffrage in England (209); he asserted that in the purer and more radical days of the French Revolution "the victories of Frenchmen" were "the victories of Human Nature" (270); and he likened Pitt to Judas Iscariot and hoped that he would be struck by a thunderbolt (167). But if these extracts, chosen as instances of candour, give an impression of rashness or bombast, as well they might, the impression is false. The tone of *The Watchman* was prevailingly temperate. . . .[15]

Moreover, Coleridge does seem to have attempted to tidy things up a bit with respect to earlier opinions. Thus, just as Southey in 1817 was enraged by the unauthorized publication of his *Wat Tyler* of 1794, Henry Crabb Robinson can note in 1816 that "I read at Montagu's Coleridge's beautiful *Fire, Famine, and Slaughter*, written in his Jacobinical days, and now reprinted to his annoyance by Hunt in the *Examiner*."[16] To make sure that he would not be further embarrassed by having raw earlier emphases thrown in his face, Coleridge significantly altered his poem *To a Young Ass*. Where in 1794 the concluding lines read:

> Yea! and more musically sweet to me
> Thy dissonant harsh bray of joy would be,
> Than Handel's softest airs that soothe to rest
> The tumult of a scoundrel Monarch's Breast

by 1834 both Handel and the scoundrel Monarch were gone, and the lines now read

> Yea! and more musically sweet to me
> Thy dissonant harsh bray of joy would be,

> Than warbled melodies that soothe to rest
> The aching of pale Fashion's vacant breast! [17]

In the same context, when the *Biographia Literaria* appeared in 1817 it contained in its tenth chapter a denial that Coleridge had at any time been sympathetic to Jacobinism, and in its third chapter presented a eulogy of Southey.[18] Hazlitt, in his ferocious review of the *Biographia* took note of both:

> Mr. Southey [writes Hazlitt] has come voluntarily before the public; and all the world has a right to speak of his publications. It is those only that have either been depreciated or denounced. We are not aware, at least, of any attacks that have been made, publicly or privately, on his private life or morality. The charge is, that he wrote democratical nonsense in his youth; and that he has not only taken to write against democracy in his muturer age, but has abused and reviled those who adhere to his former opinions; and accepted of emoluments from the party which formerly calumniated him, for those good services. Now, what has Mr. Coleridge to oppose to this? Mr. Southey's private character! . . . Some people say, that Mr. Southey has deserted the cause of liberty: Mr. Coleridge tells us, that he has not separated from his wife. They say, that he has changed his opinions: Mr. Coleridge says, that he keeps his appointments; and has even invented a new word, *reliability*, to express his exemplariness in this particular. It is also objected, that the worthy Laureate was as extravagant in his early writings, as he is virulent in his present ones: Mr. Coleridge answers, that he is an early riser, and not a late sitter up.[19]

As for Coleridge's claim that people he had met in the 1790s "will bear witness for me how opposite even then my principles were to those of Jacobinism or even of democracy," Hazlitt comments with a verbal shrug:

> We shall not stop at present to dispute with Mr. Coleridge, how far the principles of the Watchman, and the *Conciones ad Populum*, were or were not akin to those of the Jacobins. His style, in general, admits of a convenient latitude of interpretation. But we think we are quite safe in asserting, that they were still more opposite to those of the Anti-Jacobins, and the party to which he admits he has gone over.[20]

That Hazlitt, however, whose hatred for Coleridge was matched only by the extreme acuteness of his critical perceptions, does not choose actually to examine or assail the *Conciones ad Populum* is significant. For the work is Coleridge's earliest political statement, and it is there and in those terms, or ultimately nowhere and in no terms at all, that an accusation of early Jacobinism and later apostasy must be substantiated.[21] It will be the argument of this paper that neither charge can in fact be substantiated.

Indeed, this paper will argue that Coleridge's attitude can most fruitfully be understood not as an oscillation between left wing and right wing politics, but rather as a continuing concern for the human (one may in this regard point to Anya Taylor's sensitive study, *Coleridge's Defense of the Human*). As he wrote in 1818, long after the Revolution and his own youth were past, but in words that may serve as an emblem of his attitude from first to last,

> Marat had a conviction amounting in his own mind to a moral certainty that the death of 200,000 of his Countrymen was indispensible to the establishment of the Liberty and ultimate moral and physical well-being of France, and therein of all Europe. We will even assume, that events should have confirmed the correctness of this belief. And yet Marat was and will remain either execrable as a remorseless Ruffian, or frightful as an Insane Fanatic. And why? The proposal was frightfully disproportionate to the sphere of a poor fallible Mortal. It was a decisive symptom of an inhuman Soul, that, when the lives of myriads of his fellow-men were in question; the recollection of his necessary fallibility, and the probability of mistake where so many myriads of men possessing the same intellectual faculties with himself entertained different convictions with the same sense of positiveness, did not outweigh any confidence arising from his own individual insight.[22]

Marat, however, and it must be stressed, was an anomaly only by his higher degree of fanaticism, not by any difference from other Jacobins in his theoretical acceptance of reformist violence.[23] Coleridge saw from the first that violence was essential to Jacobinism, despite his sympathy and personal friendship with some of the leading English Jacobins, who were not themselves, like their French counterparts, brought to the actual test of violence. We may perhaps have some indication of what they would have done, however, from the reaction of one of them, James Watt, Junior, the son of the inventor, who happened to be in Paris at the time of the September massacres in 1792. He was appalled—yet he asserted that the deaths were absolutely necessary:[24] Coleridge, on the other hand, saw clearly that Jacobinism was inextricably bound up with a commitment to programmatic violence that necessarily desecrated the human. About this commitment there can be no convincing historical disagreement; it was the Jacobins (and Hébertists), not the Girondins, who planned and executed the Terror in all its phases. Crane Brinton points out that the Jacobin Clubs from the first, well before the actual advent of the Terror, were permeated by a tropism to violence, sometimes even in slight ways.[25]

In truth, the only real question is whether Jacobin violence arose from circumstances, which was the position of the historian Alphonse Aulard,[26] or was on the contrary an essential condition of the Jacobin way of viewing the world, which was the contention of Hippolyte Taine.[27] The implications of Taine's analysis, indeed, are that it would be better if the revolution had never occurred at all, and that, I believe, although not precisely Coleridge's view, is not far from it. Certainly the question in retrospect is not whether some good may have stemmed from the Revolution, but whether the cost of that good was historically too high.[28]

How radical such a conclusion was in terms of Romantic experience can scarcely be overemphasized, for that the revolution did occur was the overwhelming fact of the era, and that it should occur was the almost equally overwhelming hope of the finest and most ardent sensibilities among those who were young. "The French Revolution," wrote Shelley to Byron, was "the master theme of the epoch in which we live."[29] Hazlitt treated it as the originating moment of Romanticism itself;[30] and certainly no figure in the literature of the early nineteenth century is exempt from the impress of the revolutionary cataclysm.

And yet it is also true that hardly any figure is entirely consistent in his orientation toward that cataclysm. We must not forget that the most eloquent opponent of the French Revolution, Burke, had formerly been the most eloquent defender of the American Revolution. Yet the earlier event gave the later upheaval its pattern of hope and justification. Blake's *America*, it is generally agreed, is actually a poem about the French Revolution, and its statement that "The King of England looking westward trembles at the vision"[31] should in the reality of 1793 be understood as that the King is looking eastward. But as Hazlitt insisted,

> Mr. Burke, the opponent of the American war—and Mr. Burke, the opponent of the French Revolution, are not the same person, but opposite persons—not opposite persons only, but deadly enemies. In the latter period, he abandoned not only all his practical conclusions, but all the principles on which they were founded. He proscribed all his former sentiments, denounced all his former friends, rejected and reviled all

the maxims to which he had formerly appealed as incontestable. In the American war, he constantly spoke of the rights of the people as inherent, and inalienable: after the French Revolution, he began by treating them with the chicanery of a sophist, and ended by raving at them with the fury of a maniac. In the former case, he held out the duty of resistance to oppression, as the palladium, and only ultimate resource, of natural liberty; in the latter, he scouted, prejudiced, vilified and nicknamed, all resistance in the abstract, as a foul and unnatural union of rebellion and sacrilege.[32]

Notable in Hazlitt's rhetoric is the tendency to treat Burke's attitudes not as representing a legitimate approach to different situations, but as nothing less than a breakdown of character and personality: the two Burkes are "not the same person, but opposite persons—not opposite persons only, but deadly enemies." The charge may serve as an index to the extreme depth of feeling, both for and against, generated by the French Revolution and the political opinions connected with it. In France, former friends sent one another to the guillotine (for a single instance, Robespierre abandoned his boyhood friend Camille Desmoulins to the tumbril).[33] When Friedrich Schlegel repudiated his earlier revolutionary sentiments, joined the Catholic Church, became an aide to Metternich, and espoused reaction in a virtually feudal commitment—so strongly indeed that even Metternich was appalled—his brother Wilhelm would have nothing further to do with him, and the estrangement persisted to the end of Friedrich's life.[34]

Chameleonlike change, in truth, characterized even those closest to the revolution; for forces were there unleashed that tossed ordinary consistencies around like confetti. Robespierre, although it now seems difficult to credit, was, virtually at the same time that he became the foremost expediter of institutionalized murder, an opponent of capital punishment:[35] On 31 May, 1791, in fact, he delivered to the Assembly a long and humane speech calling for the abolition of the death penalty.[36] Again, the Girondin orator Vergniaud spoke with immense eloquence against the execution of Louis XVI, and for a time carried the day;[37] only shortly afterward to reverse himself completely, mount the rostrum, and vote for death.[38] In England, the stalwart friend of Revolution, John Thelwall, could look back on his own course of action and say unrepentantly, "If it be of any importance to my enemies to know that the opinions of the boy of nineteen, were not the same as those of the man of thirty, let them make what use they please of my apostasy."[39] And for a final example, John Horne Tooke,

Thelwall's mentor and the most respected of the English Jacobins, after a
few years accepted an income and became moderate and even cautious in
his opinions, for which Thelwall could never forgive him:

> I still, indeed, respect the politician, but I abhor the man. I venerate
> the sage, but I abhor the treacherous friend. . . . If Horne Tooke values
> posthumous reputation he has reason to wish my memoirs never should
> be resumed. It became not him to assist in driving me from society—to
> attempt to draw a line between his politics and mine; for though we dif-
> fered in some points most assuredly, the principle demarcation between
> us was, that I was open and sincere, he subtle and hypocritical . . .[40]

Those who turned against the French Revolution were bitter against
the Revolution's betrayal of their hopes; those who for their part remained
loyal to Revolutionary commitment were bitter against the apostates. As
Henry Crabb Robinson said in 1816, "Europe was rising morally and intellectually when the French Revolution, after promising to advance the
world rapidly in its progress towards perfection, suddenly, by the woe-
ful turn it took, threw the age back in its expectations."[41] But Hazlitt, as
Robinson also recalls on an occasion in 1815, "became warm on politics
and declaimed against the friends of liberty for their apostacy. He attacked
me, but was at the same time civil."[42] Hazlitt was not always civil. As Crabb
Robinson records of a later occasion in the same year: "debated with Hazlitt, in which I was . . . not successful, as far as the talent of the disputants
was involved, though Hazlitt was wrong as well as offensive in almost all
he said. . . . Hazlitt and myself once felt alike on politics, and now our
hopes and fears are directly opposed. Hazlitt retains all his hatred of kings
and bad governments, and believing them to be incorrigible, he from a
principle of revenge, rejoices that they are punished."[43]

Robinson's diary, indeed, provides the very feeling of the political acri-
mony that pervaded daily encounters. To avail ourselves of a pastiche
of examples, in 1812 he notes of a conversation that "On politics of the
time of the French Revolution [Wordsworth] also spoke and attempted,
but unsuccessfully, against Anthony Robinson's attacks, to defend Coleridge's consistency."[44] Again, in 1813: "A chat with Godwin. He expressed
himself in the ordinary commonplace way against Coleridge's honesty, ac-
cusing him of a vulgar hypocrisy of which I am sure he is not capable;
though he wants courage in company. And he also seemed ready to extend this reproach to Wordsworth, but did not persist in it."[45] On another

occasion, however, Godwin clearly did persist in it: "Spent from ten till half-past eleven in a call on Godwin. He was lately with Wordsworth, and after spending a night at his house seems to have left him with very bitter and hostile feelings. I believe political opinions alone kept him aloof."[46] This was in 1816. A year earlier Godwin had turned on Robinson himself: "I spent the evening by appointment with Godwin. The Taylors were there. We talked politics and not very comfortably. Godwin and I all but quarrelled. He was very rude, I very vehement, both a little angry, and equally offensive to each other."[47] The Revolutionary loyalists were bitter about the apostates; the apostates were bitter about the Revolution; but the apostates were serene about their apostasy. As Robinson writes in 1812: "On telling Burrell of my former attachment to Godwin and the French writers, he observed that I had taken exactly his course; he is now an anti-Jacobin like me, and I should infer a Wordsworthian in politics."[48]

Yet even the Revolutionary loyalists displayed variations in their attitudes. Blake himself, though he never repudiated his radical sentiments, changed very noticeably in his attitude toward the French Revolution as such. *America* had presented an ecstatic view of political freedom:

> Let the slave grinding at the mill, run out into the field:
> Let him look up into the heavens & laugh in the bright air:
> Let the inchained soul shut up in darkness and sighing
> Whose face has never seen a smile in thirty weary years;
> Rise and look out, his chains are loose, his dungeon doors are open.
> And let his wife and children return from the oppressors scourge;
> They look behind at every step & believe it is a dream
> Singing. The Sun has left his blackness, & has found a fresher morning
> And the fair Moon rejoices in the clear & cloudless night;
> For Empire is no more, and now the Lion & Wolf shall cease.[49]

A decade or so later, however, this intoxication with explicitly realized political freedom had given way to something much more internalized. In his address "To the Deists" that prefaces the third chapter of *Jerusalem*, Blake specifically says that although the "Tyrant Pride & the Laws" of "Babylon" shall "shortly be destroyed," it will be "with the Spiritual and not the Natural Sword."[50] In line with this internalization, the Revolutionary principle Orc is entirely absent from *Jerusalem*, although this figure had dominated the earlier prophetic books, as in Enitharmon's call in *Europe a Prophecy*:

Arise O Orc and give our mountains joy of thy red light.

·   ·   ·   ·   ·   ·   ·   ·   ·   ·   ·   ·   ·   ·   ·   ·   ·   ·

But terrible Orc, when he held the morning in the east,
Shot from the heights of Enitharmon;
And in the vineyards of red France appear'd the light of his fury.[51]

Blake was not the only intellectual to mute and internalize his Revolutionary commitments. John Thelwall, though he started out with Tory sympathies, became a protégé of Horne Tooke and in the 1790s was perhaps the most resolute of all the English Jacobins. About 1800, however, he abandoned revolutionary provocation for the teaching of elocution and the remedy of speech defects, veered back into politics about 1818, then back to elocution until his death in 1834.[52] William Cobbett, the most influential political reformer of the early nineteenth century, oscillated wildly in his commitments. For instance, he reversed himself from vilification of Thomas Paine in the 1790s to glorification twenty years later and even reverentially brought Paine's bones back with him from America, to the vast scorn of his enemies.

But these changes were like the turn of leaves in a California autumn. For flaming color one must visit the apostates. Wordsworth, who was the only one of the major English Romantic poets who actually saw the French Revolution first hand, changed from enthusiastic support of libertarian principles to an almost legendary reaction. "Most intensely did I rejoice at the Counter Revolution," wrote Robinson in 1816. "I had also rejoiced when a boy at the Revolution, and I am ashamed of neither sentiment"; but in the same breath he says, "I am sorry that Wordsworth cannot change with the times. . . . Of the integrity of Wordsworth I have no doubt, as of his genius I have an unbounded admiration; but I doubt the discretion and wisdom of his latest political writings."[53] The year before, Robinson noted that one evening Godwin, constantly bitter on this topic, was "abusive on Wordsworth, Coleridge, Southey, and Stoddart—for what he calls their political tergiversation."[54] And yet such reversals were not restricted to a small group in England. For a single continental instance, Schiller, who in his youth more influentially than almost any other figure idealized the doctrines of liberty, equality, and fraternity, in later years withdrew his support of the Revolution.[55]

Why was there so much "political tergiversation?" Why did so many writers change their opinions about the French Revolution and the complex of sentiments surrounding it? The answer is both large and simple.

The Revolution was not one thing, but two things: it was one thing in prospect, another in actuality and retrospect. The difference in the two introduced all the variations in attitude that afflicted the best sensibilities of the time.

In prospect, the Revolution partook almost of the idea of paradise, and it was no accident that millenarian doctrines flourished with particular intensity as it gathered to its climax. The overthrow of the Bastille seemed almost the beginning of a new order of peace, wisdom, and brotherhood:

> For, lo! the dread Bastille,
> With all the chambers in its horrid towers,
> Fell to the ground:—by violence overthrown
> Of indignation; and with shouts that drowned
> The crash it made in falling'. From the wreck
> A golden palace rose, or seemed to rise,
> The appointed seat of equitable law and mild
> paternal sway
>
> . . . .
>   Meanwhile, prophetic harps
> In every grove were ringing, 'War shall cease;
>
> . . . .
> Bring garlands, bring forth choicest flowers, to deck
> The tree of Liberty.'[56]

This, it must be emphasized, was what young and ardent spirits all over Europe looked to the Revolution to be. It was not simply that

> Bliss was it in that dawn to be alive,
> But to be young was very Heaven![57]

but that . . . "the whole Earth, / The beauty wore of promise—." It almost argued lack of soul not to participate in the great upsurge of hope. The cause was

> Good, pure, which no one could stand up against,
> Who was not lost, abandoned, selfish, proud,
> Mean, miserable, wilfully depraved,
> Hater perverse of equity and truth.[58]

Of special significance is the fact that the Revolution, as idealistic focus, did not suddenly burst upon the scene on July 14, 1789. That was merely the date at which it opened to full bloom. But the plant had been growing for years. Michelet, indeed, customarily spoke of it as an event that had been centuries in the coming, the rough beast, as it were, slouching toward Bethlehem. Thus when Hegel enrolled at the Tübingen Stift in 1788, his private readings were not devoted to the reigning king of philosophy, Kant, but toward the revolutionary prime-mover, Rousseau. With this as preamble, Hegel's circle of students in the spring of 1791 went up into a meadow outside of Tübingen one Sunday morning, and imitating the great events in France, put up a liberty tree. Then, young pedants that they were, they wrote "Vive la liberté" and "Vive Jean-Jacques" in one another's albums.[59] Earlier, in 1786, in the first movement of Mozart's Piano Concerto in C-Major, Köchel 503, the strains of the "Marseillaise" shot through the first movement like summer lightning. And we all know the Revolutionary direction of *Le Nozze di Figaro* and the subversive play by Beaumarchais on which it was based.[60]

But the plant had been growing long before. In 1762, for instance, Rousseau wrote in his *Émile* that "You trust in the present order of society without thinking that this order is subject to inevitable revolutions. . . . The nobles become commoners, the rich become poor, the monarch becomes subject. . . . We are approaching a state of crisis and the age of revolutions. . . . I hold it to be impossible that the great monarchies of Europe still have long to last." [61] But even that was a leafing in the high branches. In the lower branches, the seventeenth-century levellers and diggers discussed in Christopher Hill's *The World Turned Upside Down*, in *Milton and the English Revolution*, and in *The Experience of Defeat*, were already mature in Revolutionary ideology.[62] Still further down the trunk, a century earlier, the ever-subversive Rabelais had Pantagruel say of the portentous King Anarche: "These accursed kings are nothing but dolts. They know nothing, and they're good for nothing except harming their poor subjects, and troubling the whole world with wars, for their wicked and detestable pleasure. I mean to put him to a trade, and make him a hawker of green sauce." [63]

The very roots of that vast tree of liberty, indeed, twine round the Peasants Revolt of 1381, and the figures associated with that revolution, Wat Tyler, Jack Straw, and John Ball, no less than Danton, Marat, and Robespierre in the French Revolution, were moved to action by the great and perpetual question: Why should human hierarchies be allowed to perpetuate the exploitation of the many for the benefit of the few? When Adam delved and Eve span, who was then a gentleman? John Ball's speech to the peasants, as recorded by Froissart, seems forever modern:

Good people, things cannot go right in England and never will, until goods are held in common and there are no more villeins and gentlefolk, but we are all one and the same. In what way are those whom we call lords greater masters than ourselves? How have they deserved it? Why do they hold us in bondage? If we all spring from a single father and mother, Adam and Eve, how can they claim or prove that they are lords more than us, except by making us produce and grow the wealth which they spend? They are clad in velvet and camlet lined with squirrel and ermine, while we go dressed in coarse cloth. They have the wines, the spices and the good bread: we have the rye, the husks and the straw, and we drink water. They have shelter and ease in their fine manors, and we have hardship and toil, the wind and the rain in the fields. And from us must come, from our labour, the things which keep them in luxury. We are called serfs. . . . If we go in good earnest and all together, very many people who are called serfs and are held in subjection will follow us to get their freedom.[64]

That was the aspiration of the Revolution seen in prospect. As Wordsworth asks, "What temper at the prospect did not wake / To happiness unthought of? The inert / Were roused, and lively natures rapt away!"[65] The ardent Schiller, in his school days, was, as James Sime says,

fascinated by Rousseau's glowing pictures of 'nature,' and shared all his burning scorn for despotism and conventionality. Why had man been endowed with powers if all of them were not to be freely exercised? What reason could there be in the nature of things for the advantages heaped on one class and denied to another? And was it not the clear duty of humanity to destroy institutions and customs that had been handed down from degenerate ancestors, and to return to primitive simplicity and happiness?[66]

Schiller's youthful and sensational play of 1781, *The Robbers*, incorporated these burning ideals. It had an enormous impact. "It is past one o'clock in the morning," wrote Coleridge to Southey in November 1794, "—I sate down at twelve o'clock to read the 'Robbers' of Schiller—I had read chill and trembling until I came to the part where Moor fires a pistol over the Robbers who are asleep—I could read no more—My God! Southey! Who is this Schiller? This Convulser of the Heart? . . . Upon my Soul, I write to you because I am frightened—I had better go to Bed. Why have we ever called Milton sublime?"[67] Others beside Coleridge fell under Schiller's spell. "Schiller wrote for the great ideas of the Revolution," said Heinrich Heine, "he destroyed the Bastille of the intellect, he aided in building the temple of freedom."[68] The National Assembly of the Revolution even went so far as to make Schiller an honorary citizen of France; the diploma was signed by Danton and accompanied by a letter from Roland.

But that was the Revolution in prospect. At length there supervened the Revolution in retrospect, and that was a different entity for everyone. Hazlitt, who never gave up his libertarian commitments, nevertheless records the change from paradisal dawn to disappointment. He speaks of

> that bright dream of our youth; that glad dawn of the day-star of liberty; that spring-time of the world, in which the hopes and expectations of the human race seemed opening in the same gay career with our own; when France called her children to partake her equal blessings beneath her laughing skies; when the stranger was met in all her villages with dance and festive songs; in celebration of a new and golden era.

But then, as Hazlitt goes on to lament,

> The dawn of that day was suddenly overcast; that season of hope is past; it is fled with the other dreams of our youth, which we cannot recall, but has left behind it traces, which are not to be effaced by Birthday and Thanks-giving Odes, or the chaunting of *Te Deums* in all the churches of Christendom. To those hopes, eternal regrets are due.[69]

Hazlitt was nostalgic for the golden days of Revolutionary prospect and melancholy at the onset of reaction. Others, however, in Revolutionary retrospect felt betrayed and responded with revulsion rather than nostalgia. Burke's great attack of 1791 preceded the events that made him a true prophet: the many thousands of state murders undertaken in the name of John Ball's ideal.[70] After the execution of Louis XVI, Schiller wrote to his friend Körner: "For fourteen days I have been unable to look at a newspaper—these butchers disgust me so!"[71] He turned his back on the Revolution forever. He did not, like Friedrich Schlegel, retreat to reactionary feudalism and religious ultra-montanism. He always maintained his ideals for human freedom and brotherhood; but he separated them henceforth from the French Revolution as a means of achieving such advancement. As he says at the end of a poem that was occasioned by the advent of the new century, "Freedom exists only in the realm of dream / And beauty blooms only in song."[72]

So, too, with others. Wordsworth, who had earlier proudly become "a patriot; and my heart was all / Given to the people, and my love was theirs," now felt "That he, who would sow death, reaps death, or worse, / And can reap nothing better." Earlier he had said that "in the People was my trust," but now he confessed to a "loss of confidence in social man." The recognition of "Lamentable crimes," of "dire work, / Of massacre," began to erode his commitment to "arguments of civil polity." "O Friend!", he exclaims to Coleridge, "It was a lamentable time for man."[73] Thenceforth his social views began to move toward the ideal of a slow and natural evolution of human betterment and toward a hardening abhorrence of any and all state intervention in this process. He even threatened to leave the country if the Reform Bill of 1832 were enacted!

Thus the split between the Revolution in prospect and the Revolution in retrospect introduced a profound instability into the opinions of those who experienced both entities masquerading under a single name. Southey in his youth wrote a Jacobin play called *Wat Tyler* in which he expressed the rejection of kingship that became the insignia of all Revolutionary sentiment: "King," exclaims Tyler, "is all this just? / The hour of retribution is at hand, / And tyrants tremble—mark me, King of England."[74] This is quite worthy to occupy a place of honor besides Blake's alleged remark to the soldier Scholfield: "damn the King and Country, his Subjects and all you Soldiers are sold for Slaves."[75] It accords too with Shelley's proclamation in the Preface to *Hellas*: "This is the age of war of the oppressed against the oppressors, and every one of those ringleaders of the privileged gangs of murderers and swindlers, called Sovereigns, look to each other for aid against the common enemy and suspend their mutual jealousies in the presence of a mightier fear."[76] The compatibility of all these sentiments with Jacobin doctrine is evident, as we see by considering the 38th and last proposition of Robespierre's own *Declaration of the Rights of Man*: "Kings, aristocrats, tyrants of every description, are slaves in revolt against the sovereign of the earth, which is the human race, and against the legislator of the universe, which is Nature."[77]

Shelley, however, had never experienced the French Revolution in its two forms, nor in truth had the consistently liberatarian Hazlitt. Shelley therefore sounded in 1820 much as Thelwall sounded in 1791, and Hazlitt could heap scorn on Southey's political tergiversation. "Poor Bob Southey! How they laugh at him!"[78] This was in 1817, before Byron's immortal riposte, *A Vision of Judgment*, showed them how really to laugh at the hapless poet-laureate. Hazlitt had said that "Mr. Southey's Muse is confessedly not a vestal; but then she is what is much better, a Magdalen."[79] And Southey's

The Vision of Judgment, written in 1821 as laureate's lament for the death of George III, the erstwhile tyrant of *Wat Tyler*, was a maudlin work in all senses. Summing it up in 1825, in *The Spirit of the Age*, Hazlitt judged that Southey was "anomalous, incalculable, eccentric, from youth to age (the *Wat Tyler* and the *Vision of Judgment* are the Alpha and Omega of his disjointed career)."[80]

But although Southey elicited more scorn than any other of the figures who changed their minds about the Revolution, his career is nonetheless a pattern for the political vicissitudes of the time. *Wat Tyler* was published in 1817 without Southey's permission and to his great embarrassment. "Mr. Southey," said Hazlitt, "calls the person who published 'Wat Tyler' 'a skulking scoundrel,' . . . and says that it was published, 'for the avowed purpose of insulting him, and with the hope of injuring him if possible.'" Hazlitt went on to say that "Mr. Southey is not a man to hear reason at any time of his life. He thinks his change of opinion is owing to an increase of knowledge, because he has in fact no idea of any progress in intellect but exchanging one error for another."[81] But we see Southey in quite a different and more complex light in a diary entry by Robinson on May 2, 1817:

> I had a call from Robert Southey the laureate. I had a pleasant chat and a short walk with him. Southey spoke gaily of his *Wat Tyler*. He understood thirty-six thousand copies had been printed. He was not aware how popular he was when he came to town. He did not appear to feel any shame or regret at having written the piece at so early an age as twenty. He wrote the drama in three [months], anno 1794. We spoke of his *Letter to W. Smith* [where Southey had defended himself against the imputation of political apostasy], of which I thought and spoke favourably. I did not blame Southey, but commended him for asserting the right of all men, who are wiser at forty than at twenty years of age, to act on such superiority of wisdom. 'I only wish,' I added, 'that you had not appeared to have forgotten some political truths you had been early impressed with. . . .' Southey said: 'I spoke of the present time only. I am still a friend to reform.'[82]

So Southey, interestingly enough, regarded himself as constant in his opinions; it was the revolution itself that had proved disjointed. Certainly Southey's life in all other respects was one of enormous consistency and of a constancy in personal commitments that verged on the heroic.

Coleridge, who had known Southey in both youth and later years, wrote two letters to the *Courier* in March 1817, vindicating him from the charge of political apostasy (he actually wrote four, two of which were published; those two were scathingly criticized by Hazlitt).[83] The vindicating letters might well have served as vindications of their author as well. For like Southey and Wordsworth, Coleridge too veered from sympathy with the ideals of the Revolution to sympathy with the ideals of the established order. Indeed, although Southey was the most ridiculed apostate in his own time, and though Wordsworth changed more radically than either,[84] Coleridge has in our own day become the symbol *par excellence* of political apostasy.

Not everyone even in his day liked the apparent change. On the appearance of the *Biographia Literaria* in 1817, Thelwall annotated a copy with the comment that at Stowey in 1797 "I visited and found him a decided Leveller—abusing the democrats for moderation—" Again, Thelwall remembered in 1817 that Coleridge had in 1797 been "a down right zealous leveller," actually "a man of blood" from the "violence and sanguinary tendency of some of these doctrines."[85] (Incidentally, in view of Thompson's charge about Coleridge's "voracious appetite for hatreds," it is interesting to compare Coleridge's own later statement about Thelwall, in a lecture reported in 1813. "A friend of the Lecturer (Mr. Thelwall) at one time was called a traitor, but though he did not deserve that appellation, he was doubtless a mistaken man: it was at a period when men of all ranks, tailors and mechanics of various descriptions, thought they had a *call* for preaching politics, as Saints had a *call* for preaching the Gospel."[86] Although the report may sound somewhat patronizing, it hardly seems to exhibit a "voracious appetite for hatreds." Coleridge, as De Quincey observes, "had no real unkindness in his heart towards any human being."[87] We may infer that these doctrines, which were extensions of those of Thelwall himself, had been ones he was delighted to hear Coleridge express. In March 1798, Thelwall had written Dr. Crompton and said that "Mount him [Coleridge] upon his darling hobby horse, 'the republic of God's own making,' & away he goes like hey go mad, spattering & splashing thro thick & thin & scattering more *levelling* sedition, & constructive treason, than poor *Gilly* [that is, Gilbert Wakefield] or myself ever dreamt of."[88] But against Thelwall's Coleridge, who mirrored Thelwall so satisfactorily, we may place Coleridge's own statement in a letter to Josiah Wade of August 1797:

> John Thelwall is a very warm hearted honest man—and disagreeing, as we do, on almost every point of religion of morals, of politics, and of

philosophy; we like each other uncommonly well. . . . *Energetic Activity,* of *mind* and of *heart,* is his Master-feature. He is prompt to *conceive,* and still prompter to *execute*—. But I think, that he is deficient in that *patience* of mind, which can look *intensely* and *frequently* at the *same subject.* He believes and disbelieves with impassioned confidence—I wish to see him *doubting* and *doubting.* However, he is the man for *action*—he is intrepid, eloquent, and—honest.—Perhaps the only *acting* Democrat, that *is* honest for the *Patriots* are ragged cattle—a most execrable herd—arrogant because they are ignorant, and boastful of the strength of reason, because they have never tried it enough to know its *weakness.*[89]

Along with the dismissal here of the French Jacobins as "a most execrable herd," there is the pointed avowal of disagreement with Thelwall: "disagreeing, as we do, on almost every point of religion, of morals, of politics, and of philosophy; we like each other uncommonly well."[90]

It may be instructive to consider the implication of the flat disagreement of Coleridge's statement at the time, which is certainly friendly and admiring enough with respect to Thelwall, and Thelwall's own memories.[91] The implication can only be that there was a difference between what Coleridge thought, and what friends perceived him to think. We know that Coleridge was universally considered the greatest talker of that, or possibly any other age. "If Mr. Coleridge," said Hazlitt in 1825, "had not been the most impressive talker of his age, he would probably have been the finest writer; but he lays down his pen to make sure of an auditor, and mortgages the admiration of posterity for the stare of an idler."[92] Other testimonials abound. We know, too, that there was a difference between Coleridge's talk in later years and his talk as a youth, the later talk being more like the seamless and droning flow immortalized in Carlyle's description,[93] the earlier talk being something more dazzling and dynamic. By 1798, in the words of Leslie Stephen, "Coleridge had not only given proofs of astonishing power, but had won what was even more valuable, the true sympathy and cordial affection of young men who were the distinct leaders of the next generation."[94] We can only shake our heads in perplexity as to how Coleridge so unerringly collected future famous men as his friends; we can perhaps hope to understand, however, how he managed to win their "true sympathy and cordial affection." By being a hypocrite? That can hardly be the case; the intellectual caliber of his interlocutors of itself confutes such a conclusion. Rather it was by mirroring, in his matchless, his truly unique conversational flow, their own deepest aspirations. Thelwall himself reported in helpless admiration that Coleridge was "one of the most extraordinary Geniuses & finest scholars of the age."[95] The scarcely less radical Hazlitt, for his part, said that Coleridge was "the only person I ever knew who answered to the idea of a man of genius."[96]

As to why Coleridge gave himself so wholly to the mirroring of his friends' deepest and dearest aspirations, we surely find the answer in his lifelong sense of having been abandoned in his childhood. As he explained to Sir George Beaumont in 1803, "Who then remained to listen to me? to be kind to me? to be my friends? . . . These offices of Love the Democrats only performed to me; my own family, bigots from Ignorance, remained wilfully ignorant from Bigotry." Forever seeking the approval of surrogate brothers, Coleridge expended heroic effort in mirroring their hopes. "With an ebullient Fancy," he remembers, "a flowing Utterance, a light & dancing Heart, & a disposition to catch fire by the very rapidity of my own motion, & to speak vehemently from mere verbal associations . . . I aided the Jacobins, by witty sarcasms & subtle reasonings & declamations full of genuine feeling against all Rules & against all established Forms."[97]

Thompson finds these explanations of 1803 particularly indicative of Coleridge's chameleonlike lack of principle. Perhaps we ourselves should regard them rather as extraordinarily perceptive self-analysis. Certainly they were no change of opinions uttered specifically for the benefit of Sir George Beaumont. For instance, in 1801, two years before the explanation to Beaumont, Wordsworth wrote to John Taylor that

> Mr Coleridge and I had a long conversation [probably at Keswick on March 25] upon what you with great propriety call jacobinical pathos; and I can assure you he deeply regretted that he had ever written a single word of that character, or given, directly or indirectly, any encouragement whatever to such writings; which he condemned as arguing both want of genius and of knowledge: he pointed out as worthy of the severest reprehension, the conduct of those writers who seem to estimate their power of exciting sorrow for suffering humanity, by the quantity of hatred and revenge which they are able to pour into the hearts of their Readers. Pity, we agreed, is a sacred thing, that cannot, and will not be prophaned. Mr C is as deeply convinced as myself that the human heart can never be moved to any salutary purposes in this way; and that they who attempt to give it such movements are poisoners of its best feelings. They are bad poets, and misguided men.[98]

Wordsworth, who knew Coleridge somewhat better than is possible for Thompson, apparently found nothing chameleonlike in these sentiments; indeed, on the very same day, April 9, that this letter was written, another one, to Thomas Poole, said that Coleridge "is a great man, and if God grant him life will do great things."[99]

In any event Coleridge mirrored Thelwall's aspirations, as he had those of Hazlitt, as he had those of Southey. His first letter to Southey, in July 1794, mirrors Southey's ardent political radicalism, although no earlier letter of Coleridge's mentions anything at all of such matters. But to Southey he writes at the close, "Farewell, sturdy Republican!", and in the body of the letter he has said that "The Cockatrice is a foul Dragon with a *crown* on its head"; he has referred to "the unfeeling Remarks, which the lingering Remains of Aristocracy occasionally prompt"; and he has asked —we may well suspect the event to be an imaginary one—"is it *wrong*, Southey! for a little Girl with a half famished sickly Baby in her arms to put her head in at the window of an Inn—'Pray give me a bit of Bread and Meat': from a Party dining on Lamb, Green Peas & Sallad.[100] Scant wonder that Southey in 1809, after Coleridge in *The Friend* had defied his "worst enemy to shew, in any of my few writings, the least bias of Irreligion, Immorality, or Jacobinism,"[101] irritably commented: "It is worse than folly, for if he was not a Jacobine, in the common acceptation of the name, I wonder who the Devil was, I am sure I was, am still, and ever more shall be. I am sure that he wrote a flaming panegyric of Tom Paine, and that I delivered it in one of my lectures."[102]

If Southey's ardent Jacobinism of the early 1790s seemed wholly mirrored in Coleridge's language and action, still more dramatic examples of Coleridge's unique ability to mesmerize his friends by mirroring their most cherished opinions can be supplied elsewhere. Southey the enthusiastic Jacobin found Coleridge an enthusiastic Jacobin. The nature-loving Wordsworth, however, found him an enthusiast for nature, one who had "sought / The truth in solitude, and thou art one, / The most intense of Nature's worshippers; / In many things my brother, chiefly here / In this my deep devotion."[103] The joking Lamb, still again, found him a jokester: "*Summer*, as my friend Coleridge waggishly writes, has set in, with its usual severity."[104] And always there was the awe before Coleridge's conversational powers. On an occasion in 1823, when Lamb said he "dined in Parnassus, with Wordsworth, Coleridge, Rogers, and Tom Moore—half the Poetry of England constellated and clustered in Gloster Place!", Coleridge was at the top of his form. "Coleridge was in his finest vein of talk, had all the talk, and let 'em talk as evilly as they do of the Envy of Poets, I am sure not one there but was content to be nothing but a listener. The Muses were dumb, while Apollo lectured on his and their fine Art."[105] Significantly, to poets Coleridge talked about poetry—"his and their fine Art."

But perhaps Coleridge's mirroring powers are shown in most instructive relief in his comments on Swedenborg. Coleridge mentions Swedenborg infrequently either in his correspondence or elsewhere, although he knew Swedenborgian thought extremely well. Benjamin Kurtz, who has investigated the matter, shows that Coleridge had read at least eleven volumes of Swedenborg's works, which means that he knew the seer as well as Blake himself did.[106] On certain occasions, however, despite his usual reticence about Swedenborg, Coleridge talks about the Swedish thinker so volubly, knowledgeably, and enthusiastically as almost to seem a Swedenborgian. Remarkably, these occasions are almost always in letters to a single person, Charles Tulk.[107] Who was Charles Tulk? A wealthy Swedenborgian, whose father had been a Swedenborgian before him. The younger Tulk, with John Flaxman, formed the society for publishing Swedenborg's works and devoted much of his own later writing to elucidating the underlying rationalism of Swedenborg's doctrines. To Tulk, Coleridge seemed a Swedenborgian adept. But Coleridge did not talk of Swedenborg in his letters to Thelwall, or those to Southey, or those to Wordsworth.

So too with Coleridge's alleged Jacobinism. Republican enthusiasm mirrored the aspirations of those who testified to its reality. It did not, however, by that fact reflect the intricacy of what Coleridge really thought. That it was, moreover, very possible for those who heard Coleridge to be mistaken about what he thought may be shown from a single example. It is almost a truism that Coleridge's deepest and most constant thoughts were directed toward the Christian religion, from the Unitarianism of the 1790s to the Trinitarianism of his final position. As Walter Jackson Bate, to name only one of many scholarly investigators, concludes: "If we wish to understand and assess Coleridge's career, we must do so at least partly in terms of what mattered most to him: the hope that his life, whatever its failings, might ultimately be religious in shape, intention, meaning."[108] As Coleridge himself said, "I can truly affirm of myself, that my studies have been profitable and availing to me only so far, as I have endeavoured to use all my other knowledge as a glass enabling me to receive more light in a wider field of vision from the word of God." [109] That is the simple and ineluctable truth of Coleridge's career. And yet Henry Crabb Robinson says of Coleridge in 1812:

> He afterward entered into a long series of observations on the Trinity, from which I could learn only that he is very desirous to be orthodox. . . . Coleridge is very desirous to be both a refined and subtle philosopher and metaphysician, and at the same time conform with the people in religion. That this desire is consciously excited by any unworthy suggestions, or that he is grossly insincere in any of his assertions, I do not believe; but I believe there is in him much self-deception. [110]

It is fascinating to consider how antithetical Robinson's eyewitness but casual report is to Bate's considered conclusion. Those companions who thought Coleridge a Jacobin, I suggest, are the complement of a Henry Crabb Robinson who, despite his good intentions, thought Coleridge not serious about Christianity. We correct both misapprehensions in the same way, by considering the course and ramification of Coleridge's intellectual commitment over many years.

If we look at that course and commitment, we see Coleridge as actually quite different politically from both Southey and Wordsworth. Instead of passing from committed Jacobinism to committed reaction, Coleridge developed, very early, an original and profound theory of politics that was not only far more sophisticated than the attitudes of either Southey or Wordsworth but was, so far as one can judge, consistent throughout his adult life. For Coleridge, so weak and vacillating in all personal situations, was, as I stressed above and wish continually to repeat, almost unbelievably constant in his intellectual views.

If we turn toward the Coleridge of later years we do not quite see a Tory, though conservative opinion took much comfort from his views. But De Quincey, continually perceptive with regard to the Lake Poets, insists on the unsatisfactoriness of classifying Coleridge as a Tory.

> One character in which Mr. Coleridge most often came before the public was that of politician. In this age of fervent partisanship it will, therefore, naturally occur as a first question to inquire after his party and political connexions . . . was he Whig, Tory, or Radical? Or, under a new classification, were his propensities Conservative or Reforming? I answer that, in any exclusive or emphatic sense, he was none of these; because, as a philosopher, he was, according to circumstances, and according to the object concerned, all of these by turns. [111]

Unlike Thompson, De Quincey finds no lack of sincerity in Coleridge's political views. "In his politics, Mr. Coleridge was most sincere and enthusiastic. No man hailed with profounder sympathy the French Revolution; and, though he saw cause to withdraw his regard from many of the democratic zealots in this country, and even from the revolutionary interest as it was subsequently conducted, he continued to worship the original revolutionary cause in a pure Miltonic spirit."[112]

To the extent that Coleridge did make common cause with the Tories, De Quincey urges, it was because the Whigs themselves had deserted their principles. With regard to Coleridge's alleged "want of principle in his supposed sacrifice of his early political connexions," says De Quincey, the "explanation is involved in the strange and scandalous conduct of the Parliamentary Whigs":

> Coleridge passed over to the Tories only in that sense in which all patriots did so at that time . . . by refusing to accompany the Whigs in their almost perfidious demeanor towards Napoleon Bonaparte. . . . [H]is adhesion to the Tories was bound by his approbation of their foreign policy; and even of *that* rarely in its executive details, rarely even in its military plans . . . but solely in its animating principle . . . that Napoleon Bonaparte ought to be resisted. . . . Thus far he went along with the Tories: in all else he belonged quite as much to other parties—so far as he belonged to any.[113]

Certainly Coleridge did not move toward the hardened reaction of Wordsworth. "With respect to Mr. Coleridge," noted De Quincey, "he was certainly a friend to all enlightened reforms; he was a friend, for example, to Reform in Parliament."[114]

De Quincey saw with his customary acuteness the complexity and idiosyncrasy of Coleridge's later sympathy with conservative policies. That complexity made Coleridge as difficult to dismiss as to classify. John Stuart Mill, as Michael St. John Packe points out, thought the aged Coleridge the most formidable opponent of his own libertarian and intellectually powerful views:

> Coleridge, then at the height of his prophetic powers, wielded tremendous influence. He was writing little. . . . But he talked . . . and young men, eager and adventurous like Maurice and Sterling, sat listening to him by the hour. As the story-teller ran along in his soft sweet voice, his hearers forgot him and forgot themselves. For he told of the white marble palaces of heart's desire. . . . Mill, unlike most others, was be-

witched less by the presence than by the written word. In April 1834
he wrote, "Few persons have exercised more influence over my thoughts
and character than Coleridge has; not much by personal knowledge of
him, though I have seen and conversed with him several times, but by his
works, pieced together by what I have otherwise learned of his opinions."
   Everything about him was directly contrary to radical beliefs. While
Radicals worked industriously, building up their man-made tower to
heaven, he . . . said that heaven was already in the world, all but the
seeing of it. Where they dealt in proofs, he dispensed faith.

. . . .

   The very delicacy of his opposition to radicalism made it all the more
dangerous. The general run of intuitionist defended Church, State, and
the Aristocracy simply and for what they were—their country right or
wrong. Not so Coleridge: his distinction between the apparent shadow
and the spiritual substance enabled him to attack the existing frame-
work of the institutions while exalting the possibility of what they might
be made. None was ahead of him in deploring inhumanities and injus-
tices, the slave ships, the child labour, the presumption of the rich, the
complacency of the clergy. He was ahead of all in describing the spirit
of the whole . . . of a gracious civility between the orders of society
working together harmoniously towards a proud and placid destiny. . . .
The opposed movements of Christian Socialism and Oxford Mysticism
alike derived from him. In the great battle of the century between authority and the individual, between tradition and science, he was the
most significant of the patricians.[115]

St. John Packe's description of Coleridge's conservatism as involving
political progressivism accurately reflects the dialectical basis of Coleridge's politics. They are, like Marx's, based on the Romantic doctrine of
the progression of opposites; Marx's were borrowed from Hegel, Coleridge's arose from the same sources that Hegel himself used. At the very
heart of Coleridge's theory was an insistence on the "harmonious balance
of the two great correspondent, at once supporting and counterposing,
interests of the state, its permanence, and its progression."[116]
   The formula is characteristic of Coleridge in that it serves as illustration for his lifelong tendency not to reject but to incorporate adverse data.
Thus in order to combat Enlightenment *raison*, he changes the *raison* of
Diderot into "understanding," and nominates his own version as "reason";
both, however, remain necessary to the definition of mind. Likewise, in
order to combat the psychology of Locke's tradition, he calls that tradition's theory of mental imaging "fancy," and nominates his own version

as "imagination"; both, however remain necessary to the functioning of mind. So, too, with his great political polarity. The interests of his earlier libertarian sympathies are preserved in the word "progression," which is cast into polar opposition with his conservative interests under the word "permanence."

But certainly permanence lay deeper in the psychology and instinct of Coleridge. For, leaving aside his political opinions, his intellectual attitudes were always profoundly conservative, which, indeed, is precisely the reason for his immense and lifelong reading of other and earlier thinkers.

> What is it [asks Coleridge] that I employ my Metaphysics on? To perplex our clearest notions, & living moral Instincts? To extinguish the Light of Love & of Conscience, to put out the Life of Arbitrement—to make myself & others . . . *Worthless, Soul*-less, *God*less?—No! To expose the Folly & the Legerdemain of those, who have thus abused the blessed Organ of Language, to support all old & venerable Truths, to support, to kindle, to project, to make the Reason spread Light over our Feelings, to make our Feelings diffuse vital Warmth thro' our Reason—these are my Objects—& these my Subjects.[117]

In his commitment to "support all old & venerable Truths" we see one reason why Coleridge could never have been in any real sense a Jacobin, nor have remained one if he temporarily did espouse such radicalism. As he said, "the dreariest feature of Jacobinism" was "the contempt of the Institutions of our Ancestors and of past wisdom.[118] Coleridge, on the contrary, and it cannot be emphasized enough, found such contempt abhorrent. As he says in November of 1803, he always rejoiced "to find his opinions plumed & winged with the authority of venerable Forefathers."[119]

It is interesting that this statement about "the dreariest feature of Jacobinism" was summoned in a context that deplores "the Jacobinism of Anti-Jacobins," for it clearly reveals Coleridge's temperamental lack of radicalism, either of the left or the right.[120] He hewed to his own line, which steered between the two extremes.

That idiosyncratic line is defined by the second of the reasons why Coleridge could never have been in any real sense a Jacobin: his commitment to the Christian religion. Not only is the *Conciones ad Populum* of 1795 shot through with Coleridge's Christianity, which even Thelwall accepted, but in that same year he produced writings entitled *Six Lectures on Revealed Religion its Corruption and Political Views*. As Peter Mann, the editor of Coleridge's *Lectures 1795 on Politics and Religion* points out: "The Lectures on Revealed Religion allow one to see how deeply rooted Coleridge's religious and moral feelings were in 1795 and how they would necessarily bring him into conflict, intellectually and morally, with the extreme radical movement and lead him to a point of view that was different from that of such 'friends of liberty' as Paine, Thelwall, and Holcroft."[121] The Jacobins, on the other hand, were virulent anti-Christians. Embarking on a specific program of "Dechristianization," they replaced Christianity with a religion of reason. As Lefebvre says,

> The new religion endowed itself with symbols and a form of liturgy, honoured the 'holy Mountain' [the Jacobin side of the Assembly was called "the mountain"], and venerated its martyrs, Lepeletier, Marat, and Chalier. On 3 Brumaire, Year II (October 23, 1793) . . . the Convention adopted the revolutionary calendar. It attempted to dechristianize daily life by substituting the date of September 22, 1792, the first day of the Republic, for the Christian era; by replacing references to religious ceremonies and the saints with names borrowed from tools . . . and above all, by eliminating Sunday in favour of the Tenth day (*décadi*).[122]

Indeed a Festival of Liberty was planned for 20 Brumaire, Year II (November 10, 1793), for which the Commune seized Notre Dame, now called the Temple of Reason, and built a mountain in the choir, with an actress impersonating Liberty. As Brinton remarks, "The Jacobins unquestionably held their political philosophy as a matter of faith." Again: "Jacobinism is, then, first of all a faith. . . . 'Liberty, Equality, Fraternity,' as words, may be subject to definition and contain the seeds of infinite dispute; as symbols, they were to the Jacobins a common property above logic."[123]

It is tempting to linger over the implications of Jacobin anti-Christianity,[124] which led directly to the doctrinal atheism of Marx. What has been said, however, suffices to show how profound the division was between Coleridge and the Jacobins, especially since the Christian religion came to be elaborated into the very theory of Coleridge's view of the social organism. In his *On the Constitution of the Church and State*, which was his last published prose work, and which, as John Colmer says, is "a brief and brilliant synthesis of the political and theological thinking of a lifetime,"[125] Coleridge takes up a theme he had described twenty years earlier and adhered to tenaciously all that time. In 1810 he writes:

> Church and state—civil and religious rights—to hold these essential powers of civilized society in due relation to each other, so as to prevent them from becoming its burdens instead of its supports; this is perhaps

the most difficult problem in the whole science of politics. . . . From the first ages of Christianity to the present period, the two relations of a rational being, to his present and future state, have been abstracted and framed into moral personages, Church and State: and to each has been assigned its own domain and its especial rights.[126]

When in 1830 Coleridge published *On the Constitution of the Church and State*, the reconciliation of the two domains was effected as a large instance of the principle of interacting opposites. The "two antagonist powers or opposite interests of the state, under which all other state interests are comprised, are those of PERMANENCE AND PROGRESSION." In a footnote Coleridge distinguishes between opposites and contraries:

The feminine character is *opposed* to the masculine; but the effeminate is its *contrary*. Even so in the present instance, the interest of permanence is opposed to that of progressiveness; but so far from being contrary interests, they, like the magnetic forces, suppose and require each other. Even the most mobile of creatures, the serpent, makes a *rest* of its own body, and drawing up its voluminous train from behind on the fulcrum, propels itself onward. On the other hand, it is a proverb in all languages, that (relatively to man at least) what would stand still must retrograde.[127]

Coleridge never wanted society to stand still, but to balance its progression principles of rest were necessary. One of these was property, which he, like Burke, specifically summoned against the Jacobin spirit. As he writes in 1802, in his thirty-first year:

We were never at any period of our life converts to the system of French politics. As far back as our memory reaches, it was an axiom in politics with us, that in every country in which property prevailed property must be the grand basis of government; and that that government was the best, in which the power was the most exactly proportioned to the property.[128]

The Revolution had not initially been opposed to private property. As the *Déclaration des droits de l'homme et du citoyen*, drafted by Lafayette and decreed on August 26, 1789, emphasized in its seventeenth and final article, "Les propriétés étant un droit inviolable et sacré, nul ne peut en être privé, si ce n'est lorsque la nécessité publique légalement constatée l'exige évidemment, et sous la condition d'une juste et préalable indemnité."[129] Robespierre himself, as Louis Madelin points out, "had three dogmas: *the support of Virtue by Terror; the existence of the Supreme Being; and the abso-*

lute sanctity of Property".[130] But the Jacobin theories of taxation and of the subordination of property to personal rights—and the burgeoning social-ism of figures like Chaumette and Fouché—tended to erode the status of property, a status still more compromised by the time of the *Communist Manifesto*. "The theory of the Communists," says that enchiridion, "may be summed up in the single sentence: Abolition of private property."[131]

But property as a principle of rest, along with the church, does not exist in monolithic stagnation in Coleridge's scheme; it too is brought into the conciliating flux of permanence and progression. "We have thus divided the subjects of the state into two orders," he says in 1830, "the agricultural or possessors of land; and the merchant manufacturer, the distributive, and the professional bodies, under the common name of citizens." The first group, he says, "either by their interests or by the very effect of their situation, circumstances, and the nature of their employment," are "vitally connected with the permanency of the state, its institutions, rights, cus-toms, manners, privileges—and as such, opposed to the inhabitants of ports, towns, and cities, who are in like manner and from like causes especially connected with its progression."[132]

The one thing there was no room for in Coleridge's view of politics was reformist violence. And this, though connected with his commitment to Christianity, is the third and most unbridgeable of the reasons why he never was a Jacobin and never could have been one. Although, as Le-febvre observes, "nothing contributed as much to spreading the Terror as dechristianization,"[133] in the remainder of this essay the Christian/anti-Christian opposition of Coleridge and the Jacobins shall be muted in favor of an emphasis on the contrast between Coleridge's humanitari-anism and the Jacobin commitment to reformist violence. Thus, in his earliest political statement, the *Conciones ad Populum* of 1795, Coleridge is clearly and unarguably not a Jacobin, for he says, with epigrammatic terseness: "A system of fundamental Reform will scarcely be effected by massacres mechanized into Revolution."[134]

Even Jacobin apologists have to take note of the truth of the oneness of Jacobinism and massacre. Isser Woloch, for instance, in *Jacobin Legacy*, says that Jacobinism "had much to do with what Americans call grass-roots democracy, and a commitment to equality in the sense of mitigating social distinctions"—but in the same sentence he must also grant that Jacobinism is also synonymous "with the strange mantle of terrorism and fanaticism that the sociétaires wore in the Year II."[135] Lefebvre, whose history of the Revolution is written as a partisan both of Robespierre and the Jacobins, and though he does his best to mute the terror, nevertheless must note things like this: "Proposals involving violence were more and more frequently heard, even at the Assembly, where Merlin de Thionville demanded that wives and children of emigrés be seized as hostages, while Debry advocated a 'tyrannicide corps' to exterminate kings. Marat had many times insisted that the only way to save the Revolution was to slaughter the aristocrats en masse." Or this: "So, after Germinal the sessions of the Convention became dreary, the committees worked in silence, and the clubs disappeared, except for the Jacobins, where most of the regulars were functionaries of the Terror."[136]

That Coleridge was acutely aware of the Jacobin commitment to violence is evident at the outset. In the Introductory address to *Conciones ad Populum*—the year is 1795 and Coleridge's age is 23—he says:

> The Annals of the French Revolution have recorded in Letters of Blood, that the Knowledge of the Few cannot counteract the Ignorance of the Many; that the Light of Philosophy, when it is confined to a small Minority, points out the Possessors as the Victims, rather than the Illuminators, of the Multitude. The Patriots of France either hastened into the dangerous and gigantic Error of making certain Evil the means of contingent Good, or were sacrificed by the Mob, with whose prejudices and ferocity their unbending Virtue forbade them to assimilate.[137]

The rejection of reformist violence, the arguing for humanity, the avoidance of the "gigantic Error of making certain Evil the means of contingent Good," these indeed are the very hallmarks of Coleridge's political writings of 1795:

> We should be cautious how we indulge the feelings even of virtuous indignation. Indignation is the handsome brother of Anger and Hatred. The Temple of Despotism, like that of Tescalipoca, the Mexican Deity, is built of human skulls, and cemented with human blood;—let us beware that we be not transported into revenge while we are levelling the loathsome Pile; lest when we erect the edifice of Freedom we but vary the stile of Architecture, not change the materials.[138]

The passage is a fair glimpse of Coleridge's line of thought in the process of steering itself between the extremes of Jacobinism and Toryism. The temple of despotism must be levelled; but the edifice of Freedom must be careful not to duplicate it in a different style. This steering of a

path at once libertarian and humanitarian between the extremes of Jacobinism and reaction, so evident in 1795, is the very stuff of Coleridge's
vision clear through to 1830. As he wrote in January 1800, at the age
of 28:

> We detest equally Jacobinism and usurpation in the French, and the
> principles of despotism preached by their opponents—we look with
> equal horror on those who murder a lawful Constitution, and those
> who, under pretence of medicine, administer poison to it. We deem it
> among the most fatal errors in some friends of freedom in England, that
> they have thought it necessary to a consistent opposition to Ministers,
> that they should *slur* over the follies or wickedness of France. We think
> otherwise. TRUTH is *our* policy. We despise the absurdities and dread the
> fanaticism of France; believing, however, at the same time [and here
> Coleridge presages the position of Auland] that but for the war against
> France they would have died in their infancy.[139]

Such steering between extremes is the pilot's course throughout this exhortation of early 1800, which concludes by rejecting both Jacobinism and
monarchical reaction, and doing so in terms of the interplay of permanence and progression. He said (and proved true prophet):

> Supposing for a moment, that Royalty could be restored—what rea-
> son have we for affirming its permanency? Will not the principles of
> Jacobinism remain? Can the faction of the Royalists boast more talent,
> more activity, more energy, than the Republicans? Will it not disturb the
> present state of property infinitely more than the usurpation of Buona-
> parte? And by the very act of disturbing property, will it not necessarily
> bring Jacobinism once more into play? And will not Royalty therefore, if
> restored, perish, like a bubble, by the very agitation that produced it?[140]

Coleridge understood not only the violence inseparable from Jacobinism, but also the nobler ideals that lay behind its aspiration. As he says in
1802:

> A Jacobin, in *our* sense of the term, is one who believes, and is dis-
> posed to act on the belief, that all, or the greater part of, the happiness
> or misery . . . of mankind, depends on forms of government; who ad-
> mits no form of government as either good or rightful, which does not
> flow directly and formally from the persons governed; who—consider-
> ing life, health, moral and intellectual improvement, and liberty both
> of person and conscience, as blessings which governments are bound
> as far as possible to increase and secure to every inhabitant, whether

he has or has not any fixed property, and moreover as blessings of infinitely greater value to each individual, than the preservation of property can be to any individual—does consequently and consistently hold, that every inhabitant, who has attained the age of reason, has a natural and inalienable right to an *equal* share of power in the choice of governors. In other words, the Jacobin affirms that no legislature can be rightful or good, which did not proceed from universal suffrage. In the power, and under the controul, of a legislature so chosen, he places all and every thing, with the exception of the natural rights of man, and the means appointed for the preservation and exercise of those rights, by a direct vote of the nation itself—that is to say, by a CONSTITUTION. Finally the Jacobin deems it both justifiable and expedient to effect these requisite changes in faulty governments, by absolute revolutions, and considers no violences as properly rebellious or criminal, which are the *means* of giving to a nation the power of declaring and enforcing its sovereignty.[141]

All this is not only perspicacious, accurate, and subtly articulated, but it is eminently fair toward the aspirations of the Jacobins.

Indeed the Jacobins, in Coleridge's description here, sound more like bourgeois liberals in the Jeffersonian mold than architects of terror. Marx and Engels, in fact, distinguished Communism from the Jacobin revolution by claiming that their own revolution was to be a proletarian revolution that looked totally to the future, whereas the French Revolution had been a bourgeois venture that recapitulated the past. "The social revolution of the nineteenth century," said Marx in *The Eighteenth Brumaire of Louis Bonaparte*, "cannot draw its poetry from the past, but only from the future. It cannot make a beginning until it has stripped off all superstition of the past."[142] But Marx was not so much different from the Jacobin spirit as he affected to believe. After all, Shelley, "the most Jacobinical of poets," as Richard Holmes calls him,[143] said that "The system of society as it exists at present must be overthrown from the foundations with all its superstructure of maxims & forms."[144] Marx, however, not caring to see himself as preempted by Jacobin theorists and attitudes, disregarded this central truth of the Jacobin spirit and insisted on the bourgeois character of the French Revolution. He pointed out that it looked back to Roman Republican values as the English Revolution had looked back to Old Testament values. (Coleridge, incidentally, published three articles in 1802 on the comparison of Revolutionary France and ancient Rome.) Marx says:

Camille Desmoulins, Danton, Robespierre, Saint-Just, Napoleon, the heroes, as well as the parties and the masses of the old French Revolution, performed the task of their time in Roman costume and with Roman phrases, the task of releasing and establishing modern *bourgeois* society. The first mentioned knocked the feudal basis to pieces and cut off the feudal heads which had grown from it. The other [Napoleon] created inside France the conditions under which free competition could first be developed . . . and outside the French borders he everywhere swept the feudal form away, so far as it was necessary to furnish bourgeois society in France with a suitable up-to-date environment on the European Continent.[145]

Despite these arguments, Marx, with his acceptance of the cutting off of feudal heads, reveals himself as far closer to Jacobinism than Coleridge ever was. Violence, indeed, is cherished in Marxist theory as in Jacobin actuality. Writing on Engel's utopian phrase, "the withering away of the state," Lenin, in *The State and Revolution*, sharply reminds true believers that this refers only to the proletarian state; violence, on the contrary, must and should be used by the proletariat to abolish the bourgeois state. "In the same work of Engels, from which every one remembers his argument on the 'withering away' of the State," says Lenin, "there is also a disquisition on the significance of a violent revolution. The historical analysis of its role becomes, with Engels, a veritable panegyric on violent revolution." Lenin then quotes Engels as saying that "force" is, "in the words of Marx," the "midwife of every old society that is pregnant with the new; that it is the instrument with whose aid social movement forces its way through and shatters the dead, fossilized political forms."[146] And the conclusion of the *Communist Manifesto* proudly proclaims that "The Communists disdain to conceal their views and aims. They openly declare that their ends can be attained only by the forcible overthrow of all existing social conditions."[147]

It is the obsession with reformist violence that provides the final link in the chain joining Jacobinism to Communism. Although the Jacobin clubs were disestablished following Robespierre's fall on 9 Thermidor of the Year II (July 27, 1794), the Jacobin spirit did not die. A later strain of Jacobinism, Babouvism, transformed itself into outright communism.[148] Babeuf himself (the Chartist Bronterre O'Brien compared him to Jesus)[149] was not guillotined until 1797.[150] Coleridge, in listing the radical tenets Babouvism in an issue of *The Watchman* for April 27, 1796, is confronting an enumeration perhaps even more unequivocal than that contained in the Communist Manifesto. Certainly he understood the tendency of the Jacobin spirit from the Democrats of the original Jacobin clubs to the Terrorist functionaries of 1792 to 1794 to the Babouvian communism of 1796 and 1797 to the Communist Manifesto of 1848 to the Russian radicals described by Dostoevsky in *The Possessed* to the latter-day Jacobins called Bolsheviks, and all the way to Lenin's arrival at the Finland Station, there is one united progression of a single spirit, the spirit of Jacobinism.[151]

That spirit is unseparable from reformist violence. The Communist apotheosis of violence merely raised to theory what the Jacobins had discovered as praxis. Its institutionalization has borne the richest kind of historical fruit. As aftermath of Marxist and Leninist commandments, Pol Pot and the Khmer Rouge actually and in grotesque fact caused to be erected new temples of skulls to replace those Aztec temples of skulls metaphorically invoked by Coleridge. Stalin, using reformist violence to achieve the Communist goal of collectivizing Russian farmland, achieved also the death of staggering numbers of human beings—fourteen million of them, according to Robert Conquest's melancholy history of that late Jacobin episode.[152] The nonviolent reforms of American capitalism, on the other hand, which were undertaken in the presidencies of Theodore Roosevelt, Taft, and Franklin Roosevelt, were the sorts of action that were stigmatized by Marx, in *The Poverty of Philosophy*, as effects of "the humanitarian school," or even worse, of "the philanthropic school";[153] they were reforms, certainly, that were entirely in the spirit of Coleridge's reconciling and humane political vision.

That political vision is wholly at odds with the infatuation with force and violence that was the truest legacy of Jacobin. "To *reconcile*," said Coleridge in one of his most characteristic statements, ". . . is truly the work of the Inspired! This is the true *Atonement*."[154] The Jacobins were not interested in reconciling;[155] and in the Marxist analysis, the Terror of 1792, 1793, and 1794 was not an aberration but an accreditation, a necessary and desirable cleansing action. In Coleridge, on the other hand, one finds everywhere an express humanitarianism that stands in irreconcilable opposition to this essential of the Jacobin spirit. For instance, in the very midst of the twenty-three-year-old Coleridge's passionate democratic plea in *Conciones ad Populum*, we read of

> the awful Truth, that in the course of this calamitous Contest more than a Million of men have perished—a MILLION of men, of each one of whom the mangled corpse terrifies the dreams of her that loved him, and makes some mother, some sister, some widow start from slumber with a shriek.[156]

To the Coleridge of 1795 the slave trade was not a matter of charts and statistics and moral guidelines:

> I address myself first of all to those who independent of political distinction profess themselves Christian. As you hope you live with Christ hereafter you are commanded to do unto others as ye would that others should do unto you! Would you choose that Slave Merchants should incite an intoxicated Chieftain to make War on your Tribe to murder your Wife and Children before your face and drag them with yourself to the Market—Would you choose to be sold, to have the hot iron hiss upon your breast, to be thrown down into the hold of a ship ironed with so many fellow victims so closely crammed together that the heat and stench arising from your diseased bodies should rot the very planks of the Ship?[157]

That was the true substance of Coleridge's political libertarianism. Programmatic Jacobinism and its desecration of the human were alien to him. He avoided, if the Jacobins did not, "the dangerous and gigantic Error of making certain Evil the means of contingent Good."

If we wonder whether it was certain evil or contingent good that loomed larger in the French Revolution, we might be helped in our conclusion by Taine's great history of the revolution, *The Origins of Modern France*.[158] To Taine, the real truth of that revolution was the triumph of violence and the desecration of the human: "from the peasant, the labourer, and the bourgeois, pacified and tamed by an old civilization, we see suddenly spring forth the barbarian, and still worse, the primitive animal, the grinning, bloody, wanton baboon, who chuckles while he slays, and gambols over the ruin he has accomplished."[159] To Taine, the Revolution was an orgy of violence from the start, and he records its enormities in passionate detail. "To every impartial man," he quotes Malouet as saying, "the Terror dates from the 14th of July [1789]."[160] But Taine sees it as being brought to its edge of perfection by what he calls the "homicidal idea" of the Jacobins. For the Jacobins themselves he has only revulsion and scorn:

> From one end of the territory to the other, the machine, with its hundred thousand arms, works efficaciously in the hands of those who have seized the lever at the central point. Resolution, audacity, rude energy, are all that are needed to make the lever act, and none of these is wanting in the Jacobin.
>   First, he has faith, and faith at all times "moves mountains." Take any ordinary party recruit, an attorney, a second-rate lawyer, a shopkeeper,

an artisan, and conceive, if you can the extraordinary effect of this doctrine on a mind so poorly prepared for it, so narrow, so out of proportion
with the gigantic conception which has mastered it. Formed for routine
and the limited views of one in his position, he is suddenly carried away
by a complete system of philosophy, a theory of nature and of man, a
theory of society and of religion, a theory of universal history, conclusions about the past, the present, and the future of humanity, axioms
of absolute right, a system of perfect and final truth, the whole concentrated in a few rigid formulae as, for example: "Religion is superstition,
monarchy is usurpation, priests are impostors, aristocrats are vampires,
and kings are so many tyrants and monsters." These ideas flood a mind
of this stamp like a vast torrent precipitating itself into a narrow gorge;
they upset it, and, no longer under self-direction, they sweep it away. . . .
A plain bourgeois, a common laborer is not transformed with impunity
into an apostle or liberator of the human species.[161]

Taine speaks with equal contempt of the Jacobin clubs. "In many of the
large cities, in Paris, Lyons, Aix and Bordeaux, there are two clubs in
partnership, one, more or less respectable and parliamentary . . . and
the other, practical and active. . . . The latter is a branch of the former,
and, in urgent cases, supplies it with rioters. 'We are placed amongst the
people,' says one of these subaltern clubs, 'we read to them the decrees,
and through lectures and counsel, we warn them against the publications
and intrigues of the aristocrats. We ferret out and track plotters and their
machinations. We welcome and advise all complainants . . .'[162]

But Taine's profoundest revulsion is for the leaders of the Jacobins.
"Three men among the Jacobins," he says,

Marat, Danton, and Robespierre, merited distinction and possessed authority:—owing to a malformation, or distortion, of head and heart,
they fulfilled the requisite conditions.—Of the three, Marat is the most
monstrous; he borders on the lunatic, of which he displays the chief
characteristics—furious exaltation, constant over-excitement, feverish
restlessness, an inexhaustible propensity for scribbling. . . . From first
to last, he was in the right line of the Revolution, lucid on account of
his blindness, thanks to his crazy logic, thanks to the concordance of his
personal malady with the public malady, to the precocity of his complete
madness alongside the incomplete or tardy madness of the rest, he alone
steadfast, remorseless, triumphant, perched aloft at the first round of
the sharp pinnacle which his rivals dared not climb or only stumbled
up.[163]

Robespierre, to both Taine and Coleridge, was different. He was, says Taine, a "*cuistre*,"[164] that is to say,

> the hollow, inflated mind that, filled with words and imagining that these are ideas, revels in its own declamation and dupes itself that it may dictate to others. Such is his title, character and the part he plays. In this artificial and declamatory tragedy of the Revolution he takes the leading part; the maniac and the barbarian slowly retire into the background on the appearance of the *cuistre*. . . . If we would comprehend him we must look at him as he stands in the midst of his surroundings. At the last stage of an intellectual vegetation passing away, he remains on the last branch of the eighteenth century, the most abortive and driest offshoot of the classical spirit. He has retained nothing of a worn-out system of philosophy but its lifeless dregs and well-conned formulae, the formulae of Rousseau, Mably, and Raynal, concerning "the people, nature, reason, liberty, tyrants, factions, virtue, morality," a ready-made vocabulary, expressions too ample, the meaning of which, ill-defined by the masters, evaporates in the hands of the disciple. . . . It might be said that he never saw anything with his own eyes, that he neither could nor would see, that false conceptions have intervened and fixed themselves between him and the object; he combines these in logical sequences, and simulates the absent thought by an affected jargon, and this is all. . . . For hours, we grope after him in the vague shadows of political speculation, in the cold and perplexing mist of didactic generalities, trying in vain to make something out of his colorless tirades, and we grasp nothing. We then, astonished, ask what all this talk amounts to, and why he talks at all; the answer is, that he has said nothing, that he talks only for the sake of talking, the same as a sectary preaching to his congregation, neither the preacher nor the audience ever wearying, the one of turning the dogmatic crank, and the other of listening. So much the better if the hopper is empty; the emptier it is the easier and faster the crank turns. And better still, if the empty term he selects is used in a contrary sense; the grand words justice, humanity, mean to him piles of human heads, the same as a text from the gospels means to a grand inquisitor the burning of heretics.[165]

With Taine's reference to Robespierre's "piles of human heads," we return to Coleridge's warning in 1795 about not building again the Aztec temple of skulls in the name of freedom. Indeed, Taine's burning volumes, motivated not by political prepossession but by humanitarian concern, are especially relevant to Coleridge's attitudes. As Taine says in the preface to his third volume:

> I have again to regret the dissatisfaction which I foresee this work will cause to many of my countrymen. My excuse is, that almost all of them, more fortunate than myself, have political principles that serve them in forming their judgments of the past. I had none; if, indeed, I had any motive in undertaking this work, it was to seek for political principles. Thus far I have attained to scarcely more than one; and this is so simple that it will seem puerile, and I hardly dare enunciate it. . . . It consists wholly in this observation: *that human society, especially a modern society, is a vast and complicated thing.*[166]

Taine's implication, that human knowledge is not sufficient to balance hypothetical improvement against real massacre is identical with Coleridge's counsel to avoid "the dangerous and gigantic Error of making certain Evil the means of contingent Good."

And just as the great French savant's portrait of Robespierre brings to burning focus his rejection of the crimes of Jacobin activity, so does the twenty-three-year-old Coleridge's portrait of that same arch-Jacobin Robespierre serve as similar focus and serve to establish once and for all that Coleridge was never, and never in any true sense could have been, a Jacobin:

> Robespierre, who displaced [Brissot], possessed a glowing ardor that still remembered the *end,* and a cool ferocity that never either overlooked, or scrupled, the *means.* What the end was, is not known: that it was a wicked one, has by no means been proved. I rather think, that the distant prospect, to which he was travelling, appeared to him grand and beautiful; but that he fixed his eye on it with such intense eagerness as to neglect the foulness of the road. If however his first intentions were pure, his subsequent enormities yield us a melancholy proof, that it is not the character of the possessor which directs the power, but the power which shapes and depraves the character of the possessor. In Robespierre, its influence was shaped by the properties of his disposition. . . . [E]nthusiasm in Robespierre was blended with gloom, and suspiciousness, and inordinate vanity. His dark imagination was still brooding over supposed plots against freedom—to prevent tyranny he became a Tyrant[167]—and having realized the evils which he suspected, a wild and dreadful Tyrant.—Those loud-tongued adulators, the mob, overpowered the lone-whispered denunciations of conscience—he despotized in all the pomp of Patriotism, and masqueraded on the bloody stage of Revolution, a Caligula with the cap of Liberty on his head.[168]

This, then, is enough. Not even Taine's portrait of Robespierre can quite match the point, the compression, the Roman parallelism so beloved by the Jacobins, of "a Caligula with the cap of Liberty on his head." [169] For Coleridge's beautiful prose not only validates his idiosyncratically humane political stance against any charge of Jacobinism, but in its depth and cadence perhaps gives us as well a fleeting glimpse of the conversational power that bemused so many among his most brilliant contemporaries.

13

The *Biographia Literaria* and the Contentions of English Romanticism

Jerome J. McGann

The *Biographia Literaria* is one of the chief documents of English Romantic theory, and in recent years, thanks to the work of various critics, we have also begun to see the book as a more coherently developed text than it was earlier thought to be. This new scholarship has proved eminently Coleridgean in character, for out of it has emerged a reconciliation of much material in the *Biographia* which had before seemed rather opposite and discordant in its qualities. Today we see the book more clearly, I think, than we have ever seen it before; and the consequence of this new clarity is that we may also begin to see in exactly what ways the *Biographia* is crucial to an understanding of English Romanticism.

First of all, it is not crucial because it is the *central* theoretical document —not, at any rate, if by "central" we mean the one that incorporates all the major lines of thought associated with English Romanticism. Indeed, my present inquiry will try to *decenter* the *Biographia* in precisely this respect, to contrast it with two other important theoretical approaches that emerged in the Romantic movement. But in decentering Coleridge's book, I shall also be arguing its seminal importance for the development of the original strands of English Romanticism, as well as for our understanding of the movement as a whole. A careful look at the *Biographia* in its contemporary setting, even in the restricted terms I am proposing for this essay, brings the variety and richness of Romantic thought and practice into sharp relief.

The first thing we need to see is what Coleridge himself thought about the form and purpose of his book. It is the author of the "Essays on

Method" who glanced intramurally at the *Biographia* as an "immethodical . . . miscellany",[1] yet the same author was to say a bit later, and extramurally, that the work "cannot justly be regarded as a motley Patchwork, or Farrago of heterogeneous Effusions".[2] Following the recent work of McFarland, Jackson, Christensen, Wheeler, and Wallace, however, we have learned to see the kind of order that underlies Coleridge's often wayward and digressive procedures—indeed, to see that Coleridge's "mosaic" or "marginal" or "miscellaneous" manner of composition is precisely what is needed, in his view, if one is to execute a truly methodical and theoretically sound critical operation.[3]

None of this is to say, of course, that the *Biographia* is a formal masterpiece, or even that all of the interlaced topics are equally interesting, or handled with equal skill. What we are bound to see, however, if we want to read the book profitably, is the truth in Coleridge's own account of what he had written. "Let the following words", he said, "be prefixed as the Common Heading" of the work:

> An attempt to fix the true meaning of the Terms, Reason, Understanding, Sense, Imagination, Conscience & Ideas, with reflections on the theoretical & practical Consequences of their perversion from the Revolution (1688) to the present day, 1816—the moral of the whole being that the Man who gives to the Understanding the primacy due to the Reason, and lets the motives of Expedience usurp the place of the prescripts of the Conscience, in both cases loses the one and spoils the other. . . .[4]

This is a fair enough description, generally speaking, but troublesome because Coleridge said that it applied just as well to *The Statesman's Manual, A Lay Sermon*, and the three-volume *Friend* (1818). Yet this general application by Coleridge was both shrewd and correct. On the one hand, it called attention to the coherence of his purposes and preoccupations in these different works, and on the other it implied that the differences between them involved shifts in emphasis and in the relations established between the several topics. We need only glance at the "Essays on Method" to be clear about Coleridge's meaning. The *Biographia* moves by a process that Coleridge called *"progressive transition."* This is no "mere dead arrangement"[5] but an accumulating set of interrelations which develop gradually (with references backward and anticipations forward) under the guidance and direction of a leading Idea, or what Coleridge called a "preconception" and "Initiative":

Lord Bacon equally with ourselves, demands what we have ventured to call the intellectual or mental initiative, as the motive and guide of every philosophical experiment; some well-grounded purposes, some distinct impression of the probable results, some self-consistent anticipation as the grounds of the *"prudens quaestio"* (the fore-thoughtful query), which he affirms to be the prior *half* of the knowledge sought. . . .[6]

The *Biographia* takes up all of the same topics handled in *The Lay Sermons* and *The Friend* but disposes of them in a biographical field of relations. The emphasis of the work is therefore "literary," although literary in the broadest sense because Coleridge's literary life encompassed (besides poetry and plays) journalism, political pamphleteering, and philosophy. The *Biographia* is no different from Coleridge's other works in being committed to a critical procedure based upon what he liked to call "principles." Thus, when he speaks of an investigation or a discourse of "well-grounded purposes," the term "well-grounded" glances at the need for an initiative established on *a priori* "principles" rather than on *a posteriori* generalizations arrived at and refined through cumulative observation.

What then—to come to *my* leading idea—are Coleridge's "purposes" in the *Biographia*, what is his "distinct impression of the probable results" of this most famous of English literary lives? They are generally the same as those he specified for the Appendix to *The Statesman's Manual*: "The Object was to rouse and stimulate the mind—to set the reader a thinking —and at least to obtain entrance for the question, whether the [truth of the] Opinions in fashion . . . is quite so certain as he had hitherto taken for granted."[7] Coleridge set this attitude as the motto of most of his work, and it plainly applies to the whole thrust of the *Biographia*—in its critique of the reigning empirical school of philosophy; reviews and ideas about poetry; and gossip about Coleridge, Wordsworth, and the so-called Lake School of poetry. The *Biographia* opposed the "Opinions in fashion" on all these matters—indeed, opposes the idea that any truth at all could ever be found in fashion or grounded in opinion.

More particularly, Coleridge's purpose was to set forth a theory of poetry grounded in the distinction between imagination and fancy, for

were it once fully ascertained, that this division is . . . grounded in nature . . . the theory of the fine arts, and of poetry in particular, could not, I thought, but derive some additional and important light. It would in its immediate effects furnish a torch of guidance to the philosophi-

cal critic; and ultimately to the poet himself. In energetic minds, truth
soon changes by domestication into power; and from directing in the
discrimination and appraisal of the product, becomes influencive in the
production. To admire on principle, is the only way to imitate without
loss of originality. (1:85)

This passage, which culminates the introductory four chapters of the *Biographia*, sets forth the "well-grounded purposes" and hoped-for "results"
that Coleridge anticipated for his book. On the one hand, the *Biographia*
was to be a model of literary criticism that would be *represented* in the
practical discussions of Shakespeare, Wordsworth, and Maturin; and that
would be *polemicized* in the critique of Jeffrey and the reviewing institution
of the period. On the other hand, the *Biographia* was to establish guidelines for the writing of poetry. Both of these practical aims were to succeed
because Coleridge's was a work of "philosophical" criticism which could
be a model for critics, on the one hand, and which could show poets, on
the other, how "to imitate without loss of originality" the work of other
poets and of nature itself.

Coleridge's "well-grounded purposes" would be, finally, set forth as a
man of letters' intellectual biography. The significance of the biographical frame for Coleridge's work cannot be too greatly emphasized, for the
story he tells reveals a person whose work was steadfast in its principles
—more, was steadfast *in principles* as such, was steadfast (that is to say) in
God——from the beginning, but who only *grew* into his developing self-
conscious grasp of the operation of these principles in his own life's work
and practice. Like every human being in a world made by God, Coleridge was born a child of truth, but only gradually did he raise himself
from an ignorance of what that meant to a methodical and active assent
to its reality. In the *Biographia* he comes forth as the person he calls in
The Friend the "*well*-educated man," of whom he goes on to say: "However
irregular and desultory his talk, there is *method* in the fragments."[8] The
ultimate myth, or faith, of the *Biographia* is, therefore, that the "principles"
of all things, including the principles of a benevolently dynamic human
self-consciousness, are "grounded in nature." Coleridge's life and its narrative are important because together they "furnish a torch of guidance"
to others. According to Coleridge, the intellectual dynamic that has been
his life is the birthright of every human being—every Christian human
being, at any rate.

We need to be clear about Coleridge's explicit aims and purposes in

the *Biographia* if we are to begin an accurate assessment of its achievements. The accusations of incoherence and disorganization, installed with
the early reviews, have grown to seem much less important, and in certain respects misguided, as readers have tended to favor an aesthetic or
hermeneutical method of reading the work over a positive and critical approach. To the degree that scholars have been interested in judging the
correctness of Coleridge's various ideas and positions in philosophy, politics, and literary criticism, the consensus seems to be that (a) his critique of
the empirical tradition and of materialism, and his correlative defense of
Idealist positions, leaves that old debate more or less where it has always
been (undecided, exactly where his German mentors in philosophy had
left it); (b) his political views are independent and conservative, with both
characteristics deriving ultimately from his religious and theological convictions; (c) the representation of his views on all matters, *in order to be
objectively understood,* have to pass through the filter of Coleridge's subjectivity, and Coleridge himself must be the vehicle but not the master of that
subjectivity (that is to say, Coleridge is not always candid, even with himself); (d) the literary criticism, both practical and theoretical, is the great
achievement of the work.

For the remainder of this essay I shall be concentrating on Coleridge's
literary criticism in the *Biographia.* I have spent some time on the general
structure and method because the literary theory and criticism is of a piece
with the rest of the book. Thus, Coleridge's argument that poetry is essentially ideal relates directly to his account of Idealist philosophy. Similarly,
his critique of associationism and empirical philosophy connects just as
directly with his critique of Wordsworth's poetry, and especially the principles which underly that poetry. Finally, the history of his own life from
his early radicalism to his achieved religious conservatism—and culmi-
nating in the *Biographia* itself—argues the social and political importance
of a correct view of poetry and criticism. Coleridge repeatedly associates
radical political thought with the philosophic positions he attacks directly
and at length. Indeed, much of this kind of "philosophical" political commentary in the *Biographia* is simply jingoism, as we see very clearly in
his discussion of associationism. "Opinions fundamentally false" on these
academic matters are not, he says, "harmless" at the political and social
level:

> the sting of the adder remains venemous. . . . Some indeed there seem
> to have been, in an unfortunate neighbour-nation at least, who have

embraced this system with a full view of all its moral and religious consequences; some

> who deem themselves most free,
> When they within this gross and visible sphere
> Chain down the winged thought, scoffing assent,
> Proud in their meanness; and themselves they cheat
> With noisy emptiness of learned phrase,
> Their subtle fluids, impacts, essences,
> Self-working tools, uncaus'd effects, and all
> Those blind omniscients, those Almighty slaves,
> Untenanting Creation of its God!

Such men need discipline, not argument; they must be made better men,
before they can become wiser. (1:122–23)

These are the contexts in which Coleridge engages the question of
poetry and of literary criticism—to his credit, let it be said that whatever
one may think of his reactionary cultural and social views, he struggled
to maintain a holistic approach to all human studies. The question of
the excellences and defects of Wordsworth's poetry, and of Wordsworth's
theoretical justification of that poetry, was important for Coleridge not
simply for personal reasons, but because he felt that the poetry (in particular, the *Lyrical Ballads*) occupied a nexus of great importance for English, and even for European, society. Today we take it for granted that
Coleridge won the argument with Wordsworth.[9] I want to reconsider this
question again by examining Coleridge's position for what it is, a polemical set of ideas about the nature and function of poetry. Specifically, I want
to examine it in relation to the antithetical positions of Wordsworth and
Byron.

II

Coleridge said that, although the "Preface" to *Lyrical Ballads* was half the
product of his own brain, and although he and Wordsworth shared many
of the same ideas about poetry, a fundamental difference of opinion about
poetry separated them. He was right. Both men talked equally about the
interchanges of mind and nature, but in each the emphasis was different; and this difference of emphasis, in the end, proved radical. In the
Biographia Coleridge traced the source of this difference to eighteenth-

century theories of association and sensation, which he came to reject but which Wordsworth—if one is to judge by the "preface" to *Lyrical Ballads* —remained committed to. Chapters 17–22 of the *Biographia* argue that the defects of Wordsworth's poetry are the consequence of a defective, ultimately an associationist, theory of mind.[10]

One of the root problems with associationist thought, in Coleridge's view, was that it based itself not on "principles," or *a priori* categories, or "innate ideas," but on observation. A poetry founded on such a theory would therefore have to be in error, for "poetry as poetry is essentially *ideal*, [and] avoids and excludes all *accident*; . . . its apparent individualities . . . must be *representative* . . . and . . . the *persons* of poetry must be clothed with *generic* attributes" (2:45–46). Again and again Coleridge returns to this theme in his critique of Wordsworth's theoretical and practical defects. Laying so much stress on the language of people in low and rustic life as a model for poetic language, Wordsworth "leads us to place the chief value on those things on which man DIFFERS from man and to forget or disregard the high dignities, which . . . *may* be, and *ought* to be, found in all ranks" (2:130). Wordsworth's is a *levelling* poetry, perhaps even a democratic or Jacobinical poetry: a poetry which proposes that a "rustic's" mode of experience and discourse is a more appropriate norm for poetical experience and discourse than is the experience and discourse of "the educated man" (2:52–53). Coleridge vigorously opposes such an idea. In actual fact, Coleridge says,

> the rustic, from the more imperfect development of his faculties, and from the lower state of their cultivation, aims almost solely to convey *insulated facts*, either those of his scanty experience or his traditional belief; while the educated man seeks to discover and express those *connections* of things, or those relative *bearings* of fact to fact, from which some more or less general law is deducible. For *facts* are valuable to a wise man, chiefly as they lead to the discovery of the indwelling *law*, which is the true *being* of things. . . . (2:52–53)

The rustic is here used as a figure of what Coleridge called elsewhere "the ignorant man," the man who lacks the requisite self-consciousness to raise up out of his experience an image or reflex of subsistent harmony. For Coleridge, that image or reflex is the ground of imagination, and hence the essential feature of poetry; and it comes, he says, from "*meditation, rather than . . . observation*" (2:82). Wordsworth's views not only place entirely too much emphasis upon details and particulars, on what Coleridge calls "matters-of-fact"; they suggest that the subject of poetry lies outside the mind, somehow in "reality" or "the world." On the contrary, Coleridge insists that the poet's eye is not the observer's eye but the mind's eye, and further, that the mind's eye is directed inward, to the ideal world created and revealed through the imagination (both primary and secondary). This aspect of Coleridge's views has been insisted upon by all of his best readers: "The reality that poems 'imitate,'" as Catherine Wallace has recently put it, "is not the objective world as such but, rather, the consciousness of the poet himself *in his encounters with* the objective world. . . . the poet's only genuine subject matter is himself, and the only ideas he presents will be ideas about the activity of consciousness in the world around him."[11]

Finally, by emphasizing observation rather than meditation, and matters-of-fact rather than the ideal, Wordsworth suggests that his theory of imagination is mechanistic and associationist rather than creative and idealist. This difference which Coleridge observes leads him to stress the volitional character of poetic imagination. The whole point of chapters 5–8 of the *Biographia* is to insist upon the primacy of conscious will in the human being, and to attack associationist thought as a "mechanist" philosophy which undermines the concept of the will. Poetry is and must always be a product of what he calls "the conscious will" (1:304). When the poet "brings the whole soul of man into activity," the power of imagination is "first put in action by the will and understanding, and retained under their irremissive, though gentle and unnoticed, controul" (2:15–16).

In his best practice, and recurrently in his theory as set forth in the "Preface" to the *Lyrical Ballads*, Wordsworth (according to Coleridge) illustrates Coleridge's own ideas about the ideal, the conscious, and the volitional character of poetry and imagination. The defects in Wordsworth's poetic work are traceable to certain defects in his principles, in his theory of poetry as set forth in his famous preface. Coleridge scrutinizes the preface for residual traces of Wordsworth's associationist ideas, and he then argues that the faults in the poems in the *Lyrical Ballads* are the consequence of these residual—and, so far as Wordsworth's true genius as a poet is concerned—inessential ideas. This is the method of Coleridge's critique of Wordsworth in the *Biographia*.

And in point of fact he was right; Wordsworth's poetic theory and practice remained committed to certain associationist positions as Coleridge's did not. Where Coleridge would always stress the poet's will and self-consciousness—indeed, where Coleridge would suggest that the poet's (or at least the modern poet's) central subject ought to be the act of the conscious will itself—Wordsworth's poetic impulses drove him toward insights and revelations that stood beyond the limits of the conscious will. In contemporary terms, Coleridge's is a theory of poetry as a process of revelation via mediations—indeed, a poetry whose subject is the acts and processes of mediation. Wordsworth, on the other hand, sets out in quest of an unmediated poetry, and in the preface to the *Lyrical Ballads* he offers a theoretical sketch of what such a project involves.

Briefly, what Wordsworth aspires to is a direct perception of what he calls "the subject." This is his primary aim as a poet: "I have at all times endeavoured to look steadily at my subject; consequently, there is I hope in these poems little falsehood of description. . . ."[12] This purpose, apparently so simple, is reiterated in more emphatic and explicit terms in 1815: "The powers requisite for the production of poetry are: first, those of Observation and Description,—*i.e.*, the ability to observe with accuracy things as they are in themselves, and with fidelity to describe them, unmodified by any passion or feeling existing in the mind of the describer" (*Prose Works* 3:26). Coleridge, however, in his distinction between "copy" and "imitation," vigorously opposes Wordsworth's ideas on this matter, and later commentators—particularly 20th century critics and academics—have sided with Coleridge, and have even come to believe that his is the more innovative view. The most influential contemporary scholarship of Wordsworth's poetry—the line established through the work of Geoffrey Hartman—has armed itself with Coleridge's vision in order to save Wordsworth's poetry from the poet himself. Wordsworth, we are now urged to think, was no mystic, and least of all was he a poet of nature. He is the poet of the mind, the revealer of the operations of the consciousness. He is, in short, what Coleridge said he was and ought to be.

In trying to understand the importance of the differences that separate Wordsworth's and Coleridge's ideas about poetry, we must not abandon what we have come to learn about Wordsworth's poetry of consciousness. What we have to see, however, is that *all* his poetry—"The Idiot Boy" as much as *The Prelude*—is a poetry based in a committment to unmediated perception, on the one hand, and to a theory of nonconscious awareness on the other (what Wordsworth calls "habits"). Both aspects of his ideas about poetry are intimately related to each other. In his critique of Wordsworth, Coleridge argued that Wordsworth's attack on poetic diction in the

Preface to the *Lyrical Ballads* was not, (could not have been), fundamental, but was rather directed to peculiar circumstances which had developed in English poetry in the eighteenth century (2:40–42). This is a very conservative reading of Wordsworth's ideas, and in the end it is wrong. Wordsworth's whole argument that there neither is nor can be any real or essential difference between poetry and prose is grounded in an impulse to avert altogether the grids, the Kantian "categories," and all the complex mediations which stand between the act of perception and the objects perceived. It did not matter to Wordsworth whether the "subject" of the poet was an idiot boy, a broken pot, an abstract reality (nature, social classes or conventions, psychological events like "fidelity"), God, or even "the mind of man" itself and all its complex states of consciousness. The ideal was to set these matters free of the mediations which necessarily conveyed them, either to one's self or to others.

This could be done, Wordsworth believed, by grounding poetry not in "the conscious will" but in "spontaneous" and "powerful feelings," on the one hand, and "habits of meditation" on the other (1:127):

> Poems to which any value can be attached were never produced on any variety of subjects but by a man who, being possessed of more than usual organic sensibility, had also thought long and deeply. For our continued influxes of feeling are modified and directed by our thoughts, which are indeed the representatives of all our past feelings; and, as by contemplating the relation of these general representatives to each other, we discover what is really important to men, so, by the repetition and continuance of this act, our feelings will be connected with important subjects, till at length . . . such habits of mind will be produced, that, by obeying blindly and mechanically the impulses of those habits, we shall describe objects, and utter sentiments . . . that the understanding of the Reader must necessarily be in some degree enlightened, and his affections strengthened and purified. (1:127)

This is a highly pragmatic, even a tactical, way of stating his position. Not until Shelley would reformulate Wordsworth's ideas more than twenty years later would the theory insinuated by Wordsworth receive a comprehensive and adequate formulation. This would happen when Shelley provided Wordsworth's ideas with a broad social and political dimension, a comprehensive theory of culture in which poetry was revealed as a set of various related, and imaginatively grounded, social practices.

That subject is, however, beyond the scope of my present concerns.

Here I want only to indicate how consciousness and the structure of all forms of mediation are viewed by Wordsworth. Simply, they are impediments to clear vision. For Wordsworth, to show (in practice) or argue (in theory) that the mediations are themselves the subject of the poet is to abandon the ground of any nonsubjective experience, and hence to abandon the ground of all human intercourse and social life, which involve sympathetic relationships between persons distinct and different. To Wordsworth, Coleridge's position also involves a theoretical contradiction: for we cannot have knowledge of anything, not even knowledge of the mediations, unless an unmediated consciousness is at some point admitted to acts of knowledge and perception. In effect, Coleridge's Kantian position, by resituating the problem of knowledge, has merely reopened it at the level of epistemology. Coleridge's position stands under threat to the critique of an infinite regress: what will mediate the mediations? Coleridge's eventual response to this question, developed out of Schelling, was to argue for a continuous and self-developing process of mediated knowledge—that is to say, it was to make a virtue of necessity and turn the infinite regress into an organic process. It was also, needless to say, to have literally postponed both the problem and the answer to the problem. The move was a brilliant finesse.

Wordsworth took a different course—less spectacular and intellectually brilliant but in the end perhaps more daring and profound, at least so far as poetry is concerned. Observing and describing without the intervention of consciousness or subjective mediations, following blindly and mechanically the unselfconsciously meditated directions of unselfconscious feeling and thought: these are Wordsworth's remarkable procedures. Their object, as he says in various ways, is to avoid the veils of familiarity—the mediations—through which we experience the world. Unlike Coleridge, Wordsworth is seeking for a poetry, and a mode of perception, which will lay the mortal mind asleep in order that it may see into the life of things—in order that it may transcend the limits of experience laid down by Coleridge's self-conscious will and Kant's categorical imperatives. This program, needless to say, is anything but supernaturalist; it is in fact a deeply materialist and mundane program. What it seeks to transcend is not this world or concrete experience but the ideologies of this world and our modes of perceiving it. Coleridge was quite right to oppose this program on principle, for Wordsworth's ideal, in principle, is toward a poetry in which the mind transcends its own volitions and categories; in which the mind, following not consciousness but "feelings," "impulses," and "sensations," is suddenly confronted with the unknown, the revelation of what is miraculous. Wordsworth calls his ideal "sympathy," an experience in which

> passions and thoughts and feelings are . . . connected with our moral sentiments and animal sensations, and with the causes which excite these; with the operations of the elements, and the appearances of the visible universe; with storm and sunshine, with the revolutions of the seasons, with cold and heat, with loss of friends and kindred, with injuries and resentments, gratitude and hope, with fear and sorrow. (1:142)

At such moments—glimpsing a hedgehog or a flower, observing a peculiar encounter between two people, being wrapped in a specific atmospheric moment, perhaps of wind and humidity—the mind will be led to feel that it suddenly *understands,* that it has been brought to some moment of ultimate knowledge. In Wordsworth we are gently led on to these moments by the affections; it is not the conscious will that controls experiences of primary or secondary imagination, it is "habit," "impulse," and "feeling." Consciousness follows experience, not the other way round.

When Coleridge linked Wordsworth's poetry to materialist and associationist principles, then, his insight was acute. Equally acute was the way he attacked Wordsworth's "matter-of-factness." The "laborious minuteness and fidelity in the representation of objects, and . . . the insertion of accidental circumstances" (2:126) infects the poetry with what Coleridge sees as a sort of misplaced concreteness. Wordsworth's insistence upon treating *peculiar* experiences puts at risk the Coleridgean ideal of poetic harmony and the reconciliation of opposite and discordant qualities. In Wordsworth, Coleridge is constantly being brought up against resistant particulars, details that somehow evade—or rather, details that seem *determined* to evade—the necessary poetic harmony and reconciliation. Coleridge calls this Wordsworth's "*accidentality,*" and he says that it contravenes "the essence of poetry," which must be, he adds, "catholic and abstract" (2:126). "Accidentality" works against Coleridge's idea that poetry is the most philosophical of discourses because it alone can reveal the general in the especial, the sameness in the differences.

To Wordsworth, however, accidentality was precisely the means by which feelings and impulses outwitted the mind's catholic and abstracting censors. "I am sensible," he says, that my associations must have sometimes been particular instead of general, and that, consequently, giving to things a false importance, I may have sometimes written on unworthy subjects; but I am less apprehensive on this account, than that my language may frequently have suffered from those arbitrary connections of feelings and ideas with particular words and phrases, from which no man can altogether protect himself. . . . Such faulty expressions . . . I would willingly take all reasonable pains to correct. But it is dangerous to make these alterations on the simple authority of a few individuals, or even of certain classes of men; for where the understanding of an Author is not convinced, or his feelings altered, this cannot be done without great injury to himself: for his own feelings are his stay and support. . . . To this may be added, that the critic ought never to forget that he is himself exposed to the same errors as the Poet, and, perhaps, in a much greater degree. . . . (1:153)

Once again the ground of Wordsworth's decisions, both as regards his subject matter and his choice of words, is determined by "feelings." He means to act, as Blake said of Jesus, by impulse, and not by rules. The critical mind—even the poet's own conscious and critical operations—may suspect accidentality and arbitrariness in the poem's subject matter or language, but if the feelings which led the poet to his choices cannot be shown to be factitious, then the choices must be maintained. It is not merely that the heart has its reasons; the choice must be maintained because *the consciousness has its reasons. The mind* directs itself to the ordering of experience, to the establishment of harmonies; *the feelings* direct themselves to the enlarging of experience itself. Wordsworth's "feeling" is what Blake called "the Prolific": judge and censor of the judgmental and censorious consciousness, the feelings and their concomitant train of accidentalities refuse to let the mind settle into its *a priori* harmonies.

Coleridge is an ideologue, and his theory of poetry is not merely an ideology of poetry; it finally argues that poetry is the perfect form of ideology (more philosophical than philosophy, more concrete than history). Poetry is the revelation and expression of the Ideal, of the idea and what is ideational, of the world as a play of the mediations of consciousness. It is the product of the conscious will. But to Wordsworth, the true human will is not located in the ego or the superego, it lies in the unconscious; it is a form of desire, an eros, not a form of thought, an eidolon. A poetry of sympathy rather than a poetry of consciousness, it covets irrelevant detail and "accidentality" as the limit and test of its own imaginative reach.

Insofar as it is a poetry of the mind and consciousness, Wordsworth's work is strongest and most characteristic when it represents mind at the moment of its dawning and self-discovery, consciousness falling upon itself in its instants of wonder and surprise. In such poetry—*The Prelude* is the preeminent example—consciousness is rendered as an experience rather than as a knowledge or form of thought. The difference between Coleridge's and Wordsworth's theorizing on these matters reflects, then, a small but in the end crucial difference of emphasis: for Coleridge, poetry is an idea and is to be understood via the networks of intellectual mediations which are poetry's ultimate ground and "principles"; for Wordsworth poetry is an experience and is to be understood primarily in the event itself, but in any case only through the rhetorical and sympathetic networks which the poems set in motion. It is a matter, as Wordsworth's "Preface" says, of contracts and arrangements, not—as Coleridge insists —of *a priori* ideas and "principles."

Ultimately, Coleridge's theory of poetry sees it as a continuous play of signifiers and signifieds, and its object is to provide, in the traces left by this play, glimpses of the ordering process which is the ground of the play. For Wordsworth, however, the semiotic dance traces a referential system back into the material world. In the play of language, the dance of the signifiers and the signifieds, we glimpse the structure in which the system of symbols and the order of references hold themselves together. Coleridge, too, says that poetry affords a glimpse of a superior reality lying behind the appearances of things. But for Coleridge this superior reality is nonmaterial, in the order of platonic or ideal forms. For Wordsworth, by contrast, the order is emphatically concrete and material, an order of actual sympathies and arrangements which we have, in our getting and spending, only neglected or forgotten. In Wordsworth, the play of the signifiers and the signifieds, the spectacle of the mediations, lies under judgment to a superior reality, the order of the referents. Wordsworth's poetry is a symbolic system which aims to disappear, but with a flash that reveals the invisible world—which is to say, *this* material and human world, the very world of all of us that has too regularly "been disappeared" (so to speak) in the symbols and ideas we have made of it.

III

In the *Biographia*, Coleridge sought to replace what he felt to be an outmoded theory of poetry and poetic perception with a more adequate and advanced theory. Wordsworth's famous Preface was his point of attack, first, because he felt that Wordsworth's actual practice as a poet went far beyond his theory; and second, because he felt that insofar as the practice was weak, it reflected the poverty of Wordsworth's theory. This well-known and important theoretical struggle about the nature of poetry has had, and continues to have, weighty consequences for scholars and for poets alike. Its importance looms even larger, however, if we reflect upon an equally relevant but (so far as I can see) completely *un*known fact: that Byron's *Don Juan* was consciously conceived as a response to the *Biographia*. Scholars are of course well aware that Byron began his masterwork by lashing out at Wordsworth, Southey, and the Lake School in general. What is not realized, however, is the extent to which the *Biographia* inspired Byron's *Don Juan*.

The story begins in the autumn of 1817, when Byron received and read Coleridge's literary autobiography. In a letter to Murray of October 12, Byron refers contemptuously to the *Biographia*'s treatment of the program of Coleridge, Wordsworth, and the enthusiasts of the Lake School. His disparaging remarks on the book are concentrated, however, on the review of Maturin's play *Bertram*, which Coleridge had savaged in chapter 23.[13] This letter to Murray is also important because it contains Byron's first announcement that he had just "written a poem (of 84 octave Stanzas) humourous, in or after the excellent manner of Mr. Whistlecraft . . . on a Venetian anecdote."

Let us begin with Coleridge's attack on *Bertram*. Critics who write about Coleridge's great book rarely spend any time on chapter 23, probably because it is one of the least creditable passages, in several senses. But in fact it is one of the most *interesting* chapters in the book, because it shows Coleridge's literary criticism operating at its most polemical moral level. Coleridge's attack on *Bertram* begins with two critical indirections: first, Coleridge's argument that this kind of so-called Gothic (or "German") drama is English in origin and fundamentally Jacobinical in its moral tendencies; and second, Coleridge's extended discussion of the Don Juan tradition in drama, and in particular of "the old Spanish play, entitled *Atheista Fulminato* . . . which . . . has had its day of favour in every country throughout Europe" (2:212). The point of these indirections is to erect a model for the treatment of evil in theatrical productions. What places the *Atheista Fulminato* "at a world's distance from the spirit of modern jacobinism" in plays like *Bertram* is the following:

> The latter introduces to us clumsy copies of these showy instrumental qualities [i.e., appearances of virtue] in order to *reconcile* us to vice and want of principle; while the *Atheista Fulminato* presents . . . them for the sole purpose of displaying their hollowness, and in order to put us on our guard by demonstrating their utter indifference to vice and virtue. . . .
> (2:221)

Unlike the ideologically correct *Atheista Fulminato*, *Bertram* is typical of recent Gothic drama for "representing . . . liberality, refined feeling, and a nice sense of honour" in people that tradition teaches us are wicked, and for "rewarding with all the sympathies which are the due of virtue, those criminals whom law, reason, and religion have excommunicated from our esteem" (2:221). Coleridge was attacking *Bertram*, but he might as easily have made the same charge against all of Byron's famous tales and against Byron's recent Gothic drama *Manfred* as well. In an earlier version of this passage printed as part of "Letter II" of "Satyrane's Letters," Coleridge declared that "the whole System" of dramas like *Bertram* "is a moral and intellectual *Jacobinism* of the most dangerous kind."[14]

It is difficult to resist the impression that the very subject of *Don Juan* was chosen as an antithetical move against Coleridge's discussion of Jacobinical drama in this chapter of the *Biographia*. In the first place, his letter to Murray shows that he took personal offense at Coleridge's critique of *Bertram*. His anger was partly the consequence of his sense that Coleridge had behaved meanly and ungratefully toward both himself personally, and the Drury Lane theatre committee in general.[15] Nor could Byron have been insensible to the import of Coleridge's critique of *Bertram*, which was as much an attack on Byron's sympathetic treatment of bad men in *his* poetry.

Equally impressive are certain other internal connections between what Coleridge wrote in the *Biographia* and what Byron wrote in *Don Juan*. The first line of Coleridge's direct attack on *Bertram* is aimed at "the prodigy of the tempest at *Bertram*'s shipwreck" (2:222). Coleridge ridicules the treatment of the storm for its absurd lack of probability. The events are inherently hyperbolical and beyond belief ("The Sicilian sea coast: a convent of monks: night: a most portentous, unearthly storm: a vessel wrecked: contrary to all human expectation, one man saves himself by his prodigious powers as a swimmer"); besides, when one of the characters gives his "theory of Sicilian storms," it is, Coleridge says, "not apparently founded on any great familiarity of his own with this troublesome article" (i.e., Sicilian storms) (2:222–23). Anyone familiar with Canto II of *Don Juan* will recognize some of its essential features anticipated here: in Byron's poem we will not only see once again that "prodigious . . . swimmer" who alone escapes his shipwreck; the entire treatment of the event will emphasize the accuracy and truthfulness of its circumstantial details.

I could expatiate on a number of other specific intertextual connections between the early cantos of *Don Juan* and the *Biographia*, but I shall have to relegate them to a footnote, for the sake of maintaining the larger train of the argument.[16] Coleridge's principal criticism of *Bertram* is that it is indecent and immoral. Coleridge searches out the scenes in the play which demonstrate its apparently fixed intention to display evil and vice in a favorable or at least in a sympathetic light. Perhaps nowhere else has Coleridge's literary criticism lapsed so badly. His diatribe culminates in the discussion of Act IV, where the disasters that attend the illicit love of Bertram and Imogine begin to unfold in the play's series of deaths and madness. "I want words to describe the mingled horror and disgust, with which I witnessed the opening of the fourth act. . . . The shocking spirit of jacobinism seemed no longer confined to politics" (2:229). What Coleridge means is that "The familiarity with atrocious events and characters" seemed to "have poisoned the taste" of the people watching the play. The event leaves Coleridge in a state of moral breathlessness:

> that a British audience could remain passive under such an insult to common decency, nay, receive with a thunder of applause, a human being supposed to have come reeking from the consummation of this complex foulness and baseness, these and the like reflections . . . pressed as with the weight of lead upon my heart. . . . (2:229)

It is against this sort of bourgeois moralism that *Don Juan* was written; indeed, it is against this simplistic and narrow attitudinizing—one can call it nothing better—that all of Byron's poetry was conceived. It was a tone which Byron caught in the work of most of the Lake School writers, but especially in Southey. It is rare in Coleridge, but its appearance in the critique of *Bertram* is important to remember, for Coleridge's ideology of poetry—that is, his conviction that poetry should be the vehicle of the willed acts of a reconciling consciousness—necessarily implies the specifics of his critique of *Bertram*. Coleridge was entirely correct, and—as always—entirely consistent when he said that his work was founded on principles. The critique of *Bertram* displays the principles in an applied and specific form.

If chapter 23 suggested to Byron that he might usefully make the Don Juan legend the focus of an attack upon the Lake School and middle-class ideology in general, and if it also influenced Byron's choice of subject and approach in Canto II of his masterwork, chapter 16 seems to have brought into focus the central stylistic issues. In this chapter Coleridge establishes a contrast between "the materials and structure of modern poetry" (2:32) and "the more polished poets of the fifteenth and sixteenth century, especially . . . of Italy" (2:33). This contrast prepares specifically for the extended discussion of Wordsworth which begins in chapter 17. Coleridge's critique of Wordsworth's matter-of-factness, of the meanness of his diction, of the excessive particularity, is based in his praise of the contrasting manner of the earlier Italian poets. In the modern period, Coleridge says, "few have guarded the purity of their native tongue with that jealous care, with which the sublime Dante in his tract 'De la nobile volgare eloquenza,' declares to be the first duty of a poet" (2:30). The manner of these early poets and their "dolce stil nuovo" provides, in Coleridge's view, a challenge and critical model for the poets of the present:

> The imagery is almost always general: sun, moon, flowers, breezes, murmuring streams, warbling songsters, delicious shades, lovely damsels, cruel as fair, nymphs, naiads, and goddesses, are the materials which are common to all, and which each shaped and arranged according to his judgement or fancy, little solicitous to add or to particularize. If we make an honorable exception in favor of some English poets, the thoughts too are as little novel as the images; and the fable of their narrative poems, for the most part drawn from mythology, or sources of equal notoriety, derive their chief attractions from the manner of treating them: from impassioned flow, or picturesque arrangement. In opposition to the present age, and perhaps in as faulty an extreme, they placed the essence of poetry in the *art*. The excellence, at which they aimed, consisted in the exquisite polish of the diction, combined with perfect simplicity. This their prime object, they attained by the avoidance of every word, which a *gentleman* would *not* use in dignified conversation, and of every word and phrase, which none but a *learned* man *would* use. (2:33)

Such stylistic purity passes a judgment on the characteristic faults and defects of modern poetry, which Coleridge summarizes this way: "a downright simpleness, under the affectation of simplicity, prosaic words in feeble metre, silly thoughts in childish phrases, and a preference of mean, degrading, or at best trivial associations, and characters" (1:75).

In Byron's critique of Wordsworth's poetry in *Don Juan* he follows Coleridge's line fairly closely. Most critics have assumed that Byron was recalling Jeffrey's strictures in the *Edinburgh Review*, and in fact he may well have been. But Coleridge's critique of his friend does not disagree with the *particulars* of Jeffrey's criticisms, it simply dissents from the general tone and attitude. To Coleridge, Wordsworth is a great poet whose defects are "characteristic" of his place and epoch. In the *Biographia* Coleridge summarizes very well the typical negative judgments brought against Wordsworth by contemporary reviewers, and it may well be that *Don Juan*'s criticisms and travesties of Wordsworth's poetry owe more to Coleridge's summary presentation than to his recollection of Jeffrey and the other reviewers.

However that may be, *Don Juan* is certainly responding directly to the stylistic challenge laid down in chapter 16 of the *Biographia*. We should recall that Byron's first reference to the *Biographia* occurs in the letter which announced the completion of the first draft of *Beppo*. The latter was specifically written in imitation of "the new style of poetry very lately sprung up in England"[17] in the work of Rose, Merivale, and especially Frere. This "new style" returned to fifteenth and sixteenth century Italy for its models—that is, to the work of Boiardo, Ariosto, Pulci, and Berni. Byron adopted (and adapted) this stylistic reformation in various ways between 1817–24. His defense of Pope against his Romantic detractors was part of his program to reform and purify the language and its poetic possibilities: "There is no bearing [the atrocious cant and nonsense about Pope] any longer, and if it goes on, it will destroy what little good writing and taste remains among us" (*BLJ* 7:61). His experiments in drama were part of this effort to restore greater correctness to English poetry, his translations from Dante and Pulci were exercises and acts of homage, as were *The Lament of Tasso* and *The Prophecy of Dante*, but *Don Juan* was the capstone and masterwork in Byron's new stylistic program. No one can read Byron's letters of 1817–24 and not be aware that he looked upon his poetical work during these years as all of a piece, and that one of its principal aims was to "[guard] the purity of [his] native tongue with that jealous care, which the sublime Dante . . . declares to be the first duty of a poet":

> you know that [*Beppo*] is no more than an imitation of Pulci & of a style common & esteemed in Italy. I have just published a drama [*Marino Faliero*], which is at least good English—I presume—for Gifford lays great stress on the purity of its diction. (*BLJ* 8:114)

It was probably Rose and Kinnaird who gave Byron a copy of the *Biographia* to read in September 1817, at the same time that they brought him Frere's imitation of Pulci. Thus, the following famous passage in Byron's letters—in which he first declares his intention to set off on a new course in poetry—is haunted by the two books he was reading at that time, Frere's "Whistlecraft" and Coleridge's *Biographia*:

> With regard to poetry in general I am convinced the more I think of it—
> that he and *all* of us—Scott—Southey—Wordsworth—Moore—Camp-
> bell—I—are all in the wrong—one as much as another—that we are
> upon a wrong revolutionary poetical system—or systems—not worth a
> damn in itself—& from which none but Rogers and Crabbe are free—
> and that the present & next generations will finally be of this opinion
> —I am the more confirmed in this—by having lately gone over some
> of our Classics—particularly *Pope*—whom I tried in this way—I took
> Moore's poems & my own & some others—& went over them side by
> side with Pope's—and I was really astonished (I ought not to have been
> so) and mortified—at the ineffable distance in point of sense—harmony
> —effect—and even *Imagination* Passion—& *Invention*—between the little
> Queen Anne's Man—& us of the lower Empire—depend upon it [it] is
> all Horace then, and Claudian now among us—and if I had to begin
> again—I would model myself accordingly—(*BLJ* 5:265)

In the years that were to follow, Byron defended *Don Juan* on a number of fronts, not the least of which was stylistic. When he fought against the accusations of immorality and indecency, he was also arguing for the purity (in both senses) of his new work. In the *Biographia* Coleridge had called for the reintroduction of linguistic correctness into contemporary English poetry, and had taken his contemporaries to task—even the greatest of them—for lapses from such standards of correctness, indeed, for lapses which were the "characteristic defects" of a new "system" of poetry. *Don Juan* picks up on both of these arguments and gives them a further range of meaning not contained in Coleridge's position. Here is Byron on the "wrong revolutionary poetical system" we now call Romanticism:

> *You* are taken in by that false stilted trashy style which is a mixture of all
> the styles of the day—which are *all bombastic* (I don't except my *own*—no
> one has done more through negligence to corrupt the language) but it is
> neither English nor poetry.——Time will show. (*BLJ* 7:182)

As for writing poetry which exhibited "exquisite polish of diction" and "perfect simplicity," poetry in a language "which a *gentleman* would *not* use in dignified conversation, and . . . which none but a *learned* man *would* use," it all depended upon what one meant by the terms "conversation," "gentleman," and "learned." *Don Juan*—as Byron well knew, and as all later scholars have recognized—is an impeccable rendering of aristocratic conversational idiom. This is the discourse of well-bred gentlemen who are "learned" not in bookish and academic ways, but in what Byron called "the world." A letter to Douglas Kinnaird of October 26, 1819, states his views in that prose—at once simple, polished, and expressive—which many regard as the finest ever written in the English language.

> As to "Don Juan"—confess—confess—you dog—and be candid—that it is the sublime of *that there* sort of writing—it may be bawdy—but is it not good English?—it may be profligate—but is it not *life*, is it not *the thing*? —Could any man have written it—who has not lived in the world?— and tooled in a post-chaise? in a hackney coach? in a Gondola? against a wall? in a court carriage? in a vis a vis?—on a table?—and under it? —I have written about a hundred stanzas of a third Canto—but it is damned modest—the outcry has frightened me.—I had such projects for the Don—but the *Cant* is so much stronger than *Cunt*—now a days— that the benefit of experience in a man who had well weighed the worth of both monosyllables—must be lost to despairing posterity. (*BLJ* 6:232)

This is the prose of a man who has well-weighed the worth of all his monosyllables. Its lightness of touch, its wit, and even its outrageousness cannot, should not, disguise its precision and purity. This is also a prose which finds its poetical equivalent in the *musa pedestris* of *Don Juan*.

At this point certain generalizations seem in order. In the first place, we see in all three of these men—Wordsworth, Byron, and Coleridge— a shared interest in renovating the medium of poetic work. Each worked consciously, even programmatically, toward that end, but in each case the end took on a different appearance. Byron and Wordsworth stand opposed to Coleridge in their stylistic empiricism, if I may so call it: that is to say, both Wordsworth and Byron set as their linguistic standard a real and current idiomatic usage. The language of poetry reflects, is modelled on, an actual linguistic practice which the poet takes to be a critical standard for his own work. This stylistic empiricism stands in sharp contrast to Coleridge's idealistic—ultimately, his academic—approach to poetic discourse. Lest this characterization of Coleridge's program seem invidious, I should point out that its offspring in later work is to be found in the some of the richest traditions of symbolist poetry.

Of course, Byron reflects the idiom of the aristocracy whereas Wordsworth's poetry is modelled on the usage of the "lower and middle orders" of "rustic" society. Coleridge's critique of Wordsworth's linguistic standard —that it is a usage that often reflects no more than the unself-consciousness and even the ignorance of the classes it is drawn from (2:42–55)— helps to explain the significance of the different choices made by Wordsworth and Byron. Wordsworth precisely wants a language which can be seen to say, or to imply, or to know, more than it understands at a self-conscious level. Byron, on the other hand, chooses an idiom which reflects language being used at the very highest pitch of self-consciousness.

This difference between Wordsworth and Byron brings into sharp relief a similarity in the positions of Coleridge and Byron. In contrast to Wordsworth, both laid a premium on the self-conscious and voluntarist dimensions of poetic discourse, just as they both praised the polished and artful work of Renaissance Italian poetry. Byron was as consciously ideological in his work as Coleridge. They differed, however, not only in their politics and class allegiances, but in the salient that their poetic self-consciousness took. Where Coleridge is working toward balances, reconciliations, and a harmony of elements that might otherwise remain discordant, Byron covets surprises and the upsetting of balance, antithetical moves of every kind, and what he called, in a wonderful portmanteau word, "opposition."

Much more could and should be said on these matters. We need to specify, in a detailed way, how these different theoretical positions work themselves out in actual poetic practice. Equally important would be to incorporate the related views of Shelley, Keats, and Blake—especially Shelley. Obviously this is not the occasion for such a demonstration. In a series of unpublished papers, however, I have worked through these lines of inquiry at considerable length and depth. The *Biographia*, however, is the obvious place to begin an investigation of the variances and differentials of Romantic stylistics because it is—as scholars have always known—the key text in this area. I hope the present essay has helped to clarify precisely why and how Coleridge's greatest work was and is so crucial.

14

Poetry and Barrel-Organs: The Text in the Book of the *Biographia Literaria*

Robert Maniquis

"Christendom," Coleridge says in chapter 16 of the *Biographia Literaria*, "from its first settlement on feudal rights, has been so far one great body, however imperfectly organized, that a similar spirit will be found in each period to have been acting in all its members."[1] This historicized Christianity is common to European Romanticism. Chateaubriand and Novalis were its most lyrical advocates in France and Germany, and Coleridge was its theoretical spokesman in England. But Coleridge, unlike Chateaubriand or Novalis, is still echoed in fragmentary strains of ideas he imagined could arise only from inseparable literary and religious principles. The *Biographia*, the *Lay Sermons*, *On the Constitution of the Church and State*, and *Confessions of an Inquiring Spirit* witness his constant attempt to produce that inseparability. Christianity he finds diversely manifest and almost everywhere—in the details of Greek grammar, in the idea of the English Constitution, and obviously in Milton, Shakespeare, and Wordsworth, poets who, whatever their flaws, had divinity in their voices.

That divine literary voice Coleridge defended against something he deeply feared—its commodification in a society increasingly pervaded by commerce. The defense of that voice is central to the Christianized politics of the *Biographia*. Its renunciation of materialism, dualism, and mechanistic psychology, and the constitutional, economic and literary principles in the long critique of Wordsworth—all this leads to the object of his "literary life," which is to ". . . preserve the Soul steady and collected in its pure *Act* of inward Adoration to the great I AM, and to the filial *Word* that reaffirmeth it from Eternity to Eternity, whose choral Echo is the Universe"

(2:247–48). This announced purpose, closing volume 2, ends with the invocation, in Greek, of "Glory to God Alone," a doxology, our editors remind us, commonly placed at the end of seventeenth-century books.

This tacked-on salutation to God, like "Satyrane's Letters" and the review of Maturin's *Bertram*, helped stretch manuscript copy into the proper second volume, which emerged during his publisher's clumsy patching together of Coleridge's "literary life." Rounding off his book with Renaissance doxology is, however, even as patching, significant. Coleridge would have preferred the audience he imagined for Richard Hooker, Thomas Browne, Francis Bacon, and Jeremy Taylor. Milton confidently wrote for a "fit audience though few." Coleridge sensed that the fit and few were now unreachable except by passing through the contaminating crowd of the unfit and the many. He could dedicate his book to the glory of God, apprehended in the same inward ontological I AM that grounds poetic imagination. But this book, which he pulled and padded, and partly plagiarized into existence, is also immediately in search of a complex audience, which he imagines made up of friends, the learned, and anonymous admirers.

These make up what he calls, in a common Enlightenment phrase, a "literary republic," an idealized presence midst the ill-defined and many-headed "reading public," that which foreshadows our mass audience and for which Coleridge had only contempt. Sometimes the contempt is lightened with humorous disdain, as in this passage from *The Stateman's Manual*:

> . . . among other odd burs and kecksies, the misgrowth of our luxuriant activity, we have now a READING PUBLIC—as strange a phrase, methinks, as ever forced a splenetic smile on the staid countenance of Meditation: and yet no fiction! For our Readers have, in good truth, multiplied exceedingly, and have waxed proud. It would require the intrepid accuracy of a Colquhoun [a statistician] to venture at the precise number of that vast company only, whose heads and hearts are dieted at the two public *ordinaries* of Literature, the circulating libraries and the periodical press. But what is the result? Does the inward man thrive on this regime? Alas! if the average health of the consumer may be judged of by the articles of largest consumption; if the secretions may be conjectured from the ingredients of the dishes that are found best suited to their palates; from all that I have seen, either of the banquet or the guests, I shall utter my *Profaccia* with a desponding sigh. From a popular philosophy and a philosophic populace, Good Sense deliver us! (*SM* 36–38)

Coleridge was only one of many who feared communal catastrophe in the marketplace, from Goethe who, in *Faust II*, warned about the effects

of paper money on consciousness to Wordsworth who wrote of prefer-
ring paganism to a Christian world of getting and spending. Not everyone was horrified. Fanny Burney comforted her father, who thought her
five-decker novel *Camilla* had been roughly treated by the critics, with a
reminder of its vast success. Or as she more plainly put it:

> Now heed no more what Critics thought 'em
> Since this you know—All People bought-em.[2]

But light-hearted certainties such as this or Samuel Johnson's assurance
that no one but a blockhead ever wrote except for money were becoming
merely quaint, not appropriate to the Romantic desire for cultural sur-
vival. Johnson could speak in the 1760s of the "teeming modern press,"[3]
but it was then still not what it would be in the post-revolutionary period—
a truly mammoth machine of production and consumption. Even Byron's
satirical gaze at the city and commercial book culture has a bitterness
never quite dissolved by humor as in Pope. Gone were the days when a
Daniel Defoe or Addison and Steele, shrewd businessmen and writers,
vilified but also celebrated money and commodities in centralized circulation. Many nineteenth-century writers, successful or not, who saw their
own writing increasingly absorbed into that circulation, tended only to
vilify. But whether writers bemoaned huge literary consumption or saw its
power in rebellion or reaction, as commodity circulation increased, they
began fictitious dialogues with those who laid down their money for books.

In these dialogues, implicit or direct, setting distances or defining an
imagined common ground with the reader, the reading audience is shaped
and a personality accorded to it. Authors shaped "audiences" out of the
actual expanding audience of readers commonly sensed as driving all literary values down to the lowest level. Romantic creation, under the shadow
of vast numbers, of an imaginary audience and even its appropriate literary taste is an important and generally neglected process of literary
culture during the industrial revolution.[4] This process can be seen particularly in the *Biographia*. Unceasing commodification running up against
Coleridge's Christianizing of all things is a central antagonism in this,
the canonized text of high Romantic tradition. Coleridge's works were
certainly not sought-after commodities. Only his theatrical hit, *Remorse*,
earned a respectable return for its author who was for most of his life,
despite generous benefactors, harassed by money problems. Successful or
not, Coleridge wrote with constant consciousness of the making of newspaper and book publishing fortunes in a market where authors like Sir

Walter Scott were to produce not simply novels but European publishing booms. In this world, the narrator of the *Biographia*, seems like a vulnerable visitor, and this vulnerability is one of his generally unrecognized but prominent dramatic themes.[5] Much of this work is made with the tension of a text as a poetic and religious voice, passing self-consciously through the book as commodity, a transitory existence grudgingly accepted by the aspiring text, the soul within the body, the I AM of the filial word within commodified words. Even manuscript padding like the review of *Bertram*, necessary to the fabrication of the "book" of the *Biographia* is about the degenerate audience that reigns in the marketplace of art, where the *Biographia* seeks its proper higher place among the stalls, but where it *must* certainly seek its place.

Timeless text and consumable book confront each other mostly in volume 1, though an important theme of these passages surfaces, as we shall see, in his critique of Wordsworth. Coleridge devotes chapter 2 to the question of the "Irritability of Men of Genius" and the relation of author and audience. Here is Coleridge first of all on the situation caused by the levelling down of literature to a commodity attainable by the many:

> . . . alas! the multitude of books, and the general diffusion of literature, have produced other, and more lamentable effects in the world of letters, and such as are abundant to explain, tho' by no means to justify, the contempt with which the best grounded complaints of injured genius are rejected as frivolous, or entertained as matter of merriment. In the days of Chaucer and Gower, our language might . . . be compared to a wilderness of vocal reeds, from which the favorites only of Pan or Apollo could construct even the rude Syrinx; and from this the *constructors* alone could elict strains of music. But now . . . language, mechanized as it were into a barrel-organ, supplies at once both instrument and tune. Thus even the deaf may play, so as to delight the many. Sometimes . . . I have attempted to illustrate the present state of our language, in its relation to literature, by a press-room of larger and smaller stereotype pieces, which in the present anglo-gallican fashion of unconnected, epigrammatic period, it requires but an ordinary portion of ingenuity to vary indefinitely, and yet still produce something, which, if *not* sense, will be so like it, as to do as well. Perhaps better: for it spares the reader the trouble of thinking; prevents vacancy, while it indulges indolence; and secures the memory from all danger of an intellectual plethora. Hence of all trades, literature at present demands the least talent or information; and, of all modes of literature, the manufacturing of poems. The

difference indeed between these and the works of genius, is not less than between an egg, and an egg-shell; yet at a distance they both look alike. (1:38–39)

The shell of literature, easily fabricated and easily consumed, as distinguished from the authentic poetic voice and the holy text is clear enough here. As Coleridge goes on, however, defending genius against vicious critics and manufactured art, he invokes a more complicated and tendentious idea of property, reaching towards mean-spirited reviewers and the reading public in terms they might understand:

> . . . suppose a Review set on foot, the object of which was to criticise all the chief works presented to the public by our ribbon-weavers, calico-printers, cabinet-makers, and china-manufacturers; a Review conducted in the same spirit, and which should take the same freedom with personal character, as our literary journals. They would scarcely, I think, deny their belief, not only that the "genus irritabile" would be found to include many other *species* besides that of bards; but that the irritability of *trade* would soon reduce the resentments of *poets* into mere shadow-fights . . . in the comparison. Or is wealth the only rational object of human interest? Or even if this were admitted, has the poet no property in his works?. . . is the character and property of the individual, who labours for our intellectual pleasure, less entitled to a share of our fellow feelings, than that of the wine-merchant or milliner? . . . (1:38–45)

Property here should not be confused with commodities. Coleridge associates property and poetry at a noble level, and with nineteenth-century "high seriousness" against the reproduceable, the saleable, the "barrel-organ" of mass-constructed art designed by and sold by the deaf to the deaf. In defending genius, he implies a criterion he could expect his "literary republic" to understand. Ideal readers, republican and Christian, knew nothing of themselves if not that their political rights depended on transforming, by means of property, personal into constitutional existence. Rampant commodification of art undermines this mythical constitutional republic—the republic not simply of rights but of culture, which circumscribes both property and poetic taste.

Later on, he invokes this same sense of property in criticizing Wordsworth's theory of poetry, asserting that Wordsworth errs in attributing a privileged sense of language to "rustic life in general." He argues that "manners truly republican" and by implication the power to speak wisely, are produced only in those countries where rural populations (as in Switzerland) "live under forms of property" appropriate to pastoral life (2:44–45). What he has in mind are small familially defined holdings. Wordsworth thought the same, as we see in poems like *Michael*.[6] But his supposed theoretical error was, for Coleridge, fraught with disturbing politica! implications. To dissolve them, he arms his critical vision of commercialism with idealized property. This property is republican without being Jacobin; it implies possession with personal identity; and it makes for the cohesive link in a traditional hierarchy of minds and social classes to counter indiscriminate consumption. When Coleridge speaks of the writer's property, he implicitly claims that for which Dickens would fight so hard a few decades later—rights in a commodity. But Coleridge is less concerned with market rights than with the right not to be abused in one's person by the abuse of one's writing. He uses the word *property* as with an ancient English aura and charges into the market of literary commodities with the insignia of the constitution. The word *property* used to defend literary genius resonates here as it does in sanctioning poetic taste in rural populations. Whether property is a small plot of ground or a sonnet, real estate or literary labor, he suggests it is self-defining property. This archly conservative and yet republican combination of constitutionality and property thus produces a social ideal consonant with the ontological I AM THAT I AM of poetic genius. All this is only touched on in the *Biographia*. But from this point on and ending with *On the Constitution of the Church and State* (1829–30) Coleridge elaborates associations between aesthetic imagination, Hebraic-Christian constitutional continuity, and a Lockean sense of property that has been called possessive individualism.[7]

Or is this political individualism the ground of this romantic I AM? Coleridge would obviously not say so, for he traces an ideological one over the hermeneutical circle of the psychological subject, the I AM out of which all creation flows so that, for him, the two circles blend. Genius, individuality, originality, possessive individualism and organic communality all come together. The political dissolves into the religious and the original textual "voice" of God becomes the ground of all self-consciousness, all the order of constitutional property, and finally the immediate voice by which that Godly voice is rejoined in the ultimate symbol of the complete circle—those poems written by poets filled with the "faculty divine." Property, then, provides him with a local and a universal concept, applied to visionary texts and the works of genius as they exist in books. The implied contrary of poetry as commodity property or goods cannot do this, for commodities carry no such definitional power, no organically constituted social base. Since they can only be exchanged or "consumed" they can never enter into organicism, transcendentalism, or constitutionalism as parts of an inseparable whole. Commodities work against that social whole as merely signs of a sign, things exchanged that stand for new forms of wealth, then validated only by turning it into other commodities or signs of wealth to be exchanged in greater accumulation. Use value, of course, was for Coleridge out of the question when it came to cultural commodities and, of course, he had no theory of mass psychology. The mass, or to use the contemporary term, the *multitude,* swinish or otherwise, was a social formation without a psychology, a constitutional and cultural vacuity.

What Coleridge most disliked was that this new "READING PUBLIC," like all consuming "publics," had power, or at least imaged that commodity exchange which threatened power based on traditional concepts of property. This new commercial power of great numbers of people threatened the "IDEA" of the Constitution. Coleridge's elaboration of the threat was to be variously repeated in nineteenth-century English cultural thinking. The ultimate Coleridgean IDEA images that "one great body" of historical Christendom he speaks of in chapter 16 incorporated in the modern Christian (and, to be sure, Protestant) state, the most important social class of which is the "clerisy," a classless class (anyone is potentially a member) of the intelligentsia, the corresponding contrary of the classless consuming public. But more about this later.

After chapters 5 through 9, where Coleridge has brought his readers through his philosophical ideas, from associationism to idealism, he returns to that reading public and to a direct dialogue with his readers as readers, those at least who have survived chapters 5 through 9. He speaks to the few about the many who now, as in the past, will never understand and never purchase what Coleridge has to say and to sell. This chapter is a farrago of stories, homilies, advice about and diatribes against the publishing trade and periodical literature. Here we read about the financial details of publishing *The Friend,* his journal of 1808–1809, along with the story of his pathetic attempts to sell subscriptions to his political journal of 1795–96, *The Watchman,* a story which Coleridge amusingly tells on himself. We see him, in unforgettably humble guise, travelling from town to town, Unitarian preacher and newspaper salesman, refused by one tradesman to whom he showed his prospectus, with the excuse that he was "over-run with these articles" after having "significantly rubbed and smoothed one part against the other," before putting it into his pocket and retiring into his counting house (1:182). Turning words into merchandised things, that is to say, the turning of his articles into articles and unsaleable ones at that, Coleridge narrates with touching good humor. He was nonetheless deeply affected by these experiences. Popular rejection was, of course, largely his own fault. Reluctant audiences were to be expected when we consider how Coleridge, as R. J. White says "never ceased to speak out loud, if not clear, from somewhere above" their heads.[8] But that others may avoid this pathos, Coleridge recommends, further on, that no young writer ever "PURSUE LITERATURE AS A TRADE." "Money," he says, "and immediate reputation form only an arbitrary and accidental end of literary labor." He caps his warning with a dreamy passage on the rewards of separating writing and selling; it is worth quoting at length to show how much the fantasy of escape from the marketplace could take hold of him:

> My dear young friend (I would say—"suppose yourself established in any honourable occupation. From the manufactory or counting-house, from the law-court, or from having visited your last patient, you return at evening,
>   Dear tranquil time, when the sweet sense of home
>   Is sweetest——
> to your family, prepared for its social enjoyments, with the very countenances of your wife and children brightened and their voice of welcome made doubly welcome, by the knowledge that, as far as *they* are concerned, you have satisfied the demands of the day by the labor of the day. Then, when you retire into your study, in the books on your shelves you revisit so many venerable friends with whom you converse. Your own spirit scarcely less free from personal anxieties than the great minds in those books are still living for you. Even your writing desk with its blank paper and all its other implements will appear as a chain of flowers, capable of linking your feelings as well as thoughts to events and characters past or to come; not a chain of iron which binds you down to think of the future and the remote by recalling the claims and feelings of the peremptory present." (1:223–25)

After this idealization of the writer freed from the literary commodity, chapter 12 provides explanations of the subject and the object, preparing the way for metaphysical explanation of the I AM THAT I AM. And just as we think we are headed for another philosophical bog, there comes the famous self-interruption that stops the text running away with itself and transforms it, the genial utterance, back into its other existence as a book.

Ironically, it is the book as commodity that Coleridge invokes to help himself out of difficulty. He allows his other self, the so-called "friend," to remind Coleridge the genius of hard, economic reality. This fictious friend, wise in the business of books, speaks as an alter ego to the author of a "text." After explaining the compositional reasons why this philosophical business will never do, Coleridge recommends to himself what he previously complains of, the necessity of treating this text as a saleable item:

> This Chapter, which cannot, when it is printed, amount to so little as a hundred pages, will of necessity greatly increase the expense of the work; and every reader who, like myself, is neither prepared or perhaps calculated for the study of so abstruse a subject so abstrusely treated, will, as I have before hinted, be almost entitled to accuse you of a sort of imposition on him. [He further discusses the appropriateness of all this philosophy in a book about his literary life and then writes:] I could add to these arguments one derived from pecuniary motives, and particularly from the probable effects on the sale of your present publication; but they would weigh little with you compared with the preceding. (1:302–03)

Recognizing that his text must survive as a book does not keep the author from straining past that confining shell. The sly reference to the sound economic reason for not finishing his philosophical explanations is almost immediately dismissed, for Coleridge has already put into the mouth of his double, his editorial friend, a description of what he has read to this point. This description has forever transformed the text we are never wholly to see within the book into a supernatural utterance that floats somewhere outside and above the book. The "friend" sets a distance, and shows the practical-minded consumer-reader, dazzled before a magical text with a noble inner being, dark and mysterious, difficult but also fabular, a text impossible to confuse with a commodity. Here is the reader describing what he feels, or what Coleridge would like him to feel in reading this text:

> The effect on my feelings . . . I cannot better represent, than by supposing myself to have known only our light airy modern chapels of ease, and then for the first time to have been placed, and left alone, in one of our largest Gothic cathedrals in a gusty moonlight night of autumn. 'Now in

glimmer, and now in gloom;' often in palpable darkness not without a
chilly sensation of terror; then suddenly emerging into broad yet visionary lengths with coloured shadows, of fantastic shapes yet all decked with
holy insignia and mystic symbols; and ever and anon coming out full
upon pictures and stone-work images of great men, with whose names I
was familiar, but which looked upon me with countenances and an expression, the most dissimilar to all I had been in the habit of connecting
with those names. Those whom I had been taught to venerate as almost
super-human in magnitude of intellect, I found perched in little fret-
work niches, as grotesque dwarfs; while the grotesques, in my hitherto
belief, stood guarding the high altar with all the characters of Apotheosis. In short, what I had supposed substances were thinned away into
shadows, while everywhere shadows were deepened into substances:

If substances may be call'd what shadow seem'd,
For each seem'ed either!

                                             [Milton] (1:300–01)

There is more than a touch of good humor in this accomplished and generally neglected passage of High Romantic Irony.[9] Preserved in this ma-
jestic gibe is the presence of the *Biographia* as a text flawed by abstruseness
and Gothic intertwining in which the reader, as Coleridge well knows, will
easily get lost. Saved in this passage, indeed shrewdly and ironically *auf-
gehoben,* is the text as a supersensual power, presented metaphorically as
a Gothic Cathedral, translating shadow into substance and substance into
shadow. This is the word as transforming power, not as reproduceable
thing, the word in its spiritual textuality, not in its commercial book-ness.

This playful but earnest antagonism in the *Biographia* between text and
book, the Word and mere words, the genial utterance and the saleable
commodity is one narrative result of Coleridge's Christian politics. As I
have already suggested, one of the influential social ideas Coleridge left
to English nineteenth-century thought is that of the *clerisy*. The word did
not survive but the idea thrived in the line of Matthew Arnold all the
way down to T. S. Eliot, in *The Idea of a Christian Society*, and throughout
the cultural criticism of that American critic most valued by the British,
Lionel Trilling. While much has been written about this idea, and despite
the valuable work of Raymond Williams on the ideology of "culture" as
a principle, it is not always clearly understood.[10] To call the idea elitist
—which it is—is not enough. The clerisy or National Church, a class of
the learned who would guide the many, is a notion formed from what

Coleridge sensed to be an important social conflict, which would develop
through the nineteenth and twentieth centuries. I refer to that borne
alongside the classically defined conflict of proletarian and bourgeois, and
which in advanced technological societies is substituted for it—the conflict between educated and mass culture. Two overlapping but distinguish-
able oppositions are at work here—the opposition between social classes
and the opposition between the system of social classes and classlessness.
Coleridge may have, as Olivia Smith argues, invoked the politics of language in the *Biographia* to insist upon a "firm, binary division between
social classes."[11] But just as important in affirming such a division is the
struggle to oppose the wrong kind of classlessness with the right kind.
Both oppositions, in other words, are of similar political import, though
it is the opposition between the classlessness of culture and that of industrial production that will determine cultural discourse from Coleridge on.
Classlessness invited by the commodity always remains a political mirage,
no matter how huge the consuming audience becomes. Still, it is a powerful mirage and Coleridge realized that there was no traditional "social"
class to act as its proper adversary, since commercialism had begun to seep
through all traditional social orders—hence his idealized clerisy. The idea
of a clerisy is, of course, both reactionary and explained by that necessity
Marx implies in *The German Ideology* of all dominant classes to universal-
ize themselves. But it is just as important to see that Coleridge sets the
terms of Romantic engagement with a society of limited but increasing
consumption that are still current and that once deeply affected modernist
and avant-garde engagement with even more pervasive commercialism.

When Lionel Trilling, in a discussion about mass culture, announced
in the early 70s the death of the avant-garde—another historical extension, like the intelligentsia, of the Coleridgean clerisy—that avant-garde,
Trilling says, died because it had lost its imaginative will.

> . . . one of the characteristics of the avant-garde, as we experienced it
> in the 30's, was its continuation of the artistic effort of the 19th century.
> The avant-garde had a profound will to impose itself morally. It wanted
> to change people's sensibility, to change people's view of life. I think this
> can no longer be said. At the present time there is implicit in the concep-
> tion of the avant-garde a certain tendency to say that we are not finally
> serious in the old way. Irony has come in, a devaluation of clear moral-
> izing intention, and with it that diminution of distinction between high
> art and low art which we are so conscious of at the moment.[12]

The terms of Trilling's historical description descend from Coleridge. Admittedly the will, which in Coleridge is a psychological and aesthetical faculty filtered through Arnoldian and Eliotesque patterns, reaches Trilling as an even more self-conscious social will to moral dominance. But the terms by which Romantic imagination would become central to intellectual and avant-garde struggle, and even some of the irony that Trilling takes as the sign of ultimate defeat, are already built into Coleridge's writing, from the *Biographia Literaria* to *On the Constitution of the Church and State*. If Trilling must witness a "diminution of distinction between high art and low art" Coleridge engaged in the early conflict between the two kinds. He recognized that political rights and the classical political order were being subordinated to a new order of commodification and consumption. In sensing that the only ideological response to this was equally idealized "classless" culture, he outlined for the first time what would be taken up, both on the left and the right, as an historically necessary order of intellectuality capable of standing against the new social phenomena of consumption. The secondary Imagination that arises from the ontological I AM THAT I AM demands a presence of will. Central to that will is the idealized self-identity common in visionary texts and impossible in the merely reproduced.

When Coleridge speaks of the "multitudinous PUBLIC, shaped into personal unity by the magic of abstraction, . . . sitting nominal despot on the throne of criticism" he describes what was to become the anonymous culture of the mass to which Trilling conceded historical victory. By the 1970s, the mass audience was not only abstractly, it was so materially unified that some, especially in depressed liberal circles, were willing to say that the avant-garde's and the whole intellectual class's usefulness was at an end, their will dissolved. The importance of the intelligentia has not, however, been given up either by conservative or Western Marxists. And it is Marxists, often popularly and incorrectly seen as cramped economist thinkers, who most seek an intellectual willfulness within dominant technological and mass cultures. From Gramsci in *The Prison Notebooks* to the East German theorist Rudolf Bahro in *The Alternative*, the idea of the organic intellectual class survives, dechristianized but not dissimilar to Coleridge's clerisy, the class of interpreters of texts and the speakers of visionary ideas.[13] It may seem strange to associate ideas nurtured by Coleridge's conservatism and those nurtured in Western Marxism's reaction to both dominant capitalist and Eastern socialist state cultures. Though the politics in these historically separated sets of ideas are profoundly different, some of their cultural strategies are similar because of the continuing shift of the economic and material into the realm of cultural battles. The texts of Coleridge's Christian politics, then, are filled with both dying and prescient ideas. Even Raymond Williams's classic study, *Culture and Society: 1780–1950*, cannot simply describe but must also engage Coleridgean formulas, working out another oppositional and realistic sense of community to counter that overbearing cultural and political maneuver of setting classlessness against the monstrous masses.

The *Biographia* participates in the ideological contradictions of which it is a representative. It is an embodiment of the conflict it describes between text and book, mass audience and intelligentia, the divine Romantic artist and the growing numbers of citizens that would populate what Walter Benjamin would call, though with sanguine expectations, the age of mechanical reproduction. As we have seen, language "mechanized . . . into a barrel-organ" is Coleridge's image of modern mass-produced literature. He saw the implications of this barrel-organ literature and was one of the first in Anglo-American writing to take up a self-conscious position in modern cultural politics. He elaborates, from his traditionalist point of view, a preoccupation reflected by writers who ever after skirmish in running cultural battles. The terms have not changed much, though they are both intensified and diminished in that modernist irony which replaced the transcendent High Romantic kind. Krug, in Nabokov's *Bend Sinister*, for instance, looks down from a window to see two organ-grinders come upon each other "neither of them playing—in fact, both looked depressed and self-conscious," to which he says ". . . it is a very singular picture. An organ grinder is the very emblem of oneness. But here we have an absurd duality." [14] This is the I AM THAT I AM fallen on hard times, wandering the streets and turning a handle on a box—the "very emblem of oneness" in modernist terms, the mechanically reproduced confronting itself as the mechanically reproduced in a shrunken circle of absurdity. The offense offered to unique poetic imagination by its mirrored image in the mechanically reproduced has a long history by now. But Coleridge's comparison of poetry to the vocal reeds of Pan and Apollo has disappeared in the increased pressure upon the "unique." Coleridge's irritable men of genius, like Nabokov, are less irritable today than musing, intensely self-conscious observers of mass culture in which their vocal reeds are only straws in the wind.

The *Biographia* is ideologically tendentious, but also instructive, a kind of writing that, as Jerome McGann suggests, we must see our continuity with and distance from.[15] Looking for a way to the Glory of God by penning sacramental words within mere words, like all Romantics looking for the silent unitary language within language, Coleridge is of another historical moment. And yet, idealist sympathizer of the French Revolution turned imperialist reactionary, he was troubled by and had a fine sense of social contradictions in which we are still embroiled. We thus have no scholarly choice but to try to understand the strategies and the intelligence in that historical place where his holy and fantastical texts struggle with the social reality of his very real books.

Notes

Chapter 1 Editing and Annotating the *Biographia Literaria*

1. *Biographia Literaria*, ed. Henry Nelson Coleridge and Sara Coleridge (London: William Pickering, 1847), 1:xv. All references to editions of the *Biographia* will be cited in the text by volume and page number, with the date of publication.
2. *The Letters of Charles and Mary Lamb*, ed. E. W. Marrs (Ithaca: Cornell University Press, 1975), 1:20.
3. *Collected Letters of Samuel Taylor Coleridge*, 6 vols., ed. Earl Leslie Griggs (Oxford: Clarendon Press, 1956–1971), 6:674–75. Hereafter cited as *CL*.
4. Quoted from James Thorpe, *Principles of Textual Criticism* (San Marino: Huntington Library, 1972), viii.
5. *Memoirs and Letters of Sara Coleridge*, edited by her daughter (London, 1873), 2:40.
6. Sigmund Freud, *Introductory Lectures on Psychoanalysis*, trans. and ed. James Strachey (New York: Norton, 1966), 23.
7. "Preface to Shakespeare," in *Criticism: the Major Texts*, ed. Walter Jackson Bate (New York: Harcourt, Brace, 1952), 212.
8. *The Poetical Works of Samuel Taylor Coleridge*, ed. James Dykes Campbell (London: Macmillan, 1893), 638.
9. *The Notebooks of Samuel Taylor Coleridge*, ed. Kathleen Coburn (New York: Pantheon, 1957–), 1:§§33–36.
10. Christopher North (John Wilson), "Some Observation on the 'Biographia Literaria' of S.T. Coleridge, Esq.," *Blackwood's Edinburgh Magazine* 2 (Oct. 1817):3–18.
11. *The Autobiography of Leigh Hunt*, ed. J.E. Morpurgo (London: The Cresset Press, 1949), 67.
12. *The Works of Charles and Mary Lamb*, 7 vols., ed. E. V. Lucas (London: Methuen, 1903–05), 2:19.
13. Hunt, *Autobiography*, 109.
14. *American Monthly Magazine and Critical Review* (New York, Dec. 1817), 111.
15. *Lay Sermons*, ed. R. J. White, in the *Collected Works of Samuel Taylor Coleridge* (London: Routledge & Kegan Paul; Princeton: Princeton University Press, 1972), 214.
16. *The Complete Poetical Works of Samuel Taylor Coleridge*, 2 vols., ed. Ernest Hartley Coleridge (Oxford: Clarendon Press, 1912), 2:159.

17. *Biographia Literaria*, ed. George Sampson (Cambridge: Cambridge University Press, 1920), 276.

Chapter 2 Coleridge's Book of Moonlight

1. It may also be a direct parody of Coleridge: "My walks therefore were almost daily on the top of Quantock, and among its sloping coombs. With my pencil and memorandum book in my hand, I was *making studies*, as the artists call them, and often moulding my thoughts into verse, with the objects and imagery immediately before my senses. Many circumstances, evil and good, intervened to prevent the completion of the poem. . . ." (1:196).

2. Wordsworth repeatedly emphasizes the importance of the "meditated arrangement of my minor Poems" (1815 *Preface* 140), in the service of a two-fold order: "as composing an entire work within themselves, and as adjuncts to the philosophical Poem, 'The Recluse.' This arrangement has long presented itself habitually to my own mind. Nevertheless, I should have preferred to scatter the contents of these volumes at random, if I had been persuaded that, by the plan adopted, any thing material would be taken from the natural effect of the pieces, individually" (143). There is a useful discussion of some of the connections between Wordsworth's preface and the *Biographia* in Johnston (333–62).

3. Jerome Christensen, building on observations made by Thomas McFarland, and making use of some Derridean insights, has made some interesting observations on the way Coleridge's writing can be seen as taking place in a marginal space, dependent on the existence of a prior text. My views can readily be seen to overlap with his in places, while disagreeing in others. Lawrence Lipking considers the question of "marginalia" (a word apparently invented by Coleridge) in a broad nineteenth-twentieth-century context.

4. In a July letter to R. H. Brabant, Coleridge claims to have written "One long passage—a disquisition on the powers of association, with the History of the Opinions on this subject from Aristotle to Hartley, and on the generic difference between the faculties of Fancy and Imagination . . . as laying the foundation Stones of the Constructive or Dynamic Philosophy in opposition to the merely mechanic—" (*CL* 4:579).

5. The same split impulse hovered over Wordsworth's attempts to write *The Recluse*. As early as 1798 he could posit both "action" and "the excursive power / Of Intellect and thought" as the essential support and ground of "The being that we are" (MS 16, Gill 676–79). As with all projects like *The Prelude* and the *Biographia*, a unified identity is both the base assumption that makes subjective narration possible and that which can only be produced through narration, as demonstrated by the completion of a coherent narrative.

6. Paul Mann, "*The Book of Urizen* and the Horizon of the Book," in *Unnam'd Forms: Blake and Textuality*, ed. Nelson Hilton and Thomas Vogler (Berkeley: University of California Press, 1986), 49–68.

7. "Our language is full of indirect presentations of this sort, in which the expression does not contain the proper schema for the concept, but merely a symbol for reflection. Thus the words *ground* (support, basis), *to depend* (to be held up from above), to *flow* from something (instead of, to follow), *substance* (as Locke expresses it, the support of accidents), and countless others are not schematical but symbolical hypotyposes and expressions for concepts, not by means of a direct intuition, but only by analogy with it, i.e. by the transference of reflection upon an object of intuition to a quite different concept to which perhaps an intuition can never directly correspond" (*Judgment* 198).

8. Neil Saccamano, "Authority and Publication: The Works of 'Swift,'" *The Eighteenth Century* 25.3(Fall 1984):241–62.

9. Santa Cruz Blake Study Group. Review of David V. Erdman, ed. *The Complete Poetry and Prose of William Blake*, in *Blake* 18.1(Summer 1984):4–30.

10. In this they follow Fogle's "Compositional History," showing how conveniently it can be used to "explain" the formal and philosophical shortcomings of the work. In his "Review Essay" Fruman has argued convincingly that these "Philosophical chapters"—and in particular chapter 13—might well have been written earlier and under less trying circumstances than those imagined by Fogle, Engell, and Bate.

11. In giving cumulative page numbers I shall use the Shawcross edition, where the editor's own notes are placed at the end of the text.

12. See David Simpson, in *Irony and Authority*: "What the artist in the primary, authoritarian sense cannot do is presented to the reader as an invitation or temptation, an empty space which he must fill for himself in the cause of kindling his own torch. The central chapters of *Biographia Literaria* seem to me to make some sense in this context" (95).

13. In the year following the publication of the *Biographia*, in his lecture on "Wit and Humour" for the Philosophical Society in London, Coleridge expressed his pleasure in reading *Tristram Shandy*, and his own "acknowledgment of the hollowness and farce of the world." He also challenged the notion that the novel is chaotic, urging that "the digressive spirit [is] not wantonness, but the *very form* of his genius (*CH* 353–56).

14. Cervantes is invoked directly in chapter 21, in the extravaganza where Coleridge develops the image of a "critical machine" which is like the windmills in *Don Quixote*: "Should any literary Quixote find himself provoked by its sounds and regular movements, I should admonish him with Sancho Panza, that it is no giant but a windmill" (2:111).

15. See Brisman (33–37) and Christensen (169–75). The fictitious friend is remarkably like Carlyle's "English Editor" who provides the essential ballast for Teufelsdröckh. Closer to home, he resembles John Morgan conducting his correspondence in furtherance of Coleridge's *Biographia* project. "I am no dreamer, my *facts* are not *ideas* you know" (2:283). "I am no poet no day-dreamer you know" (2:285).

16. "Thus Fontanier in his *Figures du discours*: 'But what can give rise to apostrophe? It can only be feeling, and only the feeling stirred up within the heart

until it breaks out and spreads itself about on the outside, as if acting on its own . . . [as if it were] the spontaneous impulse of a powerfully moved soul!' " (Culler 138).

17. "Substance" here translates Paul's *hypostasis* ("that which stands under"). The meaning seems to be either that things without reality in themselves are made real (given "substance") by faith, or that there are realities for which we have no material evidence, whose real existence we can only know through faith.

18. The effect can be strong enough to provoke assertions of actual existence. Johnston argues that *The Recluse* really does exist as "twenty thousand lines of poetry susceptible of constructive reading," making it as real as works like *The Canterbury Tales* and *The Faerie Queene*. McFarland has argued that Coleridge's *magnum opus* was "not merely a concrete plan dating from a certain period around the year 1815, but an omnipresent reality, even when imperfectly expressed" (*Pantheist*, 194). My own sense of the way these works "existed" is best expressed by Melville's description of Pierre's double writing: "Two books are being writ; of which the world shall only see one, and that the bungled one. The larger book, and the infinitely better, is for Pierre's own private shelf. That it is, whose unfathomable cravings drink his blood; the other only demands his ink. But circumstances have so decreed, that the one can not be composed on the paper, but only as the other is writ down in his soul" (304).

Chapter 3 The Besetting Sins of Coleridge's Prose

1. *The Design of 'Biographia Literaria'* (London: George Allen & Unwin, 1983), chapter 1.
2. *Biographia Literaria*, ed. J. Shawcross, 2 vols (London: Oxford University Press, 1907). Subsequent references to the *Biographia* will be to this edition except where noted, and will be identified by volume and page number only.
3. I document this claim in *The Design of 'Biographia Literaria.'* See note 1, above.
4. Bishop C. Hunt, Jr., "Coleridge and the Endeavor of Philosophy," *PMLA* 91(1976):829–39.
5. Thomas DeQuincey, *DeQuincey's Collected Writings*, ed. David Masson, 2nd ed. (Edinburgh: Adam & Charles Black, 1889–90), vol. 2, 152–53.
6. See Thomas Carlyle, *Life of John Sterling*, in *The Works of Thomas Carlyle* (New York: Charles Scribner's Sons, 1897), vol. 11, 56.
7. The best I know on Coleridge's idea of history is Robert Preyer, *Bentham, Coleridge, and the Science of History*, Beiträge zur englischen Phil., 41. Heft. (Bochum-Langendreer: H. Poppinghaus, 1958). See also the debate between Rene Wellek and Thomas McFarland: Rene Wellek, "Coleridge," in *A History of Modern Criticism*, vol. 2, 151–87; Thomas McFarland, *Coleridge and the Pantheist Tradition* (Oxford: Clarendon Press, 1969); and Wellek's review of McFarland's book in *Comparative Literature* 22(1970):282–86.
8. See Thomas McFarland, "The Origin and Significance of Coleridge's Theory of Secondary Imagination," in *New Perspectives on Coleridge and Wordsworth*, ed.

Geoffrey Hartman (New York: Columbia University Press, 1972), 195–246. There is of course a considerable number of scholarly works attempting to define the originality and the origins of Coleridge's distinctions.

9. See *The Design of 'Biographia Literaria'* (above, note 1), 68–74 and following.
10. See *The Design of 'Biographia Literaria'* (above, note 1), chapter 5, esp. page 75.
11. *Biographia Literaria*, ed. James Engell & W. Jackson Bate, *The Collected Works of Samuel Taylor Coleridge*, vol. 7 (Princeton: Princeton University Press, 1983), 296,n.1.
12. George Watson, ed. *Biographia Literaria* (London: Everyman Library, 1965), 161,n.2.

Chapter 4 Coleridge and the Language of Adam

1. A view succinctly set forth by Agrippa von Nettesheim ("as [Adam] named any thing, so the name of it was, which names indeed contain in them wonderfull powers of the things signified," 153), by Kircher (see esp. p. 145 on the unity of Adamic names and the nature of the things they refer to), by Vico ("the sacred language invented by Adam, to whom God granted divine onomathesia, the giving of names to things according to the nature of each," 127), and by Warburton ("the most generally received [reading of Genesis 2:19–20], tho', perhaps, as groundless as any, is, that Adam gave every Creature a Name expressive of its Nature," 2:82). Foucault (36) offers similar observations on theories about the original "transparency" of language and its division into many tongues incompatible with one another "only in so far as they had previously lost this original resemblance to the things that had been the prime reason for the existence of language. All the languages known to us are now spoken only against the background of this lost similitude and in the space that it left vacant."
2. Cohen (21) proposes a similar division, but based on slightly different criteria. The distinction I adopt follows Todorov's differentiation of "the motivated (natural)" sign from the "unmotivated" (228). This distinction between the two schools is of course not absolute, as demonstrated by Webster's praise of Boehme's theory of divine "signatures" linking Adam's language to creation (26). For good historical surveys of the idea of linguistic motivation, see Genette, who concentrates on French texts, and McKusick (4–13).
3. The study of Egyptian hieroglyphics as motivated pictographs (for example in Warburton) is another manifestation of the same interest in ideal modes of signification.
4. Derrida has characterized the *"episteme"* of this kind of "science" as "an algebrizing, de-poetizing formulation whose operation is to repress—in order to master it better—the charged [i.e., motivated or polysemous?] signifier or the linked hieroglyph" (*Of Grammotology* 285).
5. Land's study documents this shift from a concentration on the structure of individual signs to the structure of sentences in the eighteenth century.

Slaughter convincingly demonstrates the importance of taxonomy to rationalist linguistics. Hers is the most philosophically perceptive study of seventeenth-
century language theories. Perhaps the first to see the basic thrust of Wilkins'
system was Jones, who in 1769 criticized "the arbitrary, real characters of Dr.
Wilkins and others" (11) as part of his argument for English as a universal
language.

6. Compare, for example, the views of de Mott and the reactions to them in
Salmon, esp. p. 153 note 4.

7. *Aids to Reflection*, 168–69. See also Coleridge's comment of March 13, 1827,
that "a Pun will sometimes facilitate explanation," which he then exemplifies
with an English pun and a Hebrew etymology (*Table Talk* 43). In Coleridge's
day, etymological studies consisted mainly of strings of puns directed by some
a priori notion of the origin of language—see, for example, Jacob Bryant's *A
New System, or, An Analysis of Ancient Mythology* (1774–76), and Horne Tooke,
The Diversions of Purley (1786–1805). For the latter's influence on Coleridge,
see McKusick, p. 33–52.

8. See Coleridge's letter to James Gillman of October 22, 1826: "For (as I have
long ago observed to you) it is the fundamental Mistake of Grammarians
and Writers on the philosophy of Grammar and Language [to assume] that
words and their syntaxis are the immediate representatives of *Things*, or that
they correspond to *Things*. Words correspond to thoughts; and the legitimate
Order & Connection of words to the *Laws* of Thinking and to the acts and
affections of the Thinker's mind" (*Letters* 6:60; see also 6:817). The Lockean view, however, does not answer the question of *how* reference comes into
being within the internal dynamics of the sign and makes no distinction, of
the sort Coleridge found so essential, between lower (arbitrary) and higher
(motivated) modes of referentiality.

9. *Die Kunstlehre* in *Kritische Schriften und Briefe*, 7 vols., ed. Edgar Lohner (Stutt-
gart:Kohlhammer 1963–74), 1:239. Compare Schlegel's "natural signs" with
Boehme's description of Adamic speech as "the language of Nature" (3:80).

10. See for example Wellek (*History* 2:175): "In his practical criticism Coleridge
rarely uses the term 'symbol.'" The point has been most recently reiterated by
Mileur (21–22), who summarizes de Man's view (the validity of which I argue
for herein) that there are no true symbols in "any actual act of Romantic figuration," but (quite rightly) questions de Man's conclusion that "the notion of
the symbol was a self-deceiving mystification." McKusick's fine general study
of Coleridge's linguistic concepts makes only passing references to the idea of
symbol.

11. *CN* 3:3587. Christensen (*Blessed Machine* 19) further defines and uses the term
as "the necessary artifice" and "enabling figure that makes fiction as well as
philosophy conceivable."

12. Wellek (*History* 174) suggests that Coleridge's "sail" example is fallacious, but
does not say why. Culler (263) quite correctly calls Coleridge's symbol a "motivated sign," but then equates this with "a synecdoche."

13. Todorov (137–45, 177–83) briefly summarizes the theories of motivated figu-

ration and "imitation" in Lessing, Herder, A. W. Schlegel, and Friedrich Ast (whose notion of charged and spiritualized synecdoche, published in 1808, bears some interesting similarities to Coleridge's symbol).

14. For Coleridge's distinction between "copy" and "imitation," see *Biographia* 1:cv–vi, 2:72 and note 4. His somewhat scattered definitions of the latter term indicate that it is yet another variant on the attempt to claim a motivated relationship between poetry and nature, but one which takes cognizance of inescapable differences between them.

15. See particularly the note Coleridge added in 1829: "What is an Idea in the Subject, i.e., in the Mind, is a Law in the Object, i.e., in Nature" (*Friend* 1:497).

16. See Exodus 3:13–14 and Byron's play on these words in *Don Juan* canto 1, stanza 14.

17. See also Coleridge's letter of September 16, 1829, to Hyman Hurwitz: "Pro-thesis [,] i.e. the identity or co-inherence of Act and Being of which there is and there can be but one perfect Instance—viz. The Eternal I AM, who *is* by his own *act*—who affirms himself to *be* in that he is; and who *is*, in that he *affirms* himself to be. But the Image & Representative of himself is the personal Identity, the 'I am' of every self-conscious Spirit" (*CL* 6:816–17).

18. See for example the selections from Vico, Herder, and Karl Moritz in Feldman and Richardson 58, 229, 264–65. The theory was perpetuated into the nineteenth century by eclectic mythographers such as Davies, who mixed together his primitivist notions about Celtic bards and Druids with a reading of Genesis 2:19 and a belief (somewhat like Boehme's) that fragments of original, motivated language lie hidden in modern tongues. He claims, for example, that "all expressions of the human voice . . . are not, therefore, as many have supposed, mere imitations of that which has been heard,—or unconnected with ideas of things, and of their natural affinities" (368).

19. 1:160. Wordsworth repeats this motivated/arbitrary distinction in the "Essay on Epitaphs" when he contrasts words which are "an incarnation of the thought" and those which are "only a clothing for it" (2:84).

20. *Mysterium Magnum*; Boehme 3:204. See also Coleridge's warnings about the burial of "faith . . . in the dead letter" in comments prelusive to his definition of "symbol" (*Statesman's Manual* 30).

Chapter 6 Coleridge, Habit, and the Politics of Vision

1. S. T. Coleridge, *Biographia Literaria*, ed. James Engell and W. Jackson Bate (Princeton: Princeton University Press, 1983), 1:80–81. All further quotations will be from this edition and appear in the text.

2. Shelley, Bate and Engell note, employs a similar image in "The Defense of Poetry": "Poetry . . . purges from our inward sight the film of familiarity which obscures from us the wonder of being."

3. Wordsworth repeatedly speaks in *The Prelude* of the "despotism," the "tyranny" of eye, like Coleridge responding against the inescapable materialism and

empiricism of optics. "We are restless," writes Coleridge, "because invisible things are not the objects of vision" (1:107).

4. See James K. Chandler, *Wordsworth's Second Nature* (Chicago: University of Chicago Press, 1984).

5. James Beattie in "Of Imagination," in *The Elements of Moral Science* from *The Philosophical and Critical Works* (New York: G. Olms Verlag, 1974), 3:110, writes, "Custom or habit is a very extensive principle of association. . . ." He then goes on to discuss the obvious virtues of custom, but is also interested in the ossification of habits which originate in "some perverse association": "It should be our care to guard against these and the like absurd habits, and to be very thankful to those who caution us against them . . ." (3:113). Beattie, it may be noted, like Hume, also uses "habit" and "custom" interchangeably.

6. Thomas McFarland, *Coleridge and the Pantheist Tradition*, (Oxford: Clarendon Press, 1969), 157ff.

7. Ernst Cassirer, *The Philosophy of the Enlightenment*, trans. Koelln and Pettegrove (New Jersey: Princeton University Press, 1951), 108–09.

8. John Locke, *An Essay Concerning Human Understanding*, ed. A. C. Fraser (New York: Dover, 1959), 1:186–87. All further quotations will be from this edition and appear in the text.

9. There may be another reason behind Locke's "no": a "yes" raises the specter of an innate idea, some common proto-idea that bridges visual and tactual ideas and precedes the sense data of each. J. L. Mackie's *Problems from Locke* (London: Oxford, 1976), 30, discusses this possibility, and Michael J. Morgan, *Molyneux's Question* (Cambridge: Cambridge University Press, 1977), p. 7, takes Locke's "no" as a defense of his position against innate ideas. Fraser's note refers to Reid and Leibniz. The latter disagrees with Locke's solution, and "concludes that if the born-blind man had known beforehand, by touch only, that the cube and the globe were there, he could *at once*, when he recovered sight, distinguish them by reason, in combination with the sensuous data of touch; because otherwise a born-blind man could not learn the rudiments of geometry by touch only, as he is able to do" (1:186–87).

10. For a brief account of those experiments, such as the Cheselden experiment, see for instance M. J. Morgan, *Molyneux's Question* (1977). The effect upon the newly sighted person of suddenly being able to see was often anything but happy. To the contrary he or she was bewildered and depressed (Addison has an account of one such person) because the neurological pathways that had been established by the blind person have now become a mass of confusion owing to the addition of sight. J. Z. Young, a contemporary neurologist, offers in *Doubt and Certainty* an excellent explanation of the physiological disruption.

11. One wonders if Locke did not possess some uncanny ability to visualize abstractions. Berkeley, in addition to Hume, taxes Locke with the fantasy of his abstractions: how is it possible, Berkeley wonders, for us to picture as Locke insists we can a triangle that is not equilateral, scalene, or isosceles—yet still a triangle?

12. Berkeley would argue that our saying, "I hear a garbage truck," is utterly false

to the actual experience. In reality I hear the roar of a large motor (a sound which in itself is not necessarily an engine, but a deep-throated sound that resembles what I know to be that emitted by engines), I hear the whining groan of something I associate with the sound garbage trucks make as they pick up and then press down the rubbish, etc. But perhaps most important, it happens that the trash collectors are regular. This is Wednesday, 5:30 A.M., the very hour and day I am accustomed to hearing the garbage truck. Were I near the Indianapolis Speedway and hearing the same sounds, I would not suppose I was about to watch a garbage truck race.

13. Michel de Montaigne, "Of Experience," *The Complete Essays of Montaigne*, trans. Donald M. Frame (Stanford: Stanford University Press, 1948), 827.

14. David Hume, *A Treatise of Human Nature*, ed. L. A. Selby-Bigge, rev. P. H. Nidditch (Oxford: Oxford University Press, 1978), 652. This quotation comes from the "Abstract" Hume composed; but section II, "Of scepticism with regard to the senses," Book I, provides abundant proof of Hume's conviction that "all reasoning concerning matters of fact arises only from custom, and custom can only be the effect of repeated perceptions. . . ," 198.

15. Isaiah Berlin, "Hume and the Sources of German Anti-Rationalism," in *Against the Current* (New York: Penguin Books, 1982), 162–63.

16. This is a most important concept to Locke—that of "assent" or "consent" to reasonable ideas—and appears throughout the early chapters of the *Essay*. In its broad inclusiveness and general optimism, it has obvious political implications.

17. Hume writes: "Our imagination has a great authority over our ideas; and there are no ideas that are different from each other, which it cannot separate, and join, and compose into all varieties of fiction. But notwithstanding the empire of the imagination, there is a secret tie or union among particular ideas, which causes the mind to conjoin them more frequently together, and makes the one, upon its appearance, introduce the other . . . hence the connection of writing: and hence that thread or chain of thought." The "secret tie" is association, consisting of resemblance, contiguity, and causation: ". . . as these are the only ties of our thoughts, they are really *to us* the cement of the universe . . ." (662). The emphasis here upon a universe of unrelated particulars ("everything that exists, is particular") that the mind must "compose" has an obvious bearing not only each act of perception, which insists upon composition, but upon poetry as an extension of perception. Coleridge's position is in some ways contradictory. Although inalterably opposed to Locke and Hume, he yet sharply—and I think unfairly—criticizes Wordsworth for claiming in the Intimations Ode that the child is an eye among the blind, a great seer—in both senses—and a prophet. To Coleridge this is an egregious instance of "thoughts and images too great for the subject . . . an approximation to what might be called *mental bombast* . . ." (2:136ff). Coleridge seems coyly unknowing here: "In what sense is a child of that age a *philosopher*? In what sense does he *read* "the eternal deep"? . . . Children at this age give us no information of themselves; and at what time were we dipt in the Lethe, which has

produced utter oblivion of a state so godlike?" Coleridge seems to play the philosophical redneck here, forgetting his own strictures about the relation between childhood vision and poetic genius.

18. Thomas Burnet, *The Sacred Theory of the Earth* (Carbondale: Southern Illinois University Press, 1965), 15. This is not the work by Burnet from which Coleridge takes the motto (which comes from *Archaeologiae Philosophicae*), but one Coleridge so admired he once contemplated making of it some sort of verse translation.

19. The translation I am using, as well as the "The Rime of the Ancient Mariner," appear in *English Romantic Writers*, ed. David Perkins (New York: Harcourt, Brace & World, 1967), 404–13.

20. For a somewhat different and thoroughly absorbing treatment of "rime," see "The Riming Mariner and the Mariner Rimed" in Arden Reed's *Romantic Weather* (Hanover: University Presses of New England, 1983).

21. It should be said in regard to my point about individual or particular as opposed to class or mass that Coleridge takes for a moment a different view at the end of chapter 7 of the *Biographia*. There, arguing for how one might achieve a proper memory without resorting to *memoria technica* or artificial memory, he suggests a temperamental disposition of mind: "Sound logic, as the habitual subordination of the individual to the species, and of the species to the genus . . ." is the first recommendation he makes for the intellect. Although Bate and Engell suggest this notion of subordination of the individual to the species is by then "a *leitmotif* in German philosophy" and that Coleridge is aligning himself with the notion that "when the individual becomes truly aware and creative he submerges himself in the species," I suspect that Coleridge is here thinking less in the grand political and cultural terms Bate and Engell suggest than in merely logical and mechanical ones. His use of "habitual," normally not a positive word, would support the point. Also, he concludes his recipe for a good memory with some physiological recommendations, "sound health, and above all (as far as this relates to passive remembrance) a healthy digestion; these are the best, these are the only ARTS OF MEMORY" (1:128).

22. Perkins, 491. Coleridge says in "On Poesy or Art," "The primary art is writing. . . . First, there is mere gesticulation; then rosaries or *wampum;* then picture-language; then hieroglyphics, and finally alphabetic letters."

23. Perkins, 495.

24. Perkins, 492. In a formulation reminiscent of Berkeley, Coleridge writes: "nature itself is to a religious observer the art of God. . . . Hence nature itself would give us the impression of a work of art, if we could see the thought which is present at once in the whole and in every part; and a work of art will be just in proportion as it adequately conveys the thought, and rich in proportion to the variety of parts it holds in unity."

25. William Wordsworth, "Preface of 1815," *The Prose Works of William Wordsworth*, ed. Owen and Smyser (London: Oxford, 1974), 3:32–33.

26. John Ruskin, *The Seven Lamps of Architecture* (New York: Noonday Press,

1961), 143. Ruskin goes on about our mind's groaning beneath the weight of "thoughts . . . brittle, obstinate, and icy, which can neither bend nor grow. . . . All men are liable in some degree to be frost-bitten . . . have no clear consciousness of what is around them, or with them; blind to the one, insensible to the other. . . . I would not press the definition into its darker application to the dull heart and heavy ear; I have to do with it only as it refers to the too frequent condition of rural existence, whether of nations or of individuals, settling commonly upon them in proportion to their age."

27. Friedrich Nietzsche, *The Birth of Tragedy* and *The Genealogy of Morals*, trans. Francis Golffing (New York: Doubleday Anchor, 1956), *The Genealogy of Morals*, "First Essay," i, 158. With further reference to utilitarianism, Nietzsche later remarks upon "the custom character of morals": "With the help of custom and the social strait-jacket, man was, in fact, made calculable" (190–91).

28. Walter Pater, *The Renaissance* in *Selected Writings of Walter Pater*, ed. H. Bloom (New York: Columbia University Press, 1974), 60.

29. Pater, "Coleridge," *Appreciations*, in *Selected Writings*; Bloom, 166–67.

Chapter 7 Coleridge and Energy

1. *The Complete Poetical Works of Samuel Taylor Coleridge*, ed. Ernest Hartley Coleridge, 2 vols. (Oxford: Oxford University Press, 1912), 1:111, 1.49. Subsequent references to *PW* will appear in the text of the essay).

2. The clearest articulation of this position occurs in the famous passage on the imagination in the *Biographia Literaria*. See *Biographia Literaria* ed. J. Shawcross, 2 vols. (London: Oxford University Press, 1907), 1:202.

3. Sir Philip Sidney, *Defense of Poesy*, ed. Lewis Soens (Lincoln: University of Nebraska Press, 1970), 10, provides a context for Coleridge's idea. Sidney enjoins his reader to give "right honor to the heavenly Maker of that maker [i.e., poet], who, having made man to his own likeness, set him beyond and over all the works of that second [i.e., postlapsarian] nature, which in nothing he shows so much as in poetry. . . ."

4. See Thomas McFarland, *Coleridge and the Pantheist Tradition* (Oxford: Clarendon, 1969), 184–84, 189–90.

5. *The Table Talk and Omniana of Samuel Taylor Coleridge*, ed. T. Ashe (London: George Bell and Sons, 1888). I have followed the convention of citing this edition for the convenience of the users of other editions—i.e., by date of entry rather than by page.

6. *Ibid.*

7. *Biographia*, ed. Shawcross, 1:202.

8. *The Friend*, ed. Barbara Rooke, 2 vols., in *The Collected Works of Samuel Taylor Coleridge*, ed. Kathleen Coburn, vol. 4 (Princeton: Princeton University Press, 1969), 1:467n.

9. *Biographia*, ed. Shawcross, 1:202.

10. Thomas Carlyle, "Signs of the Times," in *Thomas Carlyle: Sartor Resartus and Selected Prose*, ed. Herbert Sussman (New York: Holt, Rinehart and Winston, 1970), 16. Plate 4 of Blake's *The Marriage of Heaven and Hell* (1790–93) concludes with the observation that "Energy is Eternal Delight." In Book I of *The Prelude* (1805), Wordsworth expresses concern that an access of authentic inspiration has turned into "A tempest, a redundant energy / Vexing its own creation" (ll. 46–47). In "On Locke's 'Essay of the Human Understanding'" (1810–11?), Hazlitt talks of "the pervading and elastic energy" of the mind. In the *Essay on Christianity* (1815–19?), Shelley describes God as "the overruling Spirit of the collective energy of the moral and material world," *Shelley's Prose in the Bodleian Manuscripts*, 17. Keats argues, in the long letter of February 14– May 3, 1819, to his brother and sister-in-law in America, that "though a quarrel in the streets is a thing to be hated, the energies displayed in it are fine. . . ." If the word *energy* is not found in Byron, the concept most certainly is.

11. Morton D. Paley, *Energy and Imagination in the Development of Blake's Thought* (Oxford: Clarendon, 1970), 3–4.

12. Thomas Young, *A Course of Lectures on Natural Philosophy and the Mechanical Arts*, 2 vols. (1807; rpt. London: Taylor and Walton, 1845), 1:59–60. "The term energy may be applied . . . to the product of the mass or weight of a body, into the square of the number expressing its velocity. This product has been denominated by the living or ascending force [the *vis viva*], since the height of a body's vertical ascent is in proportion to it . . . but although this opinion has been very universally rejected, yet the force thus estimated well deserves a distinct denomination."

13. Richard Saumarez, *The Principles of Physiological and Physical Science; Comprehending the Ends for Which Animated Beings Were Created; and an Examination of the Unnatural and Artificial Means of Philosophy Which Now Prevail* (London: R. Edwards for T. Egerton, 1812), 41.

14. Coleridge, *Biographia*, 1:104n.

15. Loyd S. Swenson, *The Genesis of Relativity: Einstein in Context* (New York: Burt Franklin, 1979); and Stephen J. Gould, *Ontogeny and Phylogeny* (Cambridge, Mass.: Belknap, 1977), are exemplary for their insightful analysis of the politics that distort both the development of science and the history of that development in the fields of physical theory and genetic theory, respectively.

16. I am, of course, summarizing the scenario developed by Thomas S. Kuhn, *The Structure of Scientific Revolutions*, 2nd ed. (Chicago: University of Chicago Press, 1970). Fritjof Capra, *The Turning-Point: Science, Society and the Rising Culture* (New York: Simon and Schuster, 1982), argues that it is only in the twentieth century—and especially in the second half of the century—that the Newtonian paradigms that have ruled scientific disciplines and technologies other than physics have been replaced by more nearly Einsteinian paradigms.

17. Kuhn himself makes this point in "Mathematical Versus Experimental Traditions in the Development of Physical Science," reprinted in *The Essential Tension: Selected Studies in Scientific Tradition and Change* (Chicago: University of Chicago Press, 1977), 31–65, esp. 32–33.

18. Gerald Holton, *The Thematic Origins of Scientific Thought: Kepler to Einstein* (Cambridge, Mass.: Harvard University Press, 1973); and *The Scientific Imagination: Case Studies* (Cambridge: Cambridge University Press, 1978).

19. Abraham Rees, *The Cyclopaedia; or, Universal Dictionary of Arts, Sciences, and Literature*, 45 vols. (London: Longman, Hurst Rees, Orme, and Brown, 1819–20), 29, s. v. *Quakers*. Rees accounts Quakerism "remarkable for asserting the continuance, up to the present time, of immediate revelation, or the communication of divine instruction to the mind, by the testimony of the Spirit of God. This revelation . . . neither does nor can contradict the outward testimony of the scriptures, or right and sound reason."

20. Richard Saumarez, *A New System of Physiology, Comprehending the Laws by Which Animated Beings in General, and the Human Species in Particular, Are Governed, in Their Several States of Health and Disease*, 2 vols. (London: J. Johnson, 1798), 2:9–10, ch. 1.

21. See Trevor H. Levere, *Poetry Realized in Nature: Samuel Taylor Coleridge and Early Nineteenth-Century Science* (Cambridge: Cambridge University Press, 1981), 80, 157.

22. *Collected Letters of Samuel Taylor Coleridge*, ed. Earl Leslie Griggs, 6 vols. (Oxford: Clarendon, 1956–71), 2:709. Letter of March 23, 1801, to Poole.

23. Levere, *Poetry Realized in Nature*, 6.

24. Richard Rorty, *Philosophy and the Mirror of Nature* (Princeton: Princeton University Press, 1979), 131, argues for these assumptions, as philosophical assumptions, originating with Hobbes and Descartes, who "were fighting (albeit discreetly) to make the intellectual world safe for Copernicus and Galileo. They did not think of themselves as offering 'philosophical systems,' but as contributing to the efflorescence of research in mathematics and mechanics, as well as liberating intellectual life from ecclesiastical institutions." Paul Magnuson, *Coleridge's Nightmare Poetry* (Charlottesville: University Press of Virginia, 1974), 27, discusses the impact of Berkeley's *Siris* on Coleridge in 1796. Magnuson argues that Coleridge's self-proclaimed Berkeleian sympathies are for Berkeley's belief in the priority of soul or mind over body as a condition of ontology and epistemology alike. McFarland, *The Pantheist Tradition*, ch. 2 ("The Spinozistic Crescendo"), 53–106, elaborates the distinction between the "I am" and the "it is."

25. Aristotle, *The "Art" of Rhetoric, with an English Translation*, tr. John Henry Freese (1926; rpt. Cambridge, Mass.: Harvard University Press, 1959), 405, 407.

26. Lvs. 8r–8v. ll.342–78 (Bodleian Library Copy).

27. See my "The Re-Emergence of Energy in the Discourse of Literature and Science," *Annals of Scholarship* 4:1 (Fall 1986): 22–53.

28. See for example Elizabeth Hamilton, *Memoirs of Modern Philosophers*, 3 vols. (London: C., G., and J. Robinson, 1800), 2:19–20. Hamilton, who served Anglican orthodoxy long and well, writing a number of books of religious instruction, rated a monument to her memory, erected at Harrogate Church, where she was buried in 1816. Her orthodox, anti-energy stance comes

through in an exchange between Myope and Vallaton, the former playing
Pangloss to the latter's Candide: "'Happy it had been for the world, if not
only your arm, but every bone in your body had been broken, so that it had
been the means of furnishing mankind with a proof of the perfectibility of
philosophical energy!'" For more on Hamilton, see *DNB* 24:147–48.

29. Sermon 85, *Sermons on Several Occasions*, in *The Works of the Reverend John Wesley,
A.M.*, 14 vols. (London: Wesleyan Conference Office, 1872), 6:508.

30. *The Theological and Miscellaneous Works of Joseph Priestley, LL.D., F. R. S., &c.*,
ed. John Towill Rutt, 23 vols. (London: G. Smallfield, 1817–20), 4:20.

31. Levere, *Poetry Realized in Nature*, 6.

32. "Prospectus" to *The Excursion*, 1.55, in the *Poetical Works of William Wordsworth*,
ed. Ernest de Selincourt and Helen Darbishire, 5 vols. (Oxford: Clarendon,
1949), 5:2.

33. See M. H. Abrams, *Natural Supernaturalism: Tradition and Revolution in Romantic
Literature* (New York: Norton, 1971), 95ff., 197ff.

34. M. H. Abrams, "Coleridge's 'A Light in Sound': Science, Metascience, and
Poetic Imagination," *PAPS* 116 (1972), 458–75, esp. pp. 459–60. Speaking
of "The Eolian Harp," with its idea of "the one Life within us and abroad"
(*CPW*, 1, 101, 1.26), Abrams notes that "Coleridge suggested in several other
poems written at the time of 'The Eolian Harp' that there is in nature an
indwelling cause of the organization and consciousness of all individual exis-
tents."

35. "Dear Reynolds, as Last Night I Lay in Bed" ("Epistle to John Hamilton Reynolds"), ll. 76–77, in *John Keats: Complete Poems*, ed. Jack Stillinger (Cambridge, Mass.: Belknap, 1982), 181. Timothy Corrigan, *Coleridge, Language,
and Criticism* (Athens: University of Georgia Press, 1982), 169, notes that "the
function of the will in both its divine and human forms" is a salient concern for
Coleridge in the 1820's. Jean-Pierre Mileur, *Vision and Revision: Coleridge's Art
of Immanence* (Berkeley and Los Angeles: University of California Press, 1982),
20–21, discusses the tendency of the creative will, acting through the medium
of the symbol to produce allegory, towards self-abstraction and meanings "not
of this world."

36. Laurence S. Lockridge, *Coleridge the Moralist* (Ithaca, NY: Cornell University
Press, 1977), 62. Anthony John Harding, *Coleridge and the Idea of Love: Aspects of Relationship in Coleridge's Thought and Writing* (Cambridge: Cambridge
University Press, 1974), 31, discusses the fact that Coleridge "never lost his
childhood fascination with the products of his own mind. . . ."

37. Rorty, *Philosophy*, 17–69, esp. p. 35 ("The Invention of the Mind"), focuses
on the problem of consciousness. His list, on p. 35, of the "features which
philosophers have, at one time or another, taken as marks of the mental," contains several that were also of importance to Coleridge. These include "ability
to know itself incorrigibly ('privileged access')," "ability to grasp universals,"
"ability to sustain relations to the inexistent ('intentionality')," and "ability to
act freely."

38. McFarland, *The Pantheist Tradition*, 32, quoting *Collected Letters*, 4, 792, dis-

cusses the likelihood that Coleridge formed his opinions before reading the German philosophers, especially Fichte, Schelling, and their followers.

39. Mileur, *Vision and Revision*, viii.
40. Jerome Christensen, *Coleridge's Blessed Machine of Language* (Ithaca: Cornell University Press, 1981), 265, talks of Coleridge's "anxiety about origins."
41. See McFarland, *The Pantheist Tradition*, 193–94, 228–29, 233, 234.
42. Rorty, *Philosophy*, 35.
43. *The Complete Works of Samuel Taylor Coleridge*, 7 vols., ed. W. G. T. Shedd. (New York: Harper and Brothers, 1853), 1, 195–96.
44. See Rorty, *Philosophy*, 65; and E. A. Burtt, *The Metaphysical Foundations of Modern Physical Science* (Garden City, N.Y.: Doubleday, 1955), ch. 4, esp. p. 117. The Cartesian "move" is what Husserl objects to under the rubric of "the mathematization of nature."
45. Dorothy Emmet, "Coleridge on Powers in Mind and Nature," in *Coleridge's Variety: Bicentenary Studies*, ed. John Beer (Pittsburgh: University of Pittsburgh Press, 1974), 166–82, esp. p. 167.
46. Coleridge, *Biographia*, ed. Shawcross, 1:197–98.
47. Mileur, *Vision and Revision*, 5.
48. Richard Olson, *Scottish Philosophy and British Physics, 1750–1880* (Princeton: Princeton University Press, 1975), 4, 174–77. Levere, *Poetry Realized in Nature*, p. 157, notes Coleridge's acquaintance with Young's work on light.
49. Levere, ibid., 154.
50. As cited in Levere, ibid. The shape of the pentad brings to mind Thomas Browne's discussion of the Quincunx and its significance in *The Garden of Cyrus*.
51. See Newton, *Mathematical Principles of Natural Philosophy and His System of the World*, trans. Andrew Motte, rev. Florian Cajori (Berkeley: University of California Press, 1934), 399.
52. *Paradise Lost*, 1, 45–85, as printed in *John Milton: Complete Poems and Major Prose*, ed. Merritt Y. Highes (New York: Odyssey, 1957), 212–13. Subsequent references to *Paradise Lost*, by book and line numbers, will be to this edition and will appear in the text of the essay.
53. Julia L. Epstein and Mark L. Greenberg, "Decomposing Milton's Rainbow," *JHI* 45:1 (1984), 115–40, discuss the way that the poets appropriated the Newtonian account of the rainbow and turned it against Newton and Newtonian thought. The importance of the rainbow for the Wordsworth-Coleridge circle is suggested by a poem like Wordsworth's "My Heart Leaps Up" (1802).
54. Cf. *Adonais*, 11. 462–64, in *Shelley's Poetry and Prose: Authoritative Texts, Criticism*, ed. Donald H. Reiman and Sharon B. Powers (New York: Norton, 1977), 405.

> Life, like a dome of many-coloured glass,
> Stains the white radiance of Eternity,
> Until Death tramples it to fragments.

55. Discussed in McFarland, *The Pantheist Tradition*, 203–05.

56. See my "Blake and Newton: Argument as Art, Argument as Science," in *Studies in Eighteenth-Century Culture* 10 (1980): 205–26.
57. *The Prelude* (1805 version), Book 13, ll. 442–52, as printed in *Wordsworth's Prelude*, ed. Ernest de Selincourt, rev. Helen Darbishire, 2nd ed. (Oxford: Clarendon, 1959).
58. For a discussion of this structure, see Leslie Brisman, *Romantic Origins* (Ithaca, NY: Cornell University Press, 1978), ch. 1, 21–54.
59. See the "Prospectus" to *The Excursion*, as cited in note 32 above.
60. McFarland, *The Pantheist Tradition*, 53.

Chapter 8 Perception and "the heaven-descended KNOW-THYSELF"

1. Kant, *Kritik der reinen Vernunft* B (= 2nd ed., 1787) 68, 131–40 (§§ 16–18); in *Werke*, ed. Wilhelm Weichsedel (Darmstadt: Wissenschaftliche Buchgesellschaft, 1956; 4th ed., 1975), II. Subsequent references given parenthetically (§ or B) in text.
2. Rene Wellek, *Immanuel Kant in England, 1793–1838* (Princeton: Princeton University Press, 1931); Gian Orsini, *Coleridge and German Idealism* (Carbondale: Southern Illinois University Press, 1969); Norman Fruman, *Coleridge, the Damaged Archangel* (New York, 1971); Thomas MacFarland, *Coleridge and the Pantheist Tradition* (Oxford: Clarendon Press, 1969); MacFarland, "Coleridge's Plagiarisms Once More: A Review Essay," *The Yale Review* 63 (Winter, 1974): 252–86. Thorough cross-reference is provided in the Engell-Bate edition cited below.
3. *Biographia Literaria*, ed. James Engell and W. Jackson Bate (London and Princeton: Routledge & Kegan Paul, Princeton University Press, 1983), 1:232–94; *Logic*, ed. J. R. de J. Jackson (London and Princeton: Routledge & Kegan Paul, Princeton University Press, 1981), 60–94; *The Notebooks of Samuel Taylor Coleridge*, ed. Kathleen Coburn (Princeton: Princeton University Press, 1957–), 3:4265. References given parenthetically in text (*BL, Logic, CN*).
4. Orsini, esp. ch. 4, "Kant III—The Transcendental Unity of Apperception," 117–48, and ch. 8, "Schelling I—Metaphysics," 192–221.
5. David Hume, *A Treatise of Human Nature*, ed. L. A. Selby-Bigge (Oxford: Clarendon Press, 1888, reprint 1965), 252.
6. Engell, Bate, *BL* 1:119n, cite parallels to this statement on self-consciousness in *CL* 2:709, as well as in the subsequent discussion of the self in ch. 9:1:145–46, 158–60.
7. §17 "Der Grundsatz der synthetischen Einheit der Apperzeption ist das oberste Prinzip alles Verstandesgebrauchs," *Kritik der reinen Vernunft*, B136.
8. Orsini, 121.
9. Fichte, *Grundlage der gesammten Wissenschaftslehre* (Jena, Leipzig: 2nd ed. Christian Ernst Gabler, 1802), 153–85, appropriates the electric/magnetic/galvanic construction of Schelling's *Naturphilosophie* as principles of activity/permanence/change in the postulation of the "I" ("Das Ich . . . als *sich setzend*.")

10. Orsini, 182; Steffens, *Was ich erlebte* (1840–44), 4, 78–80; Fichte, *Versuch einer neuen Darstellung der Wissenschaftslehre* (1797) in *Sämmtliche Werke*, ed. J. H. Fichte (Berlin, 1845), 1, 522.

11. See esp. "Vorläufige Beziehung des Standpunktes der Medicin nach Grundsätzen der Naturphilosophie," which concludes with the affirmation of pantheism, *Jahrbücher der Medizin als Wissenschaft* (1805; reprint Hildesheim: Georg Olms, 1969); *Zeitschrift für spekulative Physik* (1800–01; reprint Hildesheim: Georg Olms, 1969); *Sämmtliche Werke*, ed. Manfred Schröter (1927–59; reprint Munich: C. H. Beck, 1962–71). Schröter provides pagination from the original edition (Stuttgart, Augsburg: Cotta, 1856–61) which will be cited in subsequent references (*SW*).

12. Orsini, 200. Trevore Levere, *Poetry Realized in Nature, Samuel Taylor Coleridge and early nineteenth-century Science* (Cambridge: Cambridge University Press, 1981), 68, 81, 124–25, 129, 164, 203–04, 244–45.

13. *BL* 1:250; *Kritik der reinen Vernunft*, B16–17; *SW* 3:440–50, 462–90.

14. *BL* 1:251; *SW* 3:345. The parallel between these two passages has not been previously noted. At the fourth level of "inner sense," Coleridge says, a man "attains to a notion of his notions–he reflects on his own reflections"; Schelling asserts that "das transcendentale Denken . . . , indem es des Begriffs als Akts sich bewußt wird, zum Begriff des Begriffs sich erhebt."

15. Schelling posits an "unauflösliche" or "unvermeidliche Cirkel" in his *System* (*SW* III, 359–360); in *Vom Ich* he employs the Fichtean opposition of center and circumferance in defining "die Sphäre unsers Wissens" (*SW* I, 163–5). Engell, Bate, *BL* 1, 267n, also call attention to Fichte's "image of a circle used in a way similar to C's," in *Über den Begriff der Wissenschaftslehre* (1793), *Sämmtliche Werke*, 1:61–62.

16. Coleridge's regression from "the picture of the line," "the stoke thus drawn," and "the image," to "the original line generated by the act of the imagination" (*BL* 1, 250) is more precisely descriminated in the *Logic*, 73, as ἐγεργια θεωρη-τικη, ειδος, ειδωλον. Coleridge's terms are to be contrasted with Schelling's "Unterschied des Schema vom Bild und vom Symbol," *SW* 3:508–09.

17. Jackson, *Logic*, 75n, points to similar examples of this phenomena recorded in *CN* 1:549 ("Vortices of flies") and *CL* 2:974 ("whirling round a live Coal").

Chapter 9 Annotating the Annotations

1. I have argued elsewhere that both Hegel's and Derrida's tendency to *isolate* the difference entailed by expressed force begs the question on behalf of more or less developed appeal to "not-being." That is, when in the *Phenomenology* Hegel sublates the play of force to the "law of Force" as "universal difference," he effectively reduces relational difference to a unity that can only be founded on the "unity" of negation (see Hegel 90). Derrida, I believe, does the same thing, in his approving reference to the Nietzschean notion that "force itself is never present; it is only a play of differences and quantities"—explaining further,

by way of a Deleuzean citation, that the " 'difference in quantity is the essence of force.' " (See Derrida 148). My argument is simply that relational force can be reduced neither to the unity of presence *nor* to the (albeit deferred) unity of its relational differences: hence my appeal to "power-*and*-difference."

Chapter 10 Coleridge and Milton

1. U. C. Knoepflmacher, "A Nineteenth-Century Touchstone: Chapter XV of *Biographia Literaria*," in *Nineteenth-Century Perspectives. Essays in Honor of Lionel Stevenson* (Durham: Duke University Press, 1974), 3–16. Although I disagree with Knoepflmacher's conclusion, I have found his analysis of chapter 15 of *Biographia Literaria* to be very illuminating. Knoepflmacher is also aware of Coleridge's use of Milton as "a stabilizing element and idealized *alter ego*" (4, n. 5), but he does not pursue the effect of Coleridge's personal identification with Milton on his assessment of Wordsworth in *Biographia*.

2. See Wordsworth's statement in his 1815 Preface that he had given as much evidence of the power of the imagination as Shakespeare, Spenser, and Milton, and therefore was entitled to expect that, like the works of his three distinguished predecessors, his own was "worthy to be holden in undying remembrance." "Preface to Poems (1815)" in *William Wordsworth*, ed. Stephen Gill (Oxford: Oxford University Press, 1984), 634–35. We can safely presume that this comment must have irritated Coleridge, primarily because Wordsworth reached this climax of self-regard by borrowing two important concepts he owed to Coleridge without any acknowledgment: the distinction between Shakespeare and Milton, which Coleridge discussed in his 1811–1812 course of lectures; and the difference between Greek and Christian religion (the former being characterized by "bondage of definite form," the latter by the indefiniteness of the sublime), which Coleridge had developed as early as 1799. I deal with Coleridge's response to Wordsworth's unacknowledged borrowings from him in "Coleridge and Wordsworth: The Ethics of Gift Exchange and Literary Ownership," forthcoming in *Coleridge's Theory of the Imagination Today*, ed. Christine Gallant (New York: AMS Press, 1989).

3. Harold Bloom, "Coleridge: The Anxiety of Influence," in *New Perspectives on Coleridge and Wordsworth*, ed. Geoffrey Hartman (New York and London: Columbia University Press, 1972), 247–67.

4. Bloom, 254.

5. In *Coleridge, Wordsworth and the Language of Allusion* (Oxford: Clarendon Press, 1986), Lucy Newlyn points out that in *The Prelude* Wordsworth, while seeming to praise Coleridge, introduces an allusion to *Sampson Agonistes* which has "a jarring effect." It recalls, of course, the mood of dejection in which Coleridge had last echoed the same passage, and it highlights the ambiguity of Coleridge's status. On one level, he is a hero with the capacity of a God; on the other, he is a human being whose health and vision are frail" (176–77). On Coleridge's and Wordsworth's use of the reference to *Samson Agonistes* see pp.

68–69. Newlyn also shows that in Book 6 and 8 of *The Prelude* Wordsworth echoes Adam's theory of dreams in Book 5 of *Paradise Lost* in order to draw attention "to the anarchic potential of Coleridge's thought. . . . Milton's presence within the language not only sharpens the poet's meaning, it pinpoints an underlying aggression" (178–79).

6. *Collected Letters of Samuel Taylor Coleridge*, ed. Earl Leslie Griggs, 6 vols. (Oxford: Clarendon Press, 1956–71), 2:1013. Henceforward cited as *CL* in the text.

7. Newlyn, 69.

8. Lawrence Buell argues that *Biographia* does not "meet its own criteria of poesis," as enunciated in the theory of organic unity. Its actual "principles of unfolding are finally divergent from, if not downright hostile to, Coleridge's stated notions of poesis." "The Question of Form in Coleridge's *Biographia Literaria*, *ELH* 46 (1979): 399–417. The discrepancy between Coleridge's organic theory and the actual "processes by which poems have to be produced" is also pointed out by Bloom in "The Anxiety of Influence," 265. For the incongruity between Coleridge's evaluation of Shakespeare in terms of organicism and "the history of the development of an accurate Shakespearean text" see Norman Fruman, *Coleridge, The Damaged Archangel* (New York: George Braziller, 1971), 162–63 and Clifford Davidson, "Organic Unity and Shakespearean Tragedy," *Journal of Aesthetics and Art Criticism* 30 (1971): 171–76. The difference between Coleridge's assessment of Milton and the charge of inorganicism launched against him by critics such as Pound, Eliot, Leavis, Murry, Lucas, Dobrée, and Read is discussed by Elisabeth T. McLaughlin in "Coleridge and Milton," *Studies in Philology* 61 (1964): 545–72, esp. p. 545–49.

9. I discuss Coleridge's use of Bowles as a covert strategy of criticizing Wordsworth in "Coleridge and Wordsworth. The Ethics of Gift Exchange and Literary Ownership," cited in n. 2 above.

10. *Biographia Literaria*, ed. James Engell and W. Jackson Bate, *The Collected Works of Samuel Taylor Coleridge*, vol. 7, Bollingen Series 75, 2 vols. (Princeton: Princeton University Press, 1983), 2:20. Henceforward cited as *BL* in the text.

11. Lucy Newlyn is one of the few critics who points out Coleridge's use of Milton as a weapon against Wordsworth. In referring to the letter to Southey, she argues that Coleridge quotes Milton's definition of poetry "in the context of his dissatisfaction with Wordsworth. One feels that he turns to Milton in reaction against Wordsworth, because Milton allows him to think in his customary symbolic terms" (96).

12. In other versions concerning Milton's definition of poetry, passion is usually defined by Coleridge as a counterforce to the objective dimension of poetry as constituted by sensory images, imbuing such images with "the spirit of the mind" or the *"passio vera* of humanity." See *Coleridge on the Seventeenth Century*, ed. Roberta Brinkley (Durham, N.C.: Duke University Press, 1955), 546–47.

13. On Coleridge's projected lecture on Wordsworth see *CL* 3:111 and *The Notebooks of Samuel Taylor Coleridge*, ed. Kathleen Coburn, vols. 1 and 2 (New York: Pantheon Books; London: Routhledge & Kegan Paul, 1857, 1961); vol. 3

(Princeton: Princeton University Press, 1973), 3:3257n. Henceforward cited as *CN* in the text.

14. From Sir Joshua Reynolds' second Discourse (1769) quoted by Coleridge in chapter 16, *BL* 2:35n. It is interesting to note that in the Advertisement to the 1798 edition of the *Lyrical Ballads* Wordsworth uses the same passage from Reynolds in order to encourage his readers to acquaint themselves patiently with his poetry through repeated readings rather than judge it rashly and erroneously. This is a rather conspicuously self-serving departure from Reynolds whose notion of good taste, as Coleridge adequately represented, involved not repeated exposure to the work of a contemporary, but to those works whose "*reputation*" had "matured into *fame* by the consent of ages" (*BL* 2:36n.).

15. Here Coleridge reprints the sonnet he had published in the *Monthly Magazine* under the pseudonym Nehemiah Higginbottom in which he satirized the use of "low, creeping language and thoughts, under the pretence of *simplicity*" (*BL* 1:27). As I argued in "Coleridge and Wordsworth. The Ethics of Gift Exchange and Literary Ownership," the sonnets reprinted in chapter 1 are aimed at Wordsworth, even though originally they were directed against Charles Lamb and Charles Lloyd. For Wordsworth's view that "humble subjects" written in "a naked and simple style" was one of his chief goals in the *Lyrical Ballads* poems, see his "Preface to *Lyrical Ballads* (1802)," esp. p. 609.

16. Although occasionally Coleridge used the term "simplicity" in a conventional sense, as unadorned diction, he characteristically linked it with high ideals, such as the ideal of organic unity. Thus in chapter 16, Coleridge shows how the elder writers attained simplicity in their poetry by avoiding words "which a *gentleman* would *not* use in dignified conversation" and by "the studied position of words and phrases, so that not only each part should be melodious in itself, but contribute to the harmony of the whole . . ." (*BL* 2:33). The covert critique of Wordsworth in this chapter is as pervasive as in his analysis of Shakespeare's early writings in chapter 15. It is also important to note that in two alternative versions of Milton's definition of poetry, Coleridge renders simplicity as either pointing to "the elements and the primary laws of our nature" (from the 1813 first lecture on Milton), or to singularity of conception (from *Table Talk*, May 8, 1824). See *Coleridge on the Seventeenth Century*, 546.

17. This gives weight to Lawrence Buell's claim that there is a different principle operating in *Biographia Literaria*, at odds with Coleridge's theory of organic unity. See "The Question of Form in Coleridge's *Biographia Literaria*," cited in n. 8 above.

18. As Norman Fruman points out, in Coleridge's praise of Wordsworth's virtues as a poet, we "hear nothing of organic unity, or of opposite or discordant qualities reconciled," which represent Coleridge's quintessential norms for good poetry. *Coleridge, The Damaged Archangel*, 198. Also, by resorting to a long list of quotations from Wordsworth's poetry, as illustration of his gifts, Coleridge merely reinforces the charge previously made against Wordsworth that while

parts of the poems might be excellent, they do not merge well with other parts so as to constitute an organic whole.

19. Coleridge developed the distinction between Shakespeare and Milton in a notebook entry of 1811 which he used in the fourth lecture of the 1811–1812 series (*CN* 3:4115). See also *Shakespearean Criticism*, ed. Thomas Middleton Raysor, 2 vols. (Cambridge, MA: Harvard University Press, 1930), II, 95–96. For Wordsworth's use of this distinction see "Preface to Poems (1815)," 634–35.

20. Stephen Bygrave, *Coleridge and the Self. Romantic Egotism* (London: Macmillan, 1986), 42.

21. Bygrave, 40–42.

22. Cf. Coleridge's statement in chapter 13 that "There is a philosophic, no less than a poetic genius, which is differenced from the highest perfection of talent, not by degree but by kind" (*BL* 1:299–300). While building upon the presuppositions of Schelling's system, which demonstrated the unity between philosophic and artistic consciousness, Coleridge reverses the direction of Schelling's arguments by privileging philosophy and not art, as Schelling did in the closing section of his *System of Transcendental Idealism*.

23. As I argued in "Coleridge and Wordsworth. The Ethics of Gift Exchange and Literary Ownership," in chapter 1 of *Biographia Literaria* Coleridge quotes Milton in order to reverse the implication of his apologetic statement concerning his presumably damaging interest in metaphysics as a young poet.

24. It is not fortuitous that chapter 13, which includes Coleridge's theory of the imagination, opens with a long quotation from *Paradise Lost*.

25. "Essay, Supplementary to the Preface (1815)," 640.

26. For Coleridge's defense of Milton's egotism see *CN*, 1, 904 and his Prefaces to his 1796 and 1797 collection of poems in *The Romantics on Milton*, ed. J. A. Wittreich (Cleveland: The Press of Case Western Reserve University, 1970), 158–59, and cf. Bygrave, ch. 3.

27. For the view that *Biographia Literaria* is a response to *The Prelude* see Lawrence Buell's article cited in n. 8 above.

28. Catherine Miles Wallace, *The Design of Biographia Literaria* (London: Allen & Unwin, 1983), 140.

29. In the *Biographia* every attack on Wordsworth is matched by a self-directed attack. Coleridge in fact violates almost every standard by which he achieves his victories over his friend. As several critics have noted, his critique of Wordsworth undermines the very standards of genial criticism that Coleridge sets up against the anonymous critics. Similarly, Coleridge does not maintain, as he claims, the indifference of genius in relation to public opinion. Rather, he displays fits of anger both against Wordsworth and the anonymous critics, to the point that Sara Coleridge found it necessary to suppress certain parts of the *Biographia* which she felt Coleridge himself would not have reprinted. See *BL* 2:156n.3. On Coleridge's dependence on Wordsworth in the *Biographia* see Jerome Christensen, "The Genius in *Biographia Literaria*," *Studies in Roman-*

ticism 17 (1978): 227–28 and especially William Galperin, "Desynonymizing the Self in Wordsworth and Coleridge," in *Studies in Romanticism* 27 (1988).

30. I discuss Coleridge's views concerning the ideal self in *Coleridge & the Concept of Nature* (London: Macmillan, 1985), 76–78.

31. See Edmund Burke, *A Philosophical Enquiry into the Origin of our Ideas of the Sublime and Beautiful*, ed. James T. Boulton (Notre Dame, IN: University of Notre Dame, 1968), 65.

32. I am indebted to Charles Altieri for drawing my attention to the impersonal nature of successful idealization and its theological underpinnings.

33. From *Literary Remains* (1808), quoted in *The Romantics on Milton*, 185.

34. On the Trinity see *Coleridge & the Concept of Nature*, 186–203.

Chapter 11 "Like a Guilty Thing Surprised"

1. Frank Lentricchia, *Criticism and Social Change* (Chicago: University of Chicago Press, 1983), 38–40.

2. Edmund Burke, *Reflections on the Revolution in France* (Harmondsworth: Penguin, 1969), 120. Subsequent references to this edition will appear in the text.

3. In *Interpretations*, ed. Charles Singleton (Baltimore: Johns Hopkins University Press, 1969).

4. Lentricchia, *Criticism*, 51. Lentricchia displays a curious blindness to the problem of romanticism. He rightly observes that when in his essay "Literary History and Literary Modernity" de Man writes "literature," others might "say more modestly 'romantic literature'" (47). The same substitution might be performed on de Man's use of the word "modern." Lentricchia seems to think that pointing to the substitution discredits it, whereas it merely opens the question, surely in de Man's mind, of the possibility of rewriting all literary history since the end of the eighteenth century as an elaboration of a few central romantic preoccupations or tropes.

5. E. P. Thompson, review of David Erdman, ed., *The Collected Works of Samuel Taylor Coleridge: Essays on His Times* in *The Wordsworth Circle*, 10 (Summer 1979), 263. "Disenchantment or Default?" appears in *Power and Consciousness*, ed. Conor Cruise O'Brien and William Dean Vanech (London: London University Press, 1969), 149–82. I say "renewed severity" because in "Disenchantment" Thompson self-ironically retracts his earlier "sneer" in *The Making of the English Working Class* at the "sincerity of Coleridge's professions" of fear at what he and other radicals might suffer at the hands of patriotic rioters in Nether Stowey in 1798 (162).

6. In an 1802 letter to William Sotheby, Coleridge writes "Εστησε signifies—*He hath stood*—which in these times of apostasy from the principles of Freedom, or of Religion in this country, & from both by the same persons in France, is no unmeaning Signature, if subscribed with humility, & in the remembrance

of, Let him that stands take heed lest he fall—. However it is in truth no more than S. T. C. written in Greek. *Es tee see*—" In his note to this passage Earl Leslie Griggs observes that "*Εστηοε* signifies 'he Hath placed' not 'He hath stood.' The word should have been *Εστηκε*, but then the play on Coleridge's initials would have been lost. Elsewhere he called it 'Punic Greek.'" (*Letters of Samuel Taylor Coleridge*, ed. Earl Leslie Griggs, 6 vols. [Oxford: Clarendon Press, 1956–71], 2:459.) Taking his stand on the etymon that is his proper signature requires Coleridge to put in place that which he is to stand on, to stand off his name in order that his name may be a standing place. That *apostasis* is simultaneously a theft (under the cover of resemblance) of the proper meaning of *Εστηκε* and its surreptitious importation into *Εστηοε*. The diachronic gesture serves a wholly anti-historical strategy. For Coleridge, the signature and the self which it underwrites *are* strategies.

7. Samuel Taylor Coleridge, *The Watchman*, ed. Lewis Patton, vol. 2 of *The Collected Works of Samuel Taylor Coleridge*, gen'l ed. Kathleen Coburn (Princeton: Princeton University Press, 1970), 39 and 152. Burke was not the only person subjected to this sort of ideological critique by Coleridge. Like other charges, such as plagiarism, which Coleridge both feared and cherished, the tag of "apostate" was not frugally applied. For an early example, see his denunciation of Southey for the "Apostacy" of his decision to abandon pantisocracy for the bar (*Collected Letters* 1:162–73). A later and more indirect example would be the treatment of Wordsworth in the second volume of the *Biographia*, where, in effect, the poet is accused of apostasy from the divine truth of his genius.

8. William Hazlitt, "Illustrations of the *Times* Newspaper," in *The Complete Works of William Hazlitt*, ed. P. P. Howe, 21 vols. (London: J. M. Dent, 1930–34), 7:135.

9. Early versions of Coleridge's "shaking off" occur in prose in his letters to his clerical brother George (see, especially, *CL* 1:125–27) and in poetry in the 1796 "Eolian Harp." In its final, 1817 version, "The Eolian Harp" displays a double apostasy: a turn from connubial fidelity and the domestic "Cot" to an autoerotically charged fairy fancy and a turn from that scene, now characterized in speculative, pantheistic terms, to "pensive Sara." The material artifact of the poem itself registers Coleridge's retirement in the country, a turn away from political activism.

10. As the editor of the *Marginalia* indicates, these marginalia, comprising a long series of return engagements with Boehme's texts, are difficult to date, although most fall within the period 1817–18. But the congruence of the language of those under consideration here with notebook entries of 1818 allows us to place them with some confidence near that year. (*Marginalia*, ed. George Whalley, vol. 12 of *The Collected Coleridge* [Princeton: Princeton University Press], 1:553–54. All subsequent references to *Marginalia* will appear by volume, entry, and page in the text.)

11. *The Notebooks of Samuel Taylor Coleridge*, ed. Kathleen Coburn, 3 vols. (Princeton: Princeton University Press, 1957–73), 3:4449.

12. This is the crucial metaphysical problem for Coleridge. See Thomas McFar-

land, *Coleridge and the Pantheist Tradition* (Oxford: Oxford University Press, 1969). Cf. the aborted Schellingian formulation in chapter 13 of the *Biographia* (Coleridge, *Biographia Literaria*, eds. James Engell and W. J. Bate, vol. 7 of *The Collected Works*, 2 vols. (Princeton: Princeton University Press, 1983) 1:296–300. Subsequent references to *BL* will appear in the text.

13. *Notebooks* 3:4449.

14. For a subtle treatment of this aspect of Coleridge, see Reeve Parker's *Coleridge's Meditative Art* (Ithaca, NY: Cornell University Press, 1975), 21–60 and passim.

15. J. G. A. Pocock. "Burke and the Ancient Constitution: A Problem in the History of Ideas," in *Politics, Language and Time: Essays on Political Thought and History* (New York: Atheneum, 1973), 227.

16. *Politics. Language and Time*, 229–30.

17. *Allegories of Reading: Figural Language in Rousseau, Nietzsche, Rilke, and Proust* (New Haven: Yale University Press, 1979), 273.

18. Cf. Blackstone: "LIFE is the immediate gift of God, a right inherent by nature in every individual; and it begins in contemplation of law as soon as an infant is able to stir in the mother's womb" (William Blackstone, *Commentaries on the Laws of England* 4 vols. [Oxford: Clarendon Press, 1765], 1:125).

19. I stress English history to distinguish it, as does Burke, from French. In certain respects my commentary on Burke renders *Reflections* as akin to the paradoxical formulation of Rousseau in *The Social Contract*: "The people subject to the Law must be the authors of the Law." De Man observes, "Only a subterfuge can put this paralysis in motion. Since the system itself had to be based on deceit, the mainspring of its movement has to be deceitful as well" (*Allegories of Reading*, 274). What is apt for Rousseau would be wrong for Burke just because the evaluative terms of subterfuge and deceit are inappropriate for an argument that embraces theatricality as a determinant of the English character and English history. For Burke it is because the French do not have either the English theater or the English common law tradition that they must resort to a deceit to motivate paralysis.

20. *On a Motion Made in the House of Commons . . . for a Committee to Enquire into the State of the Representation of the Commons in Parliament*: quoted in Pocock, *Politics, Language and Time*, 228.

21. The editors' translation of *"nihil in intellectu quod non prius in sensu. . . . praeter ipsum intellectum* (*BL* 1:141 and n. 1).

22. Edmund Burke, *Selected Writings*, ed. Walter J. Bate (New York: Random House, 1960), 487.

23. For an application of Hartleian associationism to the philosophical and rhetorical problem of the self-producing and self-reading text which takes up the issue of narcissism in relation to Coleridge's "The Garden of Boccaccio," see my essay, "Philosophy/Literature: The Associationist Precedent for Coleridge's Late Poems," in *Philosophical Approaches to Literature: New Essays on Nineteenth- and Twentieth-Century Texts*, ed. William E. Cain (Lewisburg, PA: Bucknell University Press, 1983), 27–50.

24. *Blindness and Insight: Essays in the Rhetoric of Contemporary Criticism* (London: Oxford University Press, 1971), 106.
25. *Allegories of Reading*, 65.
26. *Blindness and Insight*, 163.
27. *Blindness and Insight*, 162.
28. Evidence that this is de Man's *aim* would be the substitution in the late *Allegories of Reading* of the rhetorical categories "metonymy" and "metaphor" for the suspiciously intentional nouns "flight" and "return" used in the early *Blindness and Insight*.
29. N. B.: This must be not a complete cancellation of the more arbitrary terms: although it is by the necessity and purposiveness of our separation that we attest to poetry's merit, it is by the contingency and compulsiveness of that movement that the critic witnesses to poetry's "genuine power."
30. Coleridge, *On the Constitution of the Church and State*, ed. John Colmer, vol. 10 of *The Collected Works* (Princeton: Princeton University Press, 1976), p. 8 and n. 2. Subsequent references to *CCS* will appear in the text.
31. A full treatment of Coleridge's constitutionalism would have to consider in more detail the ramifications of professionalism in his argument. It is a fact that the professional groups that detached themselves from the clergy in the sixteenth century are not expected to return in the nineteenth. Call this realism or ostracism, it fits with the strong anti-professionalism that Coleridge displays in the *Biographia* where professionals and especially professional critics like Jeffrey are not exempted from the taint of trade. In terms of his relation to Burke, Coleridge was ready to accept the form of the constitutional argument but eager to rid it of all connection to the common-law tradition, which Coleridge could with considerable justice regard as being formulated in the Renaissance in order to justify legal detachment and aggrandize the legal profession. It is certainly a defensible interpretation of the remarks of Coke to James I that Pocock cites as his earliest example of mature ancient constitutionalism (*Politics. Language and Time*, 214). The demystification of the cognitive privileges of the law was already underway in Burke's *Reflections*, where veneration for English law was uneasily coupled with hatred of French lawyers. By regarding the historical act of separation under the idea of detachment and by abandoning particular professions for the general authority of the third estate, Coleridge was able to fulfill Burke's program and substitute newly invented English criticism for the law as the arbiter of all relations to precedent. It might be added that another precedent for the relations between detachment (in this case exile) and the formation of a privileged intellectual class in the late sixteenth and early seventeenth centuries, with which Coleridge would have been familiar, occurs in the experience of the Puritan saints (see Michael Walzer, *The Revolution of the Saints: A Study in the Origins of Radical Politics* [1965; rept., Cambridge, MA: Harvard University Press, 1982], esp. pp. 114–47.).
32. Coleridge vented his regrets over the first decision in chapter 11 of the *Biographia*, an extract of which was transposed to *CCS* 75–76. On the latter

decision, Hazlitt's narrative account in "My First Acquaintance with Poets" remains the *locus classicus*.

33. Lentricchia, *Criticism and Social Change*, 24.
34. De Man, *Allegories of Reading*, 8.
35. *Coleridge's Shakespearean Criticism*, ed. Thomas Middleton Raysor, 2 vols. (London: Constable & Co., 1930), 1:37, 273 (paraphrased).

Chapter 12 Coleridge and the Charge of Political Apostasy

1. E. P. Thompson, "Disenchantment or Default? A Lay Sermon," in *Power and Consciousness*, ed. Conor Cruise O'Brien and William Dean Vanech (London: London University Press, 1969), 152–53.
2. Thompson, review of David Erdman, ed., *Essays on His Times*, 3 vols., *The Collected Works of Samuel Taylor Coleridge*, 3 (London: Routledge & Kegan Paul; Princeton: Princeton University Press, 1978), in *The Wordsworth Circle* 10 (Summer 1979): 261–65.
3. Coleridge, "Mr. Southey and Wat Tyler, IV: Apostasy and Renegadoism" (2 April 1817), in *Essays on His Times*, 2:474.
4. *The Notebooks of Samuel Taylor Coleridge*, ed. Kathleen Coburn (London: Routledge & Kegan Paul; Princeton: Princeton University Press, 1957–), 2:2121.
5. *The Complete Works of William Hazlitt*, ed. P. P. Howe, after the edition of A. R. Waller and Arnold Glover (London: J. M. Dent & Sons, 1930–34), 17:318.
6. *Ibid.*, 22.
7. *Ibid.*, 316.
8. Thomas McFarland, *Coleridge and the Pantheist Tradition* (Oxford: Clarendon Press, 1969), 163–64, 358–59.
9. For a single revealing example, John Thelwall commented, on Coleridge's endorsement in the *Biographia* of "the EXISTENCE of the Supreme Being," that Coleridge "seems to have received some new light upon the signification of the syllable *ex,* since he talked to me at Keswick of his design of writing an elaborate demonstration of the truth of Christian revelation which should commence with a denial of the *existence* of god." (Burton R. Pollin, assisted by Redmond Burke, "John Thelwall's Marginalia in a Copy of Coleridge's *Biographia Literaria*," *Bulletin of the New York Public Library* 74 (1970): 88).
10. *The Table Talk and Omniana of Samuel Taylor Coleridge*, ed. T. Ashe (London: George Bell & Sons, 1888), 138–39 (September 12, 1831).
11. *Coleridge and the Pantheist Tradition*, 254.
12. *Hazlitt*, 17:133.
13. *Ibid.*, 29.
14. *Ibid.*, 12:51–2.
15. *The Watchman*, ed. Lewis Patton, *The Collected Works of Samuel Taylor Coleridge*, 2 (London: Routledge & Kegan Paul; Princeton: Princeton University Press, 1970), lviii.

16. Henry Crabb Robinson *On Books and their Writers*, ed. Edith J. Morley (London: J. M. Dent, 1938), 1:198.
17. *The Complete Poetical Works of Samuel Taylor Coleridge*, ed. Ernest Hartley Coleridge (Oxford: Clarendon Press, 1912), 1:76.
18. *Biographia Literaria*, ed. James Engell and W. Jackson Bate, *The Collected Works of Samuel Taylor Coleridge*, 7 (London: Routledge & Kegan Paul; Princeton: Princeton University Press, 1983), 1:184 and 59–67. One can, as this essay will continue to attempt to show, accept Coleridge's claim that he was "never at any period of my life a Convert to the System" of Jacobinism (184n), and that friends could "bear witness for me, how opposite even then my principles were to those of jacobinism" (184). The key word is "principles," which for Coleridge did not change; in the play of his mind and conversation, however, it might be more accurate to say that he was in his early years both inclined toward Jacobinism and inclined against it. A sonnet on Burke in 1794 exactly expresses this characteristically antithetical approach. Burke, the archenemy of Jacobinism, is hailed by "FREEDOM" as "Great Son of Genius!", but then blamed that "in an evil hour with alter'd voice / Thou bad'st Oppressions hireling crew rejoice." On the other hand, it is then said that "never, BURKE! thou drank'st Corruption's bowl"; and the poem concludes by hailing Burke as "Spirit pure" and wishing "That Error's mist had left thy purgèd eye: / So might I clasp thee with a Mother's joy!" (*Poetical Works* 1:80–81). If Jacobin sympathies here coexist with reverence for Burke, in *The Fall of Robespierre*, written in collaboration with Southey in 1794, the same antithetical pattern appears. As a commentator points out, "Its dedication, which is plainly un-Jacobin in tone, speaks of Robespierre's 'great bad actions' and of the 'vast stage of horrors' on which the two young poets have set the events of their play. . . . But the play is as anti-monarchical as it is anti-Jacobin" (George Watson, "The Revolutionary Youth of Coleridge and Wordsworth," *Critical Quarterly* 18 (1976): 53). For a rebuttal to Watson's article see John Beer, "The 'Revolutionary Youth' of Wordsworth and Coleridge: Another View," *Critical Quarterly* 19 (1977): 79–87, which argues for more consistency and less prevarication in Coleridge's views than Watson concedes them.
19. "Coleridge's Literary Life," *Edinburgh Review* 28 (August 1817), in *Hazlitt*, 16:120.
20. *Ibid.*, 129.
21. *Conciones ad Populum. Or Addresses to the People* (February 1795), in *Lectures 1795. On Politics and Religion*, ed. Lewis Patton and Peter Mann, *The Collected Works of Samuel Taylor Coleridge* (London: Routledge & Kegan Paul; Princeton: Princeton University Press, 1971), 1:21–74.
22. *Inquiring Spirit; A New Presentation of Coleridge from his Published and Unpublished Prose Writings*, ed. Kathleen Coburn (New York: Pantheon Books, 1951), 130.
23. For general background on Jacobinism see Gérard Walter, *Histoire des Jacobins* (Paris: Aimery Somogy, 1946). For an important source collection of documents see Alphonse Aulard, *La Société des Jacobins. Recueil de documents pour*

l'histoire du club des Jacobins de Paris (Paris: Librairie Jouaust, 1889–97), 6 vols. For discussion of the kinds of people who became Jacobins see, e.g., Michael L. Kennedy, *The Jacobin Clubs in the French Revolution; The First Years* (Princeton: Princeton University Press, 1982), 73–78.

24. As Watt said, "I am filled with involuntary horror at the scenes which pass before me and wish they could have been avoided, but at the same time I allow the absolute necessity of them. In some instances the vengeance of the people has been savage & inhuman." (David V. Erdman, *Commerce des Lumières; John Oswald and the British in Paris, 1790–1793* [Columbia: University of Missouri Press, 1986], 228–29.)

25. Clarence Crane Brinton, *The Jacobins; An Essay in the New History* (New York: The Macmillan Co., 1930), 111–15.

26. E.g., ". . . there was nothing systematic in the creation of the Revolutionary Government. Nearly all the facts hitherto related go to prove that this Government was not the application of any system or any preconceived idea, but that it formed itself empirically, from day to day, out of the elements imposed on it by the successive necessities of the national defences of a people at war with Europe; a people in arms for the defence of its existence, in a country which resembled a vast military camp. . . . The Revolution . . . strove to govern by law and liberty until August 10, 1792. Then, the resisting forces of the past having formed an alliance, having brought about a civil war and a war of invasion . . . then the Revolution put away and suspended the principles of '89, and turned against its enemies . . . the weapons with which it found itself attacked. The Terror consisted in the suspension of the principles of '89." (A. Aulard, *The French Revolution; A Political History 1789–1804*, trans. Bernard Miall (New York: Charles Scribner's Sons, 1910), 2:278–79).

27. Taine finds that a "homicidal idea"—*idée homicide*—characterized Jacobinism from the first: "In his narrow brain, perverted and turned topsy-turvy by the disproportionate notions put into it, only one idea suited to his gross instincts and aptitudes finds a place, and that is the desire to kill his enemies; and these are also the State's enemies. . . . He carries this savagery and bewilderment into politics, and hence the evil arising from his usurpation. . . . As representing the State, he undertakes wholesale massacres, of which he has the means ready at hand. For he has not yet had time enough to take apart the old administrative implements; at all events the minor wheels, gendarmes, jailers, employees, book-keepers, and accountants, are always in their place and under control. There can be no resistance on the part of those arrested; accustomed to the protection of the laws and to peaceable ways and times, they have never relied on defending themselves nor ever could imagine that any one could be so summarily slain. As to the mass, rendered incapable of any effort of its own by ancient centralization, it remains inert and passive and lets things go their own way. Hence, during many long, successive days, without being hurried or impeded, with official papers quite correct and accounts in perfect order, a massacre can be carried out with the same impunity and as methodically as cleaning the streets or clubbing stray dogs. Let us trace

the progress of the homicidal idea in the mass of the party. It lies at the very bottom of the revolutionary creed." (Hippolyte Taine, *Les Origines de la France contemporaine* (Paris: Librairie Hachette et Cie, 1875–93), 3:265–66).

28. The cost was not alone in lives, as has so often been rehearsed (17,000 executed in the Terror, 2,000,000 more dead in the Napoleonic wars that erupted from the Revolution), but in wealth, goods, and national treasure—irrecoverably so (the destruction of Cluny alone makes one wonder what benefit could justify it). See René Sédillot, *Le Coût de la Révolution françoise* (Paris: Perrin, 1987).

29. Letter to Lord Byron (September 8, 1816), *The Letters of Percy Bysshe Shelley,* ed. Frederick L. Jones (Oxford: Clarendon Press, 1964), 1:504.

30. *Hazlitt,* 5:161–3.

31. *America a Prophecy,* plate 4, line 12, in *The Complete Poetry and Prose of William Blake,* ed. David V. Erdman (Berkeley and Los Angeles: University of California Press, 1982), 53.

32. *Hazlitt,* 16:130.

33. See, e.g., Ralph Korngold, *Robespierre: First Modern Dictator* (London: Macmillan, 1937), 292–99.

34. Hans Eichner, *Friedrich Schlegel* (New York: Twayne, 1970), 110–11 and 112–17.

35. See, e.g., David P. Jordan, *The Revolutionary Career of Maximilien Robespierre* (New York: Free Press, 1985), 54. For an impressive catalogue of Robespierre's many humane and enlightened beliefs see 51–54.

36. See, e.g., Jean Matrat, *Robespierre; Or the Tyranny of the Majority,* trans. Alan Kendall and Felix Brenner (New York: Charles Scribner's Sons, 1971), 106.

37. Alphonse de Lamartine, *Histoire des Girondins,* ed. Jean-Pierre Jacques (Paris: Librairie Plon, 1984), 2:70–74.

38. "Au nom de Vergniaud, les conversations cessèrent, les regards se portèrent sur lui seul. Il monta lentement les degrés de la tribune, se recueillit un moment, la paupière baissée sur les yeux, comme un homme qui réfléchit pour la dernière fois avant d'agir; puis, d'une voix sourde, et comme résistant dans son âme à la sensibilité qui criait en lui, il prononça: *La mort.*" (Lamartine, 2:210).

39. *The Life of John Thelwall,* by his widow [Mrs. Cecil Boyle Thelwall] (London: John Macrone, St. James's Square, 1837), 1:47.

40. *Ibid.,* 352.

41. *Robinson,* 1:183.

42. *Ibid.,* 161.

43. *Ibid.,* 164.

44. *Ibid.,* 103.

45. *Ibid.,* 127.

46. *Ibid.,* 183.

47. *Ibid.,* 171.

48. *Ibid.,* 115.

49. *America a Prophecy,* plate 6, lines 6–15, in *Blake's Poetry and Prose,* 53.

50. *Jerusalem*, plate 52, in *Blake's Poetry and Prose*, 200.
51. *Europe a Prophecy*, plates 14–15, in *Blake's Poetry and Prose*, 66.
52. Although Thelwall always remained true to his democratic principles, he did say later that "I no longer consider a stubborn consistency to two or three political dogmas, however excellent in themselves, as sufficient to atone for all deficiencies of heart and morals." (*Life of Thelwall*, 1:352). And he became uncomfortable about the name "Jacobin." By 1817 he would say that "Nothing betrays the destitution of principle more completely than the sophistical use of really unmeaning, but yet popular cant nick names. Thus Jacobin (a term of no definable signification, but conjuring up in the minds of alarmist & zealous royalists every emotion that belongs to the hatred of all crimes & enormities) is used by the consistent [Coleridge] in such way as to be apparently applicable to all reformers & *incliners* to republicanism—in short to all who are dissatisfied with the established systems of *legitimate* despotism" ("Thelwall's Marginalia in *Biographia Literaria*," 93). Coleridge had earlier made the same point in a fuller discussion: "What *is* a Jacobin. Perhaps the best answer to this question would be, that it is a term of abuse, the convenient watch-word of a faction"—and he goes on to speak brilliantly of various uses of the term. (*Essays on His Times*, 1:365).
53. *Robinson*, 1:183–84.
54. *Ibid.*, 177.
55. Benno von Wiese, *Friedrich Schiller* (Stuttgart: Metzler, 1959), 70, 72, 335, 345–47, 456–59, 808.
56. Wordsworth, *The Excursion*, Book 3, lines 709–26.
57. Wordsworth, *The Prelude* (1850 version), book 11, lines 108–09.
58. *Ibid.*, book 9, lines 284–87.
59. Franz Wiedmann, *Hegel*, trans. Jaochim Neugroschel (New York: Pegasus, 1968), 20–21.
60. Robert Niklaus, *Beaumarchais: Le Mariage de Figaro* (London: Grant & Culler, 1893).
61. J.-J. Rousseau, *Émile*, in *Oeuvres complètes*, ed. Bernard Gagnebin and Marcel Raymond, Bibliothèque de la Pléiade (Paris: Gallimard, 1959–69), 4:468.
62. Christopher Hill, *The World Turned Upside Down; Radical Ideas during the English Revolution* (1972); *Milton and the English Revolution* (1978); *The Experience of Defeat: Milton and Some Contemporaries* (1984).
63. Rabelais, *Pantagruel, Roy des Dipsodes*, ch. 31; in *Oeuvres complètes*, ed. Jacques Boulenger and Lucien Scheler, Bibliothèque de la Pléiade (Paris: Gallimard, 1955), 304.
64. Froissart, *Chronicles*, trans. and ed. Geoffrey Brereton (Harmondsworth, Middlesex: Penguin Books, 1978), 212.
65. Wordsworth, *The Prelude* (1850 version), book 11, lines 122–24.
66. James Sime, *Schiller* (Edinburgh and London: William Blackwood and Sons, 1882), 21.
67. To Southey (3 Nov 1794), in *Collected Letters of Samuel Taylor Coleridge*, ed. Earl Leslie Griggs (Oxford: Clarendon Press, 1956–1971), 1:68.

68. Heinrich Heine, *Sämtliche Schriften*, ed. Klaus Briegleb (Munich: Hanser, 1969–75), 3:393.

69. "Character of Mr. Wordsworth's new poem, *The Excursion*" (*The Examiner*, August 21, August 28, and October 2, 1814), in *Hazlitt*, 4:119-20.

70. For the subsequent Terror see, e.g., M. Mortimer-Ternaux, *Histoire de la Terreur 1792–1794* (Paris: Michel Lévy, 1862–81), 8 vols.; Wilfred B. Kerr, *The Reign of Terror 1793–74* (Toronto: University of Toronto Press, 1927); R. R. Palmer, *Twelve Who Ruled: The Year of the Terror in the French Revolution* (Princeton: Princeton University Press, 1941). See also Colin Lucas, *The Structure of the Terror; The Example of Javogues and the Loire* (London: Oxford University Press, 1973) for a detailed study of extreme terrorist activity in one of the provinces.

71. To Christian Gottfried Körner (February 28, 1793), in Friedrich Schiller, *Briefe*, ed. Gerhard Fricke (Munich: Hanser, 1955), 281.

72. Schiller, *Sämtliche Werke*, ed. Gerhard Fricke and H. G. Göpfert (Munich: Hanser, 1962), 1:459.

73. Wordsworth, *The Prelude* (1850 version), book 9, lines 123–24; book 11, lines 67–68; book 10, lines 41–43; book 11, line 77; book 10, lines 383–84.

74. Robert Southey, *Wat Tyler*, in *Poetical Works* (London: Longman, 1840), 2:43.

75. Mona Wilson, *The Life of William Blake* (1927, rev. 1948; rpt. New York: Cooper Square, 1969), 147–149.

76. *The Complete Works of Percy Bysshe Shelley*, ed. Roger Ingpen and Walter E. Peck (New York: Gordian Press, 1965), 3:9.

77. Maximilien Robespierre, *Textes choisis*, ed. Jean Poperen (Paris: Éditions Sociales, 1956), 2:140.

78. *Hazlitt*, 7:179. Again, "Many people laugh at him, some may blush for him, but nobody envies him." (89).

79. *Ibid.*, 178.

80. *Ibid.*, 11:82.

81. *Ibid.*, 7:190, 199.

82. *Robinson*, 1:206.

83. Coleridge, "Mr. Southey and Wat Tyler" (*Courier*, March 17 and 18, 1817), in *Essays on His Times*, 2:449–60; *Hazlitt*, 7:176–86. Hazlitt says wickedly that "Instead of applying for an injunction against *Wat Tyler*, Mr. Southey would do well to apply for an injunction against Mr. Coleridge, who has undertaken his defence in *The Courier*." (176).

84. Though Thompson is apparently too intent on Coleridge's alleged apostasy to charge Wordsworth in the same way, Byron in 1818 is less benign, referring to Wordsworth's place "at Lord Lonsdale's table, where this poetical charlatan and political parasite licks up the crumbs with a hardened alacrity; the converted Jacobin having long subsided into the clownish sycophant of the worst prejudices of the aristocracy." (Note to the "Dedication" of *Don Juan*). In the "Preface" to *Don Juan* Byron calls Southey "this Pantisocratic apostle of Apostasy."

85. "Thelwall's Marginalia in *Biographia Literaria*," 82, 81.

86. Coleridge, *Lectures 1808–1819; On Literature*, in *The Collected Works of Samuel Taylor Coleridge*, 5 vols. (London: Routledge & Kegan Paul; Princeton: Princeton University Press, 1987), 1:586. Cf. Thelwall to his wife: "Why should not I equal those wonders of ancient eloquence? I have a nobler cause than antiquity ever pleaded. Cicero argued for his client—Demosthenes thundered for the glory and independence of a little city—I advocate the cause of the human race—the rights of the universe—the happiness of ages yet unborn." (*Life of Thelwall*, 1:367–68).

87. *The Collected Writings of Thomas De Quincey*, ed. David Masson (Edinburgh: Adam and Charles Black, 1889–1890), 2:209.

88. Quoted in E. P. Thompson, "Disenchantment or Default? A Lay Sermon," 162.

89. Coleridge, *CL* 1:339.

90. In 1818 Coleridge recalled that he told Thelwall what "he was so unwilling to believe—viz. that alike on the grounds of Taste, Morals, Politics, and Religion, he and I had no one point of coincidence" (*CL* 4:880).

91. Memories of course can play tricks after a certain amount of time has passed. For instance, in 1817 Thelwall at one point when Coleridge refers to Fichte as a disciple of Kant, recalls some details about Fichte. But then he says, "P. S. In the shadowy recollections of past times I have jumbled names—It was Knitch not Fichte—to whom the facts in the above note have reference." ("Thelwall's Marginalia in *Biographia Literaria*," 92).

92. *Hazlitt*, 11:30.

93. *The Works of Thomas Carlyle in Thirty Volumes*, centenary edition, ed. H. D. Traill (London: Chapman & Hall, 1896–99), 11:55–58.

94. Leslie Stephen, *Hours in a Library* (London: Smith, Elder & Co., 1909), 3:324.

95. Quoted in E. P. Thompson, "Disenchantment or Default? A Lay Sermon," 159.

96. *Hazlitt*, 5:167.

97. Coleridge, *CL* 2:1000.

98. *The Letters of William and Dorothy Wordsworth; The Early Years; 1787–1805*, ed. Ernest de Selincourt, revised Chester Shaver (Oxford: Clarendon Press, 1967), 325–26.

99. *Ibid.*, 324.

100. Coleridge, *CL* 1:84.

101. Coleridge, *The Friend*, ed. Barbara E. Rooke, *The Collected Works of Samuel Taylor Coleridge*, 4 vols. (London: Routledge & Kegan Paul; Princeton: Princeton University Press, 1969), 2:26.

102. To Charles Danvers (15 June 1809), *New Letters of Robert Southey*, ed. Kenneth Curry (New York and London: Columbia University Press, 1965), 1:511.

103. Wordsworth, *The Prelude* (1805 version), book 2, lines 475–79.

104. To Bernard Barton (16 May 1826), *Letters of Charles and Mary Lamb*, ed. E. V. Lucas (London: Dent and Methuen, 1935), 3:45.

105. To Bernard Barton (5 April 1823), *Letters of Charles and Mary Lamb*, 2:376–77.

106. Benjamin P. Kurtz, "Coleridge and Swedenborg with Unpublished Marginalia on the 'Prodromus'", *Essays and Studies; University of California Publications in English; Volume 14* (Berkeley and Los Angeles, 1943), 201.

107. Coleridge, *Collected Letters*, 4:835, 837; 5:9–10, 17–19, 86–91, 136–38.

108. Walter Jackson Bate, *Coleridge* (New York: The Macmillan Company, 1968), 213.

109. Coleridge, *Lay Sermons*, ed. R. J. White, in *The Collected Works of Samuel Taylor Coleridge* (London: Routledge & Kegan Paul; Princeton: Princeton University Press, 1972), 6:70.

110. *Robinson*, 1:108.

111. *De Quincey*, 2:215.

112. *Ibid.*, 169.

113. *Ibid.*, 223.

114. *Ibid.*, 217.

115. Michael St. John Packe, *The Life of John Stuart Mill* (New York: The Macmillan Company, 1954), 83–84.

116. Coleridge, *Constitution of the Church and State*, ed. John Colmer, in *The Collected Works of Samuel Taylor Coleridge* (London: Routledge & Kegan Paul; Princeton: Princeton University Press, 1976), 10:29.

117. Coleridge, *Notebooks*, 1:1623.

118. *Ibid.*, 2:2150.

119. *Ibid.*, 1:1695.

120. Again: "If we are not greatly deceived we could point out more than one or two celebrated Anti-Jacobins who are not slightly infected with some of the worst symptoms of the madness against which they are raving; and one or two acts of parliament which are justifiable only upon Jacobin principles" (*Essays on His Times*, 1:370).

121. Editors' Introduction, *Lectures 1795. On Politics and Religion*, lxxix.

122. Georges Lefebvre, *The French Revolution*, trans. Elizabeth Moss Evanson, John Hall Stewart, and James Friguglietti (London: Routledge & Kegan Paul; New York: Columbia University Press, 1962–64), 2:77.

123. *The Jacobins: An Essay in the New History*, 218, 240.

124. Cf. Aulard: "The peril thus run by Christianity at the time of the Worship of Reason and the Worship of the Supreme Being is the most outstanding episode in the religious history of the French Revolution." (A. Aulard, *Christianity and the French Revolution*, trans. Lady Frazer [Boston: Little, Brown, and Company, 1927], 14).

125. Coleridge, *Constitution of the Church and State*, Editor's Introduction, xxxiii.

126. Coleridge, *Essays on His Times*, 1:372–73.

127. Coleridge, *Constitution of the Church and State*, 24.

128. Coleridge, *Essays on His Times*, 1:372–73.

129. Lafayette, *Déclaration des droits de l'homme et du citoyen et ses antécédents américains*, August 26, 1789 (Washington, D. C., 1945); *Mémoires, correspondance*

et manuscrits (Paris: Fournier, 1837), 2:253–306. On the concern with property, see Louis Gottschalk and Margaret Maddox, *Lafayette in the French Revolution* (Chicago: University of Chicago Press, 1969), 88–89. For the immense role of America in the evolution of the Revolution, see, e.g., Pierre Gaxotte, *La Révolution française*, nouvelle édition (Paris: Fayard, 1970), 74–75: "La révolte américaine précipita encore l'évolution. Les Treize colonies étaient depuis longtemps un des thèmes principaux de la littérature sentimentale et humanitaire. On voyait en elles un peuple neuf, tout proche de la nature, tolérant, pieux, patriarcal, sans autre passion que celle du bien, sans autre fanatisme que celui de la vertu. Les chapitres que Raynal leur consacre sont la partie brillante de son *Histoire des Indes*. . . . La déclaration des droits rédigée par Jefferson en un style de code moral tourna la tête aux beaux spirits. Quelques-uns se firent quakers; d'autres—et des plus nobles—s'engagèrent à la suite de La Fayette dans les armées républicaines." American influence crested with the arrival of Benjamin Franklin in Paris: "Il est le grand prêtre des philosophes, le Messie des mécontents, le patron des faiseurs de systèmes. Ses portefeuilles sont plein de lettres qui montrent quelle place il tient dans l'esprit publie et quelle influence il a sur lui. On lui écrit de partout. On implore ses conseils. . . . Un cardinal—c'est Rohan, celui du Collier—organise des fêtes en son honneur. Un médecin—c'est Marat—lui soumet des expériences de physique. Un avocat—c'est Brissot—l'interroge sur le nouveau monde où il pense aller prendre une lecon de Révolution. Un autre lui dédie son premier plaidoyer: c'est Robespierre. Quand Franklin quitte la France, la légende des Etats-Unis est indestructible. . . . Les Etats-Unis avaient donné à la doctrine révolutionnaire ce que lui manquait encore: l'exemple" (76).

130. Louis Madelin, *The French Revolution*, trans. from the French (New York: G. P. Putnam's Sons, 1928), 382.
131. *The Marxist Reader; The Most Significant and Enduring Works of Marxism*, ed. Emile Burns (New York: Avenel Books, 1982), 38.
132. Coleridge, *Constitution of the Church and State*, 26–27.
133. Lefebvre, 2:119.
134. Coleridge, *Lectures 1795. On Politics and Religion*, 48.
135. Isser Woloch, *Jacobin Legacy; The Democratic Movement under the Directory* (Princeton: Princeton University Press, 1970), 12.
136. Lefebvre, 1:242; 2:92.
137. Coleridge, *Lectures 1795. On Politics and Religion*, 34.
138. *Ibid.*, 48.
139. Coleridge, *Essays on His Times*, 78.
140. *Ibid.*, 79.
141. *Ibid.*, 368–69.
142. *The Marxist Reader*, 119.
143. Richard Holmes, *Shelley: The Pursuit* (New York: E. P. Dutton, 1975), 392.
144. Shelley, *Works*, 6:219.

145. *The Marxist Reader*, 117.
146. *Ibid.*, 581.
147. *Ibid.*, 59.
148. For Babeuf's centrality in the line leading from Jacobin principles to Russian communism, cf., e.g., R. B. Rose: "As the first revolutionary communist of modern times Gracchus Babeuf has been for many years a figure of considerable veneration for Marxists. In 1845 Marx and Engels paid their own tribute in *The Holy Family* to the rôle of Babeuf and the Conspiracy of Equals of 1796 in passing on the idea of communism from the utopians of the Enlightenment, through the mediation of Buonarotti, to the nineteenth century; in the *Communist Manifesto* Babeuf was recognized as the spokesman of the proletariat in the French Revolution. In 1919, on the morrow of the Bolshevik Revolution, Leon Trotsky proclaimed Babeuf the first of a long line of revolutionary heroes and martyrs whose struggle had prepared the way for the Communist International and the world proletarian revolution." (R. B. Rose, *Gracchus Babeuf; The First Revolutionary Communist* [London: Edward Arnold, 1978], 1). Interestingly, Rose notes that "the great French Revolution scholar Albert Mathiez always obstinately refused to distinguish between the Jacobin tradition and the Babouvist tradition" (330).
149. Philippe Buonarotti, *Babeuf's Conspiracy for Equality*, trans. Bronterre O'Brien (New York: August M. Kelley, 1965 [1836]), 57n.
150. For Babeuf's career see, e.g., Gérard Walter, *Babeuf 1760–1797 et la conjuration des égaux* (Paris: Payot, 1937).
151. "After the victorious first generation of Russian Jacobins had laid the foundation of their work, the master narrative has gradually become absorbed into *their* story of foundation. Lenin's, Trotsky's and Luxemburg's generation still knew by heart what had happened in Paris in those distant days." (Ferenc Feher, *The Frozen Revolution: An Essay on Jacobinism* [Cambridge: Cambridge University Press; Paris: Editions de la Maison des Sciences de l'Homme, 1987], 153). For those who witnessed the "Jacobin mania" of our own recent decade of the 1960s, Feher's description of the character of the Jacobin will seem especially just: "The new French revolutionary . . . wanted only to live in social turbulence, promoting revolutions preferably from a position of power, but if things changed for the worse, then also to do so under persecution. These men shared three features in common. Firstly, they preferred process to consolidation. The term 'permanent revolution' was coined later, but the way of life pertaining to it had already been invented by the Jacobin militant. . . . The second feature was the strong ideological motivation of the modern revolutionary . . . [T]he real life of human beings should cede to the imperatives of doctrine. Thirdly, the modern revolutionary was a professional: revolution was his *métier*. He lived from the revolution, mostly poorly but sometimes in a dandyish, well-provided manner" (125). What Feher calls "the strong ideological motivation" Taine stigmatizes as the "theorizing mania" that scrambled the brains of the ordi-

nary people who made up the Jacobins (Taine, 3:41). Again, Brinton says that "Of the very general truth that the Jacobins were thoroughly steeped in the writings of the eighteenth century philosophers there can be no doubt" (*The Jacobins*, 210).

152. ". . . when we conclude that no fewer than fourteen million odd peasants lost their lives as a result of the events recounted in this book we may well be understating." (Robert Conquest, *The Harvest of Sorrow: Soviet Collectivization and the Terror-Famine* [New York: Oxford University Press, 1986], 305). Conquest emphasizes that the massacre was not a result of inadvertency or mismanagement, but was precisely a furtherance of Marxist doctrine as interpreted by Stalin: "In a more general sense, the responsibility for the massacre of the 'class enemy' and the crushing of 'bourgeois nationalism,' may be held to lie with the Marxist conceptions in the form given them by the Communist Party as accepted by Stalin" (328). "The main lesson seems to be that the Communist ideology provided the motivation for an unprecedented massacre of men, women, and children. And that this ideology, perhaps all set-piece theory, turned out to be a primitive and schematic approach to matters far too complex for it" (344).

153. *The Marxist Reader*, 264–65.

154. Coleridge, *Notebooks*, 2:2208.

155. As Saint Just said, "What constitutes the Republic is the destruction of everything opposed to it. A man is guilty against the Republic when he takes pity on prisoners: he is guilty because he has no desire for virtue: he is guilty because he is opposed to the Terror" (Madelin, 394).

156. Coleridge, *Lectures 1795. On Politics and Religion*, 59.

157. *Ibid.*, 247–48.

158. Taine's fury against the Revolution predictably led to counterattacks by those historians who celebrated it as a great advance in human history. Aulard wrote an entire book in an attempt to discredit Taine: "Ainsi toute la Terreur s'explique (je ne dis pas: se justifie) par les circonstances de guerre civile et étrangère où se trouvait alors la France. Taine ne parle pas de ces circonstances ou n'y fait que d'insignifiantes allusions. Les moyens de violence que les Montagnards employèrent pour assurer la défense nationale contre les insurgés vendéens, contre les Autrichiens, les Anglais, les Espagnols, Taine ne les attribue qu'à un fanatisme philosophique." (A. Aulard, *Taine; historien de la révolution française* [Paris: Librairie Armand Colin, 1907], 326). He attempts at great length but with indifferent success to impeach Taine's learning ("J'ai moins voulu critiquer les théories philosophico-historiques de Taine que son érudition, dont l'appareil, d'aspect si imposant, a donné crédit à ses théories et lui a valu, en France et à l'étranger, une grande réputation d'historien" [323]); and he concludes that Taine's "livre, tout compte fait, et en ses résultats généraux, me semble presque inutile à l'histoire. Il n'est vraiment utile qu'à la biographie intellectuelle de Taine lui-même ou à celle de quelques contemporains, ses disciples" (330). The majority of academic historians today (quite a few of whom are declared Marxists)

are content with Aulard's position, and reject Taine as intolerably biased. So far as I myself can judge, however, he is less biased than Michelet was as the extoller of Revolution, and no more biased than Aulard himself, or Lefebvre, or other academic apologists for the great upheaval. As a single random case in point, Cobb can quaintly accuse Taine of progressing "to pure insult" in his description of the personnel of the provincial armies, while Cobb himself is continually palliating their crimes. (Richard Cobb, *The People's Armies; The armées révolutionnaires; Instrument of the Terror in the Departments; April 1793 to Floréal Year II*, trans. Marianne Elliott [New Haven and London: Yale University Press, 1987 (1961–63)], 5). After all, Brinton at one point finds it fitting to speak of "the madness of true Jacobinism" (*The Jacobins*, 240). "They were in the main ordinary, quite prosperous middle-class people. And yet they behaved like fanatics. The Reign of Terror was marked by cruelties and absurdities which the greatest of misanthropes will hardly maintain are characteristic of ordinary human beings" (232).

For those who, unlike Taine and Coleridge, did and do think that the Revolution justified its cost, the classic line of argument is that eloquently pleaded by Shelley: "The oppressors of mankind had enjoyed a long and undisturbed reign in France, and to the pining famine, the shelterless destitution of the inhabitants of that country had been added and heaped up insult harder to endure than misery. For the feudal system (the immediate causes and conditions of its institution having become obliterated) had degenerated into the instrument not only of oppression but of contumely, and both were unsparingly inflicted. Blind in the possession of strength, drunken as with the intoxication of ancestral greatness, the rulers perceived not that increase of knowledge in their subjects which made its exercise insecure. They called soldiers to hew down the people when their power was already past. The tyrants were, as usual, the aggressors. Then the oppressed, having been rendered brutal, ignorant, servile and bloody by long slavery, having had the intellectual thirst, excited in them by the progress of civilization, satiated from fountains of literature poisoned by the spirit and the form of monarchy, arose and took a dreadful revenge on their oppressors. Their desire to wreak revenge, to this extent, in itself a mistake, a crime, a calamity, arose from the same source as their other miseries and errors, and affords an additional proof of the necessity of that long-delayed change which it accompanied and disgraced" (Shelley, *Complete Works*, 7:13).

159. Taine, 2:70.
160. *Ibid.*, 65.
161. *Ibid.*, 3:66–7.
162. *Ibid.*, 48–9.
163. *Ibid.*, 4:159, 174.
164. Gaxotte argues interestingly that Robespierre's special kind of mediocrity was especially fitted to be empowered by the structure of the Jacobin Club. "Robespierre est l'homme de club par excellence. Tout ce qui le dessert dans

la vie réelle lui devient au club un gage de succès. Il a l'esprit peu fécond, peu d'idées, peu d'invention? Il est au niveau de son auditoire, il ne l'effraie pas, il n'excite pas sa jalousie. Sa personnalité est apparemment faible, indistincte? Il se fond dans la personnalité collective, il se plie sans effort à la la discipline démocratique. Sa situation sociale est presque nulle? Le club est fondé sur l'égalité de tous ses membres et il supporte mal les supériorités extérieures de rang et d'argent. Ses affaires l'occupent peu? Il n'en sera que plus assidu aux séances. Il a peu vécu, son expérience des hommes et des choses est bornée. Le club est une société artificielle construite au rebours de la société véritable. Il a l'intelligence formaliste, sans grande prise sur le réel? Au club l'action ne compte pas, mais la parole." "Cet homme médiocre a le sens, ou, si l'on veut, le génie de la Révolution et de son mécanisme" (Gaxotte, 389–90, 391).

165. Taine, 4:190–92.
166. *Ibid.*, 3:i–ii.
167. Cf. Madelin: "The one and constant thought of that mediocre brain and narrow soul was to protect himself against 'his enemies.' These he discovered in every quarter; to destroy them he kept the guillotine permanently employed. . . . It was unsafe to look sad, or even thoughtful. Barras tells a story of one deputy who fancied Robespierre looked at him when he was in a dreamy mood, and exclaimed in alarm: '*He'll be supposing I was thinking about something!*'" (Madelin, 402–03).
168. Coleridge, *Lectures 1795. On Politics and Religion*, 35.
169. It detracts in no way from the magnificence and fittingness of Coleridge's metaphor to note that just as Robespierre was not actually the Emperor Caligula, so too in fact he was too much of a dandy to wear the cap of liberty. "All the same, he did not seem at all pleased that the general had arrived wearing a red cap. He never wore one himself, but only had a tricolour cockade in his buttonhole. How could he put such a covering over his powdered hair that was so carefully combed? . . . Even so, the cap had great success with the Parisians and members of the club, the majority of whom wore it. . . . At the end of the session one of those present tried to put one on Robespierre's head. No doubt he was an admirer and he did not want his idol to appear to disadvantage alongside Dumouriez. Robespierre immediately snatched it off and threw it to the ground. From anyone else but him the gesture would have seemed a sacrilege. Even so, no one protested. In fact, for a while fewer red caps were seen at the club" (Matrat, 144–45).

Chapter 13 The *Biographia Literaria* and the Contentions of English Romanticism

1. *Biographia Literaria*, ed. James Engell and W. Jackson Bate (Princeton: Princeton University Press, 1983) 1:88. This edition is used throughout and page references are given in the text.

2. See *Lay Sermons*, ed. R. J. White (Princeton: Princeton University Press, 1972), 114n.
3. For Coleridge's "marginal" method of proceeding in *Biographia* see Thomas McFarland, *Coleridge and the Pantheist Tradition* (Oxford: Clarendon Press, 1969), 27; and Jerome Christensen, *Coleridge's Blessed Machine of Language* (Ithaca: Cornell University Press, 1981), ch. 3.
4. *Lay Sermons*, 114n.
5. *The Friend*, ed. Barbara E. Rooke (Princeton: Princeton University Press, 1969) 1:457.
6. *The Collected Letters of Samuel Taylor Coleridge*, ed. Earl Leslie Griggs (Oxford: Clarendon Press, 1956–71) 2:812.
7. *Lay Sermons*, 114n.
8. *The Friend*, 1:449.
9. Even John Crowe Ransom, in his excellent discussion of Wordsworth's position, grudgingly agrees that Coleridge's views have been—in contrast to Wordsworth's—a "permanent influence on poetic theory" (see Ransom's "William Wordsworth: Notes Toward an Understanding of Poetry," in *Wordsworth. Centenary Studies*, ed. Gilbert T. Dunklin (Princeton: Princeton University Press, 1951), 92. A strong case for Wordsworth's theoretical importance has been made by Gene Ruoff, "Wordsworth on Language: Towards a Radical Poetics of English Romanticism," *The Wordsworth Circle* (1972), 204–11.
10. Compare *Blake. Complete Writings*, ed. Geoffrey Keynes (London: Oxford University Press, 1966), 782–84.
11. C. M. Wallace, *The Design of Biographia Literaria* (London: George Allen & Unwin, 1983), 113.
12. *The Prose Works of William Wordsworth*, ed. W. J. B. Owen and J. W. Smyser (Oxford: Clarendon, 1974), 1:133. References hereafter will be cited in the text to this edition.
13. *Byron's Letters and Journals*, ed. Leslie A. Marchand (Cambridge, Mass.: Harvard University Press 1973–82), 5:267. (References hereafter will be cited as *BLJ*). Byron had been instrumental in getting Drury Lane to produce Coleridge's *Remorse* in 1813, and he tried—unsuccessfully—to get Coleridge to write another play for the theater. He encouraged and praised Coleridge's poetry and also provided him with financial assistance. See *BLJ* 4:285–86, 318–19 and 5:16 and n.
14. *The Friend*, 2:220.
15. For Byron's financial and literary help to Coleridge see above, n. 13, as well as *BLJ* 9:206–08.
16. Certain other small textual details illustrate Byron's recollection of Coleridge's text when he was writing *Don Juan*. For example, the unusual phrase "olla Podrida" appears in ch. 23 of the *Biographia* as well as in Byron's (later rejected) prose Preface to *Don Juan* (see *Biographia*, p. 211 and *Lord Byron. The Complete Poetical Works*, ed. Jerome J. McGann. Vol. 5 (*Don Juan*) (London: Oxford University Press 1986), 83. Similarly, the conclusion of stanza 2 of Byron's "Dedication" to *Don Juan* glances at Coleridge's defensive remarks about his

"metaphysics," especially in *Biographia* ch. 24. Compare also *Biographia* 2, pp. 126–35 with Byron's treatment of Wordsworth in the rejected prose preface to *Don Juan*. See the discussion by McGann, 5:668.

17. *Lord Byron. Complete Poetical Works*, 4:247.

Chapter 14 Poetry and Barrel-Organs

1. *Biographia Literaria*, 2:29, in *The Collected Works of Samuel Taylor Coleridge* (London & Princeton, N.J. 1969—). All further references to Coleridge's works are to this edition and will appear in the text. Abbreviations of titles of Coleridge's works are those used in this collected edition.

2. *Camilla, or A Picture of Youth*, ed. by Edward A. Bloom and Lillian D. Bloom. Quoted in the introduction, xx.

3. Boswell's *Life of Samuel Johnson* (New York: Oxford University Press, 1933) 251. Johnson also is reported to have said that booksellers were "generous, liberal-minded men" (i,203) and that "there are few ways in which a man can be more innocently employed than in getting money" (ii,567), two opinions less and less common throughout the nineteenth century. For some useful essays on book publishing and reading in the eighteenth century, based on the most recent scholarship, see *Books and Their Readers in Eighteenth-Century England*, ed. Isabel Rivers (New York: St. Martin's Press, 1982).

4. For an illuminating study of this subject see Jon Klancher, *The Making of English Reading Audiences, 1790–1832* (Madison: University of Wisconsin Press, 1987). Thomas McFarland, in *Originality and Imagination* (Baltimore: The Johns Hopkins University Press, 1985), discusses the problem of aesthetic originality, genius, and imagination confronting the mass audience much as it must confront the endless universe. His point of view is decidedly Coleridgean, e. g. "it is against . . . encompassing darkness that originality and imagination hold aloft their flickering torches" (200). For a useful account of the self-consciousness of language and class in the works of Romantic writers and their contemporaries, see Olivia Smith, *The Politics of Language, 1791–1819* (London: Oxford University Press, 1984).

5. Criticism of the *ideas* in the *Biographia Literaria* is much more abundant than criticism of it as a piece of writing. Most books devoted to it as a book follow the traditional critical line of looking for its "wholeness" or "unity"; they invoke Coleridge's critical ideas by which to search out some more or less hidden Coleridgean organic principle. See, for instance, Catherine Miles Wallace, *The Design of Biographia Literaria* (London and Boston: Allen & Unwin, 1983) and Lynn M. Grow, "The Consistency of the *Biographia Literaria*," in Wichita State University Bulletin, University Studies No. 95, 49.2 (May, 1973). There is a driving desire in both these studies to read the *Biographia* like a well-formed meditative whole, that is to say, like a poem. Kathleen M. Wheeler's *Sources, Processes and Methods in Coleridge's* Biographia Literaria (Cambridge: Cambridge University Press, 1980) presents a somewhat more distanced read-

ing of the process of "writing" in the *Biographia* and demonstrates some of its ironical method.

6. See also Wordsworth's famous letter to Charles James Fox of January 14th, 1801, in which he speaks of the "most sacred of all property . . . the property of the Poor."

7. See C. B. Macpherson, *The Political Theory of Possessive Individualism: Hobbes to Locke* (New York: Oxford University Press, 1983 [1962]).

8. *Lay Sermons*, in *The Collected Works*, xxix.

9. One critic, as I have already suggested [see note 5] who does see the High Romantic Irony in the *Biographia* is Katherine M. Wheeler. Yet seeing the irony as a mode of high romanticism is a complicated ideological business. It allows the social antagonisms that preoccupied Coleridge into our reading only to smooth them out with one more admiring glance at the power of aesthetic order. This tendency in Romantic scholarship to turn historical and social antagonisms, sensed by Romantic writers, as nothing more or less than social, into neat aesthetic form is ubiquitous. Coleridge *does* employ an ironical mode here, but this is a stance taken towards a problem he sees unresolved, perplexing, and, above all, politically dangerous. Critics who show us the "unity" of the *Biographia Literaria* give at least the impression that something has been satisfied in a work that constantly registers serious disjunction and ideological discomfort. This critical line of "aesthetic unity" has been pushed as far as it can go by Donald Reiman, who asks us to see the *Biographia* as an epigone of *Tristam Shandy*; see "Coleridge and the Art of Equivocation," in *Studies in Romanticism* 25 (Fall 1986): 325–50.

10. Raymond Williams, *Culture and Society, 1780–1850* (New York: Columbia University Press, 1983 [1958]).

11. *The Politics of Language, 1791–1819*, 225.

12. *Commentary*, vol. 58, no. 6 (December, 1974): 35. Trilling's statement is part of a round-table discussion, whose other participants are Edward Grossman, Cynthia Ozick, Hilton Kramer, Norman Podhoretz, Michael Novak, and Jack Richardson. The entire discussion occurs at an important moment, when some American new conservative thinkers (old liberal modernists) were still staking out positions towards mass culture. There is much nostalgia in this discussion for the Coleridgean and the Arnoldean.

13. The influence of Gramsci, especially his idea of hegemony and of the intellectual class, is preeminent in all Marxist influence on American liberal and left academic cultural critics. For an example of that pervasive influence even in a critique of contemporary criticism, see Edward W. Said, *The World, the Text, and the Critic* (Cambridge, Mass.: Harvard University Press, 1983).

14. Vladimir Nabokov, *Bend Sinister* (New York: Henry Holt and Co., 1947) 123–24.

15. *The Romantic Ideology* (Chicago and London: University of Chicago Press, 1983).

Bibliography

I. Coleridge

Aids to Reflection, ed. Henry Nelson Coleridge. 4th ed. London: William Pickering, 1839.

Biographia Literaria, 2 vols. London: Rest Fenner, 1817.

Biographia Literaria, 2 vols. in 3, ed. H. N. and Sara Coleridge. London: William Pickering, 1847.

Biographia Literaria, 2 vols., ed. John Shawcross. London: Oxford University Press, 1907.

Biographia Literaria, ed. George Sampson. Cambridge: Cambridge University Press, 1920.

Biographia Literaria, ed. George Watson. London: Dent, 1956; rev. 1965, 1975.

Biographia Literaria, 2 vols., ed. James Engell and Walter Jackson Bate, in *The Collected Works of Samuel Taylor Coleridge*, 7. General Editors: Kathleen Coburn and Bart Winer. Bollingen Series 75. Princeton: Princeton University Press; London: Routledge and Kegan Paul, 1983.

Coleridge on the Seventeenth Century, ed. Roberta Brinkley. Durham: Duke University Press, 1955.

Collected Letters of Samuel Taylor Coleridge, 6 vols., ed. Earl Leslie Griggs. Oxford: Clarendon, 1956–71.

Complete Works of Samuel Taylor Coleridge, 7 vols., ed. W. G. T. Shedd. New York: Harper and Brothers, 1853.

Complete Poetical Works, 2 vols., ed. Ernest Hartley Coleridge. Oxford: Clarendon Press, 1912.

Essays on His Times, 3 vols., ed. David V. Erdman, in *The Collected Works of Samuel Taylor Coleridge*, 3. Princeton: Princeton University Press; London: Routledge and Kegan Paul, 1978.

The Friend, 2 vols., ed. Barbara Rooke, in *The Collected Works of Samuel Taylor Coleridge*, 4. Princeton: Princeton University Press; London: Routledge and Kegan Paul, 1969.

Inquiring Spirit; A New Presentation of Coleridge from his Published and Unpublished Prose Writings, ed. Kathleen Coburn. New York: Pantheon Books, 1951.

Lay Sermons, ed. R. J. White, in *The Collected Works of Samuel Taylor Coleridge*, 6.

Princeton: Princeton University Press; London: Routledge and Kegan Paul, 1972.

Lectures 1795: On Politics and Religion, ed. Lewis Patton and Peter Mann, in *The Collected Works of Samuel Taylor Coleridge*, 1. Princeton: Princeton University Press; London: Routledge and Kegan Paul, 1971.

Lectures 1808–1819: On Literature, 2 vols., ed. Reginald A. Foakes, in *The Collected Works of Samuel Taylor Coleridge*, 5. Princeton: Princeton University Press; London: Routledge and Kegan Paul, 1987.

Logic, ed. J. R. de J. Jackson, in *The Collected Works of Samuel Taylor Coleridge*, 13. Princeton: Princeton University Press; London: Routledge and Kegan Paul, 1981.

Marginalia, 5 vols., ed. George Whalley, in *The Collected Works of Samuel Taylor Coleridge*, 12. Princeton: Princeton University Press; London: Routledge and Kegan Paul, 1980–.

Miscellaneous Criticism, ed. Thomas Middleton Raysor. London: Constable, 1936.

The Notebooks of Samuel Taylor Coleridge, 3 vols., ed. Kathleen Coburn. New York: Pantheon, 1957–61; Princeton: Princeton University Press, 1973.

On the Constitution of the Church and State, ed. John Colmer, in *The Collected Works of Samuel Taylor Coleridge*, 10. Princeton: Princeton University Press; London: Routledge and Kegan Paul, 1976.

The Poetical Works of Samuel Taylor Coleridge, ed. James Dykes Campbell. London: Macmillan, 1893.

Shakespearean Criticism, 2 vols., ed. Thomas Middleton Raysor. 2nd ed. London: Dent, 1960.

Specimens of the Table Talk of the Late Samuel Taylor Coleridge, 2 vols., ed. H. N. Coleridge. London: John Murray, 1835.

The Table Talk and Omniana of Samuel Taylor Coleridge, ed. T. Ashe. London: George Bell and Sons, 1888.

The Watchman, ed. Lewis Patton, in *The Collected Works of Samuel Taylor Coleridge*, 2. Princeton: Princeton University Press; London: Routledge and Kegan Paul, 1970.

II. Coleridge Bibliography

Caskey, J. D., and M. M. Stapper. *Samuel Taylor Coleridge: A Selective Bibliography of Criticism 1935–1977*. London and Westport, Conn.: 1978.

Crawford, Walter B., Edward S. Lauterbach, and Ann M. Crawford, *Samuel Taylor Coleridge: An Annotated Bibliography of Criticism and Scholarship*, 2: 1900–39. Boston: Hall, 1983.

Haney, John L. *A Bibliography of S. T. Coleridge*. Philadelphia, 1903.

Haven, R. and J., and M. Adams, *Samuel Taylor Coleridge: An Annotated Bibliography of Criticism and Scholarship*, 1: 1793–1899. Boston: Hall, 1976.

III. Works on Coleridge

Abrams, M. H. *The Mirror and the Lamp*. London: Oxford University Press, 1953.
———. *Natural Supernaturalism: Tradition and Revolution in Romantic Literature*. New York: Norton, 1971.
———. "Coleridge's 'A Light in Sound': Science, Metascience, and Poetic Imagination," *Proceedings of the American Philosophical Society* 116 (1972): 458–75.
Appleyard, J. A., S. J. *Coleridge's Philosophy of Literature: the Development of a Concept of Poetry 1791–1819*. Cambridge, Mass.: Harvard University Press, 1965.
Ashton, Rosemary. *The German Idea: Four English Writers and the Reception of German Thought 1800–1860*. Cambridge: Cambridge University Press, 1980.
Baker, James. *The Sacred River: Coleridge's Theory of the Imagination*. Baton Rouge: Louisiana State University Press, 1957.
Barfield, Owen. *What Coleridge Thought*. Middletown, Conn.: Wesleyan University Press, 1971.
Barth, J. Robert, S. J. *Coleridge and Christian Doctrine*. Cambridge, Mass.: Harvard University Press, 1969.
———. *The Symbolic Imagination. Coleridge and the Romantic Tradition*. Princeton: Princeton University Press, 1977.
———. "Theological Implications of Coleridge's Theory of Imagination," *Studies in Literary Interpretation* 19.2 (Fall 1986): 22–33.
Bate, Walter Jackson. *Coleridge*. New York: Macmillan, 1968.
———, ed. *Criticism: the Major Texts*. New York: Harcourt Brace, 1952.
Beer, John. *Coleridge The Visionary*. London and New York: Chatto and Windus, 1959.
———. *Coleridge's Poetic Intelligence*. London: Macmillan, 1977.
———. "The 'Revolutionary Youth' of Wordsworth and Coleridge: Another View" [reply to Watson; see below], *Critical Quarterly* 19 (1977): 79–87.
Bloom, Harold, ed. *Romanticism and Consciousness. Essays in Criticism*. New York: Norton, 1970.
———. "Coleridge: The Anxiety of Influence," in *New Perspectives on Coleridge and Wordsworth*, ed. Geoffrey Hartman. New York: Columbia University Press, 1972, 246–67.
Boulger, James D. "Coleridge on Imagination Revisited," *Wordsworth Circle* 4 (1973): 13–24.
Buell, Lawrence. "The Question of Form in Coleridge's *Biographia Literaria*," *ELH* 16 (1979): 399–417.
Burwick, Frederick. "Coleridge's 'Limbo' and 'Ne Plus Ultra': The Muleity of Intertextuality," *Romanticism Past and Present* 9.1 (1985): 35–45.
———. *The Damnation of Newton: Goethe's Color Theory and Romantic Perception*. Berlin and New York: De Gruyter, 1986.
———. *Perception and the Grotesque in English and German Romanticism*. Heidelberg: Carl Winter Universitätsverlag, 1987.
Bygrave, Stephen. *Coleridge and the Self. Romantic Egotism*. London: Macmillan, 1986.

Christensen, Jerome C. "Coleridge's Marginal Method in the *Biographia Literaria*," *PMLA* 92 (October 1977): 928–40.

———. "The Genius in the *Biographia Literaria*," *Studies in Romanticism* 17 (Winter 1978): 215–31.

———. *Coleridge's Blessed Machine of Language*. Ithaca: Cornell University Press, 1981.

———. "Once an Apostate Always an Apostate," *Studies in Romanticism* 21.3 (Fall, 1982): 461–64.

———. "The Mind at Ocean: The Impropriety of Coleridge's Literary Life," in *Romanticism and Language*, ed. Arden Reed. Ithaca: Cornell University Press, 1984, 144–67.

———. "Philosophy/Literature: The Associationist Precedent for Coleridge's Late Poems," in *Philosophical Approaches to Literature: New Essays on Nineteenth- and Twentieth-Century Texts*, ed. William Cain. Lewisburg, Penn.: Bucknell University Press, 1984, 27–50.

Cooke, Michael G. "*Quisque Sui Faber*: Coleridge in the *Biographia Literaria*," *Philological Quarterly* 50 (1971): 208–29.

Corrigan, Timothy. *Coleridge, Language, and Criticism*. Athens: University of Georgia Press, 1982.

De Quincey, Thomas. "Samuel Taylor Coleridge" (1834–35), "The Lake Poets: Southey, Wordsworth, and Coleridge" (1839), "Coleridge and Opium-Eating" (1845), in *The Collected Writings of Thomas De Quincey*, 14 vols., ed. David Masson. Edinburgh: Adam and Charles Black, 1889–90, 2:138–228, 335–47; 5:179–214.

DePaolo, Charles. "Kant, Coleridge, and the Ethics of War," *Wordsworth Circle* 16.1 (Winter 1985): 3–13.

Emmet, Dorothy. "Coleridge on Powers in Mind and Nature," in *Coleridge's Variety: Bicentenary Studies*, ed. John Beer. Pittsburgh: University of Pittsburgh Press, 1974, 166–82.

Engell, James. *The Creative Imagination: Enlightenment to Romanticism*. Cambridge, Mass.: Harvard University Press, 1981.

Ferrier, James Frederick. "The Plagiarisms of S. T. Coleridge," *Blackwood's Edinburgh Magazine* 47 (March 1840): 287–99.

Ferris, David S. "Coleridge's Ventriloquy: The Abduction from the *Biographia*," *Studies in Romanticism* 24.1 (Spring 1985): 41–84.

Fischer, Michael. "Morality and History in Coleridge's Political Theory," *Studies in Romanticism* 21.3 (Fall 1982): 457–60.

Flavin, James. "Paragraph One of *Biographia Literaria*: Coleridge on Structure," *Notes and Queries*, n.s. 31.1 (March 1984): 56–57.

Fogle, David Mark. "A Compositional History of the *Biographia Literaria*," *Studies in Bibliography* 30 (1977): 219–34.

Fogle, Richard Harter. *The Idea of Coleridge's Criticism*. Berkeley: University of California Press, 1962.

Freud, Sigmund. *Introductory Lectures on Psychoanalysis*, trans. and ed. James Strachey. New York: Norton, 1966.

Fruman, Norman. *Coleridge, the Damaged Archangel.* New York: Braziller, 1971.

———. "Coleridge's Rejection of Nature and the Natural Man," in *Coleridge's Imagination: Essays in Memory of Pete Laver,* ed. Richard Gravil, Lucy Newlyn, Nicholas Roe. Cambridge: Cambridge University Press, 1985, 22–52.

———. "Review Essay: Aids to Reflection on the New *Biographia*," *Studies in Romanticism* 24.1 (Spring 1985): 141–73.

———. "Ozymandias and the Reconciliation of Opposites," *Studies in Literary Interpretation* 19.2 (Fall 1986): 71–87.

Galperin, William. "Desynonymizing the Self in Wordsworth and Coleridge," *Studies in Romanticism* 27 (1988).

Gravil, Richard. "Coleridge's Wordsworth," *Wordsworth Circle* 15.2 (Spring 1984): 38–46.

———. "Imagining Wordsworth: 1797–1807–1817," in *Coleridge's Imagination: Essays in Memory of Pete Laver,* ed. Richard Gravil, Lucy Newlyn, Nicholas Roe. Cambridge: Cambridge University Press, 1985, 129–42.

Griggs, Earl Leslie. "The Willing Suspension of Disbelief," in *Elizabethan Studies and Other Essays in Honor of George F. Reynolds.* Boulder: University of Colorado Press, 1945, 272–85.

Grow, Lynn M. "The Consistency of the *Biographia Literaria*," in *Wichita State University Bulletin* 49.2 (May 1973).

Hamilton, Paul. *Coleridge's Poetics.* Stanford: Stanford University Press, 1983.

Harding, Anthony. *Coleridge and the Idea of Love: Aspects of Relationship in Coleridge's Thought and Writing.* Cambridge: Cambridge University Press, 1974.

———. *Coleridge and the Inspired Word.* Montreal: McGill-Queen's University Press, 1985.

Haven, Richard. *Patterns of Consciousness: An Essay on Coleridge.* Amherst: University of Massachusetts Press, 1969.

Hayter, Alethea. "Coleridge, Maturin's *Bertram*, and Drury Lane," in *New Approaches to Coleridge: Biographical and Critical Essays,* ed. Donald Sultana. London: Vision, 1981, 17–37.

Hazlitt, William. "Coleridge's Literary Life" (1817), in *Complete Works,* 21 vols., ed. P. P. Howe. London: Dent, 1930–34, 16:119–30.

Hodgson, John A. "Transcendental Tropes: Coleridge's Rhetoric of Allegory and Symbol," in *Allegory, Myth, and Symbol,* ed. Morton W. Bloomfield. Cambridge, Mass.: Harvard University Press, 1981.

Hunt, Bishop C., Jr. "Coleridge and the Endeavor of Philosophy," *PMLA* 91 (1976): 829–39.

Jackson, J. R. de J. *Method and Imagination in Coleridge's Criticism.* Cambridge, Mass.: Harvard University Press, 1969.

Jang, Gyung-ryul. "The Imagination beyond and within Language: An Understanding of Coleridge's Idea of Imagination," *Studies in Romanticism* 25.4 (Winter 1986): 505–20.

Jasper, David. *The Interpretation of Belief: Coleridge, Schleiermacher and Romanticism.* New York: St. Martin's, 1986.

Jenkins, Patricia M. *Coleridge's Literary Theory: The Chronology of its Development.*

Fairfield, Conn.: University of Fairfield, 1984.

Knoepflmacher, U. C. "A Nineteenth-Century Touchstone: Chapter XV of *Biographia Literaria*," in *Nineteenth-Century Perspectives. Essays in Honor of Lionel Stevenson*. Durham: Duke University Press, 1974, 3–16.

Kurtz, Benjamin P. "Coleridge and Swedenborg, with Unpublished Marginalia on the 'Prodromus'," *Essays and Studies; University of California Publications in English* 14 (1943).

Levere, Trevor H. *Poetry Realized in Nature: Samuel Taylor Coleridge and Early Nineteenth-Century Science*. Cambridge: Cambridge University Press, 1981.

Lockridge, Laurence S. *Coleridge the Moralist*. Ithaca: Cornell University Press, 1977.

Magnuson, Paul. *Coleridge's Nightmare Poetry*. Charlottesville: University Press of Virginia, 1974.

Mallette, Richard. "Narrative Technique in the *Biographia Literaria*" *Modern Language Review* 70 (1970): 32–40.

Marks, Emerson. *Coleridge on the Language of Verse*. Princeton: Princeton University Press, 1981.

McFarland, Thomas. *Coleridge and the Pantheist Tradition*. Oxford: Clarendon Press, 1969.

———. "The Origin and Significance of Coleridge's Theory of Secondary Imagination," in *New Perspectives on Coleridge and Wordsworth*, ed. Geoffrey Hartman. New York and London, 1972, 195–246.

———. "Coleridge's Plagiarisms Once More: A Review Essay," *Yale Review* 63 (Winter 1974): 252–86.

———. *Romanticism and the Forms of Ruin. Wordsworth, Coleridge, and Modalities of Fragmentation*. Princeton: Princeton University Press, 1981.

———. *Originality and Imagination*. Baltimore: The John Hopkins University Press, 1985.

———. "So Immethodical a Miscellany: Coleridge's Literary Life," *Modern Philology* 82.4 (May 1986): 405–13.

McKusick, James. *Coleridge's Philosophy of Language*. New Haven: Yale University Press, 1986.

McLaughlin, Elisabeth T. "Coleridge and Milton," *Studies in Philology* 41 (1964): 545–72.

Miall, David S. "Coleridge's Dread Book of Judgement: A Memory for Life," *Journal of European Studies* 15.4 (December 1985): 233–46.

Mileur, Jean-Pierre. *Vision and Revision: Coleridge's Art of Immanence*. Berkeley: University of California Press, 1986.

Modiano, Raimonda. "*Naturphilosophie* and Christian Orthodoxy in Coleridge's View of the Trinity," *Pacific Coast Philology* 17 (1982): 59–68.

———. "Metaphysical Debate in Coleridge's Political Theory," *Studies in Romanticism* 21.3 (Fall 1982): 465–74.

———. *Coleridge and the Concept of Nature*. London: Macmillan, 1985.

——. "Coleridge and Wordsworth. The Ethics of Gift Exchange and Literary Ownership," in *Coleridge's Theory of the Imagination Today*, ed. Christine Gallant. New York: AMS Press, 1989.

Moffat, Douglas. "Coleridge's Ten Theses: The Plotinian Alternative," *Wordsworth Circle* 13.1 (Winter 1982): 27–31.

Newlyn, Lucy. *Coleridge, Wordsworth, and the Language of Allusion*. Oxford: Clarendon Press, 1986.

Orsini, Gian. *Coleridge and German Idealism*. Carbondale: Southern Illinois University Press, 1969.

Park, Roy. "Coleridge and Kant: Poetic Imagination and Practical Reason," *British Journal of Aesthetics* 8 (1968): 335–46.

Parker, Reeve. *Coleridge's Meditative Art*. Ithaca: Cornell University Press, 1975.

Peterfreund, Stuart. "Coleridge and the Politics of Critical Vision," *Studies in English Literature* 21.4 (Fall 1981): 585–604.

Pollin, Burton R., assisted by Redmond Burke. "John Thelwall's Marginalia on a Copy of Coleridge's *Biographia Literaria*," *Bulletin of the New York Public Library* 74 (1970): 88.

Powell, Grosvenor. "Coleridge's 'Imagination' and the Infinite Regress of Consciousness," *ELH* 39 (1972): 266–78.

Pradhan, S. V. "Coleridge's 'Philocrisy' and his Theory of Fancy and Secondary Imagination," *Studies in Romanticism* 13 (1974): 235–54.

Preyer, Robert. *Bentham, Coleridge, and the Science of History*, Beiträge zur englischen Philologie, 41 (Bochum-Langendreer: H. Poppinghaus, 1958).

Reed, Arden. *Romantic Weather. The Climates of Coleridge and Baudelaire*. Hanover: The University Presses of New England, 1983.

Reiman, Donald H. "Coleridge and the Art of Equivocation," *Studies in Romanticism* 25.3 (Fall 1986): 325–50.

Richards, I. A. *Coleridge on Imagination*. 1935; 2nd ed. New York: Norton, 1950.

Robinson, Henry Crabb. *On Books and their Writers*, 3 vols., ed. Edith J. Morley. London: Dent, 1938.

Schmitz, Eike. "Coleridge, Maas, and Tetans on Imagination: A Reconsideration," *Archiv für das Studium Neuere Sprachen und Literatur* 213 (1976): 269–88.

Shaffer, Elinor S. "Coleridge's Theory of Aesthetic Interest," *Journal of Aesthetics and Art Criticism* 27 (1969): 392–406.

——. "Coleridge's Revolution in the Standard of Taste," *Journal of Aesthetics and Art Criticism* 28 (1969): 213–21.

——. "The 'Postulates in Philosophy' in *Biographia Literaria*," *Comparative Literature Studies* 7 (1970): 297–313.

Stansfield, Dorothy. "A Note on the Genesis of Coleridge's Thinking on War and Peace, *Wordsworth Circle* 17.3 (Summer 1986): 130–34.

Storch, R. F. "The Politics of the Imagination," *Studies in Romanticism* 21.3 (Fall 1982): 448–56.

Taylor, Anya. *Coleridge's Defense of the Human*. Columbus: Ohio State University

Press, 1986.

Teich, Nathaniel. "Coleridge's *Biographia* and the Contemporary Controversy about Style," *Wordsworth Circle* 3 (1972): 61–70.

Thompson, E. P. "Disenchantment or Default? A Lay Sermon," in *Power and Consciousness*, ed. Conor Cruise O'Brien and William Dean Vanech. London: London University Press, 1969.

———. Review of David V. Erdman, ed. *Essays on His Times*, 3 vols., *Collected Works of Samuel Taylor Coleridge*, in *Wordsworth Circle* 10 (Summer 1979): 261–65.

Thorpe, Clarence D. "Coleridge and Aesthetician and Critic," *Journal of the History of Ideas* 5 (1944): 387–414.

Wallace, Catherine Miles. "Coleridge's *Biographia Literaria* and the Evidence for Christianity," in *Interspace and the Inward Sphere*, ed. Norman A. Anderson and Margene E. Weiss. Macomb, Ill.: Essays in Literature, 1978, 19–32.

———. "Coleridge's Theory of Language," *Philological Quarterly* 59.3 (Summer 1980): 338–52.

———. "The Function of Autobiography in *Biographia Literaria*," *Wordsworth Circle* 12.4 (Fall 1981): 216–25.

———. *The Design of the Biographia Literaria*. London: Allen and Unwin, 1983.

Watson, George. "The Revolutionary Youth of Coleridge and Wordsworth," *Critical Quarterly* 18.3 (1976): 49–66.

Wellek, René. *Immanuel Kant in England, 1793–1838*. Princeton: Princeton University Press, 1931.

———. "Coleridge," in *A History of Modern Criticism*, Vol. 2, *The Romantic Age*. New Haven: Yale University Press, 1955, 151–87.

Whalley, George. "The Integrity of *Biographia Literaria*," *Essays and Studies*, n.s. 6 (1953): 87–101.

Wheeler, Kathleen. *Sources, Processes, and Methods in Coleridge's* Biographia Literaria. Cambridge: Cambridge University Press, 1980.

Wilkie, Brian. "The Romantic Ideal of Unity," *Studies in Literary Interpretation* 19.2 (Fall 1986): 5–21.

Willey, Basil. *Samuel Taylor Coleridge*. London: Chatto and Windus, 1972.

Wojcik, Manfred. "The Mimetic Orientation of Coleridge's Aesthetic Thought," *Zeitschrift für Anglistik und Amerikanistik* 17 (1969): 344–91.

———. "Coleridge and the Problem of Transcendentalism," *Zeitschrift für Anglistik und Amerikanistik* 18 (1970): 30–58.

———. "Coleridge: Symbol, Organic Unity, and Modern Aesthetic Subjectivism," *Zeitischrift für Anglistik und Amerikanistik* 18 (1970): 355–90.

———. "Coleridge: Symbolization, Expression, and Artistic Creativity," *Zeitischrift für Anglistik und Amerikanistik* 19 (1971): 117–54.

Woodring, Carl. *Politics in the Poetry of Coleridge*. Madison: University of Wisconsin Press, 1961.

Wordsworth, Jonathan. "'The Infinite I AM': Coleridge and the Ascent of Being," in *Coleridge's Imagination: Essays in Memory of Pete Laver*, ed. Richard Gravil, Lucy Newlyn, Nicholas Roe. Cambridge: Cambridge University Press, 1985, 22–52.

IV. Other Works Cited

Agrippa von Nettesheim, Heinrich Cornelius. *Three Books of Occult Philosophy*, trans. J. F. London: G. Moule, 1651.

Aristotle. *Categoria*, in *The Works of Aristotle*, 11 vols., ed. W. D. Ross. Oxford: Clarendon, 1928.

———. *The "Art" of Rhetoric, with an English Translation*, trans. John Henry Freese. 1926; reprint Cambridge, Mass.: Harvard University Press, 1959.

Aulard, Alphonse. *La Société des Jacobins. Recueil de documents pour l'histoire du club des Jacobins de Paris*, 6 vols. Paris: Librairie Jouaust, 1889–97; trans. Bernard Miall. New York: Charles Scribner's Sons, 1910.

———. *Taine; historien de la révolution française*. Paris: Librairie Armand Colin, 1907.

———. *Christianity and the French Revolution*, trans. Lady Frazer. Boston: Little, Brown, and Company, 1927.

Beattie, James. *The Elements of Moral Science* (1790). *Philosophical and Critical Works*. Vol. 3 of 4 vols. Hildesheim: G. Olms Verlag, 1974.

Belsey, Catherine. "The Romantic Construction of the Unconscious," in *1789: Reading Writing Revolution*, ed. Francis Barker et al. Essex: University of Essex, 1982.

Berkeley, George. *The Works of George Berkeley*, 4 vols., ed. Alexander Campbell Fraser (Oxford: Clarendon, 1871).

Berlin, Isaiah. "Hume and the Sources of German Anti-Rationalism," in *Against the Current*. New York: Penguin Books, 1982, 162–3.

Blackstone, Sir William. *Commentaries on the Laws of England*, 4 vols., Oxford: Clarendon, 1765.

Blake, William. *The Complete Poetry and Prose of William Blake*, ed. David V. Erdman, commentary by Harold Bloom, rev. ed. Berkeley and Los Angeles: University of California Press, 1982.

———. *The Book of Urizen*, ed. Kay Parkhurst Easson and Roger Easson. Boulder: Shambala; New York: Random House, 1978.

———. *The Notebook of William Blake: A Photographic and Typographic Facsimile*, ed. David V. Erdman with the assistance of Donald Moore. Oxford and New York: Oxford University Press, 1973; rev. Readex Books, 1977.

Boehme, Jacob. *The Works of Jacob Behmen, the Teutonic Theosopher*. ["Law's edition," ed. G. Ward and T. Langcake, mostly from translations of John Sparrow]. 4 vols. London: M. Richardson, 1764–81.

Boswell, James. *The Life of Samuel Johnson*. London and New York: Oxford University Press, 1933.

Brinton, Clarence Clay. *The Jacobins: An Essay in the New History*. New York: Macmillan, 1930.

Brisman, Leslie. *Romantic Origins*. Ithaca: Cornell University Press, 1978.

Browne, Thomas. *The Works of Sir Thomas Browne*, 6 vols., ed. Geoffrey Keynes. London: Oxford, 1928–31.

Buonarotti, Philippe. *Babeuf's Conspiracy for Equality* (1836), trans. Bronterre O'Brien. New York: August M. Kelley, 1965.

Burke, Edmund. *Selected Writings*, ed. Walter Jackson Bate. New York: Random House, 1960.

———. *A Philosophical Enquiry into the Origin of our Ideas of the Sublime and Beautiful* (1756; rev. 1757), ed. James T. Boulton. South Bend, IN: University of Notre Dame, 1968.

———. *Reflections on the Revolution in France* (1790). Harmondsworth: Penguin, 1969.

Burnet, Thomas. *The Sacred Theory of the Earth.* 2 vols. London, 1684–90; Carbondale: Southern Illinois University Press, 1965.

Burney, Fanny. *Camilla, or A Picture of Youth*, ed. Edward A. Bloom and Lillian D. Bloom. Oxford: Oxford University Press, 1983.

Burns, Emile, ed. *The Marxist Reader. The Most Significant and Enduring Works of Marxism.* New York: Avenel Books, 1982.

Burtt, E. A. *The Metaphysical Foundations of Modern Physical Science.* Garden City, NY: Doubleday, 1955.

Byron, George Gordon, Lord. *Byron's Letters and Journals*, 10 vols., ed. Leslie A. Marchand. Cambridge, Mass.: Harvard University Press, 1973–82.

———. *The Complete Poetical Works*, 5 vols., ed. Jerome J. McGann. Oxford: Clarendon, 1980–86.

Capra, Fritjof. *The Turning-Point: Science, Society, and the Rising Culture.* New York: Simon and Schuster, 1982.

Carlyle, Thomas. *The Works of Thomas Carlyle*, 30 vols., ed. H. D. Traill. London: Chapman and Hall, 1896–99.

———. *The Works of Thomas Carlyle*, 30 vols. New York: Charles Scribner's Sons, 1897.

———. *Sartor Resartus*, ed. Charles Frederick Harold. New York: The Odyssey Press, 1937.

———. *Sartor Resartus and Selected Prose*, ed. Herbert Sussman. New York: Holt, Rinehart and Winston, 1970.

Cassirer, Ernst. *The Philosophy of the Enlightenment*, trans. Koelln and Pettegrove. Princeton: Princeton University Press, 1951.

Cervantes, Miguel de. *Don Quixote de la Mancha*, trans. Samuel Putnam. New York: Modern Library, 1949.

Chandler, James K. *Wordsworth's Second Nature.* Chicago: University of Chicago Press, 1984.

Cobb, Richard. *The People's Armies; The armées révolutionaires; Instrument of the Terror in the Departments; April 1793 to Floréal Year II*, trans. Marianne Elliott. New Haven: Yale University Press, 1987.

Cohen, Murray. *Sensible Words: Linguistic Practice in England 1640–1785.* Baltimore: The John Hopkins University Press, 1981.

Coleridge, Sara. *Memoirs and Letters of Sara Coleridge*, ed. by her daughter. London, 1873; New York: Harper, 1874.

Collins, William. *The Works of William Collins*, ed. Richard Wendorf and Charles

Ryskamp. Oxford: Clarendon Press, 1979.

Conquest, Robert. *The Harvest of Sorrow: Soviet Collectivization and the Terror-Famine.* New York: Oxford University Press, 1986.

Culler, Jonathan. "Literary History, Allegory, and Semiology," *New Literary History* 7 (1976): 259–70.

———. *The Pursuit of Signs.* Ithaca: Cornell University Press, 1981.

Dalgarno, George. "A Discourse of the Nature and Number of Double Consonants," in *Works.* Edinburgh: Constable, 1834.

Davidson, Clifford. "Organic Unity and Shakespearean Tragedy," *Journal of Aesthetics and Art Criticism* 30 (1971): 171–76.

Davies, Edward. *Celtic Researches on the Origin, Traditions and Language of the Ancient Britons.* London: Davies, 1804.

de Man, Paul. "The Rhetoric of Temporality," in *Interpretation: Theory and Practice,* ed. Charles S. Singleton. Baltimore: The Johns Hopkins University Press, 1969.

———. *Blindness and Insight: Essays in the Rhetoric of Contemporary Criticism.* London: Oxford University Press, 1971.

———. "The Epistemology of Metaphor," *Critical Inquiry* 5.1 (Autumn 1978): 13–30.

———. *Allegories of Reading: Figural Language in Rousseau, Nietzsche, Rilke, and Proust.* New Haven: Yale University Press, 1979.

de Mott, Benjamin. "The Sources and Development of John Wilkins' Philosophical Language," *Journal of English and German Philology* 57 (1958): 1–13.

Derrida, Jacques. *Of Grammatology,* trans. Gayatri Chakravorty Spivak. Baltimore: The Johns Hopkins University Press, 1974.

———. "Differance," in *Speech and Phenomena,* trans. David B. Allison. Evanston: Northwestern University Press, 1981.

———. "White Mythology: Metaphor in the Text of Philosophy," in *Margins of Philosophy,* trans. Alan Bass. Chicago: University of Chicago Press, 1982.

Dyer, George. *Poems.* London: 1792.

Eichner, Hans. *Friedrich Schlegel.* New York: Twayne, 1970.

Epstein, Julia L. and Mark L. Greenberg. "Decomposing Milton's Rainbow," *Journal of the History of Ideas* 45.1 (1984): 115–40.

Erdman, David V. *Commerce des Lumiéres; John Oswald and the British in Paris, 1790–1793.* Columbia: University of Missouri Press, 1986.

Feher, Ferenc. *The Frozen Revolution: An Essay on Jacobinism.* Cambridge: Cambridge University Press; Paris: Editions de la Maison des Sciences de l'Homme, 1987.

Feldman, Burton, and Robert D. Richardson, eds. *The Rise of Modern Mythology 1680–1860.* Bloomington: Indiana University Press, 1972.

Fichte, Johann Gottlieb. *Grundlage der gesammten Wissenschaftslehre.* 2nd ed. Jena, Leipzig: Christian Ernst Gabler, 1802.

———. *Über den Begriff der Wissenschaftslehre* (1793) and *Versuch einer neuen Darstellung der Wissenschaftslehre* (1797). Vols. 1 and 2 of *Sämtliche Werke,* ed. J. H. Fichte. 8 vols. Berlin: Veit, 1845-1846.

Foucault, Michel. *The Order of Things.* New York: Vintage Books, 1973.

————. "What is an Author?" in *Language, Counter-Memory, Practice*, ed. Donald Bouchard, trans. Bouchard and Sherry Simon. Ithaca: Cornell University Press, 1977.

Froissart, Jean. *Chronicles*, ed. and trans. Geoffrey Brereton. Harmondsworth, Middlesex: Penguin Books, 1978.

Gaxotte, Pierre. *La Révolution française*, rev. ed. Paris: Fayard, 1970.

Genette, Gérard. *Mimologiques: voyage en Cratylie*. Paris: Editions du Seuil, 1976.

Gottschalk, Louis and Margaret Maddox. *Lafeyette in the French Revolution*. Chicago: University of Chicago Press, 1969.

Gould, Stephen J. *Ontogeny and Phylogeny*. Cambridge, Mass.: Harvard University Press, 1977.

Gerard, Albert. *An Essay on Genius*. London: Printed for W. Strahan, T. Cadell, 1774.

Hamilton, Elizabeth. *Memoirs of Modern Philosophers*, 3 vols. London: C., G., and J. Robinson, 1800.

Hartley, David. *Observations on Man*. 2nd ed. London: J. Johnson, 1791.

Hazlitt, William. *Complete Works*, 21 vols., ed. P. P. Howe. London: Dent, 1930–34.

Heine, Heinrich. *Sämtliche Schriften*, 6 vols., ed. Klaus Briegleb. Munich: Hanser, 1969–75.

Hill, Christopher. *The World Turned Upside Down, Radical Ideas during the English Revolution*. New York: Viking, 1972.

————. *Milton and the English Revolution*. London: Faber, 1977; New York: Viking, 1978.

————. *The Experience of Defeat: Milton and Some Contemporaries*. New York: Viking, 1984.

Holmes, Richard. *Shelley: The Pursuit*. New York: E. P. Dutton, 1975.

Holton, Gerald. *The Thematic Origins of Scientific Thought: Kepler to Einstein*. Cambridge, Mass.: Harvard University Press, 1973.

————. *The Scientific Imagination: Case Studies*. Cambridge, Mass.: Harvard University Press, 1978.

Hume, David. *A Treatise of Human Nature*, ed. L. A. Selby-Bigge. Oxford: Clarendon Press, 1888; reprint 1965; rev. P. H. Nidditch, 1978.

Hunt, Leigh. *Autobiography*, ed. J. E. Morpurgo. London: The Cresset Press, 1948.

Johnson, Samuel. "Preface to Shakespeare" (1765), in *Criticism: The Major Texts*, ed. Walter Jackson Bate. New York: Harcourt, Brace and Company, 1952, 207–17.

Johnston, Kenneth. *Wordsworth and The Recluse*. New Haven: Yale University Press, 1984.

Jones, Rowland. *The Philosophy of Language*. London: J. Hughs, 1769.

Jordan, David P. *The Revolutionary Career of Maximilien Robespierre*. New York: Free Press, 1985.

Joyce, James. *Finnegans Wake*. New York: The Viking Press, 1957.

Kant, Immanuel. *Werke*, 7 vols., ed. Wilhelm Weischedel. Darmstadt: Wissenschaftliche Buchgesellschaft, 1956; 4th ed. 1975.

————. *Critique of Pure Reason*, trans. J. M. D. Meiklejohn. London: George Bell and Sons, 1884.

———. *Critique of Judgment*, trans. J. H. Bernard. New York: Hafner Publishing Company, 1951.

Keats, John. *John Keats: Complete Poems*, ed. Jack Stillinger. Cambridge, Mass.: Harvard University Press, 1982.

———. *The Letters of John Keats*, 2 vols., ed. Hyder Edward Rollins. Cambridge: Harvard University Press, 1958.

Kennedy, Michael L. *The Jacobin Clubs in the French Revolution; The First Years.* Princeton: Princeton University Press, 1982.

Kerr, Wilfred B. *The Reign of Terror 1793–4.* Toronto: University of Toronto Press, 1927.

Kierkegaard, Søren. *Concluding Unscientific Postscript*, trans. David F. Swenson and Walter Lowrie. Princeton: Princeton University Press, 1968.

———. *The Point of View for My Work as An Author: A Report to History*, ed. Benjamin Nelson, trans. Walter Lowrie. New York: Harper and Row, 1962.

Kircher, Athanasius. *Turris Babel.* Amsterdam: Janson, 1679.

Klancher, Jon. *The Making of English Reading Audiences, 1790–1832.* Madison: University of Wisconsin Press, 1987.

Korngold, Ralph. *Robespierre: First Modern Dictator.* London: Macmillan, 1937.

Kuhn, Thomas. *The Structure of Scientific Revolutions.* 2nd ed. Chicago: University of Chicago Press, 1970.

———. *The Essential Tension: Selected Studies in Scientific Tradition and Change.* Chicago: University of Chicago Press, 1977.

Lafayette, Marie-Joseph, Marquis de. *Déclaration de droits de l'homme et du citoyen et ses antécédents américains*, 26 August 1789. Washington, D.C., 1945.

———. *Mémoires, correspondance et manuscrits*, 2 vols., Paris: Fournier, 1837.

Lamartine, Alphonse de. *Histoire des Girondins*, 2 vols., ed. Jean-Pierre Jacques. Paris: Librairie Plon, 1984.

Lamb, Charles and Mary. *The Letters of Charles and Mary Lamb*, 3 vols., ed. Edwin W. Marrs, Jr. Ithaca: Cornell University Press, 1975–78.

———. *The Works of Charles and Mary Lamb*, 7 vols., ed. E. V. Lucas. London: Methuen, 1903–05.

Land, Stephen K. *From Signs to Propositions: The Concept of Form in Eighteenth-Century Semantic Theory.* London: Longman, 1974.

Lefebvre, Georges. *The French Revolution*, 2 vols., trans. Elizabeth Moss Evanson, John Hall Stewart, and James Friguglietti. London: Routledge & Kegan Paul; New York: Columbia University Press, 1962–64.

Lentricchia, Frank. *Criticism and Social Change.* Chicago: University of Chicago Press, 1983.

Lipking, Lawrence. "The Marginal Gloss," *Critical Inquiry* 3.4 (Summer 1977): 606–56.

Locke, John. *An Essay Concerning Human Understanding*, 2 vols., ed. Alexander Campbell Fraser. New York: Dover, 1959.

Lodowick, Francis. *Common Writing.* London: Lodowick, 1647.

———. *The Ground-Work and Foundation Laid, or so Intended, for the Framing of a New Perfect Language.* London: n.p., 1652.

Lucas, Colin. *The Structure of the Terror; The Example of Javogues and the Loire.* London: Oxford University Press, 1973.

Mack, Maynard. "The Muse of Satire," *Yale Review* 41 (1951): 80–92.

Mackie, J. L. *Problems from Locke.* London: Oxford, 1976.

Macksey, Richard, and Eugenio Donato, eds. *The Stucturalist Controversy: The Languages of Criticism and the Sciences of Man.* Baltimore: Johns Hopkins University Press, 1972.

Macpherson, C. B. *The Political Theory of Possessive Individualism: Hobbes to Locke.* New York: Oxford University Press, 1983.

McGann, Jerome. *The Romantic Ideology: A Critical Investigation.* Chicago: University of Chicago Press, 1983.

Madelin, Louis. *The French Revolution.* New York: G. P. Putnam's Sons, 1928.

Mann, Paul. "*The Book of Urizen* and the Horizon of the Book," in *Unnam'd Forms*, ed. Nelson Hilton and Thomas Vogler. Berkeley and Los Angeles: University of California Press, 1985.

Matrat, Jean. *Robespierre; Or the Tyranny of the Majority*, trans. Alan Kendall and Felix Brenner. New York: Charles Scribner's Sons, 1971.

Melville, Herman. *Pierre, or The Ambiguities*, ed. Harrison Hayford, Hershel Parker, G. Thomas Tanselle. Evanston and Chicago: Northwestern University Press and The Newberry Library, 1971.

Milton, John. *Complete Poems and Major Prose*, ed. Merritt Hughes. New York: Odyssey, 1957.

Montaigne, Michel de. *The Complete Essays of Montaigne*, trans. Donald M. Frame. Stanford: Stanford University Press, 1948.

Morgan, Michael J. *Molyneux's Question.* Cambridge: Cambridge University Press, 1977.

Mortimer-Ternaux, M. *Histoire de la Terreur 1792–1794*, 8 vols. Paris: Michel Lévy, 1862–81.

Nabokov, Vladimir. *Bend Sinister.* New York: Henry Holt and Co., 1947.

Newton, Sir Isaac. *The Mathematical Principles of Natural Philosophy*, trans. Andrew Motte. London: Benjamin Motte, 1729; rev. Florian Cajori, Berkeley: University of California Press, 1934.

Nietzsche, Friedrich. *The Birth of Tragedy* and *The Genealogy of Morals*, trans. Francis Golffing. New York: Doubleday Anchor, 1956.

Niklaus, Robert. *Beaumarchais: Le Mariage de Figaro.* London: Grant and Culler, 1893.

Olson, Richard. *Scottish Philosophy and British Physics, 1750–1880.* Princeton: Princeton University Press, 1975.

Owens, Joseph. *The Doctrine of Being in the Aristotelian 'Metaphysics.'* Toronto: Pontifical Institute of Medieval Studies, 1978.

Packe, Michael St. John. *The Life of John Stuart Mill.* New York: Macmillan, 1954.

Paley, Morton. *Energy and Imagination in the Development of Blake's Thought.* Oxford: Clarendon, 1970.

Palmer, R. R. *Twelve Who Ruled: The Year of the Terror in the French Revolution.* Princeton: Princeton University Press, 1941.

Pater, Walter. *Selected Writings of Walter Pater*, ed. Harold Bloom. New York: Columbia University Press, 1974.

Perkins, David, ed. *English Romantic Writers*. New York: Harcourt, Brace and World, 1967.

Peterfreund, Stuart. "Blake and Newton: Argument as Art, Argument as Science," *Studies in Eighteenth-Century Culture* 10 (1980): 205–26.

——— . "The Reemergence of Energy in the Discourse of Literature and Science," *Annals of Scholarship* 4:1 (Fall 1986): 22–53.

——— . "Organicism and the Birth of Energy," in *Approaches to Organic Form*, ed. Frederick Burwick, Boston Studies in the Philosophy of Science (Dordrecht: Reidel, 1987), 113–52.

Pocock, J. G. A. *Politics, Language and Time: Essays on Political Thought and History*. New York: Atheneum, 1973.

Pope, Alexander. *Selected Poetry and Prose*, ed. William K. Wimsatt, Jr. New York: Rinehart and Winston, 1963.

Priestley, Joseph. *The Theological and Miscellaneous Works of Joseph Priestley, LL.D., F.R.S., &c.*, 23 vols., ed. John Towill Rutt. London: G. Smallfield, 1817–20.

Rabelais, François. *Oeuvres complétes*, ed. Jacques Boulanger and Lucien Scheler. Bibliothèque de la Pléiade. Paris: Gallimard, 1955.

Ransom, John Crowe. "William Wordsworth: Notes Toward an Understanding of Poetry," in *Wordsworth. Centenary Studies*, ed. Gilbert T. Dunklin. Princeton: Princeton University Press, 1951.

Read, Herbert. *Art and Society*. New York: Pantheon Books, 1945.

Rees, Abraham. *The Cyclopedia; or, Universal Dictionary of Arts, Sciences, and Literature*, 45 vols. London: Longman, Hurst, Rees, Orme, and Brown, 1819–20.

Reynolds, Joshua, Sir. *Discourses*, ed. Helen Zimmern. London: Walter Scott, 1887.

Rivers, Isabel. ed. *Books and Their Readers in Eighteenth-Century England*. New York: St. Martin's Press, 1982.

Robespierre, Maximilien. *Textes choisis*, 2 vols. ed. Jean Poperen. Paris: Éditions Sociales, 1956.

Rorty, Richard. *Philosophy and the Mirror of Nature*. Princeton: Princeton University Press, 1979.

Rose, R. B. *Gracchus Babeuf; The First Revolutionary Communist*. London: Edward Arnold, 1978.

Rousseau, Jean-Jacques. *Oeuvres complètes*, 2 vols., ed. Bernard Gagnebin and Marcel Raymond. Bibliothèque de la Pléiade. Paris: Gallimard, 1959–69.

Ruoff, Gene. "Wordsworth on Language: Towards a Radical Poetics of English Romanticism," *Wordsworth Circle* 3 (1972): 204–11.

Ruskin, John. *The Seven Lamps of Architecture*. New York: Noonday Press, 1961.

Saccamano, Neil. "Authority and Publication: The Works of Swift," *The Eighteenth Century* 25.3 (Fall 1984): 241–62.

Said, Edward W. *The World, the Text, and the Critic*. Cambridge, Mass.: Harvard University Press, 1983.

Salmon, Vivian. *The Study of Language in 17th-Century England*. Amsterdam: John Benjamins, 1979.

Santa Cruz Blake Study Group. Review of David V. Erdman, *The Complete Poetry and Prose of William Blake*, in *Blake* 18.1 (Summer 1984): 4–30.

Saumarez, Richard. *A New System of Physiology, Comprehending the Laws by Which Animated Beings in General, and the Human Species in Particular, Are Governed, in Their Several States of Health and Disease*, 2 vols. London: J. Johnson, 1798.

———. *The Principles of Physiological and Physical Science; Comprehending the Ends for Which Animated Beings Were Created; and an Examination of the Unnatural and Artificial Means of Philosophy Which Now Prevail*. London: R. Edwards and T. Egerton, 1812.

Schelling, Friedrich W. J. *Sämtliche Werke*, ed. Manfred Schröter. 1927–59; reprint Munich: C. H. Beck, 1962–71.

———. "Vorläufige Beziehung des Standpunktes der Medicin nach Grundsätzen der Naturphilosophie," in *Jahrbücher der Medizin als Wissenschaft*. 1805; reprint Hildesheim: Georg Olms, 1969.

———. *Zeitschrift für spekulative Physik*. 1800–01; reprint Hildesheim: Georg Olms, 1969.

Schlegel, August Wilhelm. *Die Kunstlehre*, in *Kritische Schriften und Briefe*, 7 vols., ed. Edgar Lohner. Stuttgart: W. Kohlhammer, 1963–74.

Schiller, Friedrich. *Briefe*, ed. Gerhard Fricke. Munich: Hanser, 1955.

———. *Sämtliche Werke*, 5 vols., ed. Gerhard Fricke and H. G. Göpfert. Munich: Hanser, 1962.

Sédillot, René. *Le Coût de la Révolution française*. Paris: Perrin, 1987.

Shelley, Percy Bysshe. *Shelley's Poetry and Prose*, ed. Donald H. Reiman and Sharon B. Powers. New York: Norton, 1977.

———. *The Complete Works of Percy Bysshe Shelley*, 10 vols., ed. Roger Ingpen and Walter E. Peck. London: Ernest Benn, 1926–30; reprint New York: Gordian Press, 1965.

———. *The Letters of Percy Bysshe Shelley*, 2 vols., ed. Frederick L. Jones. Oxford: Clarendon, 1964.

———. *Shelley's Prose in the Bodlein Manuscripts*, ed. A. H. Koszul. London: Henry Frowde, 1910.

Sidney, Sir Philip. *Defense of Poesy*, ed. Lewis Soens. Lincoln: University of Nebraska Press, 1970.

Sime, James. *Schiller*. Edinburgh and London: William Blackwood and Sons, 1882.

Simpson, David. *Irony and Authority in Romantic Poetry*. Totowa, NJ: Rowman and Littlefield, 1979.

Singleton, Charles, ed. *Interpretations*. Baltimore: Johns Hopkins University Press, 1969.

Skelton, John. *Poems*, ed. Robert S. Kinsman. Oxford: Clarendon Press, 1969.

Slaughter, M. M. *Universal Languages and Scientific Taxonomy in the Seventeenth Century*. Cambridge: Cambridge University Press, 1982.

Smith, Olivia. *The Politics of Language, 1791–1819*. London: Oxford University Press, 1984.

Southey, Robert. *Poetical Works*, 10 vols. London: Longman, 1840.

————. *New Letters of Robert Southey*, 2 vols., ed. Kenneth Curry. New York: Columbia University Press, 1965.

Steffens, Henrik. *Was ich erlebte*, 10 vols. Breslau: Max & Co., 1840–44.

Stephen, Leslie. *Hours in a Library*, 3 vols. London: Smith, Elder, & Co., 1909.

Stevens, Wallace. *Collected Poems*. New York: Alfred A. Knopf, 1955.

Sterne, Lawrence. *The Life and Opinions of Tristram Shandy, Gentleman*, 3 vols., ed. Melvyn and Joan New. The University Presses of Florida, 1978.

Swenson, Loyd S. *The Genesis of Relativity: Einstein in Context*. New York: Burt Franklin, 1979.

Swift, Jonathan. *The Writing of Jonathan Swift*, ed. Robert Greenberg and William Bowman Piper. New York: Norton, 1973.

Taine, Hippolyte. *Les Origines de la France contemporaine*. 6 vols. Paris: Librairie Hachette et Cie, 1875–93.

Thelwall, Mrs. Cecil Boyle. *The Life of John Thelwall*. London: John Macrone, St. James's Square, 1837.

Thompson, E. P. *The Making of the English Working Class*. New York: Pantheon Books, 1963.

Thorpe, James. *Principles of Textual Criticism*. San Marino, Ca.: Huntington Library, 1972.

Todorov, Tzvetan. *Theories of the Symbol*, trans. Catherine Porter. Ithaca: Cornell University Press, 1982.

Valesio, Paolo. *Novantiqua: Rhetoric as a Contemporary Theory*. Bloomington: Indiana University Press, 1980.

Vico, Giambattista. *The New Science*, trans. Thomas Goddard Bergin and Max Harold Fisch. Ithaca: Cornell University Press, 1968.

Walter, Gérard. *Babeuf 1760–1797 et la conjuration des égaux*. Paris: Payot, 1937.

————. *Histoire des Jacobins*. Paris: Aimery Somogy, 1946.

Walzer, Michael. *The Revolution of the Saints: A Study in the Origins of Radical Politics*. Cambridge, Mass.: Harvard University Press, 1965; reprint, 1982.

Warburton, William. *The Divine Legation of Moses*, 2 vols. London: Fletcher Giles, 1738–41.

Webster, John. *Academiarum Examen*, London: Giles Calvert, 1654.

Wesley, John. *The Works of the Reverend John Wesley, A. M.*, 14 vols. London: Wesleyan Conference Office, 1872.

Wiedmann, Franz. *Hegel*, trans. Joachim Neugroschel. New York: Pegasus, 1968.

Wiese, Benno von. *Friedrich Schiller*. Stuttgart: Metzler, 1959.

Wilkins, John. *An Essay towards a Real Character, and a Philosophical Language*. London: S. Gellibrand, 1668.

Williams, Raymond. *Culture and Society, 1780–1850*. New York: Columbia University Press, 1983.

Wilson, John (Christopher North), "Some Observation on the 'Biographia Literaria' of S. T. Coleridge, Esq.," *Blackwood's Edinburgh Magazine* 2 (Oct. 1817): 3–18.

Wilson, Mona. *The Life of William Blake*. 1927, rev. 1948; reprint New York: Cooper

Square, 1969.

Wittreich, Joseph Anthony, Jr. *The Romantics on Milton*. Cleveland: The Press of Case Western Reserve University, 1970.

Woloch, Isser. *Jacobin Legacy; The Democratic Movement under the Directory*. Princeton: Princeton University Press, 1970.

Wordsworth, William. *The Poetical Works of William Wordsworth*, 5 vols., ed. Ernest de Selincourt and Helen Darbishire. Oxford: Clarendon Press, 1949.

——. *The Prelude* (1805, 1850 texts), ed. Ernest de Selincourt, rev. Helen Darbishire. Oxford: Clarendon Press, 1959.

——. *The Prose Works of William Wordsworth*, 3 vols., ed. W. J. B. Owen and Jane Worthington Smyser. Oxford: Clarendon Press, 1974.

——. *William Wordsworth*, ed. Stephen Gill. London: Oxford University Press, 1984.

——, and Dorothy Wordsworth. *The Letters of William and Dorothy Wordsworth; The Early Years, 1787–1805*, ed. Ernest de Selincourt, rev. Chester Shaver. Oxford: Clarendon Press, 1967.

Young, Edward, "On Lyric Poetry" (1728), in *Works*, 4 vols. London, 1757.

Young, J. Z. *Doubt and Certainty in Science: A Biologist's Reflections on the Brain*. London: Oxford University Press, 1960.

Young, Thomas. *A Course of Lectures on Natural Philosophy and the Mechanical Arts*, 2 vols. 1807; reprint London: Taylor and Walton, 1845.

Contributors

FREDERICK BURWICK, who studied German literature and philosophy at Göttingen and continued his work in Anglo-German literary relations with Gian Orsini at the University of Wisconsin, is now Professor of English and Comparative Literature at the University of California, Los Angeles. He has published over thirty articles on the English and Continental Romantics. His most recent books, *The Damnation of Newton: Goethe's Color Theory and Romantic Perception* (de Gruyter, 1986) and *The Haunted Eye: Perception and the Grotesque in Romantic Literature* (Carl Winter, 1987), have been devoted to perception theory. Drawing from his familiarity with perception theory in the Romantic period, his essay for this volume explains, at long last, precisely what Coleridge was doing in the *Biographia Literaria* with the "theses" stolen from Schelling.

JEROME CHRISTENSEN, Professor of English at Johns Hopkins University, is the author of *Coleridge's Blessed Machine of Language* (Cornell University Press, 1981), *Hume and the Formation of a Literary Career* (University of Wisconsin Press, 1987), and various articles on Coleridge and the English Romantics. A leader in the recent critical trend demonstrating Coleridge's centrality to poststructuralist criticism, Professor Christensen continues that work in the present volume to highlight the significance of the *Biographia Literaria* in relation to critical "deconstruction."

ROBERT N. ESSICK, Professor of English at the University of California at Riverside, is the author of *William Blake Printmaker* (Princeton, 1980), *The Separate Plates of William Blake* (Princeton, 1983), *The Works of William Blake in the Huntington Collections* (Huntington Library, 1985), and essays on Wordsworth, Blake, Shelley, and D. G. Rossetti. He is currently engaged in comprehensive research on Romantic language theory. This investigation has brought him to the *Biographia Literaria*, which he finds to be central to his concern with the concept of Adamic language. His essay presented here provides an important reference point for the concerns with language, cognition, and imagination which inform many of the studies in this collection.

RICHARD FADEM, Professor of English and the Humanities at Scripps College, has just completed a book on *Wordsworth's Equilibrium*. In addition to his reviews for *Philosophy and Literature* and his articles on Wordsworth and Coleridge for

329

Humanitas and *The Wordsworth Circle*, Professor Fadem has explored applications of psychoanalytic theory in Dickens's *Great Expectations*. His essay for this volume examines philosophical and psychological ramifications of "habit" in Coleridge's reaction to Associationist doctrine.

NORMAN FRUMAN, Professor of English at the University of Minnesota, is author of *Coleridge, the Damaged Archangel* (George Braziller, 1971), one of the most comprehensive and controversial studies of Coleridge ever published. His new edition of the *Biographia*, forthcoming from Oxford University Press, promises to be just as comprehensive and just as controversial. Professor Fruman's analysis of editorial and annotative measures necessary to balance and correct earlier editions—including the recent edition by James Engell and Walter Jackson Bate for the *Collected Coleridge* (Princeton University Press; Routledge & Kegan Paul, 1983)—addresses the autobiographical, editorial, and critical issues which are dealt with throughout this volume.

J. H. HAEGER, Professor of English at San Jose State University, has published essays on Coleridge's later writings, including his manuscript speculations on race and his *Hints Towards the Formation of a More Comprehensive Theory of Life*. Professor Haeger is currently at work on a book tentatively titled *The Altering Eye: Perception, Imagination, and Illusion in Romantic Poetry*. His essay here offers a stylistic dimension to the pattern of interest in interrelations between perception and conception, language and motive that emerges in this collection.

ROBERT MANIQUIS, Associate Professor of English and Comparative Literature at the University of California, Los Angeles, is the author of *Lonely Empires: Public and Personal Visions of Thomas De Quincey* (University of Wisconsin Press, 1976) and many essays on Romantic literature and literary theory. He is now completing a book on Coleridge and Romantic ideologies of the family. The interaction of metaphysical and political discourse in Coleridge's thought is the subject of his ideological analysis of the *Biographia* in the concluding essay of this volume.

THOMAS MCFARLAND, Murray Professor of English Literature at Princeton University, is author of the seminal study, *Coleridge and the Pantheist Tradition* (Clarendon Press, Oxford, 1969) and other important studies of Coleridge and the Romantics, including *Romanticism and the Forms of Ruin: Wordsworth, Coleridge, and Modalities of Fragmentation* (Princeton University Press, 1981), *Originality and Imagination* (Johns Hopkins University Press, 1985), *Shapes of Culture* (University of Iowa Press, 1987), and *Romantic Cruxes: The English Essayists and the Spirit of the Age* (Oxford: Clarendon, 1987), in addition to many influential journal articles. From the time of Thelwall and Hazlitt, critics have mined the *Biographia Literaria* for revelations of political or ideological bias in Coleridge's representation of himself as never a Jacobin. Arguing that the pattern of Jacobin become anti-Jacobin (as with Southey or Wordsworth) does not apply, McFarland takes issue with the accusations of political apostasy levelled against Coleridge.

JEROME J. MCGANN, Commonwealth Professor of English, University of Virginia, is a leading exponent of sociohistorical methods in literary studies. He is the editor of *Lord Byron: The Complete Poetical Works* (Clarendon Press, Oxford, 1980–), and the author of a wide variety of works on Romanticism and on textual and critical methodologies, including *A Critique of Modern Textual Criticism* (University of Chicago Press, 1982), *The Romantic Ideology* (University of Chicago Press, 1982), and *The Beauty of Inflections. Literary Investigations in Historical Method and Theory* (Oxford University Press, 1985). His most recent book is *Social Values and Poetic Acts* (Harvard University Press, 1987). In his essay for this volume he demonstrates the critical advantage in "decentering" the *Biographia Literaria*, shifting it from its position of canonical authority in order to examine its relation to other important trends in the Romantic period.

RAIMONDA MODIANO, Professor of English and Comparative Literature at the University of Washington, is the author of *Coleridge and the Concept of Nature* (Florida State University Press, 1985) as well as numerous articles and reviews on Coleridge and English Romanticism. She is also a co-editor of volumes 2–5 of the *Marginalia* for the Bollingen *Collected Coleridge* (Princeton University Press; Routledge & Kegan Paul, in press). For the present study, she examines the Miltonic and Shakespearean principles which Coleridge developed in his Lectures and utilized in his critique of Wordsworth in chapters 17–20 of the *Biographia Literaria*.

STUART PETERFREUND, Associate Professor of English at Northeastern University, is co-editor of *Nineteenth-Century Contexts* (formerly *Romanticism Past and Present*) and editor of *PLSL*, newsletter of the Society of Literature and Science, of which he is a founding member. He is currently completing a book on the concept of energy in the early nineteenth century for Duke University Press and is editing a collection of essays on literature and science for Northeastern University Press. He has published articles on English Romanticism in such journals as *ELH, Genre, K-SJ, MLQ, SECC,* and *SEL.* His essay on the concept of *energy* in Coleridge's thought in general, and in the *Biographia Literaria* in particular, relates Coleridge to a major cultural shift in his time—a turning from transcendent, externalist metaphysics to an immanent, internalist alternative, and a turning from mechanical explanatory models to a dynamic alternative. The shift, as Professor Peterfreund demonstrates, was not without its literary, philosophical, and religious problems for Coleridge.

J. FISHER SOLOMON teaches critical theory and history of criticism at the University of California, Los Angeles. He is the author of *Discourse and Reference in the Nuclear Age* (1988), as well as numerous essays on semiotics and critical theory. His essay here reexamines Coleridge's theory of the imagination both historically and critically, approaching it not merely as a brilliant, though fragmentary, philosophical component of the *Biographia Literaria* but as an important contribution to epistemology.

THOMAS VOGLER, Professor of Literature at the University of California, Santa Cruz, is editor (with Nelson Hilton) of *Unnam'd Forms: Blake and Textuality* (University of California Press, 1986) and author of *Preludes to Vision: The Epic Venture in Blake, Wordsworth, Keats, and Hart Crane* (University of California Press, 1971) and articles on authors and topics ranging from the eighteenth to the twentieth century. Professor Vogler's contribution here explores the literary and rhetorical dimensions of the *Biographia* to show how it simultaneously creates the appearance of philosophical argument while resisting the possibility of a satisfactory philosophical interpretation.

CATHERINE MILES WALLACE is a freelance writer whose scholarly essays have appeared in *Philological Quarterly* and in *The Wordsworth Circle*. She analyzed Coleridge's methods of organizing critical discourse in *The Design of Biographia Literaria* (Allen & Unwin, 1983), one of the few book-length studies on Coleridge's major critical work. In her essay for the present volume, she describes Coleridge's most misleading habits as a writer.

Index